A Mechanical People

Carl Siracusa

A Mechanical People

PERCEPTIONS OF THE INDUSTRIAL

ORDER IN MASSACHUSETTS

1815–1880

WESLEYAN UNIVERSITY PRESS

Middletown, Connecticut

The publisher gratefully acknowledges support of the publication of this book by the Andrew W. Mellon Foundation.

Library of Congress Cataloging in Publication Data

Siracusa, Carl.
    A mechanical people.

        Bibliography: p.
        Includes index.
        1. Labor policy—Massachusetts—History.   2. Labor
and laboring-classes—Massachusetts—History.   3. Fac-
tory system—Massachusetts—History.   4. Massachusetts
—Industries—History.   I. Title.
HD8083.M4S55   331.1′1′09744   78–26715
ISBN 0–8195–5029–9

Manufactured in the United States of America
First edition

For

IVAN KRAKOWSKY

who taught me more than he knew

Contents

Tables

Figures

Acknowledgments

THIS BOOK has grown by stages, and at each step I have received gener-
ous assistance. Most of the primary source material was found in the
Boston Public Library, the Massachusetts State House Library, the
Boston Athenaeum, and the Harvard College Library. The staffs of
these institutions, especially the first, were quite helpful. I have also
used material in the New York Public Library, the New York Historical
Society, the Massachusetts Historical Society, Dana Library of Rutgers
University in Newark, and the Massachusetts State Archives in Boston.

In its first incarnation, the study was a doctoral dissertation at Brandeis University. Professor Eugene Black provided the original inspiration for the topic, and along the way I received ideas, criticisms, and
support from my fellow graduate students, Carl Washburn, Avi Decter,
Marilyn Smith, and Jack Larkin. I owe a great deal to Brandeis University, and especially to the Irving and Rose Crown Fellowship Fund, for
providing the financial support that allowed me to devote three full
years to assembling the dissertation. My principal debt is to my thesis
supervisor, Professor Marvin Meyers, whose unfailing insight into the
history of ideas and whose patient guidance more than anything else
shaped the final product.

After the thesis was submitted in 1973, it underwent extensive
changes: new areas were researched and the text was expanded greatly.
I received valuable advice on British history from William Stockton and
David Hosford, and editorial criticism from Elliot Rosen. Finally, I must
thank some close friends—particularly David Trainer—and my parents,
Carmine and Anne Siracusa, for offering encouragement at a time when
it was most needed. In the long and often difficult task of revision, it was
good to know were others besides myself who thought it could be done.

Carl Siracusa

New York City
April 1978

A Mechanical People

PART I
The Worker in an
Industrial Setting

"The people of Massachusetts, to a greater extent than those of any other State in the Union, are a mechanical people."

— Horace Mann, 1845

Chapter 1

Confronting Industrialization

FOR MORE THAN two centuries, the Western world has been acquainted with the machine and all its consequences. The devising of an effective steam engine by the Scottish tinkerer James Watt opened the way for a spate of mechanical inventions that, more than anything else, divides our age from those preceding it. For the human race these years have been strangely bittersweet. The new technology has produced an unprecedented abundance of material goods. At the same time, it has brought in its wake wrenching dislocation, anxiety, controversy, and sheer misery. The machine is a potent, Janus-faced god that demands to be reckoned with.

How odd that this should be so. Those eighteenth-century Prometheans who gave us their wonderful inventions — Watt, Richard Arkwright, Edmund Cartwright, and others — apparently were unaware of all they had wrought. Confident children of an age just starting to flex its technological muscles, they assumed they were unalloyed benefactors to mankind. As far as human memory reached, wearying, consuming toil had been the rule of survival. Their ingenious new devices promised a long-awaited respite; beyond that, an incredible new productive power. Anticipation mounted as these instruments were adopted, first in England, then a short time later in America and on the Continent.

It was not long, though, before the machine — and its extension, the factory — began to arouse some serious doubts. William Blake's "dark Satanic Mills" dates from 1804. How much earlier had the same condemnation been uttered in more humble prose? The new economic arrangements the machine made possible — the "factory system" was the convenient tag — engendered far more than riches and comfort. The familiar cast of society was being radically, irretrievably altered, in what seemed to be threatening and awful ways. For many decades to come the history of almost every industrializing nation in the West would echo with the anguished protests that greeted the new order.

Yet not all of these nations responded in the same way. Most conspicuous is the contrast between the experience of the United States and that of Western Europe. In the latter, almost from the very beginning the factory provoked, along with the usual hosannas, turmoil, disruption, and bitter debate. In America, until nearly the twentieth century, the criticism and disturbance were much less violent. During the antebellum years only a few authors, southern politicians, and the small trade union movement (and just a part of it, at that) voiced deep reservations about the new economic system. After the Civil War the Knights of Labor conducted their abortive campaign against the "wage system." But it is not until the 1890s that one encounters a large-scale ideological assault on the ramparts of industrialism — one mounted, ironically enough, by a combination of socialists, agrarian populists, and "liberal," middle-class, urban political reformers. By then nearly a full century had elapsed since the first cotton-spinning factories had been established in America.

Why these strangely different reactions? What was it about America's experience with industrialization, about its people and their circumstances, that delayed for so long serious opposition to (or even discussion of) the factory and the changes it brought? And until that opposition emerged, how did Americans perceive, feel about, and cope with the rise of the factory system? It is to these questions that this work is addressed.

In periods of social transformation the early stages are usually the most difficult. The United States as it industrialized proved no exception. During the first seventy or eighty years of the nineteenth century many people were channeled into life patterns radically unlike any they had known before. Americans now have no recollection of their society as anything other than an industrial one, but most who lived in the last century had vivid memories of a quite different social order. To them fell the difficult yet imperative task of reconciling the past with the future. They were compelled to deal with the social implications of industrialization and to make some sort of judgment about its worth.

The national destiny was not yet irrevocably fixed on an industrial course. They stood at the crossroads, and they knew it.

Industrialization in the United States, as elsewhere, imposed a profound redirection on economic life. First and most obviously, it revolutionized man's manufacturing capabilities, giving him more power, precision, and, in some cases, skill to produce the things that formerly had to be laboriously turned out by hand. Yet it did much more than this; indeed, had this been its only result no one would have objected. As it flourished and spread, traditional ways of producing wealth became outmoded. Before long the factory system was so preponderant that it began to set the course for the rest of the economy. Farmers, for example, their share of the population steadily dwindling, turned to feeding the urban industrial masses. Many other people took up jobs whose very existence was made possible by, or whose chief purpose was to serve, industrial production. They furnished the raw materials or distributed the finished products of manufacturing. They built the cities, buildings, and transportation facilities that the factory system required. Or they benefited in a more general way by producing the goods and services demanded by a people made richer by the new order. In time there was hardly any significant occupational group in nineteenth-century America whose fortunes were not in some way (and usually in a major way) tied in with those of industry. The result was predictable. A populace composed in the eighteenth century largely of self-sustaining farmers was replaced by one where the labor force served predominantly in nonagricultural jobs. Concomitantly, a rural people migrated in a steady stream to the urban centers where those jobs were to be found.

These economic changes had a profoundly unsettling effect on the traditional order. Everything seemed to come unhinged. People began losing that restrictive, almost instinctual sense of "place" that had for so long served as the universal social gyroscope. Movement, growth, a new freedom expanded the individual's options immeasurably. What each would become he himself (or so he thought) would decide. His work, abode, style of life were no longer foreordained. Ambition kindled, he would let nothing deter him. The old, solid social institutions began to lose their hold. Village, "rank," even family, seemed less important. More than ever before, everyone was on his own. As these kinds of life patterns and attitudes spread, some observers worried about the disturbing world they were entering. Their sense of order and continuity was dissolving under the impact of bewildering, constant change. The worst side of human nature was coming to the fore: Serious crime and poverty and an excessive love of money seemed to betoken a general decay in all moral standards and institutional restraints. People were floating free from the old tight social fabric, self-absorbed, heedless of their obligations to others. Yet for other commentators the new system brought little to worry about. They readjusted their lives easily and filled their heads with exciting visions of liberty and opportunity.

The most tangible social consequence of industrialization was a new hierarchy of status and wealth. The vehicles of industrial production required men of uncommon traits: technical know-how, organizational skills, extensive resources, a certain willingness to take risks. Governments aided their endeavors with bounties, protective tariffs, patent laws, special charters and acts of incorporation, much of which, by its very nature, benefited a designated few. Almost from the start, then, the core of the reordered economy was not only owned but managed and controlled by a small group of "capitalists." Few were able to compete with them in the making of the world's goods.

Most other people became "workers." The machine was imperfect; it needed human assistance. Workers were most crucial in the factory, which required many,[1] but job openings also proliferated at the semimechanized craft shops, the railroads and canals, and with construction contractors and suppliers of raw materials, warehouses, banks, and commercial houses. As these positions were filled an ever greater fraction of the population entered the employ of others, selling the only commodity they possessed that capitalists wanted: their unadorned power to labor. The modern "working class" was created.

In preindustrial America most people had worked not for others, but for themselves. Employees existed, but their status was an unusual, often temporary one, confined mainly to the very lowest strata of the social order: day laborers, merchant seamen, schoolteachers, personal servants, apprentices, and helpers of all sorts. Even the many indentured servants who migrated to America had no intention of remaining in that inferior caste. This poorly paid minority was barely noticed — or deemed worth noticing — by the great mass of self-employed farmers, artisans, tradesmen, fishermen, and others engaged in "honest" callings. Industrialization changed all this. Gradually the worker became the typical, rather than the aberrant figure of society.

To appreciate the social readjustments this enlargement of the working class brought about, one has only to recall what it means to be an employee. The most basic fact is that the occupation of an employee, by definition, takes the form of a job. It provides a livelihood only when someone is willing to hire him and abruptly ceases to do so if he is fired. Of course a self-employed individual can also be thrown out of work. The farmer and the fisherman are at the mercy of natural calamities; an artisan may feel the pinch of a sudden decline in trade; and the merchant may fall victim to shifts in public taste. But these are more general, seemingly more providential reverses, not the doing of one man or set of men. In a real sense, then, the work done by the employee is controlled by another, bestowed upon him from outside. The assurance of being personally responsible for one's own economic fate, so strong in the self-employed, has been severely undermined.

It follows that the *nature* of the employee's occupation is also largely out of his control. A self-employed individual can (within the limits set by nature and the market) arrange the circumstances and patterns of his work to suit his own inclinations. Not so the employee. The length of time he works, the method and amount of his remuneration, the effort he puts into his job, the pace at which he toils, the conditions under which he works — all these aspects of his occupation are either limited or determined by his employer. Naturally, the worker is free to offer suggestions, to bargain, even to try to pressure his boss into making changes — and in certain labor market situations he may well have a chance of succeeding. But normally the only way he can alter his situation is by the extreme remedy of stopping work, either temporarily (as in a strike) or permanently (by transferring to another employer or another occupation altogether). This *dependence* of the employee is his peculiar burden. Historically, it is to be the major source of his distress under industrial capitalism.

An equally decisive feature of the employee's predicament springs from the way he is usually rewarded for his labor. Self-employed persons (if they are not also self-sufficient) are paid directly for their product or service by the consumer. The connection between what they make or do and what they receive is clear. It is noteworthy that in the early stages of American industrialization this method of remuneration was often carried over, when feasible, to the employed laborer. Shoe workers in small craft shops, hatmakers and dressmakers working at home, even some early textile mill operatives were paid on a piecework basis; that is, pay varied according to how much of the product (or part of the product) the individual worker turned out each day. Even the "share" system, by which whalers and some fishermen were reimbursed, was, if not exactly piecework, based on roughly the same notion. Very little research has been devoted specifically to piecework, but impressionistic evidence suggests that the practice lingered well into the nineteenth century, even in the most "advanced" industries.[2]

Before long, however, piecework gave way to what proved to be for the employer a much more functional method of remuneration: wages based on the amount of *time* put in at the job. Hourly or weekly pay rates became standard in one field after another.[3] More than a merely technical shift, the introduction of such rates ultimately altered the worker's attitude toward his job. No longer was he being paid for a specific product made or task accomplished, for something he could see or touch or at least have a solid sense of. Now, simply the duration of his toil determined his reward. Moreover, he received the same pay whether he worked fast or slowly, hard or lazily, carefully or sloppily (within, of course, the limits set by the stringency of the boss). The ultimate indignity came when he realized that it was not his exertions as an individual that mattered. Rather, he "earned" whatever rate he was getting because he belonged to a certain class of employees, all of whom received the same rate (though increments were often given based on length of service).

As an understanding of his situation penetrated, the wage worker came to look upon his job in a new light. His remuneration had little tangible connection with the specific work he was doing. He was being paid primarily for his labor power. And if he had any doubts on this score he had only to look around at his coworkers, all toiling with different aptitudes and varying degrees of efficiency, yet all getting the same wage rate. It was bewildering; worse, it was demeaning. The worker's personal contribution had been reduced to a trivial common denominator. His mode of reward stamped him as an easily replaceable source of mechanical effort — an impression that would grow stronger as, with the progress of industrial technology, jobs became simpler and thus required less skill and intelligence. He now appreciated fully what it meant to be a member of that generalized category, "worker."

Weak and dependent in economic terms, alienated from their jobs, their prestige and self-esteem slipping: these were the salient attributes of the working class in almost every industrializing nation of the eighteenth and nineteenth centuries. In time the full implications of their new circumstances would be clearly spelled out. For all but a lucky few skilled laborers, life became harder and more precarious. The home ceased to be the locus of economic activity, as the worker's employ brought him into a shop, factory, store, or some large bureaucracy, often a good distance from his residence. His job itself was often hazardous or unhealthy, and usually boring and unfulfilling. His formerly easy-going work habits had to yield to the demands of the machine. Efficiency, productivity, discipline, and punctuality were the watchwords of the new system. He was earning little, and found he could make ends meet only by sending his family out to work. His chances of rising to a better station, while varying from place to place, rarely were bright. In many instances, in fact, opportunities for upward mobility were fading rapidly: His training was now in unskilled or semiskilled occupations, which rendered him unfit to move up by the traditional route of becoming a self-employed craftsman. He generally lived in a town or city, amid conditions generally agreed to be deplorable. Finally, he was not alone. Once the economy was well along the path of industrialization, the working class embraced a majority of the population. It took its place at the lowest stratum of society, the human base upon which the industrial order rested.[4]

The rise of a large working class, then, was the leading social consequence of industrialization, particularly in its crucial early decades in America. And American workers shared most of the traits exhibited by their fellows abroad. It is sometimes argued that the young nation's industrial experience, especially in this initial stage, was not as brutalizing or exploitative as Europe's. Perhaps. But the fact (if indeed it is one) that the American worker was somewhat better fed should not be allowed to obscure the more important point — that his status as a worker was fundamentally analagous to his European counterpart's and marked just as great a change from the ways his immediate forebears had earned their daily bread.

In seeking, therefore, to understand nineteenth-century America's unique response to industrialization, one can hardly do better than to focus on its attitudes toward the worker. In Europe, the worker's sudden prominence — and precarious circumstances — lay at the heart of the stormy debate over the new order. How did Americans come to terms with his intrusion into their world?

One may start by observing that industrialization was not at this time a nationwide phenomenon. It sprang up in the Northeast, spread after a while to the Midwest, and up to the last decades of the nineteenth century had made but limited progress elsewhere. To apprehend the response to the working class in these years we must go to where there *was* a working class. (Conversely, if workers excited little concern there, all the more reason for other parts of the country to be apathetic.) The Northeast, then, becomes the logical choice for closer study. This work will focus on Massachusetts, one of the leading manufacturing states during the greater part of the century, as measured both by overall and per capita production, and the first (along with Rhode Island) to welcome the factory. Its inhabitants are thus ideally pristine subjects. They came to the experience of industrialization "raw," so to speak, and were forced to cope with it unaided by the trials of other Americans. The period between 1815 and 1880 will be the particular target here, as these were the years when the modern factory was introduced into Massachusetts and a large working class was established.

A stickier problem arises in deciding where, exactly, to look to discover "the response" to the working class. The ideal solution would be to sample a representative cross section of the population — everyone from tinsmiths to greengrocers to poets — collect their ideas on the subject, and somehow meld them into a generalized response. But the difficulties with this approach are formidable. What weight should be allotted to the opinions of each group? What about the many who leave no historical traces — letters, diaries, speeches? Would not any such sample in fact have an inherent bias towards the more literate, the wealthier, and the better educated?

There is a more indirect but, at the same time, sounder way of making contact with the public mind. One can choose to focus on the group that claims to speak for all the others, and whose success in doing so is continually being judged by society: its political figures. By selecting a large cross section of the political leadership of Massachusetts — government officials, aspirants for public office, and party chieftains — between 1815 and 1880 and examining their statements, it should be possible to get a clear impression of how people thought and felt about the working class.

At first glance this procedure may seem questionable. Living in an era when the stock of politicians has fallen abysmally, one tends to be unusually suspicious of the breed. It appears they hardly can be relied on to say honestly what is on their own minds, much less their constituents'. Then too, the time has long passed when government officials were assumed to be disinterested public servants. Legions of social scientists have confirmed what every legislative reporter always knew: that it is a rare politician who is not closely allied with some economic, ethnic, religious, or other kind of special interest group. When he acts, it is often for their benefit, whatever the masquerade of public concern he may assume. And his shrewd interest in his own survival inspires a good deal of the demagoguery, tricky dealing, and tawdry huckstering that so often mar political debate.

Yet granting all this, one is still left with a conundrum: These same men keep getting elected. They come before the public seeking the highest offices of trust and power their society has to bestow (a public that is usually well aware of their shortcomings, America's disdain for politicians being proverbial) and manage to win its approval. To see their success as a supreme triumph of cunning and deceit would overestimate their talents — and the voters' credulity. Other factors are at work here, and by recognizing them one can begin to understand how political discourse can serve as a significant index of public opinion.

At the root of every politician's career is the task of getting elected. In the course of running for office he soon discovers an important axiom: It will not do for him to appear as he really is. If he puts himself forth as hungry for office for its own sake or as representing a limited interest group, chances are he will lose. So the candidate learns that he must appear *larger* than he is, in order to widen his circle of support, to build a majority power base that will elect him, not only once, but, with luck, again and again. How this may be done he can determine by trial and error or by consulting his more experienced colleagues. More often he gains this knowledge haphazardly, simply by joining an established party organization, which, in its program, its appeal to the voters, and its ethos, embodies the accumulated political wisdom of a host of predecessors who faced the same problem. From these sources what he discovers is this: that he can handily improve his chances of winning by identifying himself with the citizens' deepest desires, hopes, anxieties, and fears; with their outrage or their pride; and with their most cherished values and image of themselves as a people and nation. If, in his talks on the campaign trail or at public gatherings or in the halls of the legislature, he can strike this crucial responsive chord, he will build up a fund of support that may prove nearly inexhaustible.

This strategy is particularly effective in times of far-reaching economic and social change, which tend naturally to excite the public mood. Those who find themselves riding the crest of the new wave are elated. They want recognition, congratulations, encouragement, perhaps reassurance that in entering untried paths they are not abandoning old ways. On the other hand, those who are bypassed, or worse, victimized by these transformations are apt to feel confused or angry, betrayed, lost, exploited, forgotten. In either instance there are bound to be great numbers of voters ripe for a skillful political appeal that will address their new situation. They will be seeking, too, some sort of guidance. They want explanations for what is happening to them, to know what they are leaving behind, and where they are headed. All this the adept politician can provide.

The point is, then, that whether he sincerely cares or does not, the politician must try to speak *for* the people as he is speaking to them. He needs to reach out effectively to his constituents, touching what is most vital to them. Only occasionally may he ignore this imperative. For example, he may find he can succeed by exploiting some narrow, temporary issue or, in special constituencies, by representing diligently some ethnic or racial group; he may also rely on personal charisma. And, of course, voters do pay attention to more mundane matters, such as where he claims to stand on a range of particular issues. But in most cases, in any large, diverse constituency, over an extended period — and especially in troubled times — it is incumbent on a politician to make deeper contact with the electorate. In so doing, he endows political discourse with an expressive function: It becomes an approximate, but nevertheless reliable barometer of public moods and concerns.

During most of the years being considered here, political figures in Massachusetts had every incentive and means to reach out to the electorate in this manner. From the mid-1820s onward state politics was in constant turmoil, with intense factional strife and well-developed, competing party organizations. These organizations were of special significance. One of the hallmarks of the Jacksonian party system (and of the one that succeeded it) was the great effectiveness with which it managed to read the public pulse and get its message across to the voters. Observes one historian: "Parties tended to become lively two-way channels of influence. Public opinion was heard with a new sensitivity and addressed with anxious respect. . . . As never before, the parties spoke directly, knowingly, to the interests and feelings of the public."[5] These responsive party mechanisms reflected a new spirit among politicians themselves. The old days of deference politics were gone. Now they were expected to mingle with the citizens, explain and defend their positions, listen to the electorate's views and take them into account. In the Age of the Common Man the adroit politician had to have the common touch.

Furthermore, politicians in Massachusetts were invested by their constituents with certain rather unique responsibilities. Since the revolutionary era its public figures had taken pride in the state's official designation as a commonwealth, which meant to them that overarching the particular interests of various classes and individuals was a paramount common interest, which it was the state's duty to promote. "That all shall be governed by certain laws for the common good" was how the constitution of 1780 defined the end and guiding principle of the form of government it set up. During the antebellum years this organic view of the duties of the state was to prove influential. It allowed the government to make the fullest use of its powers, often in quite creative ways, to unleash the state's economic potential and to supervise or even control the economic activities of its citizens. Massachusetts politicians were consequently expected by the voters to be attentive to the larger social and economic trends in order to shape them for the benefit of the entire polity.[6]

The electorate, it should be noted, did not include the entire adult population. The franchise was restricted to adult male citizens who could pay a small poll tax. But these men took an enthusiastic interest in public affairs. Residing in a state undergoing massive changes, they almost certainly must have wanted their leaders to talk about the unsettling, unprecedented phenomenon of industrialization. Moreover, there is every reason to believe that when those leaders did so talk, they chose their words carefully. To misapprehend the public mood could be disastrous. Crying alarm where none was felt would make them look like fools; trying to glide over a keen popular unrest would brand them as callous. To hit the right note, however, would win respect — and a following. They must have sensed too that with an experience as new as industrialization they could have a hand in actually shaping mass opinion. So long as they stayed within the bounds of plausibility and did not flout popular temperament or ideals, political leaders could crystallize half-formed thoughts, articulate vague stirrings, explain the confusing, or define an uncertain future. Yet whether they merely conveyed public concerns or went further to help set the terms through which those concerns were expressed, what they had to say was aimed at coming to grips with the way the populace was reacting to industrialization. As long as care is taken to insure that the sample of politicians covers the spectrum of political opinion — and includes the more popular among them — an analysis of their statements should yield a reasonably faithful portrait of the public's state of mind.

One last qualification is in order. Statements by politicians had this expressive function only so long as they were made in public. For only there were they held accountable for what they said (and only there could they influence the popular mind). In private conversations and letters they may have said something quite different, revealing much about their sincerity but very little else. Since we are concerned here with these men as conduits and shapers of public opinion, only those writings and speeches they intended for general consumption have been consulted.

The plan, in sum, will be this: to try to gauge the American response to industrialization by looking at the publicly expressed statements of Massachusetts politicians, between 1815 and 1880, on the rise of the working class and its place in the new order of things. Throughout, special attention will be given to comments on factory workers. These operatives were so intimately a part of the key transformations of the age that they became the exemplars of the working class. The more politicians spoke to their particular situation, the more plainly they voiced their opinion of industrialism generally. But whether they referred to factory workers specifically or to the larger working class, these leaders were forced to account for a veritable revolution in the social order of their state. The explanations they offered can tell us much about the equanimity with which America made way for the machine.

Chapter 2

Massachusetts: Building an Industrial State

To THE CASUAL observer Massachusetts at the start of the nineteenth century would hardly have appeared an auspicious setting for industrial development. Located on a poor, hard soil, it was devoid of any major natural resources save a potential for water power and its great forests (and in 1820 it lost much of the latter when its northeastern arm became the state of Maine). There was virtually no iron or coal, both so intimately connected with industrialization elsewhere. The shortage of manpower posed another problem. Workers were difficult to find for such tasks as building a road or fencing a field, much less staffing a factory. And few persons had even a rudimentary knowledge of the mysteries of modern industrial technology.

Yet first impressions can be misleading. Beneath this seemingly unpromising exterior the people of Massachusetts had been — unwittingly, of course — preparing themselves for industrialization. The configuration of the state's economy and the particular aptitudes of its citizens did much to ease the way for the factory system in the ensuing decades.

Perhaps the most crucial economic factor in this preindustrial phase was a negative one. The Bay State was *not* locked happily into a strictly agricultural mold. Farming, it is true, enlisted a healthy majority of the populace; even as late as 1820 it accounted for nearly three out of five in the labor force. But enthusiasm for tilling the soil could not have been very great. Outside the Connecticut River valley the ground was hard to work and minimally productive. Opportunities for growing crops for market were limited. Experimentation with new agricultural techniques languished. The farmer's standard of living hence was poor. In fact, a goodly number of farmers were reported in the early decades of the century to be leaving Massachusetts for the (literally) greener fields further west.[1]

With the prospects for success in agriculture mediocre at best, many, since the very first settlements, had explored other avenues of enterprise. Two for which the state had gained renown were fishing and trade. Both were doing well, despite the setbacks they incurred immediately before and after the War of 1812. The commercial and fishing towns along the coast also harbored a busy corps of artisans, turning out shoes, hats, cloth, candles, and other items by traditional handicraft techniques. In other words, before the advent of the factory the Commonwealth's productive apparatus was divided into several distinct fields of endeavor. This incipient diversification meant that the state's economic energies and ambitions, its capital and distributive mechanisms would not be closely geared to a single, all-embracing pursuit (as, say, those of the antebellum South were to cash-crop agriculture). Where a number of enterprises already existed it would be difficult to argue that the launching of a new one was somehow disruptive or improper.

Paralleling this economic adaptability was a certain looseness in occupational categories. Preindustrial Massachusetts, however primitive it may have been, was not a throwback to the medieval world. While most people probably slid into the same vocations as their parents (and continued in them for the rest of their lives), this was not an inflexible rule. It was generally understood that the path to success could well entail moving to a new place, essaying a new trade, or even carrying on several different trades at once. The biographies of the leading merchants and politicians of the preindustrial years are studded with examples of sons who left the rural areas where they were raised to migrate to the coastal towns, there to acquire fortune and fame. Early nineteenth-century census figures are notoriously inaccurate due to the large number of people engaging in two or more pursuits in the space of a single year. A farmer or fisherman in the summer months might well be a cobbler or blacksmith in the winter. What occupation he reported depended on when the census taker knocked on his door. Under these circumstances the introduction of a new set of occupational categories through industrialism would be viewed as a welcome expansion of opportunity. In England the coming of the factory was hotly resented by craftsmen and weavers whose families had been making a living at those hand trades for generations, and who could no more think of changing jobs than of changing religion. Such a reaction would have been unthinkable in Massachusetts.

Finally, it should be emphasized that most of the traditional nonagricultural occupations in Massachusetts were also capitalistic in nature. Artisans, fishermen, and, of course, merchants were men who made a living by seeking a profit in what were often chancy, shifting markets. This seems to have encouraged a certain opportunistic spirit in commercial affairs, one that would bode well for industrialization. As the historian Daniel Boorstin puts it, "The greatest resource of New England was resourcefulness."[2] New Englanders had through decades of experience refined the knack of seizing the main chance into a high art. They were willing to experiment with seemingly the most quixotic inventions, explore any business project with the barest hint of success, tinker with any established procedure in order to make a dollar. In fact, the early promoters of manufactures in Massachusetts were curious blends of probity, honesty, and frugality and of a commercial recklessness that would have made the crassest western land speculator blanch.[3] When they began sinking their funds into the newfangled factories, they were merely following the example of those intrepid ancestors who had smuggled tea into prerevolutionary Boston or opened up the China trade.

It is possible to pick out other, more concrete factors that helped pave the way for manufacturing in the Commonwealth. There were, for instance, its large capital resources, its adequate (though still primitive) system of roads and canals, its merchant marine.[4] But the context must be kept in view. A certain flexibility, openness, and even ambition were built into the economic and social fabric of preindustrial Massachusetts. These qualities inspired if not a passion then a definite readiness to experiment with new economic forms. The gate on the path to industrialization was at least unlocked.

With the first efforts in the years just prior to the War of 1812 surviving uncertainly into the decade following, the factory system was established in Massachusetts. Actually, to be technically correct one could point to still earlier experiments: the iron and paper mills of the revolutionary period and the cotton spinning works that George Cabot and friends started in Beverly in the late 1780s. These were, however, small, isolated, primitive efforts, often short-lived. The years surrounding the war marked the real breakthrough, as is made graphically clear by the record of charters granted to manufacturing corporations by the state legislature[5]:

Years	Number of charters
1789–1796	3
1800–1809	15
1810–1819	133
1820–1829	146
1830–1835	100

In the vanguard of industrialization was the manufacture of cotton cloth, which for many years to come would symbolize the state's industrial progress. Spurred by the embargo and the devastating curtailment of transatlantic trade during the War of 1812, several of the state's leading merchants diverted their spare capital into this fledgling enterprise. What is usually regarded as the first modern factory in America was a cotton textile plant that began operation in Waltham in 1814. This operation made such healthy profits that by the 1820s its backers were encouraged to erect a new, much larger mill complex at Lowell. Within a few decades the entire coast and the Connecticut River valley were dotted with cotton factories. Places like Lawrence, Fall River, New Bedford, and Chicopee — some of which had before been little more than sleepy agricultural villages — quickly grew into major industrial centers. By about 1830 the allied field of woolen manufacture was also recording notable advances, as the introduction of new power looms made it possible for the first time to incorporate all the stages of cloth production under one factory roof.

The other mainstay of Massachusetts industry was the making of boots and shoes. In the colonial period every town of decent size had boasted its own shoemaker, but after the Revolution the craft was extensively reorganized by merchant-capitalists. Central shops were set up in Boston and nearby towns, where expert artisans undertook the critical operations of shoe production, the simpler work being let out to semiskilled laborers in the surrounding villages and farms. Soon boxes of mass-produced shoes and boots were pouring into markets throughout the United States and abroad. Lynn, Haverhill, Brockton, Randolph, Brookfield, and other towns on the periphery of Boston, as well as Boston itself, became well known as shoe manufacturing centers. With the adaptation of the sewing machine to shoemaking in the 1850s true shoe factories appeared, substantially supplanting the independent craftsman. The tasks he had performed in making a single pair of shoes by himself were, by 1880, being done by over thirty different types of semiskilled operatives in the factory.

Paced by textiles and shoe manufacturing, industry advanced in Massachusetts, tentatively during the first few decades, vigorously after rebounding from the hard times of 1837–1839. The state's practically inexhaustible sources of capital, the technical capabilities of its engineers and inventors, the organizational skills of its promoters, and the distributive mechanisms perfected by its merchants all contributed to the factory's progress. In time the state became home to quite a variety of manufactures. The 1880 census lists among its major enterprises machinery and tool making, metals and various forms of metal-working, wooden goods and cabinet-making of all descriptions, paper, printing, and men's clothing. From before the Civil War there was little doubt that manufacturing would figure large in the Bay State's economic destiny.[6]

When one tries to represent Massachusetts's industrialization in numerical terms, difficulties arise. Strangely, for a century so enamored of statistics, reliable data are difficult to come by. The fact-gathering efforts of census officials were hampered by inadequate funding and disagreement over which manufacturing units were large enough to be worth counting. Moreover, when the incomplete and inconsistent figures are finally collated another problem complicates analysis: past definitions of what constituted "manufacturing" differ considerably from the one used today.[7]

Nevertheless, some informative figures, although crude, do survive, mostly for the later decades of the period 1815–1880. As presented in Table 1,[8] they show that by 1850 manufacturing was well established in Massachusetts and over the next three decades flourished handily. Other data indicate that throughout the antebellum period the Commonwealth was the leading industrial state in the Union. Later on it

TABLE 1. Statistics of Manufacturing, Massachusetts, 1850–1880

	1850	1860		1870		1880	
	amount	amount	decade increase in percent	amount	decade increase in percent	amount	decade increase in percent
Total state population	994,514	1,231,066	23.8	1,457,351	18.4	1,783,085	22.4
Number of manufacturing establishments	8,852	8,176	-7.6	13,212	61.6	14,352	8.6
Capital invested in manufacturing[a]	$ 88,940	$132,792	49.3	$231,678	74.5	$303,806	31.1
Value of products[a,b]	$157,744	$255,546	62.0	$553,913	116.8	$631,135	13.9

[a] In thousands of dollars.
[b] Includes "custom work and repairing."

slipped somewhat but definitely remained in the front ranks. A recent study of census material for 1880 puts Massachusetts in third place (behind New York and Pennsylvania) in the total amount of capital invested in manufacturing establishments and in the total value of its manufactured products. A more significant finding is that in per capita terms it remained first by far in both those categories. Quite simply it was — as it nearly always had been before this period — the most *thoroughly* industrialized state.[9]

TABLE 2. Occupational Categories of the Labor Force
in Massachusetts, 1880, by Percentage[a]

Occupational Category	Percentage
Agriculture	10
Forestry and fisheries	1
Mining	[b]
Construction	8
Manufacturing	42
Transportation	7
Trade, finance, etc.	14
Services and public administration (private household, 8%; all other, 11%)	19

[a] To nearest percent. Figures do not total 100 because of rounding.
[b] Less than 1%.

The growing ascendancy of the industrial system is also reflected in occupational statistics. Whereas in 1820 nearly three out of every five members of the labor force were engaged in agriculture, by 1880, as Table 2 indicates,[10] manufacturing alone engaged two of every five, and all nonagricultural occupations combined accounted for almost nine of every ten. (And these proportions, other tables will show, had obtained from roughly the early 1850s.) Even as late as 1880 virtually no other state had caught up. Massachusetts was second only to Rhode Island in the proportion of the labor force involved in manufacturing and second to none in the proportion in nonagricultural occupations.[11]

A final concrete measure of industrialization is the substantial increase in wealth that the factory induced. In 1840 Massachusetts had the highest total income per worker (and was the second highest, after Rhode Island, in overall per capita income) of any state east of the Mississippi.[12] Forty years later the Bay State was doing almost as well, with, according to one survey, the third-highest income per worker (behind New York and New Jersey) and the third-highest overall per capita income (behind Rhode Island and Connecticut).[13] Another survey shows that, in terms of personal income per capita, it was still first in the East.[14] While this income was quite unevenly distributed, to many people these solid material benefits were convincing proof of the awesome wealth-producing power of the machine.

As the factory system became firmly lodged at the base of the Massachusetts economy it began to agitate the state's traditional enterprises. After a while most of them fell under its sway. The new mode of production was not merely a *primus inter pares* but *the* vital economic activity. Its fluctuations came to spell prosperity or want for almost the entire populace.

The enterprise that felt most keenly the impact of industrialization, in radical and often unexpected ways, was agriculture. Until the coming of the factory most Massachusetts farmers probably fell under the heading of subsistence farmers, growing food for their own families and shipping but a small fraction of their crop to market. Only a lucky few residing close to the bigger towns could take a chance with the large-scale operations of commercial agriculture. Industrialization changed all this. By attracting laborers into urban areas it swelled the demand for food. The average farmer was only too willing to supply this new market. He boosted his output and even began specializing in those crops his location, soil, and climatic conditions rendered most profitable. Those near the industrial centers of Essex and Middlesex counties in the east turned to dairy farming and the growing of perishable vegetables and fruits, along with the usual grains. Others in the western part of the state found that raising cattle and sheep (for wool) yielded a handsome return. For quite some time industrialization made available opportunities for which the struggling farmer must have been grateful.

This happy symbiosis did not last for very long. In the 1830s the railroad made its appearance in Massachusetts. Promoted in good part by manufacturers seeking easier access to raw materials and to wider markets for their products, rail lines were quickly extended across the state. At first the farmer was pleased; better transportation gave him a wider market too. But the railroads' backers had grander ideas: After 1840 the state's rail network was linked up with the systems of the Northeast and Midwest. Almost overnight the Massachusetts farmer was forced into competition with the more fertile fields of those regions, with disastrous consequences. Trainloads of cheap western agricultural products began arriving in Boston, Lowell, and Fall River at prices the hapless local husbandman could not begin to meet. Especially hard hit were wool, wheat, pork, and cheese production, all of which, according to state census figures, fell dramatically between 1845 and 1875.

Once more farmers were compelled to make sharp readjustments to survive. Most shifted to dairy and truck farming, which soon became predominant throughout the state. Even then their condition remained precarious. After the Civil War they found it increasingly harder to hire adequate help. Industry and the towns were siphoning off the usual sources of farm labor from the countryside; the workers who remained were able to command higher pay. As farm costs escalated, the amount of capital necessary to carry on a successful operation rose markedly. Moreover, farmers who found themselves in a financial bind could no longer depend on supplementing the family income as before, by working at some craft, such as shoemaking, in the winter. Cheap manufactured goods cut them out of the market. Perhaps most disheartening of all, their own sons (and daughters) were no longer interested in following in their footsteps. Nonagricultural work promised greater and more certain rewards. As a contemporary observer noted, farmers were unable to keep up with "the present style of living": "their whole life becomes a continual struggle and deceptive show." He concluded, wistfully, that "the poetry and rhetoric of farming are very different from the reality of it." It is safe to guess that by 1880 the typical farmer must have been fairly bewildered (not to say exhausted) by the violent changes in fortune he had endured over the preceding sixty-five years. Yet he surely must have known that it was an ordeal for which industrialization was largely responsible.[15]

While not experiencing quite the same convulsions as agriculture, ocean-going trade, another traditional pursuit, was nonetheless palpably affected by industrialization. As late as the War of 1812 ships were embarking from Boston, Salem, and other ports laden with much the same goods carried by their Puritan predecessors: agricultural commodities, lumber, dried fish, and a varied assortment of handmade products. The dramatic opening of the China and East Indian trades in the 1790s had made maritime commerce more intricate and lucrative but had only a minor impact on the kinds of freight carried. With the introduction of the factory system new avenues of commerce were presented. Merchants started importing wool from South America and Turkey, coal from Philadelphia, hides from South America (for shoe leather), raw cotton and food from various southern ports to feed the burgeoning cities. In return they found a ready market in other states and abroad for the Commonwealth's manufactured products. Shoes and textiles were the most popular exports, most of them going to the South and to Latin America. All of this new, industry-related trade gave the state's ocean-going commerce a timely boost. In the 1840s and 1850s, in fact, commerce enjoyed its "golden age," as exports and imports flourished. Boston in particular, with its extensive rail connections into the interior, grew fat and wealthy. It was only after the Civil War that Massachusetts began to lose out to New York and other more southerly ports in the race for foreign trade. Even then, though, manufacturing continued to be a mainstay in the Commonwealth's dealings abroad.[16]

The prominent contribution of industry to maritime commerce points up indirectly one of its unique characteristics in Massachusetts. It relied on interchanges beyond the state's borders. How much is not yet known. In 1900 the national census reported that nearly all the materials used in manufacturing in the Commonwealth were brought in from elsewhere and that most of its manufactured products were consumed outside the state too. But for the earlier decades being treated here hard data are lacking. If one were forced to make a guess, though, a safe estimate would be that from at least the 1840s (if not before) the state's dependence on out-of-state markets and supplies must have been very great.[17]

These remote commercial ties inspired still another alteration in the state's economy, the growth of land transportation. By the 1820s the Commonwealth could rely on a fair number of roads, turnpikes, and short canals to join its major towns and connect them with nearby states.

A manufacturing economy, however, required a cheaper, more efficient transportation network — and one that would give the state access to the entire country. The ideal answer was the railroad. At the outset its promoters were cautious. The earliest railroads built (in the 1830s) were chiefly short feeder lines from Boston to Lowell, Worcester, and Providence, and of these, only the first carried large quantities of manufactured goods. More ambitious projects came later, with the construction of the Western Railroad in 1842 (united after the war with the Boston-Worcester line to form the Boston and Albany) and the merging of several lines into the Hoosac tunnel route in the 1870s. The hope of their backers was that these transstate lines would at last enable Massachusetts (and Boston especially) to tap the profitable western trade, draining off at least some of the wealth that was making New York the busiest port on the Atlantic.

In the end the railroads worked much as intended. They served industry well, and the carrying of manufactured goods was a vital ingredient in their own success. From across the nation came the resources the factory needed: raw cotton, wool, iron, coal. The industrial towns themselves demanded western wheat, flour, corn, livestock, and dressed meat, supplementing the already sizable quantity of those items sent to Boston for export. On the return trip the trains carried westward and southward the state's various manufactured products. Eventually even the most isolated areas of Massachusetts asked to be connected to this essential circulatory network. By the early 1850s every town, but one, with more than 5,000 people was linked to a railroad (as were three-fourths of the towns with populations of 2,500 to 5,000). The impact of the factory reached into every corner of the state.[18]

There were many other sectors of the economy that were affected one way or another by industrialization. The growing urban population offered a new market for the fisherman's catch. Merchants stocked their shelves with cloths and shoes of domestic manufacture. Carpenters, painters, plasterers, granite cutters, and those in other construction trades were employed to build the roads, houses, bridges, and various edifices that the expanding cities required. Not everyone prospered. Families engaged in household manufacturing and some skilled craftsmen found they could not compete with factory goods. In time they had to abandon their trades, often signing up as laborers in the very shops and mills that had thrown them out of work. But whether the effects were beneficial or harmful, the point is they did occur, extensively and with lasting impact. By 1880 industry had worked a profound transformation of the economy. Massachusetts had truly become an "industrial state."

Large economic changes usually force people's lives into new patterns. As men and women try to find their place in the revised order, they often must move from one area to another. The size and density of the entire population rise (or fall) in relation to the range of new opportunities made available to its members. Massachusetts in these years was a perfect example of these trends, which in fact its people were keenly interested in. Jesse Chickering, a contemporary student of demography, expressed a popular view when he wrote:

> Population is only one of the elements which constitute a community; still it is an essential element, and one to which all interests are subservient. By the increase or decrease of the inhabitants, and by the changes in their number and proportions in the several parts of the country, we may, to some extent, judge of the state of all the other elements of society.[19]

Gathering information on these matters, Chickering and others uncovered remarkable new evidence of the power of industrialization.

First they examined the overall size of the state's population. This was, for them, a grave subject. Like their compatriots across the United States they subscribed to the old principle that a steady rise in the number of people was an accurate gauge of the health of society (and they meant health in more than a medical sense). As they examined population figures for the earlier years of the century they must not have been pleased with what they found. As Table 3 shows, from 1800 to 1820 the decennial rate of increase of the state's population was barely one-third that of the United States as a whole.[20] Apparently the unappealing prospects in agriculture were persuading many of its inhabitants to emigrate.[21] By 1830, however, the state's rate of population increase had risen to one-half the nation's; by 1840, almost two-thirds; and in 1850 they were practically the same. In these years the Commonwealth also started to match the rates of other large states like New York and Pennsylvania. Thereafter its population would constantly grow more rapidly than that of the entire North Atlantic region (though it once again fell behind the national rate, albeit not nearly so far as before).

TABLE 3. Comparative Decennial Population Increases, Massachusetts and Other States, 1800–1880, by Percentage[a]

Decade	Massachusetts	New York	Pennsylvania	North Atlantic states[b]	United States
1800–1810	12	63	35	32	36
1810–1820	11	43	30	25	33
1820–1830	17	40	29	27	34
1830–1840	21	27	28	22	33
1840–1850	35	28	34	28	36
1850–1860	24	25	26	23	36
1860–1870	18	13	21	16	23
1870–1880	22	16	22	18	30

[a] All figures rounded to nearest whole percent.
[b] Comprises all states north and east of, and including, Pennsylvania.

Here was one area, then, where Massachusetts was clearly making "progress" — at least, as contemporaries understood it. But with a surging population came a predictable problem: crowding. As its inhabitants multiplied the state struggled to accommodate them. Traditionally thickly settled in comparison with other states, Massachusetts remained throughout the century the most densely populated of any in the Union, except for Rhode Island. Its number of people per square mile was at various points between two to four times higher than that of the entire North Atlantic region, and far higher than in the nation as a whole. There was such a thing, it was discovering, as too many people.[22]

What was behind this drastic increase in population? No doubt it was due partly to improvements in health conditions and medical practice. But the leading cause was the great influx of newcomers into the state. While information about people's place of birth began to be collected on a statewide basis only in 1830, the trends revealed are significant.

Table 4 indicates that in the decades of higher population growth rates between 1830 and 1880 there was a net gain of immigrants from other states (chiefly, the census tabulations show, the contiguous ones).[23] Be-

TABLE 4. Nativity Statistics for Massachusetts, 1830–1880

| Year | Total state pop. | Residents of Massachusetts[b] | | | | | | Residents of other states born in Massachusetts |
| | | Born within state | | Born in other states | | Foreign-born | | |
		Number	% of total[c]	Number	% of total[c]	Number	% of total[c]	
1830	610,408	a	—	a	—	8,735	1	a
1840	737,699	a	—	a	—	34,818	5	a
1850	994,514	695,236	70	134,830	14	160,909	16	199,582
1855	1,132,369	a	—	a	—	245,263	22	a
1860	1,231,066	805,546	65	163,637	13	260,114	21	235,039
1865	1,267,031	828,256	65	171,720	14	265,486	21	a
1870	1,457,351	903,297	62	200,735	14	353,319	24	243,880
1875	1,651,912	973,011	59	252,818	15	418,904	25	a
1880	1,783,085	1,088,565	61	251,029	14	443,491	25	267,730

[a] Not tabulated.

[b] Figures given under "residents of Massachusetts" may not add up to figure given under "total state population" for any given year because varying numbers are classified as having "unknown" place of birth and are not included in this table.

[c] To nearest whole percent.

tween 1850 and 1880 the number of people born in Massachusetts yet living in other states rose by 34%, an outflow more than made up for by the 86% increase in the number of Massachusetts residents born in the rest of the United States. However, even more responsible for the higher population increases was another source: the sudden arrival of great numbers of immigrants from foreign lands. The sharp jump between 1830 and 1850 in the number of the state's aliens reflects principally the emigration due to the great Irish famine, which commenced in the mid-forties. Ireland would continue to provide the bulk of the foreign-born settlers up to the Civil War. After the war (during which immigration practically ceased) immigrants came pouring in anew, only this time from other nations, predominantly Canada and Germany. All told, the proportion of foreign-born in the state's population mushroomed from 1% in 1830 to about 25% by the 1870s. And these totals do not include the large numbers of second-generation immigrants, classed officially as "native-born," whom many whose native stock went further back considered American only by a technicality.[24] It was these waves of aliens that swelled the Commonwealth's population so suddenly, and, just as crucial, so vividly altered its ethnic character.[25]

Why did all these people come to Massachusetts? The evidence points solidly to one factor: the jobs available in its industrial economy. On this most analysts, from Jesse Chickering to present-day historians, agree. Chickering, for instance, found that even in the relatively early period 1820–1840 the segment of the populace engaged in manufacturing was advancing at a much faster rate than the one in farming (and much of the increase for the latter occurred around thriving commercial or manufacturing towns). He reported as well that the aggregate population of eighty-eight of the "principal manufacturing towns" grew at a rate almost twice that of the state as a whole, and almost ten times that of a group of agricultural towns. "We may infer . . . ," he concluded, "that the whole increase during the 20 years, has been owing to manufactures, while that of the agricultural population, independent of the aids of manufacturing, has been little or nothing."[26] Later, a state official examining the 1860 national census discovered that, between 1830 and 1860, the population increase of certain "manufacturing towns" in six large counties was anywhere from two to as much as twenty-eight times greater than the growth of all the other towns in those counties.[27]

Another researcher, during World War I, dealt with population trends for all of southern New England between 1810 and 1860. His study revealed that those counties recording the greatest increase in manufactures also had the highest proportional increase in population. Particularly noteworthy was the effect of industry on urban growth: of twenty-six towns with a population of over 10,000 in 1860, most (with the exception of the major fishing ports) owed their growth wholly or in part to manufacturing. Conversely, towns in agricultural regions had either steady or declining populations.[28]

Admittedly, the preceding figures do not directly *prove* that it was economic opportunity that attracted people to Massachusetts. They merely show that areas where manufacturing was well established had disproportionately high growth rates. That growth could, theoretically, have resulted simply from an *internal* redistribution of the population — native farmers and other rural types pulling up roots to work in factories. To some extent, no doubt, this was the case. But if these trends are considered in conjunction with what is already known about where migrants from outside settled and what they did for a living, they suggest very strongly that the abundance of jobs (particularly factory and construction jobs) was the Commonwealth's strongest attraction. Certainly, in most other respects — such as climate, opportunity to own land, religious toleration — many other states were more desirable.[29]

These studies also point up another trend: As the population grew, so did urban areas. The proliferating factories gathered their labor force around them in clusters. Inevitably these concentrations boosted the population of adjoining towns — or even bred new ones, some of which matured into cities. The extraordinary growth of the textile towns of Lawrence, Lowell, and Fall River are but exaggerated examples of a process occurring all over Massachusetts.[30] Between 1810 and 1880 the state, which had always had somewhat of an urban cast, saw the fraction of its citizens living in towns and cities rise from 21.3% to 74.7%.[31] In the nation it was second only to Rhode Island as the most urbanized state. In particular, Boston and the neighboring towns within a twenty-five-mile radius, embracing a little more than one-third of the state's population in 1790, had by 1865 amassed more than half. As late as 1875 the Commonwealth's center of population still lay within one mile of the State House — although its geographical center was somewhere near

Worcester.[32] Boston and other cities were clearly acting as great magnets for rural natives, out-of-staters, and immigrants. And at the core of these cities' appeal were the jobs available in their shops and factories and in those enterprises sustained by manufacturing.

In short, the industrialization of Massachusetts at once augmented substantially and relocated the state's population. It is not difficult to imagine how this must have altered the average citizen's view of his world. In preindustrial times the slow, even increase of a people rooted for the most part in the country rather than the town had probably endowed society with a happy sense of stability. To be sure, the state *was* changing, becoming more prosperous, even in those days. But it was no doubt fairly easy to form a clear, closely defined image in one's mind of the social system of one's particular locality. A homogeneous community grew gradually within limited bounds. People tended to stay in the same place, sometimes for generations. The same faces kept reappearing, the same lives intertwined themselves with one's own. There was an undeniable *sureness* to social relations.

Industrialization disrupted this comfortable pattern. Suddenly new, usually very strange faces showed up to work in the factories. Sons left the land their fathers had plowed to seek more certain gain. Towns sprang up out of nowhere, or else grew so rapidly as to seem equally the work of some conjurer. People now thought nothing of moving from place to place and especially from city to city. In Boston, to take an extreme example, it has been estimated that between 1830 and 1860 one-half the city's population left and was replaced every one or two years! By 1860 less than 11% of its inhabitants had been born there.[33] Society, in other words, presented a far different image — one of flux, motion, restlessness. This does not necessarily mean that it was a more disturbing image. People, like children on a merry-go-round, may revel in the excitement of rapid change. Yet it certainly was an image that called for a sharp readjustment in the way the Commonwealth's inhabitants thought about their society.

The most visible social consequence of industrialization in Massachusetts was the creation of a large working class. The populace, composed in 1815 chiefly of self-employed farmers, artisans, merchants, and

fishermen, had by 1880 been fashioned into one in which a great majority of the labor force worked in the service of others. One would expect
that for a change of this magnitude mountains of hard data would be
available, but oddly enough, this is not so. National censuses did not
begin to specify the employer/employee status of even a limited number
of individuals until the second half of the nineteenth century and did not
include this question as a regular part of their tabulations until well after
the period described in this study. Still, using what information is available in these censuses and correlating it with material found in state
censuses of manufacturing for these years, it is possible to make some
rough guesses about the proportions of self-employed and employees in
various broad categories of labor. This has been done in Tables 5 and 6.
It should be emphasized that these figures are estimates only. They are
not derived directly from the censuses listed as their source.[34]

TABLE 5. Estimated Numbers, Various Divisions of the Labor Force,
Massachusetts, 1837–1880

Employment status	1837[a]	1845[b]	1855[b]	1870[b]	1880[b]
Independent					
Agricultural	85,000	71,500	51,300	41,800	42,400
Nonagricultural	39,000	65,000	80,400	103,000	122,000
Total independent	124,000	136,500	131,700	144,800	164,400
Nonindependent					
Agricultural	1,000	5,000	10,000	31,000	42,600
Manufacturing	79,000	109,500	187,500	256,400	312,400
Construction	7,000	16,400	18,300	32,200	34,900
Transportation and commerce	5,000	8,200	5,300	23,400	36,800
Fishing and extractive	15,000	17,300	19,100	11,800	12,000
Domestic service	10,000	16,300	31,400	45,800	52,800
White collar (all)	7,000	14,800	22,400	43,400	63,400
Total nonindependent	124,000	187,500	294,000	444,000	554,900
Grand total	248,000	324,000	425,700	588,800	719,300

[a] To nearest thousand.
[b] To nearest hundred.

TABLE 6. Various Divisions of the Labor Force, Massachusetts, 1837–1880, by Percentage[a]

Employment status	1837		1845		1855		1870		1880	
	Share of subtotal	Share of grand total	Share of subtotal	Share of grand total	Share of subtotal	Share of grand total	Share of subtotal	Share of grand total	Share of subtotal	Share of grand total
Independent										
Agricultural	69	34	52	22	39	12	29	7	26	6
Nonagricultural	31	16	48	20	61	19	71	17	74	17
Total independent		50		42		31		25		23
Nonindependent										
Agricultural	1	[b]	3	2	3	2	7	5	8	6
Manufacturing	64	32	58	34	64	44	58	44	56	43
Construction	6	3	9	5	6	4	7	5	6	5
Transportation and commerce	4	2	4	3	2	1	5	4	7	5
Fishing and extractive	12	6	9	5	6	4	3	2	2	2
Domestic service	8	4	9	5	11	7	10	8	10	7
White collar (all)	6	3	8	5	8	5	10	7	11	9
Total nonindependent		50		58		69		75		77

[a] All figures rounded to nearest percent. Percentages may not add correctly because of rounding.
[b] Less than 1%.

As these tables demonstrate, the data currently available permit calculations of the size of the working class as early as 1837. To attempt any
statewide estimates using the scanty figures collected for prior years is
tricky. It is easy, for instance, to put too much stress on some recent
investigations into the social structure of Boston in the revolutionary
period. This research shows that even then Boston was a city sharply
and clearly demarcated along class lines. While a mercantile and professional elite had amassed great wealth, a substantial part of the citizenry
— almost half by 1790 — could be classified as "poor" or "near poor,"
usually barely managing to scrape by. Many of these poor people (and of
the middle classes too) were probably employees. Artisans comprised
half the Boston labor force in 1790, and since the typical master craftsman of the time usually hired a small number of apprentices and journeymen (rarely more than five), a good number of those artisans were
therefore workers. Another fifth of the labor force served as clerks or
scribes, in service trades, as sailors, or in unskilled occupations; nearly
all of them must have been employees too. Adding these various groups
together one might safely conclude that from 40% to 60% of Boston's
labor force in 1790 consisted of employees. It is hence possible to argue
that a large working class was present in Massachusetts well before the
coming of industry.[35]

This hypothesis sounds plausible, but it ignores one crucial fact. In
this period Boston, even Boston and the state's other cities combined,
were not mirrors for Massachusetts. In 1790 fewer than one out of every
seven people in the state lived in an urban area; most lived on farms or
in small villages. Very little is known about the social structure of the
countryside, but all indications are that class divisions there were much
less extreme and the proportion of employees far smaller than in the
cities. The crude enumeration of occupational categories given in the
1820 United States census is also instructive:

Agriculture	63,460 (58%)
Commerce	13,301 (12%)
Manufactures	33,464 (30%)

Judging from the state of the Massachusetts economy at this time, one
may assume that nearly all the agricultural classification, and a good part
of those in commerce and "manufactures" (in 1820, still mostly artisans)

were self-employed people. It is hard to believe that the Massachusetts working class in 1820 constituted more than one-quarter of the labor force, if that. Ultimately these Boston studies serve only to reinforce a point made before: The working class did not originate with the factory but arose in the commercial cities quite some time before. However, it was definitely a minor, geographically isolated phenomenon until its numbers mushroomed under industrialization.[36]

Tables 5 and 6 offer clear evidence of its growth. Even in 1837, less than a quarter century after the Waltham mill was erected, fully one-half the laborers in the state worked for others. From then on the working class expanded steadily, as the proportion of self-employed correspondingly fell. The tables illustrate too the components of these trends. The decline in self-employed was due almost entirely to a drop in the number of independent farmers, not only in percentage terms but absolutely. The self-employed in nonagricultural fields fluctuated between one-fifth and one-sixth of the entire labor force. The reasons for the rise in the employee sector are more complex. Workers in manufacturing, the majority of this group, increased somewhat in relation to the whole. But so did, most noticeably, employees in farming, domestic service, and white-collar jobs of all descriptions. Combined, their numbers mushroomed: by 1880 over three-fourths of those laboring in Massachusetts were members of the working class.

Hence it was in these industrializing years that the working class became a significant, conspicuous, permanent feature of the social order. No longer was it confined to a relative few in the coastal towns or associated with trades where the status of employee was a mere steppingstone on the way to becoming one's own master. Now it could be found across the entire state, and increasingly it was a status that individuals retained all their lives. The manner in which the average person earned a living had undergone a veritable revolution.

It is instructive to compare the growth of the working class in Massachusetts with its contemporaneous development in the rest of the nation. A recent attempt to classify the American labor force in 1870 is presented in Table 7,[37] with the relevant figures for Massachusetts in Table 6 inserted alongside. (The groupings in that table have been realigned where necessary to match the categories of the study cited.) Interestingly enough, the Massachusetts working class was not much bigger in proportion to the whole labor force than the national one. But its composition was very different. Whereas in the nation more than two of every five employees were farm laborers, in Massachusetts not one in fourteen was. The vast majority of the state's workers were in all sorts of nonagricultural jobs, most of them in "industrial" occupations (here, a catchall category for all nonagricultural, nonservice, and non–white-collar positions). Even the figures for the self-employed reflect the state's industrial and commercial orientation. The Commonwealth's working class, in short, was not only a more prominent feature of the social landscape than it was in virtually any other state. It was also — even as late as 1870 — quite atypical of the working class of America as a whole.

TABLE 7. Divisions of Labor Force, United States and Massachusetts, 1870, by Percentage[a]

Employment status	United States	Massachusetts
Independent		
Agricultural	24	7
Nonagricultural[b]	9	18
Total independent	33	25
Nonindependent		
Agricultural	29	5
Nonagricultural:		
Industrial	27	55
Domestic	8	8
White collar	3	7
Total nonagricultural	38	70
Total nonindependent	67	75

[a] To nearest percent.
[b] Includes in United States figures "company officials" who in Massachusetts figures are classified under white collar employees.

One last statistical series is in order. Considering the large part that employees in manufacturing played in the total working class of Massachusetts, it is useful to break that category down further. Table 8 presents estimates for the major constituent groups of employees in man-

TABLE 8. Estimated Number of Dependent Workers in Nine Major Manufacturing Groups in Massachusetts, 1837–1880[a]

Manufacturing group	1837	1845	1855	1870	1880
Textiles and related industries	27,600	32,600	49,600	70,200	93,000
Boots and shoes, leather	35,300	43,200	71,800	52,000	61,500
Metals and metal-working[b]	3,100	4,300	7,900	12,400	16,000
Clothing	1,700[c]	14,800	16,300	21,900	23,300
Machinery and tools	1,500	3,200	9,500	2,200	3,200
Furniture, wooden goods, etc.	1,600	1,100	4,200	2,600	5,900
Paper	1,100	1,300	2,400	3,600	6,800
Printing and publishing	1,000	800	1,200	4,000	6,100
Boats and vessels	2,500	1,000	3,600	2,900	1,700
Total for nine groups	75,400	102,300	166,500	171,800	217,500
Total manufacturing employees in state[d]	79,000	109,500	187,500	256,400	312,400

[a] All figures to nearest hundred.
[b] Excluding blacksmiths.
[c] Does not include straw bonnet domestic industry, which is included for later years.
[d] From Table 4.

ufacturing between 1837 and 1880.[38] Not surprisingly, those engaged in the textile and shoe industries (and their allied fields) formed a majority — though a dwindling one — of the entire class. As their ascendancy weakened and the state's industry diversified, other groups came to the fore, notably those in metals and clothing manufacture. Even in the later years, though, there were still far more workers in textiles or shoes than in any other field. It is no wonder that they were regarded throughout this period as the "typical" workers.

The statistical record of industrialization in Massachusetts leaves a vivid impression of the transforming power of the factory. A short time after the machine was introduced the Commonwealth became a manufacturing leader; more important, it was the state most thoroughly given over to extensive industrial development. Almost all the older forms of enterprise eventually fell under its sway.

As it spread the factory reshaped the social order. Like some mighty hand it gathered in masses from other states and abroad, then collected the populace in urban aggregations. And, as its scale grew larger, its operations more diverse, its organization more complex, it became preeminently the instrument of those who could accumulate enough capital to make it work. The great majority of people abandoned the self-sufficient ways of their forebears and entered the employ of those who owned and managed the beneficent giant.

Ever more insistently the economic and social implications of the industrial system forced themselves on the common awareness of the people of Massachusetts. The political leaders of the state were called on to analyze, explain, and most important to justify the new order. So, with a mingling of apprehension and pride, they set about doing just that.

PART II
The Bright New Order,
1815–1865

"There is, indeed, no subject which so much requires an essay to set forth all its prominence, importance, and peculiarity, as American labor; there is nothing like it on the globe; and there never was anything like it."

— Daniel Webster, 1843

Chapter 3

The Bounteous Factory

THE RESPONSE of Massachusetts political figures to industrialization may be understood more fully by looking at it first from another perspective. To appreciate what they did one should also know what they might have done, yet did not. Since the American reaction to industrialization differed so noticeably from Europe's, it would be instructive to take a look at how some European politicians approached the same question. The best example for study is that contemporary archetype of all industrial development, Great Britain. This exercise, it should be stressed, is not meant to imply that Britain and Massachusetts in this period are "the same." Obviously, Britain was a more complex and ancient society with unique customs and institutions. But the two were definitely related, somewhat like cousins. Massachusetts in fact had long been (and would continue to be) the state most nearly like the former mother country. Hence there should be enough parallels to make a comparison illuminating.

It has become something of a fashionable game among historians to argue about when the English Industrial Revolution "started." But if one asks simply, at what point in time national manufacturing output begins accelerating noticeably because of the use of new machines and processes, the evidence points fairly decisively to the period just after the "American war" — the 1780s and 1790s. At this juncture, T. S. Ashton has observed, nearly every measure of British industrial output veers sharply upward. More than half of the century's increase in coal shipments and copper production, more than three-fourths of the increase in broad cloth manufacture, four-fifths of the rise in printed cloth production, and nine-tenths of the climb in the exports of cotton goods are compressed into its last eighteen years. Thereafter industrialization would proceed at full steam.[1]

The story of Britain's industrialization hardly needs recounting, but there are some analogies between the British experience and that of Massachusetts worth noting. Both started from the same base, heavily committed to agriculture, yet boasting a well-developed ocean-going commerce and a thriving collection of artisans (though in these latter areas Britain had made much more progress). With both, "foreign" trade[2] and foreign wars proved crucial in encouraging factory production. Each society's first industrial efforts were in cotton textiles, which for a long time remained its leading manufacturing enterprise. (Where Britain would soon outpace Massachusetts was in its rapid development of mature industries in producers' goods — coal, iron, transport vehicles, and machinery. In this area Massachusetts was to make little headway.) In other words, to quite a striking extent the Bay State followed in Britain's wake.

It was in Britain, of course, that the classic example of a modern working class emerged. Throughout the Western world the Lancashire cotton mill operatives, Durham coal miners, Sheffield steel workers, and Spitalfields silk weavers became renowned as symbols of the new order. Still, they were only the most conspicuous examples of a much larger trend. From the mid-eighteenth century an ever growing flood of people crowded into already teeming London and the northern industrial towns to seek work in the prosperous shops and factories. A drastic shift in the occupational structure of British society ensued as more and more men and women entered the employ of others. Whether they benefited thereby or not is still hotly contested. It is evident, though, that for all but a small, highly skilled "labour aristocracy" their lives were generally marked by enervating and dangerous toil; cramped, unhealthy living quarters; barely adequate food for their families; uncertain employment; and, looming over all, a haunting and only slowly receding poverty. To be sure, masses of poor had existed before industrialism. But they had been closely bound with the rest of society in a hierarchical network of dependence and responsibility. The new working class was far more of a segregated, alienated, even threatening class than the cottagers and paupers of old had ever been.[3]

Since British population statistics of the late eighteenth and early nineteenth centuries are about as primitive as America's, it is difficult to illustrate the growth of the working class in quantitative terms. One must resort to inferring its size from trends known to be associated with a working class, such as urbanization and the number of people in manufacturing and in nonagricultural occupations generally. The data for these areas are presented in Figures 1–3, with the comparable statistics for Massachusetts included.[4]

What is first apparent from these figures is how large Britain's "manufacturing" and nonagricultural populations were *before* the Industrial Revolution. This is not surprising: from the Middle Ages on there had always been a fair number of people working in commerce, trade, and handicrafts, even in rudimentary factories in such fields as brewing, shipbuilding, and pottery making. Yet, as with Massachusetts, one must be careful in trying to extrapolate the size of the British working class from population figures for the preindustrial years. The average shop or store was then quite small. Correspondingly, the proportion of self-employed in the nonagricultural population must have been fairly high, the proportion of workers low (even granting the many servants, miners, military personnel, and domestic workers). It is only with industrialization that one finds a significant, even striking increase in the size of the work place — and along with it, a sharp jump in the size of the working class.[5] In interpreting these figures, then, one can assume that those for the later dates covered include higher proportions of workers. But even taking the percentages at face value, without trying to guess how many workers they "hide," the increases after 1800 are remarkable: a continual, rapid rise in every index (though the size of the manufacturing population tapers off by midcentury). Despite periodic depressions and setbacks, the Industrial Revolution rolled onward. A conservative estimate would be that as early as 1800 at least half the labor force consisted of workers (both agricultural and nonagricultural). By 1850 the figure must have risen to at least two-thirds. The worker had come to cast his shadow over all of British society.

How did British political figures, in the century after 1780, respond to this momentous transformation?[6] For a while, their reaction was sluggish, distracted, muted. The intense political infighting of the 1780s gave way to a furor over the French Revolution and two decades of desperate war with the new republic. With Britain persuaded that its very existence hung in the balance, almost all questioning of the social order — and some incipient popular unrest — was quashed by a jingoistic public sentiment and, where necessary, diligent government pros-

FIGURE 1. Urban Population as Percentage of Whole, England and Wales, London, and Massachusetts, 1685–1885

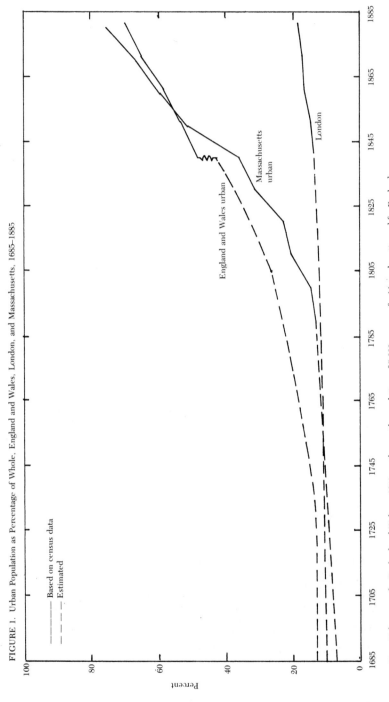

——— Based on census data
– – – Estimated

England and Wales urban

Massachusetts urban

London

Note: Urban areas for England and Wales to 1841 are those with populations of 5,000 or more; for Massachusetts, and for England and Wales from 1841 those with populations of 2,500 or more.

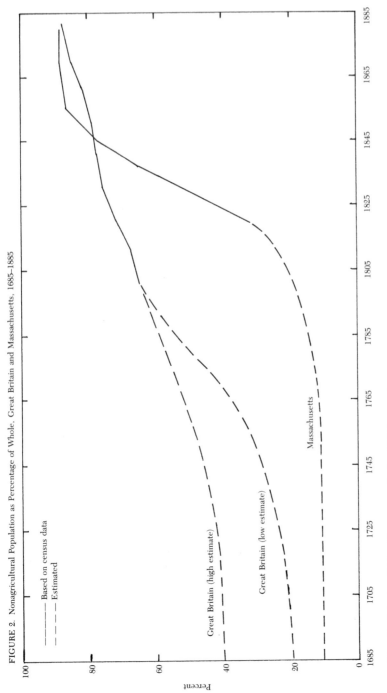

FIGURE 2. Nonagricultural Population as Percentage of Whole, Great Britain and Massachusetts, 1685–1885

Based on census data
Estimated

Great Britain (high estimate)

Great Britain (low estimate)

Massachusetts

Percent

1685 1705 1725 1745 1765 1785 1805 1825 1845 1865 1885

0 20 40 60 80 100

Note: For derivation of high and low estimates for Great Britain, see note on sources.

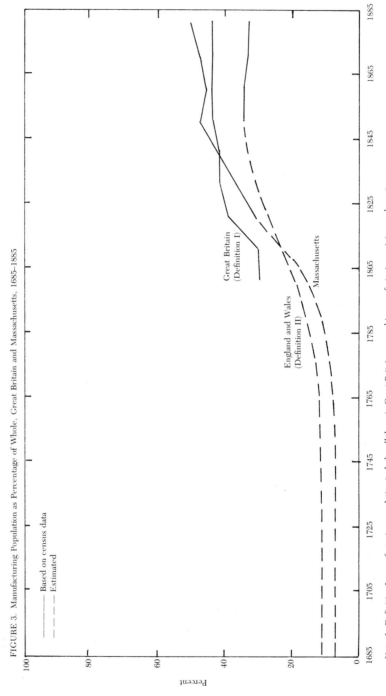

FIGURE 3. Manufacturing Population as Percentage of Whole, Great Britain and Massachusetts, 1685–1885

Based on census data
Estimated

Great Britain
(Definition I)

England and Wales
(Definition II)

Massachusetts

Percent

Note: In Definition I, manufacturing population includes all those in Great Britain engaged in manufacturing, mining, and construction. In Definition II, it includes all those in England and Wales engaged in manufacturing only.

ecution of "seditious" speech, writings, meetings, and organizations. The attention of politicians, in other words, was turned from the internal revolution by revolution abroad.

It is quite likely, though, that politicians would have been slow to respond in any case. The British political structure at the turn of the century, and for many years thereafter, hardly was geared to take into account the needs of the manufacturing sector, much less those of the working class. Power rested firmly in a narrow elite that stood fast against all democratic innovations. This tight-knit, interrelated, fairly closed hereditary group, with its roots in the countryside (and, to a lesser degree, the great mercantile houses), was only half-heartedly attentive to the desires of the grubby new industrial entrepreneurs. The only possible avenue of influence for these industrialists (and their employees), the House of Commons, was chosen largely by an upper social stratum — fewer than one in ten adult males in the kingdom — and, in the distribution of its seats, grossly underrepresented the burgeoning manufacturing towns. Only the more well-off workers — securely established skilled artisans, usually — had formal political power, and even then not very much at all. The great bulk of the working class could catch the attention of Parliament and Crown only by taking to the streets.

Not surprisingly, it was easy for this kind of political system to virtually ignore the growth of industry and the working class — not necessarily out of malice but simply because its base lay in another, older world. Some aid was offered to manufacturing: Restrictions on internal commerce and laws regulating work and wages were eliminated; protective duties were instituted.[7] However, two episodes early in the nineteenth century showed clearly that the statesman's first concerns lay elsewhere. The Orders in Council of 1806 and 1807, curtailing neutral trade with enemy ports on the Continent, provoked American retaliation and soon brought about severe setbacks in British manufacturing, heavily dependent on American raw materials and markets. Ineffective against Napoleon, the orders nevertheless remained in force until 1812, principally because of pressure from mercantile interests. Only numerous petitions to Parliament and rioting by the desperate unemployed in Birmingham, Sheffield, and Leeds finally brought about their repeal — just in time to avert severe civil disorder, but too late to prevent war with the United States.[8] Then, in 1815, in response to agricultural distress, the government passed the Corn Laws, unconcerned that the high duties on foreign grains would drive up the price of flour and bread. Once more petitions poured in from the provinces, manufacturers protested, a violent mob ran through London. All to no avail. The laws stayed on the books, a source of rancor in British politics for the next three decades. In short, Parliament was willing to assist manufacturing but in the end was to be found squarely on the side of the landed interests (and their ally, trade) whatever the consequence to the industrialist or the working class.[9]

This indifference, even hostility, to the demands of the industrial sector was to be challenged forcefully upon the conclusion of the Napoleonic wars. During the struggle's closing years the poor, and particularly the workers, were called upon to shoulder a disproportionate share of its burdens. Inflation, high taxes, high duties, and a general industrial depression hit them hard. In the North of England displaced handicraft workers lashed out against the machine in the Luddite attacks. France's defeat raised hopes that relief would soon follow. It did not: Hard times persisted until 1820. In the provinces and in London laborers began to band together for the first time to bring public attention to their predicament and to demand action. It is in these years, according to one historian, that the working class as a self-conscious, unified entity was forged. "Radical" organizations sprang up in Westminster. Similar reform clubs surfaced in the North, spreading radical papers, "educating" the workers, in some instances holding military drill to prepare for attack. As discontent festered, violence broke out. Riots and protest marches were common. Serious strikes occurred. The turmoil culminated in "Peterloo," a bloody charge in 1819 by armed troops on a huge workers' meeting near Birmingham, which shocked the country.[10]

This outburst of worker agitation marked a turning point. It had pathetically little concrete effect: Indeed, it brought only stern government repression. But it did produce a startling change in the political climate. Now, for the first time, the established leaders of the nation were *aware* of the workers, of their numbers and their grievances, and above all of their revolutionary potential. In a country that had not experienced severe, prolonged, massive internal disruptions since the seventeenth century this came as a shocking discovery. The voiceless masses had finally spoken, indeed roared. It was plain that the old combination of deference and intimidation that had for so long kept "the lower orders" in their place was fast crumbling. From this point on no English political figure could be oblivious to the working class.

The workers themselves made sure they were not ignored. The history of the next fifty years is charged with their ominous presence, hovering outside the system and demanding stridently to be taken into account (and ultimately, to be let in). Workers' organizations of all types proliferated. Despite government opposition and continuing legal harassment after the repeal of the Combination Laws (1824), an effective trade union movement developed, especially among skilled workers. By midcentury the "New Model" unions were well established on a nationwide basis, securing modest gains for their members and even starting to play a role in politics. A fair number of workers found a home in the nascent socialist movement. But it was in their more issue-oriented political organizations — pressure groups devoted to achieving some immediate change — that the voteless laborers (helped by middle-class sympathizers) had their greatest impact. Scores of associations were set up in these years, holding meetings, propagating reform ideas, running petition drives, publishing newspapers and pamphlets, and in general arousing enthusiasm for their various programs. They were most successful in drumming up public support for what eventually became the Reform Act of 1832. When that measure proved to be of meager benefit to the working class, new efforts were undertaken. Much of this coalesced around the Chartist movement. For ten years, until the mid-1840s, many workers threw their energies and hopes into this vigorous campaign to democratize the political system. It ended, however, in nothing but frustration. Only after another two decades did the workers gain at least some of the political influence they were seeking, and the Reform Act of 1867 owed much to their labors. These parliamentary reform associations, along with a host of similar ones agitating for changes in the Poor Law, the Corn Law, for factory legislation, and the like, transmitted the worker's voice into the halls of power.

Finally, there was the awesome effect the working class could have as an *un*organized mass. Time and again laborers would gather in huge meetings to express their discontents. At the peak of the reform agitation in 1831 the Birmingham Political Union was able to bring together as many as 150,000 people. This display of force was not lost on the politicians of the day. Nor were they any less impressed by the darker manifestations of worker strength, the numerous riots and mobs that scar the history of the first half of the nineteenth century, especially during hard times or moments of political excitement. Though Britain never went through anything like the Continental revolutions of 1830, 1848, or 1871, the sporadic labor violence served as a warning of the immense potential for destruction that lay within the working class.[11]

All this agitation, if it accomplished nothing else, stimulated nation-wide soul-searching and controversy. Through every rank of British society the meaning and value of industrialization became one of the leading public questions of the day. On the one side were those who had severe reservations about the new order. They included such independent spirits as William Cobbett, Robert Owen, John Ruskin, William Morris, Charles Dickens, John Henry Newman, Thomas Carlyle. All very different men, their diversity was their strength, for together they appealed to many constituencies. Then there were others who, just as vehemently, defended industrialism and dismissed the workers' complaints as ungrounded: the persuasive economists of the Manchester School, apologists such as Andrew Ure, and of course the manufacturers themselves. The clash of this debate sounded a continuing obbligato to the history of the early and middle 1800s. Occasionally the argument grew to an intense pitch, as in the dark violent period of the late thirties and early forties, when "the condition of England" was on everybody's lips and Disraeli penned his famous portrait of English society as "two nations between whom there is no intercourse and no sympathy." At other times, as in the sedate fifties, the debate was muted although, despite all that has been written about "Victorian consensus," still very much alive. Britain's politicians ascended to power with these arguments raging around them. Many decided to join in.[12]

Quite a few statesmen allied themselves with the detractors of industrialism and even became open advocates of the worker's cause. They were a curious lot, ranging from the most highly principled to the most crassly opportunistic. Included in their ranks were a small but energetic band of Philosophical Radicals; some representatives of the landed interest; philanthropic Dissenters and Evangelicals like Lord Ashley,

Richard Oastler, and Michael Sadler; Conservatives like Disraeli; even a group of factory owners headed by John Fielden. On occasion these critics of the new order were able to go beyond talk, to combine forces to achieve significant reforms. But only on occasion. Usually they were in fact men crying in a wilderness. As one reads through the historical literature on this period one is struck by how *little* the political system as a whole favored the worker's cause, or, for that matter, was even seriously moved by his plight. The old landed and commercial interests, still firmly in control of Parliament after the Reform Act of 1832, were no more concerned about the worker than before. And although manufacturers, entrepreneurs, small merchants, and the middle class generally did start amassing political strength, as a rule they were too closely identified with the "respectable" portion of society to care much about those on the other side of the (ever-widening) class gap. Hence it is scarcely surprising that almost every government from Liverpool's to Palmerston's resolutely turned a deaf ear to workers' demands. Most continued the traditional policy of impeding union activities and creating obstacles for working class organizations and newspapers. Nearly every important measure that helped workers had to be won through a long, hard struggle on their part — and sometimes, as the Chartists learned so bitterly, even that was insufficient. Often measures that workers desired were watered down to make them more palatable, and it seemed there was nothing they could do to avert inimical legislation, most notably the Poor Law of 1834. The workers quickly learned not to count on most politicians' compassion: Only pressure achieved results.

Yet despite this, there is a larger truth about this political system that must be acknowledged. However begrudgingly it acceded to their wishes, it nevertheless *was vitally aware that workers had to be taken into account.* Even if a politician despised them, he knew full well they constituted a problem that could not be ignored. It was conceded by all that they represented a fundamental, even alarming alteration in the traditional social hierarchy. They had to be studied, reckoned with, provided for. For political leaders to do anything less would be to abdicate their responsibilities and, more pragmatically, could be potentially dangerous.

For these reasons the discussions of nearly every major social and economic issue of the times were studded with references to the working class. To learn more about it special commissions were set up to look into conditions in factories and mines and study the operation of the Poor Law, unions, municipal health problems, and other worker-related topics. On the floor of Parliament the working class was considered in the deliberations on many important areas of legislation. Parliamentary reform is a notable example. The intense debates that led to the Reform Act of 1832 took place against a background of popular unrest, fomented in large part by working class political associations. That any act was passed at all was due principally to this pressure. Later workers took an even more active role in the struggle for reform, first through Chartism, then in the maneuvering that produced the Reform Act of 1867. Since the various bills under consideration would enfranchise substantial numbers of workers, the wisdom of doing so was hotly debated in Parliament, while outside workers' reform associations and violence again had a telling effect. The act that resulted added a million workers to the lists in the boroughs, giving them for the first time a significant formal voice in the political process.

One can cite many other controversies in which the status of workers figured prominently. In the prolonged Corn Law debates, for example, a persistent theme was the effect of the law (and of its repeal) on the price of workers' bread and wages. Proposals for expanding government aid to education and to promote public health evoked — actually, grew out of — concern for the lack of schooling and the poor sanitary conditions that prevailed in working class districts. The laws that were passed barely made a dent in these problems, but a great deal was done by men like Edwin Chadwick and Sir James Kay-Shuttleworth to focus parliamentary attention on them. The conflict over the Poor Law of 1834 and over the activities of the commission that law established dealt inevitably with the subject of working class poverty and the causes thereof. The issue most germane to the worker's situation, the hours and conditions of labor, was the subject of extensive discussion. Parliamentary investigations disclosed shocking treatment of employees in textile mills and coal mines. Working class political associations and Short Time Committees in the northern cotton towns worked tirelessly for ameliorative laws. Joining their cause were eloquent and effective allies, like Chadwick, Oastler, Sadler, and Lord Ashley, whose speeches in Parliament sparked a lively dispute on the plight of the factory operative.

Their tenacity resulted in substantial legislation: the Factory Acts of 1833 and 1844, the Coal Mines Act of 1842, the Ten Hours Act of 1847, and the Factory and Workshops Act of 1867. These laws curtailed the working hours of women and children (and indirectly, men) and required at least elementary schooling of young workers in most important industries.[13] There were still other issues: the power of trade unions, working class support of foreign revolutions, the general unrest among laborers in times of distress, the workers' role in the nation's prosperity. The list was fairly interminable.

In the first century or so of the Industrial Revolution, then, the British political system, after a slow start, was continually engrossed in argument over the situation and practical implications of the new working class. During most of this time that class itself was formally excluded from power and able only by extraordinary effort to win concessions from a series of antagonistic governments. Yet if the state did not always respond favorably, it did at least listen. Political leaders realized that in most important areas of decision the circumstances and wants of the laborer would have to enter into their calculations. And a good number of them were coming around to the view that workers were now such a major component of the social order that government would have to move in unprecedented ways to provide for them. To paraphrase Marx, the specter of the working class haunted the political arena. No one in a position of authority, whether sympathetic or not, could afford to ignore it.

This excursion into English history done, it is time to return to Massachusetts as it was industrializing to see how its politicians' reaction to the growth of the working class compares with Britain's. Since, as will be demonstrated, the substance of that reaction evolved with time, it is appropriate to divide the rest of this study into two segments. This one, part 2, will cover the years 1815–1865. Part 3 will deal with certain changes that occur in an overlapping period, 1840–1880.

For both of these periods a large and, I believe, representative sample of political speeches, pamphlets, and other literature was inspected. I selected forty-two leading figures of the major political factions of the era and read most of their extant writings.[14] Where these sources ran thin, they were supplemented with the political opinions expressed in the editorials of two newspapers that served as spokesmen for the major parties during these years: the Democratic Boston *Post* (for 1831–1860) and the Republican Boston *Daily Advertiser* (for 1865–1880). I also examined the official addresses and statements of the major parties' state committees and conventions; the messages of the state's governors to the General Court and the legislative replies to those messages; the speeches of the state's senators and representatives in Congress; the reports of the state Board of Education, the Bureau of Statistics of Labor, and the Board of State Charities; political articles in the *North American Review*; the record of the proceedings of the state constitutional conventions of 1820 and 1853; and other scattered material.

As one sifts through this vast political literature, a rather astounding trend emerges. Through all of it there is relatively little discussion of industrialization, much less the working class! Massachusetts politicians debated intensely (and interminably) the major issues of the day — tariffs, public lands, constitutional reform, transportation improvements, economic regulations, legislative charters and monopolies, immigration, banking and currency, slavery, the Civil War and Reconstruction — and managed to do so with minimal reference to the way the factory was restructuring their state's economy and society. It is noteworthy that not until 1878 does "the condition of manufactures and labor" earn a separate section of the governor's annual message — a distinction long before bestowed upon such topics as education, agriculture, and inland fisheries.[15] What in Britain was a ruling obsession was in Massachusetts a phenomenon that simply did not excite great concern. The circumscribed nature of this response is, I believe, one of the major findings of this study.

What happened when Massachusetts's leaders did finally address the subject? In what context did they do so, and what was the character and extent of their observations? Here again, the contrast with the English experience is remarkable.

In Britain, as shown earlier, the changes brought about by industrialization and the expansion of the working class were an integral part of the debate on many issues and, indeed, were themselves major issues. This, for the most part, was not the case in Massachusetts, especially before 1865. Rarely was an entire speech or a pamphlet given over to these subjects. The exception was usually a stump address before laborers in a manufacturing town or an oration before a workers' "improvement" club — in other words, when the occasion or the audience seemed to call for it. That such themes might have had a more universal appeal evidently did not occur to these politicians.

One does come across mention of industrialism and the working class somewhat more frequently in discussions of the leading issues of the day. For example, in tariff debates proponents of higher duties would often single out the worker as a prospective beneficiary of their proposals (as would, naturally, those advocating lower duties). The state's notable band of antislavery politicians, in attacking the "peculiar institution," would sometimes pause to refute the South's claim that the "wage slavery" of the North was a greater injustice than the bondage of blacks. Supporters of state aid to education mentioned the various ways schools helped the worker. Politicians addressing farm groups considered how agriculture would be affected by the progress of manufacturing. Advances in industry were cited in paeans to the prosperity of the state or the nation.

Yet on these occasions industrialism and the growth of the working class, though referred to, are given only cursory attention as points made to buttress a larger argument. This poses special difficulties for the scholar trying to analyze what politicians "thought" on these matters. The literature yields few extended discussions whose reason or complexities, sources or implications can be unraveled and explored. There are only a few sentences in one speech, maybe a paragraph in another, once in a while a few pages. These scattered references do not go deep enough to set these subjects in a particular context or to trace them through one individual or set of individuals. They should be treated rather as signposts, pointing the way to larger, often unspoken assumptions. Such fragmentary passages have to be collated, and then, working backwards, one must reconstruct as best as possible the system of ideas from which they sprang. This is the method that has been adopted in this study.

Once this task is done, a final disparity with the British historical record emerges. Whereas in Britain industrialization and the working class were matters of *controversy* among politicians, in Massachusetts one finds from the start an almost unbroken consensus on these questions. While the state's political parties fought enthusiastically over a host of issues, they did not choose to go to the firing line over this one (nor did they apparently feel there were many votes to be gained by doing so). From time to time some of the lesser factions did challenge the prevailing view: those politicians identified with the mercantile interests in the 1820s, some "radical" Democrats of the 1830s, or various spokesmen for labor groups. But (aside from the first) these were distinctly weak minority voices, easily overwhelmed in the hubbub of Massachusetts politics by the multitude on the other side.

And what was this consensus? Quite simply, it was that industrialization, far from posing a threat to the established order, was a beneficent and entirely welcome metamorphosis. Most politicians were convinced that Massachusetts had everything to gain from its formidable wealth-producing power. And so, they assumed, did the worker. The heated criticisms of the industrial order that did so much to exacerbate political tensions in Britain were nearly absent. Even when they did start to be heard, in the 1840s, they constituted a definitely minor theme.

The Commonwealth's politicians, in short, chose to pay little attention to industrialization and the rise of the working class, and when they did speak of these trends it was with complacent satisfaction. These two aspects of their reaction, in fact, reinforced each other. Had they been willing to probe deeper and think more seriously about the subject, most likely some of their serenity would have dissipated. And that serenity, in turn, made it possible for them to focus instead on other, more "pressing" issues. Thus they managed to pass over the most fundamental social and economic transformation of the nineteenth century.

How is one to account for this? Why, with Britain and Massachusetts undergoing essentially the same social process, did they have such radically different responses to it? It may be argued that Massachusetts was, as chapter 2 pointed out, a state well-prepared for the factory, and thus it is not surprising that there was so little consternation when it finally arrived. Some might claim that industrialization in Massachusetts was a much less extreme experience than it was in Britain. The well-publicized horrors of that nation's factories and mines found no parallel in Massachusetts. Similarly, the Commonwealth's cities were not so badly scarred. Lowell and Fall River did not degenerate to the level of Sheffield and Leeds, and Boston was certainly no London. Finally, it might be objected that the two societies being compared are chronologically out of phase. Massachusetts from 1815 to 1880 had not reached the same stage Britain was at during those years. The latter's Industrial Revolution had begun thirty or forty years earlier and it took some time before British politicians got excited about it. Is it any wonder, then, that there was a similar "lag" of response in Massachusetts?

These demurrals do have some force, but not, I think, a great deal. It is true that Massachusetts was "ready" for the factory, but so was Britain (in fact, even more so). That industrialization was somewhat easier on Massachusetts is also correct, but the difference was not great. And as to the delay in the British reaction to industrialization: True, there was one, but in large part it was due to the fact that for most of the years between 1780 and 1815 Britain was engaged in a struggle for national survival. Criticism of the social order was therefore suppressed as "unpatriotic." Who knows how much earlier there might have been a Peterloo had Napoleon lost at Austerlitz? Indeed, there had been signs of internal unrest as early as the late 1780s and early 1790s, before the war broke out. And no matter what the cause of the lag in the British response, it *was* only a matter of some three decades before the situation changed. Massachusetts' lag was at least six decades, during only four years of which it was at war.

There are other considerations to keep in mind as well. If one consults again Figures 1–3 (pp. 46–48), one finds that for each of these measures of industrialization the numbers for Massachusetts, during the years it underwent industrialization, rise far more abruptly than Britain's. Its cities grew faster, its nonagricultural and manufacturing populations swelled more rapidly. Indeed, despite its much later start, Massachusetts had, by around 1850, caught up with Britain in all three categories. Should not this so much more sudden, drastic industrialization in fact have caused an even greater awareness and apprehension among its politicians? Also, since Massachusetts' political system was far more democratic than Britain's, it should have been *more* responsive to popular concern over industrialization and to working class discontent. Finally, the Bay State's politicians were, as will soon be shown, very much aware of conditions in contemporary Britain and found them horrifying. They, unlike the British themselves, at least had a vicarious taste of what was to come. Should not that have warned them to take special care lest the same ruinous trends develop on their soil?

Without answers to these difficult questions, the puzzle remains, perhaps insoluble. Yet I think a good part of the solution may be discovered by looking carefully at what Massachusetts politicians did say — meager as it was — about the working class. Their perceptions and judgments offer clues as to why they reacted in the manner they did. For this section of the book, on the years 1815 to 1865, the logic of their argument suggests a two-part approach. Their notions about workers, it turns out, were colored by their view of industrialization as a purely economic process affecting the entire state. So the present chapter will examine that view, while the next will focus on the central theme of this study, the new working class itself.

Since the most conspicuous, immediate result of industrialization is usually the economic one, it is natural that as Massachusetts politicians began to deal with the factory system they should examine this aspect of it most carefully. Would the factory system bring prosperity? Or, to refine the point, would it bring more prosperity than the customary economic arrangements? How much of the latter would have to be sacrificed if they decided to encourage the new system's growth? In seeking answers to these questions they came more and more to regard industrialization as a generous and benign force. The factory, they became convinced, would prove a bounteous source of material wealth.

These leaders set out by confronting the doubts that must have been nagging at many of their constituents. Why change? Why embrace this radically new mode of production and the far-reaching economic reorganization it would inevitably entail? To understand their handling of these doubts one needs first to grasp how they thought about the economic system they already had.

Often in history what is not there is as important as what is. One of the chief reasons the Commonwealth's politicians had so few qualms about the factory as it was making its appearance is that they were *not* in the habit of positing a fixed, static definition of their state's economy. To their minds there was no single set of economic institutions peculiarly appropriate to their state, sanctioned by tradition and incumbent upon them to preserve. Therefore there would be no preexisting ideal to stand in the way of industrialization. Working upon this fairly blank slate they were able to sketch in easily a new portrait of the economy in which manufacturing occupied a large space.

Frequently historians assert that a major obstacle facing the early proponents of the factory in America was the strong objections voiced by the nation's agrarian interests. It is therefore necessary to state emphatically that this was not the case in Massachusetts. One must be wary of presupposing the universality of the ideas of such undeniably important figures as Jefferson, inflating their strictures against manufactures into a nationwide sentiment. The "agrarian myth" may have loomed large in Virginia, but in antebellum Massachusetts it was of almost no account. Politicians hardly ever portrayed the Bay State as an agrarian society. If one recalls what has been said about the state's economy, the reason is readily apparent. Though farming had always been the dominant occupation (and continued to be until the 1820s or 1830s), its leadership had not gone unchallenged. From colonial times it was forced to share prominence with allied enterprises, trade, fishing, and handicraft manufactures. Its supremacy, moreover, had always been shaky: The agricultural life in Massachusetts had never promised more than mediocre rewards. The struggling farmers (not to mention everyone else) would have laughed at any politician who asserted that agriculture was the glory of the state.

This is not to say that politicians did not frequently (and for a surprisingly long time) single out the farmer for special praise. Many of them, after all, came from farm families themselves. A still greater number represented constituencies where farmers cast a healthy portion of the votes. So whether out of sympathy or calculation they were careful to appear properly reverent. Often they were willing to grant, for instance, that the farmer's time-honored occupation was a spiritual step ahead of everyone else's. His constant grappling with providential forces, his wearying toil, his close communion with nature were held to endow him with a rough simplicity and honesty, virtue and contentment. "We may talk as we will of well-fed and well-clothed day-laborers or journeymen," said Daniel Webster, representative from Boston in Congress; "they are not . . . to be compared, either for happiness or respectability, with him who sleeps under his own roof and cultivates his own fee-simple inheritance." His colleague Edward Everett stated flatly that the "American Yeomanry" is "perhaps, the most substantial, uncorrupted, and intelligent population on earth."[16]

Their compliments grew even more effusive as they developed the social and political implications of these traits. The farmer's moral fiber and stable habits conferred a welcome rigor on popular manners. His "independence" — he tilled his own soil — made him a vital contributor to a republican form of government. The freeholder, according to Webster, because he owned his land

> thereby obtains a feeling of respectability, a sense of propriety and of personal independence which is generally essential to elevated character. He has a stake in society, and [is] inclined, therefore, rather to uphold than demolish it. He does not look on all property as the envied possession of others, and as a proper prey for him and his fellows . . . , but as a stock in which he has a share and which he is interested, therefore, to protect.

Similarly, Governor Levi Lincoln:

> The moral virtues of the *yeomanry*, place them in the front rank of Republican Citizens. Standing upon the soil of freedom, and holding their estates by the tenure of personal independence, the happiness of their individual condition is necessarily identified with the prosperity of the nation. It is upon this class of men . . . that a free government may always securely rest.

These kinds of encomiums regularly punctuated the political dialogue of this era. Indeed, it was easy for politicians to overdo them, especially when speaking to farmers themselves. Addressing a cattle show at Danvers in 1836, Edward Everett, at this point governor, heartily informed his audience that it was upon their condition "that the social, political, and moral character of countries mainly depends."[17]

Few, however, were willing to go so far. The farmer may have been a social and political asset, but he was not usually regarded as indispensable. Most politicians, despite occasional perfunctory references to Massachusetts as an "agricultural community" or "agricultural state," carefully refrained from describing farming as the central economic activity or the economic underpinning of a just and happy society (other than in the trivial sense that the farmer was essential because he fed everyone else). Indeed, as time passed and the state's agriculture underwent the convulsions mentioned before, politicians even felt freer to point up its shortcomings. They spoke, for instance, of how too great a reliance on agriculture encouraged social instability, as the state's poor soil made migration westward so attractive. "There is not a farm in New Hampshire or Massachusetts," offered Senator Isaac Bates, "which . . . I would take as a gift, and be obliged to cultivate it." By the 1850s the lot of the farmer was eliciting open commiseration — and some unusually frank comments. George Boutwell, secretary of the state Board of Education, noted that farming was no longer a "cherished pursuit" even among farmers themselves: "the head of the family often regards his life of labor upon the land as a necessity from which he would willingly escape," and his children naturally pick up his cues. Robert Winthrop, running for governor in 1851, bravely announced to a meeting of the Middlesex Agricultural Society that he had not come to "flatter farmers" by labeling them "the best part of the population" and ended by conceding only that they were among the best. A year later (significantly or not, he lost the election) he was proclaiming what nearly everyone had known for quite some time. Massachusetts would never be a great agricultural state. "Nature has marked and quoted her for a different destiny."[18]

What that destiny was became increasingly clear during these years. It was expressed in a clever improvisation: the Commonwealth's leaders made their state's very *lack* of a focal enterprise into a virtue. Out of this they evoked a vision of the economy in which flexibility, change, and growth were the norms — a vision that could accommodate itself easily to the factory. The idea they so confidently put forth was that of a diversified economy.

The roots of this idea go back to before the War of 1812. The ravages of Jefferson's embargo on the state's maritime commerce made government officials more acutely aware of trade's pivotal role in the economy. Besides being "a source of profit and employment" to those directly involved, its fluctuations were said to bear upon the farmer's fortunes as well. "In the channels of husbandry and commerce," affirmed Governor Elbridge Gerry, "flow in a great measure, the active prosperity of this State." They were "natural allies": "the aid of one, is indispensable to the other." As factories began sprouting up in these years similar claims were made for them. The Massachusetts house of representatives, while modestly noting that "it is hardly to be expected that we should soon become an extensively manufacturing people," nevertheless felt it important to designate certain kinds of manufacturing as "of the first necessity, and others of great utility," worthy of active support from the legislature.[19]

In the immediate postwar decades this notion of the interdependence of different types of economic endeavor was more fully elaborated. However, with the infant cotton textile industry securely established, manufacturing received more attention. The politicians welcomed the new mode of production, commenting regularly on its progress and advantages. "It is with pleasure, not unmingled with pride," ran a typical boast, "that we can particularly recognize the high degree of perfection to which some branches of the manufactures of this State have attained." The triptych of agriculture, commerce, and "mechanical industry" became a familiar adornment to speeches on economic matters.[20]

As industry was admitted into the hierarchy of enterprise, politicians were quick to note its potential benefits for the other branches of the economy, especially agriculture. Farming in the Bay State was plainly stagnating. Many farmers were abandoning the soil to move west — drawn, the state senate complained, by the lure of "speculation" and "delusive tales of milder climates and unexampled products." A thriving manufacturing sector could reverse this blighting trend. A growing population of industrial laborers, it was thought, would create new markets for the farmer's crops. Without such markets there was little hope for him. As Governor John Brooks remarked,

> agriculture is unsusceptible of an independent existence. Unsolicited by the demands of commerce and manufactures, would the rural economist extend his care and toil beyond the supply of his own immediate consumption? Men do not act without motives. The hope of profit sweetens and originates labor. But if the surplus products of the soil become a worthless incumbrance [sic] to the producer, languor, inaction and scarcity will be the result.

A few others pointed out that if the husbandman must leave the land, then factories would at least be able to provide him with work and thus keep him on as a productive member of the state. By furnishing markets and employment manufacturing would thus contribute solidly to the overall economic health of the Commonwealth. In a tariff speech on the floor of Congress in 1828 Representative John Reed offered what was by then a common observation. "I desire," he said, "to see all the various interests of agriculture, manufactures, navigation, and commerce, flourish together. In my deliberate opinion, they can flourish only together. . . . Our mutual dependence, and mutual interests, are close and indissoluble."[21]

The only noteworthy dissent from these happy assumptions in this period came from politicians associated with the maritime interests. Manufacturing did not immediately give foreign trade much of a boost; that would come only later. Meanwhile that venerable enterprise was in trouble. Commerce had long been sluggish. Oft-burned investors were shifting large sums of capital from the trading houses to manufacturing corporations. When the state's industrial entrepreneurs began pressing Congress for protective tariffs, the representatives from the coastal towns balked: Higher duties, they believed, would curtail foreign trade even more. So for a number of years (the early twenties, mainly) they went about assiduously poking holes in the standard arguments for manufacturing. Webster, in a speech at Boston's Faneuil Hall, feebly tried to show that money invested in factories was not as productive as when invested in other economic activities. Others claimed that a protective tariff would "artificially" force the growth of the factory system, to the detriment of trade. If that system is destined to prosper, they argued, let it do so on its own. In the words of Salem's Representative Benjamin Crowninshield, "It was in vain to expect to draw about the capital of a trading people at your will, by silken cords; it must be done slowly, gradually, surely, and by natural causes." It is interesting, though, that even these protests were directed primarily against the tariff itself. That the factory might ultimately prove helpful to other sectors of the economy was rarely questioned. By the late twenties, when the maritime interests at last gave up their fight against a higher tariff, serious doubts about manufacturing virtually disappeared from political dialogue.[22]

From the 1830s on, the idea of a diversified economy became widely accepted, an almost axiomatic truth that few dared to challenge. The state was by then firmly embarked on an industrial course. The advantages of movement along several economic lines were manifest. What earlier might have seemed an incongruous mixture of economic endeavors came to be viewed as the key to prosperity. An assortment of different occupations, most politicians were persuaded, made the most effective use of the "variety of talent and capacity which are bestowed by nature" among men, and even permitted society to tap the labor of those who might otherwise be drones: the elderly, women, and children. This same division of labor gave the economy as a whole a greater productive power. Specialization in discrete, narrowly defined tasks was more efficient and allowed the economy to better satisfy the varied wants of mankind. The overriding goal, according to Edward Everett, was to arrange things so that "the inhabitants of any given country will be most likely to take up and pursue those branches of industry for which, as a whole or in its separate parts, it is best adapted, by the quality of the climate and soil, other natural advantages, and the various causes which affect the character of a people." By the forties and fifties the Commonwealth's strikingly multifaceted economy had become cause for self-congratulation. "Probably no State in the Union has so great a diversity of important interests . . . ," proclaimed Governor John Davis. "We are Agriculturists, Manufacturers, Mechanics, Navigators, Fishermen, Merchants — each class following its own pursuits, but all united closely together by innumerable strong ties in a common interest." "The interests of labor are one and the same, in whatever departments it is employed," echoed Robert Winthrop; "and . . . the industrial classes, instead of thriving at each other's expense, find their highest interest and advantage in each other's prosperity." A few politicians were bold enough to confirm an increasingly obvious but still reluctantly acknowledged truth: The factory was not only well ensconced, it was fast becoming dominant. The usual place of manufacturing at the tail end of the catch phrase "agriculture, commerce, and mechanical industry" would soon be obsolete. "We are," admitted Governor Marcus Morton as early as 1840, "a manufacturing and commercial people."[23]

By setting industry on an equal footing with the ancient pursuits of commerce and agriculture and by demonstrating the benefits it bestowed upon them, the idea of a diversified economy helped pave the way for the eventual acceptance of the machine. This economic configuration was an open-ended one, rejecting a concentration on one form of enterprise for a confident welcome to all. It was predicated on the interaction of those forms, adding a new dimension to the traditional notion of a "commonwealth." And by emphasizing the strictly economic aspects of the various kinds of enterprise, this theory shifted attention away from the older view that there were particular virtues (or liabilities) inherent in each. Instead, politicians' audiences were asked to pay attention to such down-to-earth points as the advantages of the division of labor, the effects of economic linkages, the flows of capital and labor. This more businesslike approach to economic endeavor played a critical role in all the arguments for industrialization, for it was in these terms that the factory had its greatest appeal. The idea of a diversified economy thus gave industry a practical function and purpose in the existing scheme of things, at the same time that it was transforming that scheme. With that accomplished, it qualified for closer scrutiny.

A pair of ancillary arguments — not primarily economic ones, but having economic implications — were instrumental in the early stages of industrialization and should be mentioned here. The first related manufacturing to the long record of government aid to artisans and to the early crude efforts at factory production. Since the Revolution the Commonwealth had supported these kinds of enterprises through tariffs (in the 1780s), loans, exemptions from taxation, lotteries, special charters, and even outright bounties.[24] The framers of the state's constitution had considered the topic of sufficient import to specify in that document assistance to "manufactures" as one of the duties of the government they were setting up. Regularly in the 1790s and early 1800s governors and legislators commented approvingly on such measures. Recommending state aid to cotton factories "and other labour saving machines," Lieutenant Governor Levi Lincoln called it "seed sowed on good ground, which would produce, to the present and succeeding generations, an harvest of an hundred fold." The General Court agreed. "It has always been the practice of the Legislature of Massachusetts," observed its lower house, "to extend the fostering hand of encouragement to all manufactures, undertaken within the Commonwealth, with any prospect of success, or publick utility." By the time the factory system was growing in earnest, therefore, the government had long been sympathetic to the idea of stimulating the output of manufactured goods. These early officials could not have envisioned a Lowell, of course, but they had been willing to endorse on a much smaller scale the same category of enterprise. To this extent, at least, manufacturing had the sanction of tradition.[25]

The second line of reasoning — a related one which also had its traditional components — associated manufacturing with political independence. Throughout its early history Massachusetts, in common with other states, had relied on foreign nations (especially Great Britain) for the bulk of the artisan-produced goods it needed. Indeed, up to the Revolution it hardly had any choice. British mercantile theory decreed that manufacturing should be discouraged in the colonies, and the government tried by various means to secure their dependence on the mother country's looms and forges. When independence was won the Bay State resumed its imports of manufactured goods, but with very ambivalent feelings. Politicians had to walk a tightrope, on the one hand proclaiming their devotion to foreign trade and on the other decrying their state's consumption of foreign products.[26]

The calamitous effects of Jefferson's embargo brought home with full force the advantages of economic self-sufficiency. Many politicians began declaring without reservation in favor of domestic manufactures as a prerequisite for unhindered economic development. The pursuits of the artisan and the manufacturer, contended Governor Elbridge Gerry, are "practicable patriotism": "whilst our national and state parchments, establish our independence *of right*, their measures, more solid, are establishing for us, our independence *in deed.*" The War of 1812, with its prolonged curtailment of foreign imports, merely buttressed this argument. Thereafter it would be used repeatedly by the proponents of industry — and considering the fervent patriotism of the times, it must have had substantial effect. The success of the Commonwealth's manufacturing towns, Representative Edward Everett told a Fourth of July crowd at Lowell, "may with propriety be considered as a peculiar triumph of our political independence. They are, if I may so express it, the complement of the revolution." The factory thus found itself carried along on a rising tide of nationalism, rendering even more secure its newly acquired tokens of legitimacy.[27]

With these various arguments the politicians wrote what might be termed industry's letter of introduction to Massachusetts. An acceptable place was constructed for manufacturing within the limits of the existing order, one carved out of economic logic, patriotism, and precedent. Once this was done, the factory system was allowed to grow, with the trust that it would do no serious violence to what had been inherited from the past and with the hope that it might enhance the future well-being of the state.

As factory production made its great strides in these years, politicians were given the chance to elucidate its unique advantages. They did not hesitate to do so. The advantage that struck them more forcibly than any other was the obvious one, its productive power. In this they were no different from the proponents of manufacturing in nearly every other place and time. The material benefits of industry were indubitably its strongest selling point.

At the heart of industry's productive power was the machine. The political leaders of this period, in common with more ordinary folk, had a childlike fascination with these seemingly magical inventions. A tour of Lowell to view the power looms was a standard item in the itinerary of out-of-state and foreign visitors. In the words of someone like Daniel Webster machines could take on almost human form:

> Spinning-machines, power-looms, and all the mechanical devices, acting, among other operatives, in the factories and work-shops, are but so many laborers. They are usually denominated labor-*saving* machines, but it would be more just to call them labor-*doing* machines. They are made to be active agents; to have motion, and to produce effect; and though without intelligence, they are guided by laws of science, which are exact and perfect, and they produce results, therefore, in general, more accurate than the human hand is capable of producing. When we look upon one of these, we behold a mute fellow-laborer, of immense power, of mathematical exactness, and of ever-during and unwearied effort. And while he is thus a most skilful

and productive laborer, he is a non-consumer, at least beyond the wants of his mechanical being. He is not clamorous for food, raiment, or shelter, and makes no demands for the expenses of education. The eating and drinking, the reading and writing, and the clothes-wearing world, are benefitted by the labors of these coöperatives, in the same way as if Providence had provided for their service millions of beings, like ourselves in external appearance, able to labor and to toil, and yet requiring little or nothing for their own consumption or subsistence; or rather, as if Providence had created a race of giants, each of whom, demanding no more for his support and consumption than a common laborer, should yet be able to perform the work of a hundred.[28]

This ability of machines "to perform the work of a hundred" set visions dancing before politicians' eyes. The prime deficiency of the struggling American economy had always been its lack of sufficient laborers. The machine would transcend that obstacle — and in the most humane way possible. Let other nations exploit the toil of the masses; America would drive this "race of giants." In these years Americans were also starting to appreciate the potential of the country's vast natural resources. "Science and Invention . . . ," wrote the educator Horace Mann, "found that nature, in all her resources, had hidden stores of power, surpassing the accumulated strength of the whole human race, though all its vigor could be concentrated in a single arm." Yet without some way of extracting this wealth it would in effect remain what it had always been: in Everett's words, "an element of prosperity which we held in unconscious possession." The machine would solve that problem too. It was the instrument through which mankind would at last be able to realize this God-given boon.[29]

It was clear, in other words, that the machine — and a factory system based upon it — could open up unprecedented possibilities for the Commonwealth. Caleb Cushing, as a young man just starting on a long political career, expressed this new awareness concisely:

> The industry of the nation is productive in proportion to the capital and skill employed through the medium of machinery in aid of labor to accelerate production; and not in proportion to the number of its laborers. It is in manufacture, that capital and skill are employed in the greatest degree in proportion to labor; and it is there, that by their means, labor is rendered more productive than it is in any other employment.

Working from these assumptions it was not unnatural for Massachusetts politicians to expect much from the factories sprouting up in their midst.[30]

They were not disappointed. As the years passed the factory system amply fulfilled its bright promise. And every new evidence of its success was greeted by politicians with unadulterated delight. Their accolades made up in enthusiasm what they lacked in originality. "Within a few years, what a happy change has taken place!" Edward Everett was exulting as early as 1824.

> The substantial clothing of our industrious classes is now the growth of the American soil, and the texture of the American loom; the music of the water-wheel is heard on the banks of our thousand rural streams; and enterprise and skill, with wealth, refinement, and prosperity in their train, have studded the sea-shore with populous cities, are making their great "progress" of improvement through the interior, and sowing towns and villages, as it were, broadcast through the country!

High state officials started remarking publicly on the advance of industry. "In *Manufactures*," Governor Levi Lincoln reported to the legislature,

> the progress of the country has exceeded the anticipations of the most sanguine. A few years since, and scarce a water-wheel moved in our Commonwealth. . . . Now there is hardly a water-fall in our streams, but is improved to the propelling of machinery for the manufacture of fabrics of clothing, and of articles of domestic economy.

This new mode of production, he noted the following year, was having advantageous effect.

> Domestic fabrics now furnish the means of an extensive trade, and the best markets for the products of the soil are found at the doors of our own workshops. The surprising influence of these [manufacturing] institutions, in promoting the general improvement of the Country, may be witnessed wherever they are situated.

The same theme was echoed by George Bancroft, just on the verge of a long career as one of the state's leading Democrats. Applauding the increase of manufactured goods, he found "in whatever direction we turn our eyes, . . . one unclouded scene of prosperity, every where marks of advancement and increasing opulence."[31]

The striking growth of industrial centers like Lowell and, later, Lawrence and Fall River from tiny villages (or just farmers' fields) afforded cause for wonderment. Governor Lincoln depicted them as "places where the very wastes of nature, as if by the magic of machinery, have been suddenly converted into scenes of busy population, of useful industry, and of wealth!" Others reacted similarly. Edward's brother, Alexander H. Everett, a former diplomat about to enter state politics, returned to America after an absence of five years "astonished" and "delighted" at the "visible signs of . . . progress" in manufacturing. But he was most impressed by the "flourishing villages and even considerable towns springing up, as if by enchantment, on spots that were recently uninhabited." Caleb Cushing, by then a representative in the state legislature, spoke in the same vein of "populous cities, with their busy throng of industrious and educated freemen, springing up around every waterfall . . . like the gorgeous palaces raised by the genius of Alladin's [sic] lamp." There was, though, "this happy difference, that our magician is the hand of manufacturing enterprise, which builds no illusive works for time and chance to remove, [but?] the secure habitations of abounding contentment, wealth, and activity." Congressman Edward Everett's eye was particularly caught by Lowell. "No event, consequent upon the establishment of our independence," he told an audience there, "has been of greater public benefit" than the development of manufacturing. Eight years later he was lauding the city anew for "the palaces of her industry, side by side with her churches and her schoolhouses, the long lines of her shops and warehouses, her streets filled with the comfortable abodes of an enterprising, industrious, and intelligent population." It was nothing less than a "wonderful and beneficent creation."[32]

By the forties and fifties the factory's vital role in the state's economy was widely acknowledged, even taken for granted. Politicians of every stripe found common ground on this.[33] Marcus Morton, for example, the only Democrat to win the governorship in the Jacksonian years, made a point in his first inaugural address of putting in a kind word for the "shrewd, intelligent and sharp-sighted manufacturers, whose industry and skill are the just pride of New-England." Indeed, by this time it became possible to reflect contentedly on how far Massachusetts had come in this respect. In 1850 Horace Mann, now a congressman, reminisced about how in the 1820s

those establishments were founded which have produced so marvel-
lous a change in our household condition, surrounding all with so many
comforts, and filling our dwellings with so vast a variety of the refine-
ments and luxuries of life. Those of you who have arrived at my age,
and are therefore acquainted with the condition of things throughout
our country towns thirty years ago, know that the change is almost
magical.

In these fits of self-congratulation, there were even those who would
argue that few societies of comparable size were "reaping more fully the
fruits of persevering industry and intelligent, voluntary labor, than are
the present population of Massachusetts."[34]

Several politicians decided to take this panegyric to industry one last
step: They associated it with the idea of "progress." They could hardly
have done less. No other single theme appears more consistently in the
political literature of the day. A stump speech, an editorial, or a legislative address was not complete without some lofty account of how the
state (or nation) had progressed, would progress, *must* progress. "The
spirit of improvement," Massachusetts-bred President John Quincy
Adams justly remarked, "is abroad upon the earth."[35] Progress was
conceived to be the ruling tendency of the age; some even claimed it
was a unique endowment of America. The standard definitions of the
word were notably vague. Normally it was taken to mean movement in
some generally beneficial direction — as, in the political realm, greater
"liberty" and self-government, or, in the cultural realm, a "higher"
civilization. But progress did have an economic component as well. The
advance of prosperity and its diffusion through society were said to
liberate human capacities and enable the race to surmount natural limitations. As Alexander Everett put it,

> the principle of the most important change for the better which we can
> imagine in the present condition of society, lies precisely in the exten-
> sion, to a much larger number of persons, of the facilities for the
> material enjoyments of life, and for moral and intellectual culture,
> which have hitherto belonged to comparatively few individuals.

Amasa Walker, a Democratic leader and something of an economist,
even went so far as to declare that "the continued improvement of the
race *depends* upon the constant and gradual increase of wealth. Each

succeeding generation ought to be, and, in a normal state of society, will be, richer than the preceding."[36]

The facile syllogism that resulted was a boon for manufacturing. If it were true that the increase of wealth was a prime ingredient of human progress and that the factory's leading economic contribution was its ability to increase man's productivity, and thereby, his wealth, then it followed the factory was a prime ingredient of human progress. The more ebullient politicians joyfully announced the conclusion. Manufactures, Representative Rufus Choate contended, "are indispensable to the higher attainments of national greatness." The "useful arts" of "machinery and enginery" were for his colleague Edward Everett those which

> form the difference between the savage of the woods and civilized, cultivated, moral and religious man. . . . These arts are now . . . a representative of human civilization; and the moral and social improvement of our race, and the possession of the skill and knowledge embodied in them, will advance, stand still, and fall together.

Admittedly, such grandiloquent claims for industry were not common. Most other public figures were content to point out its more mundane attractions. But given the assumptions of the period, they were not all that far-fetched either.[37]

Manufacturing as a new-found complement to agriculture and commerce, as the long-time recipient of governmental aid and a bulwark of national independence, as an unmatched provider of material wealth and even, to some minds, the very symbol of progress and civilization — it was in this light that the Commonwealth's politicians looked upon industrialization as an economic process. These perceptions were of critical importance for the future. In the most practical, easy to grasp sense, the factory was a manifest good, and the inhabitants of Massachusetts, like their fellow countrymen, were an eminently practical people. An infant nation with great potential but limited means *needed* something like manufacturing to move ahead. The factory, they thought, might be its economic salvation.

It is difficult to believe that this basically favorable, optimistic view of the economic aspects of industrialization did not sway these politicians when they started judging it as a social force. They had every incentive to suppose that a process offering so much material good for society as a whole would have to be beneficial for its separate parts. That would be only logical. Besides, to believe otherwise might mean that some kind of restraint would have to be placed upon industrialism, with a sacrifice of its full effectiveness. These leaders, in short, wanted very much to believe the best of this awesome phenomenon. It was with this predisposition that they proceeded to explain the new working class.

Chapter 4

The Respectable Worker

THE WORKING CLASS must have made its way uncertainly into the social consciousness of Massachusetts. It may be spoken of now as a "dramatic" result of industrialization, but historical hindsight can foreshorten what were in reality much more gradual changes. Most likely, the growth in the number of workers was at first as unobtrusive to contemporaries as the budding of trees in spring. Workers had always existed, even before the factory arrived; few people considered them important or worthy of much attention. For some time their increase probably went almost unnoticed. In the early stages of industrialization they accumulated in hard-to-see pockets: Merchants and artisans took on help as their businesses expanded; fishermen hired extra hands to haul in bigger catches; farmers sought more day laborers; domestic handicraft workers found employ with the rising merchant capitalists. The early factories, tucked away in their rural isolation, procured their operatives from the fringes of the labor force — down-and-out families, unmarried farm girls. All these occupations were perceived as temporary. Indeed, they hardly seemed "occupations" at all, in the sense of something fit for a man or a woman to devote a life to. They were more in the nature of mere jobs, taken up to carry one through hard times, or as an interval between or preparation for more steady, reputable toil, or (in the case of women especially) as an alternative to no occupation at all. They were the loose ends in the regular occupational fabric of the state.

The new working class thus came upon the rest of the population, so to speak, through the back door. But its inexorable rise made it hard to disregard for very long; inevitably it crossed the threshold of public awareness. By the late thirties it was one-half the labor force; by the mid-fifties, over two-thirds. It became abundantly clear that this was no transitory phenomenon. A working class was an essential, permanent concomitant of the industrial order, and it had to be reckoned with.

Helping to define this encounter and to give it a greater urgency was the state's growing acquaintance with the working class emerging in Europe. The citizens of Massachusetts were keenly interested in news from abroad: Tidings from overseas were quickly inserted into the papers upon the arrival of every ship, tourists came back with their breathless reports. Through these sources many began to learn of a rather unsettling development. The people of England, the most advanced industrializing nation in the world, were *not* enjoying either prosperity or contentment.

Almost immediately after the War of 1812 this portentous news started to work its way into the state's political dialogue and soon became a cliché. Politicians of every persuasion joined in a solemn chorus of lament over the "degraded" condition of the European working class. They became convinced that the standard of living of the typical laborer abroad, especially of the English factory operative, was dreadful. His wages were abysmally low, they said, his housing filthy and crowded, his diet pitiful. Even southern slaves were treated better. "No small portion" of the British working class, observed Democratic Representative Henry Williams, "without fault of their own, are doomed, from early childhood to premature old age, to unremitting toil, to gain the barest subsistence, to keep body and soul together." Others nodded in sorry assent: Terms like "famishing poor," "miserable laborers," "ignorant, brutal, and squalid poor," "half-starved laborers" became the standard way of describing European workers. "It would seem," concluded Edward Everett after reading British parliamentary reports, "that the industrial system of Europe required for its administration an amount of suffering, depravity, and brutalism, which formed one of the great scandals of the age. No form of serfdom or slavery could be worse."[1]

It was not just the poverty of the European laborer that alarmed these statesmen. They were also upset about his depraved "character" and the hopelessness of his situation. As they saw it the worker was abandoned to all kinds of sordid vices, most prominently drunkenness and loose sexual habits. Typical was Horace Mann's account of how in England there were

thousands of wretched, degraded female operatives, who earn scarcely a shilling a day. After their day's work is done, they visit the dram-

> shops, roam the streets till midnight, and if not invited away by vicious men, they huddle by scores into filthy lodging-houses, where they sleep, men and women promiscuously, till morning summons them back to their tasks.

The high crime rates in manufacturing towns and the British practice of recruiting there for soldiers were taken as solid proof of the moral trough into which the laborers had slid. And their prospects for escaping this way of life were said to be very remote. Almost no schooling was available to give them the skills and moral instruction they so plainly lacked (and since many children worked in factories they could not go to school even if offered the chance). Most did not qualify to vote and therefore had little chance of pressuring the government to come to their aid. The worker was pretty much locked into his lowly position. "In Europe, generally speaking," Daniel Webster noted, "the laborer is always a laborer. He is destined to no better condition on earth, ordinarily he rises no higher."[2]

A few political spokesmen envisioned serious consequences. This downtrodden working class, they warned, could well prove the seed of Europe's destruction. Far from succumbing meekly to their fate, they were, by all reports, embittered. "They have no stake in society," Webster said. "They hang loose upon it, and are often neither happy in their own condition, nor without danger to the State." In any country where the poor beget only more generations of poor, Horace Mann forecast, "the race may go on, degenerating in body and soul, and casting off, one after another, the lineaments and properties of humanity." The lower classes will

> swarm into life by myriads, and crowd upwards into the ranks of society. But in society, there are no vacant places to receive them, nor unclaimed bread for their sustenance. Though uninstructed in the arts of industry, though wholly untaught in the restraints and the obligations of duty, still the great primal law of self-preservation works in their blood as vigorously as in the blood of kings. It urges them on to procure the means of gratification; but, having no resources in labor or frugality, they betake themselves to fraud, violence, incendiarism, and the destruction of human life. . . . Such, literally, is the present condition of large portions of the human race in some countries in Europe.

This was the grisly fate of any society in which the poorer classes outnumbered the richer, suppressed by the wealthy few and with no sizable middle class to serve as buffer or balance. A skewed, hate-ridden, rigid class stratification could bring only social upheaval and, ultimately, anarchy and revolution.[3]

Whether this picture was an accurate rendering of the European working classes is beside the point. What does matter is that the citizens of Massachusetts were regularly presented by their leaders with a frightening account of what a working class could actually be like. A few officials tried to reassure their constituents by arguing that such trends were the product of uniquely European circumstances: the over-crowded populations, resulting in a scarcity of land and an excess of labor, or the aristocratic, even despotic systems of government that traditionally ground down the lower orders.[4] But these explanations can hardly have seemed adequate. Many people must have conceived the same dire premonition: Would the industrial society being created in the United States come to the same end? For if the chances were likely that it would, there was plainly every reason to stop manufacturing from developing any further.

Recommending industrialization as a purely economic process was, for the Commonwealth's leaders, fairly easy; few could discount its obvious benefits. But its capacity to reorder social relations had more disruptive political implications. Inevitably, there would be many people who would gain and others injured; some whose lives and families would be harshly uprooted, and some eager to break away from tradition-bound routine to make a new start. Above all, a steadily rising portion of the populace would be finding work as employees rather than among the time-honored ranks of "independent" laborers. Each of these groups — as well as those not directly involved — would be looking to political spokesmen for guidance and, perhaps, relief. And since the major parties of the state represented recognizably different constituencies, one would expect differences, even marked contrasts, in the way they dealt with the new working class.

For the most part, as indicated before, such differences failed to develop. Politicians who were fiercely at odds (especially after 1830) on a number of critical issues quite remarkably disagreed hardly at all about the role and value of the worker. In fact it is possible, as one reads through their pronouncements on this subject, to pick out a complex of ideas that was accepted by the leaders of all the major parties. I have chosen to call it the image of the respectable worker.

Foremost in contriving this image were the state's two dominant parties in this period: first, between 1830 and the early 1850s, the Whigs; then, from the mid-1850s to 1865, the Republicans. One can almost speak of *one* dominant party, for in many respects the latter was a reincarnation of the former. The new party did have some infusion of Democratic blood, most notably in such figures as George Boutwell, Benjamin F. Butler, and Nathaniel P. Banks. But by far the greater part of Republican leaders — and its supporters at the polls — had formerly been affiliated with the Whigs (though in many cases becoming Republicans after a brief apostasy in the Free Soil party). The Whig-Republican domination of Massachusetts politics was virtually total. Their perennial rivals, the Democrats, and various third parties labored hard to mount a successful challenge but nearly always in vain. Between 1830 and 1848 the Whigs elected their candidate for governor every year but two, often by lopsided margins. (And in one of the two years they lost, the Democrat squeaked through only on the strength of temporary public discontent with a liquor-control law passed by the Whig legislature.) During this same period the Whigs captured both houses of the legislature every year but one; several years *all* the members of the state senate were Whig. From 1834 to 1848 they furnished every United States senator and twenty-seven of the thirty-one representatives elected to Congress. Without exception the state's electoral votes went to the Whig candidates for president — even when, as in 1832 and 1852, the Democrats swept most of the other states in the Union. Through all these years the leading national figures contributed by the state — men like Daniel Webster, John Quincy Adams, Edward Everett, Joseph Story, Rufus Choate, Robert Winthrop — came almost exclusively from the Whig party.[5]

The only time the Whig-Republican ascendancy was broken for any sustained period was in the transitional years of the early fifties, when the older party was crumbling and the new one not yet born. Taking advantage of a sharp division in Whig ranks over slavery and territorial expansion, the Democrats succeeded in arranging a *mariage de convenance* with the Free Soilers and in 1850 took over the state government.

Within two years the alliance, shaky from the beginning, collapsed. The Whigs regained control and in 1852 once again carried the state's electoral vote in the presidential contest. This was, however, their last gasp. In 1854 the bitter controversy over the Kansas-Nebraska Act, coupled with increasing unrest over foreign immigration, brought several years of major political realignment. In the confusion the nativist American party gained power for several years. It was not long, though, before the new Republican party superseded the moribund Whigs. In its infancy, in 1856, the Republicans won the state's electoral vote for John C. Frémont. The following year their nominee Nathaniel Banks became governor. There ensued a string of electoral victories for the party stretching uninterrupted to the end of the Civil War. By the later years of the war its gubernatorial candidate was getting a steady three-fourths of the vote. Lincoln carried the state easily. Its two Republican senators, Charles Sumner and Henry Wilson, were among the leaders of Congress. A Republican hegemony was established that would last well into the postwar decades.

Both the Whigs and the Republicans were closely allied with the economic elite of the state. Particularly in Boston, but in other towns as well, the richer entrepreneurs in mercantile, commercial, banking, and manufacturing enterprises looked to these parties to convey the businessman's point of view to the larger public. They also found strong backing among the professional classes, most notably lawyers, clergymen, and the teachers and administrators of Harvard University. In short, they were clearly on the side of all that was comfortable, responsible, high-minded and well-born. Their opponents, by contrast, were never able to persuade the voters they were anything more than scruffy outsiders.[6]

Of course, easy, continuing triumphs at the polls are not built solely on the votes of a wealthy few. The Whig-Republican platform and aura appealed to many other groups. The very religious — especially the more orthodox Congregationalists — were won over by the support given these two parties by the clergy and by their devotion to temperance, education, and other worthy reforms. Those interested in getting ahead probably joined with them to facilitate their rise. People living in out-of-the-way regions of the state no doubt liked their stand on internal improvements. Factory operatives, along with many other employees in manufacturing and commerce, held great hopes for the Whig-Republican protective tariff. And many must have voted for them simply out of disagreement with the policies of their opponents. By managing to represent at the same time tradition and progress, stability and change, the Whigs and Republicans effectively monopolized political power in Massachusetts.

Because they were so securely in control, and so well attuned to the views of the economically powerful, these parties, more than any other, were faced with the task of commenting on the working class. The public knew they spoke for the employer. And since they preened themselves on being the best and brightest of their day, the public also expected them to come up with some convincing explanations about the worker's recent rise to prominence. They accepted the challenge, or more accurately, they were more interested in the subject than their opponents. Even their concern, as noted before, was slight, compared with the other issues they addressed. Then too, because of their political preeminence a great many Whig and Republican speeches and writings were published — and survive to be examined. So it is to these two parties that one must look for a full articulation of the image of the respectable worker.

How did the Democrats react to their opponents' views of the worker? This is a hard question to answer. Their extant published writings are scanty and are notably less attentive to the subject. But by and large their leaders seem to have agreed with the statements of the opposition. In any event, if they differed significantly there is no such sign in the materials examined for this study. And it is certainly true that they did not make any such difference an important part of their appeal to the voters (except in one case: their support of the secret ballot). In the remainder of this chapter, therefore, the notes will indicate sources where the Whig-Republican views found support among Democratic politicians. In chapter 5 I propose to look more closely at the Democrats' stand in the context of their larger position in order to explain why they did not formulate an alternate view of the worker in their frustrating struggle to gain power.

What follows, then, is a portrait of the respectable worker image as set forth by Massachusetts' Whig and Republican politicians (and Free Soilers, if they came from the Whig party). This is not, I repeat, an image propounded only by these men. They were merely the most coherent, forceful advocates of ideas shared by the vast majority of the state's politicians. In any case, their striking domination of the political scene suggests that their statements on the subject may well have struck a responsive chord among the electorate (or at least, were not so absurd as to scare voters away). The discussion will draw also on the writings of politicians active in the years between 1815 and 1830. Most of these spokesmen were Republicans of the Jeffersonian type and progenitors of both the Whigs and Democrats. Some of the Whigs' later arguments originated with them. Through these groups, I submit, one can achieve a clear understanding of how the working class was treated in the political dialogue of Massachusetts.[7]

How the image of the respectable worker evolved cannot be conveyed without reference to the two larger categories of which it was a part. First, the working class was, by definition, a group of people who *worked*, that is, who were engaged during most of their waking hours in producing some good or providing some service, for which they were remunerated. It follows from this that their society's attitude towards work in general must have shaped popular ideas about their particular kind of toil. Then too, they were, obviously, not the only people who worked for a living. All sorts of self-employed individuals did too, from the wealthy capitalist to the humblest blacksmith. How accurately society managed to distinguish among the various groups of the labor force would also mold the prevailing image of the working class. Therefore, before looking specifically at these politicians' ideas about the worker himself, it is necessary to examine their approach to these more inclusive categories.

Little was more greatly admired in antebellum Massachusetts than good, hard work. Since the colonial era the citizens of the Bay State had been hauling, chopping, weaving, building, plowing, trading, and performing innumerable other productive tasks with weariless vigor. In common with their fellow Americans, they faced formidable labors: clearing a wilderness, erecting houses, churches, villages, even cities, indeed the entire apparatus of civilization. What in Europe had required centuries they were trying to achieve in decades. It must be remembered too that their Puritan ancestors had brought with them from England a strong belief in the duty of every man to follow assiduously his calling and in the redeeming value of labor generally. This concept of work survived long after the Puritans had become historical oddities. As Governor Samuel Adams reminded the legislature in 1795, "Industry naturally leads to sobriety of sentiment, rectitude of manners, a due observance of wise and constitutional laws, and of course to public and private virtue." Work was thus embedded in the ancient foundations of the Commonwealth. "From the earliest period of the history of the people of this State," noted Governor John Brooks, "industry appears to have been a prominent trait of character, accompanied by a talent of judiciously applying its powers to the purposes of subsistence and accumulation." "We are," echoed Horace Mann, "an industrious and a frugal people."[8]

The need for energetic, willing labor was even more pressing in the antebellum period. The state was still in a rather unenviable situation. Its soil was poor, its other resources meager; even its weather was nasty. It was saddled with a remote location in the northeastern corner of the nation. Nature, in short, had not treated Massachusetts kindly. To fashion prosperity out of such unpromising material would demand ingenuity and shrewdness, and, above all, prodigious labor. Then too, in a modern industrial economy there was so much more work to do. The state would need new means of transport, new buildings, new products, towns, and, of course, the factories themselves. The machines at the base of the system invited constant improvement (again, Mann: "A true Massachusetts boy seems to take to ingenious labor and to labor-saving contrivances from his birth"). For quite some time, it seemed, Bay Staters would have to struggle as their forefathers had done. "Labor," in Senator Rufus Choate's words, "is the condition — I will not say, of our greatness, but — of our being."[9]

The Commonwealth's politicians strove to make the best of this inescapable burden. Instead of scorning labor, they exalted it. "The great interest of this great country, the producing cause of all its prosperity, is labor! labor! labor! We are a laboring community." So said Webster. Rufus Choate turned lyrical:

> This it is, labor, ever labor, which, on the land, on the sea, in the
> fields, in all its applications, with all its helps, from the straw bonnet

braided or plaited by the fingers, up to those vast processes in which
. . . it takes the shapeless ore from its bed, the fleece from the felt, the
cotton from the pod, and moulds them into shapes of beauty and use
and taste, — . . . this it is which is to enrich and decorate this unlovely
nature where our lot is cast, and fit it for the home of cultivated man!

The spiritual benefits of work were usually played down in favor of more
practical ones. Webster, in fact, defined it "in a philosophical view" as
not merely physical exertion but "any active agency which, working
upon the materials with which the world is supplied, brings forth products useful or convenient to man." It was popular to cite David Ricardo's
maxim that work is the source and measure of all wealth. "Labor acts
upon materials furnished by Nature; but Nature is gratuitous in her
gifts, and it is only when acted on by man that her productions acquire
value in his estimation." As Edward Everett saw it, "Nature is so ordered, as both to require and encourage men to work" to satisfy their
ever-increasing material wants. To ignore these self-evident postulates
was to invite ruin. Without labor, warned Governor Brooks, "all our
hope of future prosperity must wither and die":

> By the power of industry, the American wilderness has been re-
> claimed, and our fields, enriched by culture, are made to teem with
> plenty. Industry has erected our temples of religion, of learning, and of
> justice. It has raised and furnished and beautified our habitations, built
> and navigated our ships, and filled our stores and garners with the
> products of various climes. Industry, in fine, has established, and is
> perfecting our various manufactures, and rendering them productive
> sources of individual wealth and comfort.

Nearly three decades later, in 1847, Governor George Briggs was
sounding the same theme. "Massachusetts . . . cannot forget, and ought
not to forget, that, under Providence, the important element of her
prosperity has been, the ceaseless, diversified and persevering industry
of her population." It was to this that "she mainly owes her present
character and standing among the States of this confederacy."[10]

Whatever the formula, the message was the same: Labor was a manifest, prodigious good. It is difficult to conceive how this assumption
could have failed to influence the politician's view of the working class.
The employed laborer, regardless of his other traits, worked. He per-

formed one of society's most noble tasks, contributing to its strength and well-being. If he was engaged directly in manufacturing, so much the better. His labor power was magnified through the agency of machines. The worker's *function*, in other words, was an eminently valuable one. That his *status* was not equally valuable was a proposition that would have to be proven. And given the enthusiasm which common sentiment bestowed upon labor, the evidence would have to be awfully persuasive.

Just as politicians were in the habit of praising work in the abstract, no matter who did it, so they were vague about distinguishing the working class from the self-employed or employer (collectively, the "independent") classes. This is not to say that they never spoke directly of the working class as it is commonly understood. Often, they did, as when talking about "the wages of labor." But they did not feel it was necessary *to consistently and clearly define that class* as a group distinct from the rest of society. What resulted was a confusion of terminology that made intelligent discussion of the worker's situation very difficult.

This point is illustrated most clearly in their use of words like "labor" (for a group of people), "worker," or "working classes," none of which had a single, universally agreed upon denotation. Only through the context can one grasp what exactly is being referred to. The possibilities were several.

Often these words were modern expressions of a very old way of identifying social groupings. Since medieval times it had been customary in England to divide society, for all practical purposes, into two parts: a small "gentry" and a vast, nameless mass comprising everyone else. The former consisted of the titled landed classes (excluding the upper nobility), various professional groups, and merchants. The latter included farmers (both freehold and tenant), craftsmen, cottagers, laborers, servants, and others. This was not an independent class–working class split. While the self-employed included the gentry, of course, it also took in many in the lower orders, the working class being then quite small. In truth this social division corresponds more closely to today's division between white-collar and blue-collar occupations.[11]

This long-standing duality was carried over into nineteenth century Massachusetts, where "laboring classes" and "labor" frequently meant simply the great majority of people who did honest manual work — including such self-employed individuals as craftsmen and farmers. The same idea was expressed in the differentiation between "labor" and "the rich" or, in a usage popular among Democrats, between "producers" and "non-producers." Thus we find Edward Everett talking about "the working classes" as opposed to "the privileged orders" in Europe, or John Quincy Adams telling Alexis de Tocqueville that in New England there are "upper classes and working classes." Senator Rufus Choate spoke of "the whole labor of the country, agricultural, navigating, mechanical, and manufacturing" or, in an earlier speech as a representative, of "the laborious, trading, and business portions of the community." Webster probably had this division in mind when he estimated that "nine tenths of the whole people [of the United States] belong to the laborious, industrious, and productive classes." Similarly, in another speech: "Strike out the laborers of the United States, . . . and you reduce the population . . . from sixteen millions to one million." Representative Levi Lincoln assigned to "the working classes" "the practical agriculturalist and husbandman, the manufacturer, and the mechanic, in the infinitely diversified departments of industry." All these speakers were plainly referring to the great majority of the population that performed any sort of manual labor.[12]

Semantic distinctions grew still more uncertain when politicians turned to another favorite theme, the differences between "labor" and "capital." This dichotomy grew popular in the thirties, as Democrats put themselves forward as the defenders of labor against greedy capital and the Whigs, in response, tried to justify their ties with the state's business leaders. Yet despite their quarrels on this score, both parties assigned these terms the same meaning. Capital did not mean the entire body of men who used accumulated resources to set up their own businesses and, perhaps, hire others to help them, but was applied only to the *richest* of those who did so. Labor, in turn, covered at the very least all those who possessed no resources and were forced to live off their ability to perform useful toil for others. But the term could also include the small businessman or shopkeeper, who owned a limited amount of capital (tools, shop, store, inventory, and so forth) but not enough to qualify as a capitalist as the word was used then. In short, capital was the group of large entrepreneurs; a laborer was either a worker or all those who were not large entrepeneurs.[13]

Complicating the picture further was Whigs' insistence that, no matter how labor was set off from capital, their similarities were far more substantial than their differences. Capital as a commodity was, after all, nothing more than the accumulation of the fruits of previous toil — "labor in possession," Nathan Appleton called it, as distinct from "labor in action." The capitalist was usually just a former laborer who had availed himself of opportunities constantly being presented to (and taken up by) many working men. "With us," Webster asserted, "labor is every day augmenting its means by its own industry; not in all cases, but in very many. Its savings of yesterday become its capital, therefore, of to-day." Consequently, he noted in another speech, "the proportion of those who have not capital, such as to render them independent without personal labor, and who are yet not without some capital, is vastly larger in this community than any other. They form indeed the great mass of our society." Where all laborers were in fact quasi-capitalists, the clear demarcation between the two groups common in Europe ceased to be very meaningful. These Whig politicians also contended that under the American system the benefits of capital accumulation would eventually filter down to the laborer. Invested as it usually was in large shops and factories, capital supplied employment and consumer goods at low prices. Conversely the capitalist, far from overawing the poor laborer as he did in Europe, was said in fact to *need* him to make his investments profitable. Between the two there was a mutually beneficial relationship — a *"holy alliance,"* Everett termed it, with both equal partners in the system's advance toward prosperity.[14]

This grudging, imprecise distinction between labor and capital was nevertheless an improvement over the third sense in which words like "worker" and "laboring classes" were used — which was, simply, to mean *everyone* who worked for a living. This all-inclusive definition was tempting to politicians straining for the grand effect. Representative William Calhoun, replying indignantly to an accusation by southern congressmen that northern banks "enslaved" labor, proclaimed that "the laboring classes of the North comprise the whole population of the North. The great rule of existence there is labor, and only labor." Representative Edward Everett scoffed at the idea of a "workingmen's party," for, as he told a gathering at Charlestown, the term "workingmen" properly included "all those who, by any kind of honest industry, employ the talent which their Creator has given them." Isaac Bates, one of Everett's colleagues, expressed the idea quite succinctly: "We are all laborers."[15]

It is true that on occasion Bay State politicians would, as mentioned before, focus on the particular problems of the working class or use the words "labor" or "laboring classes" to refer specifically to that group.[16] The point is, these types of remarks were made *only* on occasion. More often they spoke (and evidently thought) in terms of one of the more inclusive meanings outlined above. They simply did not feel it was important to define the working class as an occupational group with characteristics and interests of its own — ones quite different from those of the self-employed. It was much easier to lump that class with various independent groups to form one vast, amorphous category called labor. More is at issue here than mere semantic neatness. The way people think about social phenomena is in part determined by the way they conceptualize them. This unwillingness, or inability, of Massachusetts politicians to separate the working class from the self-employed for special consideration presented a twofold danger. First, the discussion of the condition of these two groups would tend to concentrate on those elements held in common and minimize their differences. Second, since the self-employed group preceded the working class historically and was thus more familiar, its characteristics might easily be ascribed to the newer group — which people were more likely to be ignorant of or reluctant to deal with. These confusions were to permeate the politicians' descriptions of the working class.

With these assumptions, the Commonwealth's leaders set about inquiring into the condition of the worker. They discovered, not surprisingly, just what they had hoped for: The employed laborer of Massachusetts resembled his European counterpart in name only. As they saw it, the state's nascent industrial economy had been translated by uniquely American institutions, traditions, and circumstances so as to produce a different kind of worker — one who, instead of posing a threat, was an asset to the community. As in so many other endeavors, where the Old World had stumbled, America had triumphed.

At the heart of their image of the worker was his alleged material well-being. They never tired of pointing out how wages in America — and particularly in Massachusetts — were higher than in any other society. This was, as Webster put it, "the greatest of all proofs of general happiness."[17] Several explanations were proposed. Some took note of the growing use of machinery and the resulting increase in productivity, providing more jobs and greater wealth for all. Others extolled the aforementioned advantages of a diversified economy. One factor often cited was the scarcity of population (and hence, labor), stemming from the newness of the nation and, above all, from the abundant opportunities for purchasing land. This last factor acted like, in Everett's words, "a safety-valve to the great social stream engine," enticing potential laborers westward and opening new opportunities for those who remained behind.[18] Whatever the cause, labor was in continual and great demand and thus well-rewarded. The worker was not, as was so often the case in Europe, reduced to a cramped, miserable existence. He led a comfortable life, was relatively well-fed, well-housed, and could provide for his family. Want was not continually staring him in the face.

A larger issue was at stake, however, than acquiring the primitive elements of survival. Political spokesmen repeatedly stressed that the worker in Massachusetts was "free." What they meant by this, apart from its political dimension, was the liberating effect of the worker's escape from poverty: His horizons were considerably broadened. As Representative John Davis put it, "he aspires to objects beyond physical want. He aims at something higher than food, raiment, and lodging. He lifts his hopes to those moral and intellectual attainments which qualify him to become a free, enlightened, independent citizen." A well-paid worker simply had the energy and time for (not to mention an interest in) other activities. He could improve himself by reading, attending lectures, perhaps even continuing his education. He could participate intelligently and responsibly in politics. Because he did not have to send his family out to work, his wife could provide him (as was her duty) with a happy, stable home life and his children were able to attend school. He and his dependents, finally, could abide by the moral precepts of religion and society, for they were insulated from the temptations to vice that poverty inevitably entailed.[19]

The worker's well-being also rendered him to a large degree "independent" of his employer. In most cases, politicians argued, he was easily able to set aside some of his more than adequate wages, becoming in time a sort of capitalist in miniature. (As already noted, this caused a great deal of confusion in distinguishing "labor" from "capital.") According to Nathan Appleton, "The labor of a single year gives to every laborer, if he choose to save his earnings, a very considerable capital. He takes at his pleasure a place in society." This nest egg put the worker in a strong bargaining position vis-à-vis his boss. He could effectively threaten to quit his job unless he were granted a decent wage, fair hours, or safer working conditions. He could move from place to place in search of a better job. He might even be able to survive an economic depression. In short, the worker had a buffer between the loss of employment and starvation and therefore did not need to act the obsequious slave to his current employer. For these reasons Appleton rejected the assumption of the English free traders "that labor is every where in excess, waiting to be employed by capital, in itself powerless, dependent, only asking to live." That may be true in Europe, he said, but not in the United States. "With us labor assumes a higher tone: it treats with capital on equal terms; it shares in the profits hand in hand with capital." The worker, echoed Representative John Davis,

> leans not on the rich for bread, nor does he look to the poor-house as his ultimate home; but carries forth to his daily toil a proud consciousness that he can depend safely on his own hands; that the dependence between him and the rich is mutual, and as necessary to the one as to the other.[20]

This feeling of security that high wages bestowed upon the worker was reflected in his attitude toward his job. His mind at ease, he went to work with a will. Politicians habitually characterized the worker in the United States, and in Massachusetts especially, as "spirited," "proud," "cheerful," "contented," "active," "enterprising" — all in bold contrast to the "drudgery" that was the lot of the European laborer. The worker was not alienated from his toil. It gave him a good living, so he could be positive and enthusiastic about it.

From this point the argument moved to a different plane. What implications might the practical, personal benefits of the worker's economic condition have for society as a whole? As with any participant in a given social system, the worker both contributed to the functioning of that system and in turn found his life patterns molded by it. The working class was rapidly enlisting a greater proportion of the state's people. What place would it establish for itself? How would its presence affect the existing arrangement of social classes? In what ways would its great numbers shape the future direction of society? Political leaders had optimistic answers to all these questions.

As the working class grew politicians professed themselves entirely satisfied with the new social hierarchy. Since the worker was fairly comfortable economically, most of the population remained, as it had been before, clustered at the middle-income levels. There was no sudden, devastating enlargement of the impoverished class. Indeed, few were poor, they said, clearly implying that most of those who were had only their own laziness and improvidence to thank. The citizens of Massachusetts exhibited a greater degree of social equality than those of any other place in the world. It was, the Whig leader Rufus Choate went so far as to declare, "a State perfectly homogeneous . . . , without ranks, orders, classes; without antagonisms of interests, institutions, pursuits, or moral sentiments; . . . it is . . . a Commonwealth thus absolutely kindred, and the same everywhere."[21]

Choate's description is a bit too extravagant to be representative. Most political spokesmen would have conceded that differences in wealth did indeed exist among the state's citizens. Perfect equality could never be obtained, given the uneven distribution of talents among mankind. One or two spokesmen, like Horace Mann, even worried about a growing polarization of wealth in the state. Yet the general run of politicians chose to emphasize the fact that differences in wealth meant far less in the United States than in Europe. They were not impressed upon the social fabric in the form of rigid, insular classes perpetuated through time by legal and customary privileges (or disabilities). "We are characterized by no Asiatic casts [sic]," boasted Governor John Brooks. The original settlers of Massachusetts introduced no such groupings, and the republic's tradition of equality under the law prevented any from taking root. There was rather, in the words of the eminent jurist Joseph Story, "a *gradation* of property from the highest to the lowest." This gradation lent a welcome fuzziness to social distinctions based on wealth.[22]

But if Massachusetts was not segmented into "ranks, orders, classes," the absence of clear lines of demarcation was but one reason. The other, cited more frequently, was that there was a continuing turnover of the membership of the various social divisions, however loosely defined. In modern terms, the rate of social mobility was high. The thriving, advancing economy, coupled with the country's unique system of laws (especially its partible inheritance laws), constantly opened up new opportunities — both for success and for failure. "Property," according to Story, "is continually changing like the waves of the sea." With us, former mayor Josiah Quincy told a Boston crowd, "the distinctions of wealth, or of power, are not fixed in families; . . . whatever of this nature exists to-day, may be changed to-morrow, or, in a coming generation, be absolutely reversed." The most vivid proof of these contentions was the precarious status of the wealthy. Most of them, it was said, were not like the lucky aristocrats of Europe, whose great fortunes had been handed down from generation to generation. Rather, they had amassed their property by dint of their own hard labor, and could lose it as quickly as they had earned it. Recent history showed that in fact this was an all too common occurrence. "If, in some instances," remarked Webster, "capital be accumulated till it rises to what may be called affluence, it is usually disintegrated, and broken into particles again, in one or two generations." Everett's observations were similar. "In our large cities, it is almost proverbial that the splendid mansion of one generation is a boarding-house in the next. I do not remember a family rich by inherited wealth for three generations." The result was "a constant infusion of new, untainted blood" into the upper ranks of society. As he put it in another speech, "the wheel of fortune is in constant revolution, and the poor, in one generation, furnish the rich of the next."[23]

The worker, of course, helped create this happy situation by providing the labor power which fueled the growing economy, and for this he was duly rewarded. The mobility that the economy made possible was said to be as available to him as it was to anyone else. The fluid social system and equality under the law assured, Everett said, that "as a general rule, the place to which each individual shall rise in society is precisely graduated on the scale of capacity and exertion — in a word, of merit." In short, everyone got what he deserved. The Massachusetts worker, well prepared by the state's common schools, was thus in an excellent position to take advantage of the opportunities being presented to him.

He had, according to the Commonwealth's Secretary of State John Palfrey, "every reasonable opportunity for improvement and advancement,
that money could buy, or heart desire. Every thing there is in him has
its fair chance to come out." To corroborate these contentions political
spokesmen often pointed to the dramatic examples among the wealthy
of how hard work and perseverance could bring handsome rewards.
"I hazard nothing in saying," ran Representative Charles Upham's
confident declaration, "that there is no part of the world where men
rise, without patrimony or patronage, by the inherent force of merit and
talent, to high positions in society, more surely or more generally than
in Massachusetts." A delegate to the state constitutional convention of
1853 said it was common knowledge that in Boston over the last twenty
years "the most successful and the wealthiest business men, and those
standing highest in the legal profession, and in social position, have
been the poor boys that came in here, if not with packs upon their backs,
yet with pen in their hands, to enter as clerks in the business houses of
the city." Representative Robert Winthrop spoke of "the noble specta-
cle which is so often exhibited in this country . . . of what are called
self-made men, the printer's boys, or ploughboys, or mill-boys of a few
years back, elevating themselves to the highest stations of social or of
public life." To the politicians such well-known facts demonstrated con-
clusively that there was hardly any position in life to which the worker
might not realistically aspire. There was always room at the top. In
Story's words, "the child with scarcely clothes to cover his nakedness,
may rise to the highest office in our government, and the poor man,
while he rocks his infant on his knees, may justly indulge the consola-
tion, that if he possess talents and virtue, there is no office beyond the
reach of honorable ambition."[24]

These early strains of Horatio Algerism make one wonder how seriously public figures believed in the rags-to-riches myth. Obviously, few
workers were able to succeed in climbing to the uppermost ranks of
wealth and power. Perhaps, in more sober moments, these politicians
would have suggested that the examples of dramatic rise they so fondly
cited were extreme but nonetheless real proof of a fluidity that characterized the entire social system. Those who had risen from the bottom to
the very top rungs of society demonstrated that there were places for
many others at the steps in between.

Occasionally politicians did talk about the more limited kinds of improvement a worker might realistically make in his circumstances, especially when expounding the advantages of factory work per se. Only on this point their testimony was divided. There were those, like Edward Everett, Levi Lincoln, and Rufus Choate, who argued that factories, by extending the range of jobs available, offered employment to many who otherwise might have difficulty finding work at all. "A diversified, advanced, and refined mechanical and manufacturing industry, cooperating with [the] other numerous employments of civilization which always surround it, offers," said Choate, "the widest choice, detects the slightest shade of individuality, quickens into existence and trains to perfection the largest conceivable amount and the utmost possible variety of national mind." Yet other politicians conceived of factory jobs differently, not so much as desirable ends in themselves but rather as way-stations on the path to better positions. Massachusetts, they bragged, was not saddled with a permanent "factory population" as was to be found in England. The turnover in this type of work was high. Typically factory operatives came from a healthy rural environment, were (if they were children) educated as they worked, and ordinarily spent no more than a few years at their jobs before quitting either to return home to enjoy their modest wealth or to undertake other endeavors. But however it was presented — as a mobilizer of society's untapped skills or as useful lower rungs on the ladder of success — factory work, all agreed, provided the laborer with a host of new options for getting ahead.[25]

Close attention to the blessings of social mobility added a dynamic and still more optimistic emphasis to politicians' treatment of the worker's economic status. While his relatively high wages supplied him with a cushion of security, the knowledge that he could improve his lot by applying his God-given talents offered reassurance about the future. The "hope of bettering his condition," Robert Winthrop noted, ". . . is the sweetest cordial to the heart of man, and the surest stimulus to industry, economy, and virtue."[26] Thus inspired, the worker, with luck, could describe in miniature the greater progress of society as a whole. Indeed, the argument went, as each man strove to better his condition all men would necessarily advance, for the qualities needed for personal success promoted the perfection of the race. The worker's opportunities for improvement, along with his ample income, joined him to the social order in a circle of felicity, establishing him in the most practical terms as a worthy and respectable citizen.

For the portrait of the new working class to have ended with this economic profile would have left it only partially complete. These political leaders were addressing (and themselves were formed by) a society that was vitally concerned with questions of public morality and religion. For them the good society was one where, above all, the moral injunctions of God and Christ, as set down in the Bible and interpreted through the Protestant tradition, were recognized and obeyed. All else, in the ultimate scheme of things, was peripheral. To talk about the working class without mention of its inner estate would therefore have struck their audiences as crude and moreover, as a dereliction of duty: Politicians were *expected* to weigh the moral implications of social trends. Hence they were careful to balance their enthusiastic view of the worker's temporal status with a more cursory but, it turns out, just as favorable description of his spiritual one.

It would not have been surprising if they had approached this whole question expecting the worst. Many were pessimists about human nature. Man, they were convinced, exhibits constantly a strong propensity to satisfy his personal desires at the expense of others. He is "born neither wise nor good," Governor John Brooks observed, and therefore must be inculcated with the rules of ethical behavior. "Knowledge and virtue result from instruction, and discipline and effort."[27] Even then the struggle for mastery over selfishness could be a trying one. The good society was hard to attain even in the best of circumstances. And the circumstances of the new age of the machine were hardly the best, by any means. It was an age of extensive social and geographic mobility, rapidly growing cities, a greater emphasis on wealth and material goods — none of these fostered close attention to time-honored standards of rectitude. In addition, the British experience with industrialization was a disturbing omen. The rise of a working class there had dragged down steadily the moral level of all of society. The shocking "degradation" of the workers showed that it was primarily those at the lowest rungs of the social ladder who had the least incentive to curb their instincts for self-aggrandizement and violence. When life becomes hard, the tenuous bonds of moral obligation are easily snapped. All the signs, in short, pointed to an inevitable moral deterioration of Massachusetts society — with the working class in the vanguard.

With great relief, the Commonwealth's politicians reported to their constituents that nothing of this sort was happening. Some of them *would* occasionally point with alarm to evidence of moral backsliding. Antislavery men, for instance, were fond of accusing their opponents of moral insensitivity and even cowardice. Nativists bemoaned what they claimed were the slovenly ethical standards of immigrants. Temperance advocates warned that society's values stood in imminent danger of drowning under a sea of liquor. And political parties were constantly taunting each other with charges of demagoguery and selfish opportunism. Yet despite this the vast majority of the leading politicians, while probably willing to concede a few blemishes here and there, pronounced the state's general moral tone to be quite healthy. As Edward Everett summed it up:

> May we not with reason rejoice, . . . that the quiet and humble virtues are respected; that frugality and temperance are held in honor; that luxury has made but limited progress; that the relations of domestic life are so generally deemed sacred; that Religion commands the reverence of the vast majority of the people; and that as large a proportion of the citizens are engaged in enterprizing, successful, and contented pursuit of some industrious occupation, as in any part of the world?[28]

Why *hadn't* the worker in Massachusetts descended into a slough of vice? Evidently there had been some qualms expressed in the earlier years about the possible ill effects of factory lork on the operatives' morals.[29] But the unique way that the working class developed in Massachusetts, politicians later said, kept it on the path of righteousness. The workers' material well-being and abundant opportunities to advance, coupled with their education in the state's public schools, had had the expected result: They allowed, even encouraged workers to abide by the moral injunctions of church, state, and society in general.

In this connection politicians scrutinized quite closely those who toiled in the factories. If the English experience was any guide, it was there that any signs of moral decay would show up first. What they found was encouraging. The factory workers, they said, were maintaining the same high standard of virtue that marked the state as a whole.

Optimistic accounts began coming in as early as the 1820s. Governor Levi Lincoln told the legislature in 1825 that the record of "large manufacturing establishments" so far demonstrated "that the richest sources of wealth to our country may be cultivated without danger to the moral habits and chaste manners of a numerous class of our population." Edward Everett, in whose congressional district Waltham and Lowell were located, could barely contain his enthusiasm. In an 1828 speech he commended Lowell for its "population as moral, as intelligent, as substantial, as any in the Union." A couple of years later he exulted that the factories had not proved to be the "seminaries of vice and immorality" that early skeptics thought they might be: "those establishments are as little open to reproach, on the score of morals, as any other in the community." Speaking before the inhabitants of Lowell themselves, he declared that the town

> might safely enter into a comparison with any town or city in the land. Nowhere, I believe, for the same population, is there a greater number of schools and churches, and nowhere a greater number of persons whose habits and mode of life bear witness that they are influenced by a sense of character. . . . You have gained, for the skilled industry required to carry on these mighty establishments, a place of honor in the great dispensation by which Providence governs the world. You have shown that the home-bred virtues of the parental roof are not required to be left behind by those who resort for a few years to these crowded marts of social industry; and, in the fruits of your honest and successful labor, you are daily carrying gladness to the firesides where you were reared.

Alexander Everett, previously doubtful about the value of manufacturing, by the late twenties came to share his brother's zeal. The morality of the "well conducted manufacturing establishments," he went so far as to say, ". . . is probably superior to that of any other portion of the community." At Waltham, he noted, despite the presence of hundreds of operatives of both sexes, only one instance of "irregular intercourse" had occurred since the plant's founding. "Intemperance and the vices punishable by law were unheard of." Soon thereafter he was writing, smugly, that the matter had been firmly settled: "The complaint that manufactures have an injurious effect on the morals of the people, has become, we imagine, nearly obsolete."[30]

In fact, he was right. From this point on almost no important political figure seriously questioned the morality of factory operatives (unless, as later chapters will show, they also happened to be immigrants). Most had nothing to offer but praise.[31] The factory hand stood revealed, as he was in so many other ways, as a worthy exemplar of the working class as a whole.

Intimately related to the question of public morality in the eyes of many of these leaders was that of education. Intellect and conscience, after all, were the two halves of man's inner estate. Massachusetts in these years was a pioneer in developing a government-financed network of schools intended to make available to the mass of the populace (hence the name "common" schools) the fundamentals of what was then deemed a sound education. How successfully it achieved this end has been called into question by recent scholarship;[32] even at the time the school system was continually criticized for not doing as good a job as possible. But despite these doubts, the common schools still managed to garner countless bouquets of praise. (Just after the Civil War, Governor Alexander Bullock would recommend to the legislature that the state send a model of a typical schoolhouse as its exhibit to the Paris exposition of 1867.) Horace Mann, the secretary of the state Board of Education for many years and the prime architect of the system, explained its importance succinctly: "the true business of the schoolroom connects itself, and becomes identical, with the great interests of society. . . . As 'the child is father to the man,' so may the training of the schoolroom expand into the institutions and fortunes of the State."[33]

Schools had existed in Massachusetts since the earliest colonial times. However, the nineteenth century witnessed the first attempt to extend the benefits of education to almost the entire state population — and that included, of course, the working class. So before long political leaders began citing as one of the virtues of their state's workers the fact that they were educated.

For them this was significant in several ways. First, education was perceived as being intimately related to public morality: the worker who had gone to school, they contended, was much more likely to become a virtuous citizen. In this period, as before, there was a great deal of interest in the role of "moral education" in the curriculum. With the influence of church and family palpably waning in places like Boston, the school was to serve as the main agent in teaching children fundamental moral precepts — worthy for their own sake as well as essential ingredients of social discipline. Horace Mann constantly stressed this aspect of its mission. In a republican system such as ours, he held, "the human faculties . . . glow with an intense life, and burst forth with uncontrollable impetuousity." Unfortunately, among those faculties were a group of rather unsavory ones — "the strictly selfish part of our nature, which consists of a gang of animal appetites" — especially, in the United States, "the love of gain and the love of place." To try to extirpate these dangerous passions would probably be folly. (In moderation they were in fact useful.) Rather, he maintained, the schools must put a check on such passions in the formative years of childhood. Schools must "establish the authority and extend the jurisdiction of reason and conscience." Edward Everett reiterated this idea:

> It is of utmost importance, in this country, that the active walks of life should be filled with an enlightened class of men, with a view to the security and order of society, and to protect it from those evils which have been thought, in Europe, to be inseparable from the great increase of the laboring population. What is done in other countries by *gens d'armes* and horseguards, must here be done by public sentiment, or not at all.

This was one of the prime responsibilities of the common schools, and all reports indicated they were carrying it out quite effectively.[34]

On a more practical level, political leaders took pleasure in enumerating the economic advantages the worker — and indeed all society — derived from education. The common schools, they firmly believed, were a cornerstone of the state's prosperity. As Mann put it, "An ignorant people not only is, but must be, a poor people. They must be destitute of sagacity and providence, and, of course, of competence and comfort." Schools were said to make the state wealthy by increasing the worker's productivity. An educated worker was more apt to come up with useful inventions or make improvements in existing machines or processes, a very important consideration in manufacturing. As George Boutwell, one of Mann's successors, observed: "There is no branch of manufactures without its appropriate machine; and every machine is the product of mind, enlarged and disciplined by some sort of culture." "The number of improvers will increase," wrote Mann, "as the intellectual constituency, if I may so call it, increases." As the worker advanced the art of his industry, he augmented its earnings, and thereby, his own. Then, more generally, an educated worker usually earned more because he was a better worker, understood his job better, was usually more reliable, and had greater powers of concentration. These qualities were again especially desirable in the complex, demanding world of the factory. Last, the educated worker was likely to be in a better position to rise, since in the hierarchy of occupations knowledge was one of the crucial differentiators. The laborer who had gone to school would find it easier qualifying for a higher-paying job. In short, the evidence was overwhelmingly in favor of the proposition that, in Boutwell's words, "an intelligent laboring community will soon become a wealthy community."[35]

Perhaps the school's most enduring contribution was to give the worker the means to understand and appreciate the advances in knowledge made by his contemporaries. Not so long ago, noted the politicians, knowledge was the preserve of a privileged few, the mass of men having neither the leisure nor the resources to obtain it. "Unceasing and perpetual manual toil," said Webster, "is not consistent with any considerable degree of mental improvement." Happily, this was not true of Massachusetts. "One of the most striking characteristics of the present age is the extraordinary progress which it has witnessed of popular knowledge. A new movement towards higher attainments, in science and arts, has been communicated to the whole mass of society." The Commonwealth's working classes had the time — and what was more, the incentive — to educate themselves and their children. And the schools, along with the state's many libraries, workers' "improvement" clubs, newspapers, lyceums, and the like, gave them the tools to do so. With the doors of knowledge open to them, their comprehension of their society and their world could be immeasurably enriched. Governor John Davis defined the purpose of the common school system in this way:

> To extend to a whole people the means of moral and intellectual improvement; to employ the resources of the State to make all wise and good, by enlarging their capacities for enjoyment and usefulness, is a noble conception, as it unfolds the mental strength of the poor and opens the way for all to attain honor and fame. We see among us at all

times the powerful workings of education, in the fact, that a large
portion of those who embellish the walks of literature, or adorn the
learned professions, or signalize themselves in the halls of legislation,
are the sons of persons comparatively poor. Thus the schools are constantly exerting a great influence upon our destiny by adding fresh
vigor, power, and moral energy to the popular mind, and qualifying it
to sustain the great cause of equality of rights in the most comprehensive sense.

Through public education the workers became full-fledged citizens of
the intellect, sharing in and, with luck, contributing to the enlighten-
ment of the age.[36]

In sum, the evidence of the worker's moral and intellectual condition
was most encouraging. Massachusetts had no "vicious" working class,
stultified by ignorance and wallowing in depravity. The laborer was
instead raised by his virtue and his instructed intelligence to his full
stature as a human being, ready to stand comparison with any other
group in society. His spirit as well as his body was amply provided for.
In fact there was a close relationship between the two. His physical
comforts made it easy for him to follow the moral laws of society and
gave him the chance to develop his mental capacities. And his virtue and
education, aside from their intrinsic value, repaid him handsomely in
material rewards. Each aspect of his situation reinforced the other,
confirming his sense of self-worth and making his life more righteous
and more fulfilling.

Like most other American politicians in these nationalistic times, the
leaders of Massachusetts rejoiced that the nation's forms of government
were thoroughly democratic (or as they put it, "republican"). Political
speakers on almost any topic regularly and monotonously congratulated
their listeners on their good fortune in living under such a system. "To
no other people on earth has so large a portion of personal and public
happiness been vouchsafed. Of no nation does the history of past or of
present time exhibit such a picture of true moral grandeur." And the
reason, according to Governor Levi Lincoln? "To the character of our
republican institutions we are indebted under Heaven, for whatever is
thus enviable in our condition. The continuance of our public enjoy-

ments must depend on the purity in which these institutions are preserved."[37] The thoughts, even the words of his statement, are representative of scores of others. Since the very form of government was responsible for the nation's progress and since that form derived its authority and mandate from the people, these leaders were led inevitably to consider the possible political implications of that group that was so rapidly becoming such a large part of "the people," the working class.

They did not doubt that the worker, just like any other person, benefited enormously by living in a democracy. For in Massachusetts (and across America) he was a participating citizen. After 1821 only a small poll tax was required to vote; all except the very poorest laborers must have qualified.[38] Political spokesmen were well aware of how unprecedented this situation was. The worker here had a measure of political influence denied him everywhere else on earth. "In other States," said Representative Isaac Bates, "the laboring people have little or no agency in the Government, except in the form and by the terror of the mob. But here, they are the sovereign himself." Instead of being a political pariah, the worker shared in the noble effort of self-government — and was thereby ennobled himself.[39]

The worker's role as voting citizen counted for more than mere status, however, having some very practical advantages. By the instrument of his vote he had a say in the government's policies. His interests and wants would be attended to. And given the way the democratic system usually worked in the United States, he could be sure that his property rights would be respected, that he would be treated fairly and equally under the law, and that he would be granted an exceedingly large range of personal liberties. As the politicians phrased it, in fact, the argument became a circular one. The worker was a subject of a government that dealt with him equitably, they said, in large part because it involved him and his fellows so extensively in its operations. He was at the same time the heir and the benefactor of democracy.

Statesmen cited all the aforementioned characteristics of the respectable worker to explain this fortuitous symbiosis. For example, because the protection of property was one of the chief purposes of the state, the fact that the worker was well-paid was crucial. He owned some property (and knew he had a good chance to acquire even more), so he appreciated the importance of safeguarding it. "The industrious mechanic is quite as much concerned as the rich capitalist, to have property safe, and to see that the laws protect its acquisition and enjoyment," wrote Everett. Webster, in a speech before the 1820 constitutional convention, held that a widespread distribution of property, as obtained in Massachusetts, was a necessary precondition for a free government. Where other formally republican nations were divided between a very wealthy minority and a huge, destitute lower class, one of two outcomes was inevitable. Either the rich, aided by the paupers they could bribe to help them, would establish a despotism, milking the rest of society, or the poor would in desperation try to take control, with disastrous results:

> those who have not property, and see their neighbors possess much more than they think them to need, cannot be favorable to laws made for the protection of property. When this class becomes numerous, it grows clamorous. It looks on property as its prey and plunder, and is naturally ready, at all times, for violence and revolution.

Fortunately, neither of these dire eventualities was likely in Massachusetts — or America.

> With property divided, as we have it, no other government than that of a republic could be maintained, even were we foolish enough to desire it. There is reason, therefore, to expect a long continuance of our systems. Party and passion, doubtless, may prevail at times, and much temporary mischief may be done. Even modes and forms may be changed, and perhaps for the worse. But a great revolution in regard to property must take place, before our governments can be moved from their republican basis, unless they be violently struck off by military power. The people possess the property, more emphatically than it could ever be said of the people of any other country, and they can have no interest to overturn a government which protects property by equal laws.

As long as this condition prevailed, property rights would be respected. The worker could toil with the assurance that what he earned would be indubitably his, safe from confiscatory or unjust legislation.[40]

A well-ordered democracy depended on more than a broad distribution of property, however. Scarcely any politician would have disagreed with Webster's dictum that "the actual character of the government can never be better than the general moral and intellectual character of the community." So often, in fact, was this principle cited in education-conscious Massachusetts that in 1833 Webster conceded it was a "trite maxim," and by 1849 Horace Mann was calling it "so trite . . . as to have lost much of its force by its familiarity." Triteness, of course, has never hindered any politician worthy of the name, so the state's leaders proclaimed this idea regularly. "To be free, the people must be intelligently free," was Webster's way of putting it. The Commonwealth's founders knew, according to Levi Lincoln, that "a government, founded upon the popular will, . . . can be maintained no longer than the people are enabled to comprehend their rights, and are enlightened in the proper manner of their exercise." What good was a popular franchise, for instance, unless intelligently exercised? "By a corrupt, or a mechanical cast of votes, men may be raised to the high places of trust, who would deride the feeble restraints of paper Constitutions, which have not the spirit of freemen for their guarantee." And how else, unless it was educated, could the citizenry make wise decisions in judging matters of public policy? We ignore public education at our peril, warned a delegate to the 1853 constitutional convention. It must be supported "if we wish that the ballot-box, rather than the paving stone of the street should be the engine of political revolution." It was for Webster the instrument by which "we endeavor to give a safe and proper direction to [the] public will."[41]

A democracy relied in similar fashion on public virtue. Bestowing political power on the masses would hardly work if the voters were not inspired by some notion of the public good — in short, by altruism. "As each citizen is to participate in the power of governing others, it is an essential preliminary," wrote Mann, "that he should be imbued with a feeling for the wants, and a sense of the rights, of those whom he is to govern; because the power of governing others, if guided by no higher motive than our own gratification, is the distinctive attribute of oppression." Self-government implies, Robert Winthrop said, literally the government of each individual over himself, "by intellect and conscience over mere appetite and passion." Only when each citizen had a fundamental respect for the needs of his fellows could so fragile a mechanism as democracy survive.[42]

As these intangible prerequisites for democracy were spelled out, the worker assumed even greater importance. For not only did he possess property: the politicians had also demonstrated that he *was* enlightened, was virtuous. He could assist in making democratic institutions work wisely and fairly. The worker, in sum, would be a model citizen. He would pay heed to affairs of state, judge well the competing arguments and candidacies of politicians, and take care that the government respected personal liberties and did not overstep its constitutional bounds. Through his participation, he himself would benefit, and the government would not turn into an exploitative arm of some ruling elite. He would be free to advance and prosper under the aegis of equal, just laws. And what, after all, was the entire point of government except to insure that each person is able to exercise that freedom? Governor John Davis expressed it well:

> Individual liberty coupled with intellectual improvement is manifestly the vital principle that distinguishes us and moves us on by its own inherent power, crowning our efforts with triumphant success. It creates impulses that nothing else can give, and in its great and general results exhibits in strong contrast the difference between those who enjoy it, and such as have no voice in their destiny, but from generation to generation labor quietly on, to sustain animal existence, unconscious of the capacities that sleep within them. Almost all we witness around us, is only proof of what man is capable of accomplishing for himself when free scope is given to his mental and physical faculties.

The working class gained immeasurably by contributing toward, living under, and helping to perpetuate a democratic form of government.[43]

Thus, the image of the worker presented in political discourse in Massachusetts portrayed him as well-rewarded and independent, socially mobile, virtuous and enlightened, a worthy citizen of the republic. It all belied the prognosis of doom that issued from the factory towns of England. Only one element is missing from this profile, what was probably for these leaders the most compelling proof of everything else they thought about the worker: how he was regarded by others.

In the Old World the workers were a caste apart, very much removed from and subordinate to the rest of the social order. They were shunned, pitied, mocked, stepped on, treated almost as slaves were in the United States. And they themselves were conscious of their inferiority — or at least, of their separateness. In Massachusetts, on the other hand, the worker was said to be accorded the esteem he deserved. He was — and the words were used often — "honored," "respectable."

In part he earned this respect because work was universally applauded as a valuable social function. In Britain many people (especially the aristocracy) despised labor and those who labored as menial; it was far preferable to live off one's inheritance. Not in the United States, where from the beginning, Nathan Appleton wrote, "industry was the only road to wealth. . . . In this state of things, it is not surprising that the acquisition of property by one's own labor and skill should be held in equal, or even higher estimation, than the inheritance by the accident of birth." Moreover, the Massachusetts worker was accomplishing something worthwhile with his labor: He achieved a good life for himself and his family and helped build up a new nation. As George Boutwell put it, "labor, labor of the hands merely and for a subsistence only, is and ever must be menial; but it is dignified and ennobled, when, guided by intellect, it overcomes the obstacles which lie in every man's path." The community saw this, appreciated and admired it. It saw too the worker's mental capabilities brought to fruition by the common schools. "Ignorance is the degradation of labor," contended Boutwell. But: "If all men are learned, the work of the world will be performed by learned men; and why, under such circumstances, should not every vocation that is honest, be equally honorable?" The same could be said of the worker's manifest virtue. "His sober, methodical, industrious habits," in Representative John Palfrey's words, "are such as sustain self-respect, and claim respect from others."[44]

Every facet of the worker's condition combined to win him social approval. "The laboring man of New England is any man's equal," Palfrey confidently stated. He had a crucial sense of pride and belonging and a knowledge that he was as good as the next man. "The fears and jealousies, which in other countries separate classes of men and make them hostile to each other, have here," claimed Josiah Quincy, "no influence, or a very limited one." It constituted an unparalleled achievement for America. Senator Henry Wilson summed it up best: "Here, the laboring men in all the fields of manly toil are working out a condition of society for the toiling masses more elevated than can be found in any other portion of the globe."[45]

With this last facet of the image of the respectable worker one comes closer to the underlying assumption that firms up the entire structure. Why, finally, was the worker treated with such respect by society as a whole? Because he was *not that different* from those who labored on their own account. Indeed, in most ways the two groups were barely distinguishable. Both enjoyed virtually the same prosperity and prospects, exhibited the same intellectual and moral characteristics, were regarded as equals by the community. The real thrust of what the politicians were saying is that industrialization, so overwhelming a transformation of the economy, had had as a social process . . . not merely a salutary effect, but almost no effect at all! It had produced a new class practically identical to those that had existed before. The respectable worker image simply shoved aside as irrelevant (or severely played down) most of what was new and radically different about the position of the worker under industrialism. It portrayed him as a modern version of the "traditional" social classes of Massachusetts, thus making it easier to understand and, ultimately, to accept him. A profound social change has been assimilated by disregarding its novelty.

The dimensions of this "accomplishment" become strikingly apparent when one recalls the realities this image purports to describe. Although the actual portrait of the Massachusetts worker in these years is a long way from finished, the fragments that are available (in some areas, fairly large fragments) — studies of laborers in specific cities, or specific trades — taken together form a definite outline. What it indicates, quite simply, is that the respectable worker was a myth.[46]

The average worker's economic situation was extremely precarious. From the 1830s on, contemporary estimates suggest, a yearly income of roughly $500 to $600 was the bare minimum required for a married laborer to live in anything approaching decency and comfort. Yet the large majority of male workers never earned that sum. Sending other members of the family out to work, as many husbands and fathers did, did not help all that much, for women and (especially) children were paid abysmally for their toil. An unmarried female laborer almost always had to live at home (or in company boardinghouses) to survive. Poverty was the normal way of life for the working class. From their meager wages most workers were able to save relatively little, usually owning property worth less than $200, almost always worth less than $1,000. A large proportion was literally propertyless. And no matter how unremunerative his job might be, a worker faced the added burden of struggling to hold on to it. Almost nothing prevented his being fired at his boss's merest whim, and he was almost certain to be let go, sometimes for long stretches, when business in his field was slack, or in times of general depression (as in 1837–1842 or 1857–1859). All these hardships were especially severe for the large, and rapidly growing, group at the bottom of the pile, unskilled or common laborers, whose lives were truly miserable.

The conditions under which they labored were extremely harsh too. The benevolent, paternalistic employers of the early cotton textile industry were far from typical. For most workers long hours were common, twelve–thirteen a day being the rule in the factories (for a six-day week), though by the 1850s many factories had cut back to eleven. Only the most fortunate skilled workmen labored ten hours a day. Much work was hazardous and unhealthy, especially in factories. There is evidence also that in some fields — notably cotton textiles and shoes — employees were being forced to toil a lot harder at their jobs as the decades wore on.

Very little is known about the worker's chances of improving his lot, but some generalizations may be made. His opportunities to escape the working class altogether by becoming self-employed were sharply restricted: He rarely had either the capital or skills to strike out on his own, and even if he could, the odds of a small store or artisan shop prospering were fairly dim. It is equally clear that very few workers could make the big jump from a blue-collar to white-collar job. Lack of education, unfamiliarity with middle-class standards of propriety, speech, and work discipline effectively closed off that avenue of ambition. What progress he might make usually had to occur within the manual trades. Yet even here the available evidence suggests it was not easy to move, say, from an unskilled to a skilled position. The mobility most workers achieved, if any, was not job but property mobility, seeking to add a few pennies to their daily wage or, at great sacrifice, slowly trying to save a small nest egg. These "improvements," incidentally, usually had to be made without the help of a union, which was a device most had only heard about.

The environment in which the typical worker lived, the very pattern of his life, was not of the sort to offer encouragement. At best his housing was modest, often far less adequate; large, foul slums had already made their appearance in major cities. Normally he lived in a given area only fleetingly. Recently computed statistics testify to an extraordinarily high rate of movement among workers, especially the poorest. This meant, of course, that he had little chance to establish himself in a neighborhood or community that might offer him support and lend stability to his harried life. Similarly, he lost contact with family and friends. If he turned to more formal social institutions for help, he was usually stymied. The churches (Protestant ones, at least) had little interest in his plight. Poor relief was brutally designed to discourage him from taking advantage of it and to shame him if he dared do so. The vaunted common schools, which offered the hope that his children, at least, might escape his fate, were degenerating into ineffective, overcrowded, custodial institutions. Everywhere he turned, in short, society seemed in league against him. And if he was at all "different" — particularly if he was an Irish immigrant — he faced added burdens of discrimination and hostility.

Finally, the last thing most workers qualified for was "respectability." The line between respectable and nonrespectable was growing hard and clear — and nearly always, the laborer was on the wrong side. A rising, increasingly secure middle class hastened to distinguish itself from the rabble. By countless subtle (and not so subtle) snubs, insults, and condescensions, the message was conveyed to the worker that he was a lesser sort of being.

This is not to say there were no workers who led comfortable lives. While rags-to-riches was a dream, a decent existence was possible for many in clerical and other white-collar positions. Highly skilled workers, like shoe cutters or those involved in such technical fields as textile machinery, iron making, watch or arms manufacture, often did fairly well. (A job at the Springfield Armory was so highly prized that the right to hold it was called a "privilege," which, for a while, one could actually sell, like a modern taxi medallion, for $100 to one's successor.) But these kinds of jobs were few and very hard to procure. The masses of working men and women bore scant resemblance to the figure celebrated by their political leaders.

One can of course contrive explanations for politicians' ignorance of these unhappy facts. After all, they rarely came from working class

backgrounds themselves and apparently mixed little with workers —
except, to be sure, at election time. But this explanation is hardly convincing. Ultimately one must acknowledge nothing less than a massive
failure of social awareness and imagination. These political leaders were
unable to grasp the one overwhelming fact about the rise of the working
class: that it constituted a radical transformation of the structure and
functioning of society. And if it were true, as they alleged, that this
change had not produced very many problems so far, it was almost
certain to do so in the future. In short, they grossly *misinterpreted* the
situation of the worker. Seen in this light, the question of whether
politicians were attempting some kind of whitewash really misses the
point. They were painting the wrong fence.

Why this sweeping epidemic of social blindness spread through Massachusetts, and lasted so long, is hard to explain. I would like to delay
trying to do so until some other trends in the politicial thought of these
years (and after) have been explored. What the practical consequences
of the respectable worker image were is rather easier to unravel. Above
all it was a reassuring image. Through it the recognized leaders of the
state advised the citizenry not to worry, that the striking economic
changes occurring all about them would not alter in any basic way the
familiar face of society. They should feel quite free to exploit and enjoy
industrialization's obvious benefits without fear of paying the heavy
price that had been exacted in Europe. Evidently this message was
convincing to many people, even those who, as the next chapter will
show, might be expected to reject or at least question it. The factory
system did spread rapidly in these years, unhindered by protest or
convulsions. By the end of the Civil War the state's economy was
predominantly industrial. The image of the respectable worker surely
must have encouraged this easy accommodation. Whatever its defects,
it helped wed the Commonwealth's destiny securely to the machine.

Chapter 5

Variations and Dissents

FOR ALL ITS breezy confidence, the image of the respectable worker was at bottom a rather fragile contrivance. Indeed, the very term "image" is somewhat extravagant. It was really more of a loose conglomeration of half-formed, unexamined ideas, propounded in an offhand way to serve other and larger purposes. That it managed to win such overwhelming assent is a tribute less to its inherent persuasiveness than to the fact that for so long no significant, clear alternatives were devised that might have undermined its authority. Moreover, as subsequent chapters will reveal, by the time doubts were raised this image had become so firmly embedded that it proved very difficult to dislodge. It triumphed, in other words, largely by default.

Nevertheless, it is rare for any body of ideas to gain unquestioning, universal acceptance. One always expects to encounter a few nay-sayers chipping slowly, stubbornly, sometimes fervently at the pillars of conventional wisdom. Or at least one can look for variations on the main theme, divergent emphases and formulations that may later become the fulcrum for a new departure in thought. The history of even so solid an ideological edifice as Marxism is rife with such deviations. It would hardly be surprising to find similar cracks in the more flimsy image of the respectable worker.

The present chapter, therefore, will consider this matter from two angles. What dissents from and variations upon the prevailing view of the working class began to emerge in the political arena during the years 1815–1865? And, are there any important segments of Massachusetts society which one might *expect* to generate variations or dissents, but in fact did not? The latter of these questions will be considered first.

The dominant scenario of most histories of industrialization depicts an old order being abruptly displaced by the new. Incorporated into this scheme, usually, is a subplot: the strongest dissatisfaction with industrialization and its attendant working class is sounded by those who held positions of power and influence in — or by more common folk whose livelihoods were inseparably connected with — the *pre*industrial order. It is they who are injured most palpably by the factory — their lives altered, their economic security threatened, their prestige deflated. In retaliation they launch an attack on the entire industrial system in a poignant but ultimately futile attempt to stem the tide of modernization.

Why is it that, for the most part, this did not occur in antebellum Massachusetts? The answer lies in some of the trends brought out in chapter 2. Hardly any of the leading economic groups in preindustrial Massachusetts felt their fortunes were inextricably caught up in *only* that stage of development. When the factory appeared, they were willing to make the necessary readjustments.

In the case of the agricultural sector, most farmers before industrialization were not, as has been pointed out, happily working thriving, remunerative plots of land. Quite a few had already quit their ancestral homesteads to move west. To them, the factory system must have seemed initially more of a promise than a threat. The growing working class translated into a larger demand for food, hence an expanded market for their crops and livestock. For several decades, in fact, agriculture rebounded. As for the farmer who still could not make ends meet, he (or his family) could always find seasonal, or even permanent, employment in the industrial plants themselves. Of course, as time went on, industrialization — and the transportation revolution it inspired — caused quite severe problems for the local husbandman, but by then it was too late to protest: The new system was too solidly entrenched. True, there were occasional sputterings of discontent. When a workingmen's party surfaced in the early thirties, it found a fair amount of support among, oddly enough, farmers in the western part of the state. And as the Civil War approached, legislators from rural constituencies became notably reluctant to vote for state aid to railroads, which had already done so much to undercut the farmer's position by bringing in agricultural products from the West. For the most part, however, farmers, demoralized from the start and lulled for so long by false hopes about the factory system, never developed into a vanguard of resentment against industrialism.

The state's mercantile class, at first glance, would seem a more promising source of potential dissent. Though far fewer in number than the
farmers, they were much wealthier and more powerful. Indeed,
throughout the entire preindustrial period, stretching all the way back
to the Puritans, they had been recognized (particularly in the larger
towns) as the "natural" social and political leaders of the Commonwealth. With so much to lose, and with the resources to make their
opinions known, might not this class be expected to complain vigorously
about being superseded by rising manufacturers?

As it turns out, they did protest — for a while. During the decade
after the War of 1812 spokesmen for the mercantile interests, then
suffering from a temporary decline in trade, demurred from the new
idea that manufacturing would prove a boon to the state's economy (and
hence should be protected by higher tariffs). But they went further. In
the course of their protests they sometimes issued bleak forecasts about
what a "manufacturing population" might be like.

Daniel Webster, at this phase of his career an ardent defender of New
England's merchant class in Congress, thought manufacturing was fine
— so long as it was restricted to the household level. But encourage
"great manufacturing establishments," he warned, and one invites trouble. The inevitable tendency in such large plants was toward a greater
division of labor. The operatives, after spending a fair portion of their
lives there, are fit for nothing else and eventually become "among the
most dependent of human beings": "One of these laborers, utterly in-
capable of making and carrying to the market on his own account the
smallest entire article, is necessarily at the mercy of the capitalist for the
support of himself and family." Out of this dependence flowed all sorts
of baneful consequences. The factory operative, Webster held, was
much more likely to become unemployed (being unable to do anything
else if his factory shut down or he was fired). Hence he was prone to
pauperism, and forced to take desperate measures to provide for his
family. Also, factories often hired women and children, to his mind a
pernicious practice. There they toiled "in dust, and smoke, and steam,
to the perpetual whirl of spools and spindles, and the grating of rasps
and saws." The children could easily be overworked and deprived of
proper parental supervision; the moral taint of factory labor might render the single women employed there less attractive potential marriage

partners to "respectable young men." Finally, the expansion of the
factory system encouraged people to leave the countryside for the city, a
trend Webster viewed with suspicion. "Habits favorable to good morals
and free Governments, are not usually most successfully cultivated in
populous manufacturing cities." And, "I am not in haste to see Sheffields
and Birminghams in America." The lesson of all this, according to Webster, was that the factory system should be developed *slowly*, in keeping
with "the general progress of our wealth and population." If "pushed to
excess," it would "make the poor both more numerous and more poor,
and the rich less in number, but perhaps more rich." "Two generations
. . . would change the whole face of New England society."[1]

Boston being the state's foremost port, some of its other politicians
took up these themes in the early twenties. James T. Austin, the county
attorney for Suffolk and a prominent Republican, feared that the prolif-
eration of factories would prove "decidedly hostile to republican principles, and to the moral character of the community." The operative's lot
was to toil incessantly at low pay, a "miserable existence." "The
employment is enervating, and the place where it is carried on is not
congenial to activity or health." Working so hard, he had little chance to
acquire a decent education. "With the want of instruction comes of
course the want of moral susceptibility," and, as the experience of
Europe showed, "a diseased, depraved, ignorant, and factious population" was the likely result. The "natural tendency" of the factory system
"is to divide the community into two great classes, the very rich and the
very poor, and thereby to destroy that equality on which our institutions
are universally founded." The fate of democratic institutions also concerned the city's mayor, Josiah Quincy. Addressing the 1820 constitutional convention, he foresaw a time when "the establishment of a great
manufacturing interest in the Commonwealth" would produce a large
class of "manufacturers" (that is, factory operatives) who were "absolutely dependent upon their employers, here as they are everywhere
else." Hardly the stuff of which independent citizens were made; rather,
they were "dead votes, counted by the head, by their employer." With
only a few factories in a county, "one great capitalist" could exert immense political power. Edward Everett observed that in no place in the
world did factory workers earn a decent living, for they were almost
always unskilled. The situation might turn out differently in the United

States, but since the American worker always expected more than the European, he doubted that it would.[2]

These few scattered brief speeches and articles at the dawn of industrialization in Massachusetts managed, astonishingly enough, to adumbrate all the criticisms of the respectable worker image that would appear decades later. Equally astonishingly, almost as suddenly as these objections arose, they ceased. The protective tariff did not prove the disaster that merchants predicted. Moreover, the raw materials required by the factories and the finished products they turned out were stimulating a revival of trade. Soon these political spokesmen altered their stance. Webster and Everett became avid proponents of industry and eulogists of the worker. Symbolically, in the congressional election of 1830 the incumbent free-trader Henry Lee was ousted by Nathan Appleton, merchant, industrial capitalist, and high-tariff advocate, as the representative from the Boston district. From that point on the mercantile class found little fault with the condition of the worker.

A final quirk of economic history helped still all doubts: Many leading merchants were rapidly coopted into the new order. Instead of being "displaced" by rising manufacturers, they *became* rising manufacturers. In the textile industry, for example, the first efforts at setting up a big, modern plant were undertaken by wealthy merchants like Francis Cabot Lowell and Patrick Tracy Jackson. Their success prompted others to get involved. One study of large Massachusetts and New Hampshire cotton mills has found that throughout the antebellum period the Commonwealth's mercantile class was by far the greatest single source of investment capital in these ventures. For all the years studied but one they controlled at least one-third of the corporations' equity holdings, and in some years it was over half. These men, who had prospered as merchants by risking their money in new schemes, were willing, once again, to gamble.[3] In extreme cases, as with Nathan Appleton, they transferred all their attention from trade to industry. Appleton made his fortune as an importer, but when business faltered during the War of 1812 he reluctantly consented to take a chance on the Waltham plant. Impressed with its earnings, he added to his holdings greatly in the twenties, becoming a major industrial capitalist. During the thirties and forties he was the largest holder of stock in cotton manufacturing corporations in the United States, his annual portfolio usually ranging between $600,000 and $700,000. He helped organize many new companies, served as a director of several, and almost until his death was president of one of the largest, the Merrimack Company. Admittedly, he was atypical, but other merchants, while they probably did not turn away from commerce so completely, were heavy investors in the industry nevertheless.

A similar trend manifested itself in the boot and shoe industry, although in different form. Mechanization and factory production did not appear in the industry until the 1850s and did not become dominant until after the war. Before this, however, the entire trade was reorganized through a complex system of central shops and the farming out of work to individual shoemakers at their homes. The new system was devised by "merchant capitalists," wholesale merchants in the larger towns and Boston interested in selling large quantities of cheap "store shoes" to the South and West and abroad. These merchants became the kingpins of the entire industry: They worked out its structure, directed its operations, supplied the capital and raw materials, and marketed the finished product. Without them there would have been no "boot and shoe industry," properly speaking, at all. Eventually parallel reorganizations would transform the manufacture of straw hats and men's clothing.

Thus, merchants who had amassed (and were continuing to amass) large fortunes in shipping and in commerce generally were often actively involved in the financing and operations of major industries (as well as, incidentally, railroads). Their overlapping interests had some crucial political implications. Manufacturing enterprise was not brought to Massachusetts by "foreign" meddlers or nouveau-riche upstarts.[4] Those who introduced and managed it had firm ties to the old mercantile elite. There was a comforting continuity of leadership, technique, style, even family. The most influential political class of preindustrial Massachusetts came to have a vital stake in promoting the new order. They were hardly about to deprecate the workers upon whom that order relied.

In like fashion, most of the other traditional groups of preindustrial Massachusetts came to some sort of accommodation with the factory. Fishermen and whalers, happy with the growing urban markets and (unlike the farmers) secure from out-of-state competition, were unperturbed by the new system. Small shopowners stocked their shelves with a wide range of profitable manufactured goods. Men in the professions found their services in greater demand. In fact, of all the traditional classes only self-employed artisans, who faced the prospect of becoming workers themselves, had reason to criticize the status of the worker. So different was their situation — and their reaction — that I would like to deal with them in a later chapter. The remaining groups had no *economic* motive, at least, to dissent from the image of the respectable worker. Except for the farmers, they were not dislocated economically, nor did they suffer a serious "status revolution." In short, they did not harbor any gnawing resentment of the factory system that might take the form of an attack on the condition of the worker. The sense of betrayal and loss, even futility, that did so much to evoke sympathy for the "laboring poor" in England was, among these groups, virtually absent. And the tides of political opinion reflected their serenity.

The political scene in Massachusetts between 1815 and 1865 was, as previously noted, anything but fluid. Instead of different groups and coalitions continually jockeying for power and frequent shifts in political control (as was the case, say, in neighboring New York), one political organization effectively dominated the state. In the thirties and forties this was the Whig party; after a brief transitional period in the early fifties, the Republicans. These parties were primarily responsible for fashioning the image of the respectable worker. However, if there existed a clearly defined, well-entrenched "in" group in Massachusetts politics, there must also have been one, or several, "out" groups as well. What of them? In their efforts to storm the citadel of power — or, at least, to elicit sympathy among those in power for their point of view — would they not be strongly tempted to mount a challenge to prevailing notions about the working class? To find out, it is instructive to consider the case of the two most prominent groups of political outsiders — the Democrats and the "reformers."

The lot of a Democrat in antebellum Massachusetts must have been exasperating. Across the nation, both North and South, the Democratic party was strong, bold, advancing, "progressive." At home (indeed, in all of New England) it was a perennially weak also-ran, contending against formidable odds. The state's recognized social and economic leaders were lined up almost solidly against the party. Only in the fifties did a few, like Rufus Choate, Robert Winthrop, and Amos Lawrence, temporarily join its ranks, largely out of disgust with Whig policies. Also, most newspapers were hostile to the Democrats. With such influence among the molders of public opinion and with such noted supporters, their opponents were nearly unassailable. In contrast, they seemed not quite proper, a shade unbalanced, "wild"; shabby little men lusting for power.

The Democrats struggled with other problems, too, largely self-imposed. They had an unlucky knack for taking stands that offended many respectable, middle-class, native-born voters. Their party was identified nationally with slavery, and while they never explicitly defended it, they belligerently attacked abolitionists and all others who would deny the South "justice." They opposed prohibition and curried favor with the Irish immigrant, thereby fixing the party firmly, in the eyes of many, on the side of the devil. Finally, they suffered serious internal divisions. In the thirties and forties they disagreed on how far to carry their fight against chartered corporations, banks, and the system of "privilege" generally. Later they split over the expansion of slavery. (Some, in fact, would feel so strongly on this issue that they ended up defecting to the Free Soil or Republican parties.) Rarely could they rally their quarrelsome forces for a concerted effort against their opponents. In short, theirs was a party that seemed doomed to continual defeat. Only their unfailing optimism, and their convictions, kept them in contention. "To advocate Democracy in Massachusetts," wrote George Bancroft, "is no holiday pastime. . . . Our course is not too often enlivened by success; we are wounded sometimes even by our friends. We tread a thorny path, but it leads upwards to the home of freedom, of justice, of truth."[5]

In view of their plight, the respectable worker image devised by their opponents would seem to present the Democrats with a tailor-made opportunity. The working class was not, in actuality, in very happy circumstances. Moreover, it probably comprised by the 1850s a majority of the electorate (and before then, a substantial portion of it). What better strategy than to take on the "cause" of the worker: to point with alarm at his true situation, expose the respectable worker image as a fraud, demand remedial legislation? The grateful workers would rush to their banner, and the Democrats would parlay this huge bloc of votes into victory — even permanent domination.

Even if pragmatic considerations did not lead them in this direction, one would expect that their principles might, for their party, according to the standard works on Massachusetts political history in this period, was particularly well attuned to the wishes of the "common man." Who fell into that category better than the worker? Arthur Schlesinger, Jr., the most influential modern historian of Jacksonian democracy, presents this interpretation most cogently.

Schlesinger finds Massachusetts (as well as New York) the scene of "the most serious discussion of Jacksonian issues" because it was among the states "most dominated by the new industrialism." Initially, Jackson's supporters made little progress there. The "Custom House" clique, led by David Henshaw, did push for some genuine reforms, including the destruction of the Bank of the United States, but they were fundamentally conservative, business-oriented men, little different from the powerful elite that backed the Whigs. Increasingly they found themselves out of step with the national administration; they failed, too, to respond to swelling discontent within their own state. In the early thirties the great changes wrought by industrialism gave rise to various "workingmen's" organizations and parties, which denounced the exploitation of labor by the privileged business class. Reformers like Samuel C. Allen, Seth Luther, and Theodore Sedgwick began formulating "a general theory of class oppression," a radical, urban-oriented, antimonopoly, hard-money philosophy. The remedies they proposed were ineffectual, but their ideas began to attract the attention of a new breed of Democrat.

It was, according to Schlesinger, these "radical" Democrats — George Bancroft, Robert Rantoul, Amasa Walker, Marcus Morton, B. F. Hallett, and others — who were instrumental in steering their party onto a vital new course. Aggressive, skillful politicians, they started making open appeals for the support of workingmen — and won it. As the party's vote increased with each election, their influence in party councils grew. By 1836 they had captured effective control of the organization, nominating strong radical candidates for state and national offices and drawing up a platform based firmly on hard-money, anti-banking principles. In 1839 they achieved their first notable victory with the election of one of their own, Marcus Morton, as governor. Though their actual accomplishments were few, their efforts did not go unrewarded: From this point on the Democratic party of Massachusetts was clearly aligned with the common man, championing his cause in his unending (and uneven) struggle with the business community.[6]

If this interpretation is correct, the Democrats should have had every reason to question the image of the respectable worker. They supposedly were aware of working-class discontents, sympathized with their plight, fought against a common enemy. Both principle and calculation, in short, should have shifted their organization into a posture of dissent.

Yet they never assumed such a posture. All the evidence I have looked at demonstrates, as indicated in chapter 4, that the Democrats agreed with the image of the respectable worker in most of its particulars. Where they did not do so explicitly, they often simply said nothing at all. And in the few areas where they demurred, they rarely made that disagreement a major part of their appeal. So the real question becomes, why not? The answer can be found in their political philosophy.

At its core the Democratic party of Massachusetts was a vehicle of discontent. Formed simply to promote the presidential ambitions of Andrew Jackson, it quickly, in the early thirties, adopted a larger mission. For some time a sense of trepidation had been spreading through the Commonwealth as many found the social order, especially the traditional apportionment of wealth and power, changing radically. New and apparently threatening forces were at work, striving to place control of the economy in the hands of a few and to subvert democratic institutions. Since Jackson's iconoclastic stands had given his faction a reformist tinge, the discontented looked hopefully to the Democrats to oppose these trends. Slowly at first, then enthusiastically, the party responded. For more than two decades this campaign was to be the focus of their efforts.

To the Democrats the burgeoning economy of industrial, commercial Massachusetts was a mixed blessing. That it was bringing unprecedented prosperity they could hardly deny, but its hectic growth was also encouraging a certain heedlessness, even greed. "The love of gain," the address of one Democratic convention lamented, "is become the ruling passion of an immense part of our population. . . . the whole tide

of national feeling has rushed with an irresistible current into the chan-
nel of commercial enterprise."[7] Unfortunately, in their haste to get rich,
some were taking advantage of their position to secure special favors
from the government in a way that had rarely happened before. These
men were variously identified as "the capitalists," "the aristocracy," or
simply "the rich" — the wealthy elite at the helm of the new commercial, manufacturing, banking, and transportation enterprises. They constituted the enemy: "those who endeavor to enjoy the advantages of
wealth by obtaining privileges not possessed by the mass — who are too
lazy and selfish to acquire a fortune by industry and frugality."[8]

Democrats charged that these businessmen, in conjunction with their
political arm, the Whig party, had succeeded in building up a formidable phalanx of power that in effect ruled the Commonwealth. Through
their wealth and influence over the press the Whigs had cajoled voters
into supporting them. Their success at the polls gave them an iron grip
on the state government, which became, for the most part, an instrument for their own ends. Laws were being passed "by means of which
wealth as well as power, is stealing from the many to the few, and raising
up a favored class in the Commonwealth that will be as far removed from
the working masses in process of time, as the like class are by hereditary
distinctions in monarchical institutions." The state had turned into "a
commonwealth of property, of stocks, of machinery, and of exclusive
privileges, instead of a commonwealth of MEN."[9]

To the Democrats the most offensive of these unjust laws were those
that conferred corporate charters on small groups of wealthy capitalists.
According to Democratic legislator Frederick Robinson, these corporations were nothing less than "so many facilities granted by the representatives of the people, to the few, to enable them to gather wealth
from the hard earnings of their constituents." The Boston *Post*, the
state's leading Democratic newspaper, claimed that such great "engines
of wealth and power . . . deprive the honest and industrious mechanic
and artisan, of all chance of competition." Their creation was equivalent
to "clothing wealth by law with privileges that private citizens do not
possess." The whole corporate system constituted "a convenient arrangement by which wealth might be aggregated and finally subject not
only the finances but the business of the community to a central
influence." Democrats devoted much of their energy to denouncing the

"monopoly" charters granted by the legislature and detailing the abuses committed by the corporate giants. Commencing in 1835 they agitated for a general incorporation law to open the benefits of the corporate form to all and finally, in 1851, helped to get one passed. "By this system the monopoly of corporations will be broken up, the privileges which they confer, will be placed within the reach of all." As that, of course, did not happen, for the remainder of the fifties they had to content themselves with demanding more state regulation and greater corporate accountability to stockholders. As the *Post* finally admitted, "practically speaking, the manufacturing of Massachusetts on a large scale, is irrevocably committed to corporations for an unlimited future."[10]

Two other types of "privilege" aroused Democrats' ire: "the banking system" and the protective tariff. Party leaders differed on whether to confine their opposition to the Bank of the United States or to extend it to all banks, but their denunciations were usually suitably vague so as to apply to either. Banks, said Representative Henry Williams, were "irresponsible privileged associations." Their "necessary tendency," the *Post* charged, "has been, and still is, to subject the honest productive laborers to the control of the non-producers, and thereby to place undue power in the hands of the monied aristocracy." Bankers grew wealthy while the populace suffered. The evils of the system were manifold: a fluctuating currency, which expanded and contracted erratically, and inflation, which by raising prices ahead of wages hit the common man hard. Furthermore, the excessive issue of bank notes induced "the extravagant speculations, the visionary projects, and the enormous over-trading of the times." The Democrats wanted the Bank of the United States shut down, and, at the very least, the regulation of state banks and their note issue.[11]

The protective tariff seemed equally a piece of class legislation. It imposed, they contended, an unconscionable tax on the average man's necessities of life, decreased imports, and reduced government revenue, while benefiting only one group, the manufacturers. The Democratic party stood for a reduction of the tariff — but *not,* it often stressed, because it was opposed to manufacturing itself. "The manufacturing interest," the *Post* conceded, "is a great interest; is entitled to consideration as well as other interests." The frequent allegation that Democrats were "enemies to American industry" was "stale and stupid stuff . . . , hardly worthy of notice." And in fact, in all the Democratic literature surveyed, I could find only one (very minor) attack on manufacturing per se. Democrats even granted that some industries needed protection. What they resented was *exorbitant* rates: Where such rates obtained they worked to lower them.[12]

Massachusetts Democrats eventually made their views known on many issues, but those just discussed remained foremost (until the 1850s, when the national questions of slavery and slavery expansion displaced them). They believed they had identified an awesome, insidious new combination of power and wealth in the affairs of the state, which unless checked, would undermine democracy, take control of the economy, and exploit and oppress the masses. It was nothing less than a modern variant of European-style despotism.

Underlying the Democrats' complaints was a vision of society and of the economy that is worth examining — indeed, must be examined if their position on the working class is finally to be understood. Democrats tended to be pragmatic. They did not think deeply about these abstract matters. The nearest to a theoretician among them was Robert Rantoul, and even he hardly compared with an Everett or Webster or Choate, in the other camp, as a social philosopher. Perhaps their energies were too absorbed in their uphill fight against their opponents to spend time elaborating their fundamental beliefs. But there is a deeper reason. What they were fighting for was in good part a restoration of an older world, and for certain deeply-felt and widely shared ideals. The very familiarity of their vision made theoretical explication unnecessary. Their chief task was to convince the voters that the forms and ideals they treasured were in danger, and could only be maintained by supporting their party. As one of their conventions aptly put it, they were the "true conservatives."[13]

At the core of their vision was a strong belief — one actually should call it a faith — in egalitarian political democracy. They stated repeatedly that they were the only party concerned with making government truly representative of the popular will, as it was intended to be. "Democracy," said its leading eulogist, George Bancroft,

> is the institution of government by the many, for the common good. Its energy is derived from the will of the people; its object is the welfare of the people; its strength is in the affections of the people. It is the most

powerful element of modern civilization; it is the greatest discovery
ever made in political science.

For Democrats, the genius of democracy was its egalitarian aspect. An
equal political voice for all assured that the state would treat everyone
alike. To preserve that equality was of paramount importance. Hence,
Democratic support was strong for such measures as the abolition of the
poll tax, legislative districts of equal population, the protection of the
immigrant's right to vote (though not the Negro's, which they remained
silent on), as well as for popular agitation like Dorr's rebellion in Rhode
Island and the democratic movements in England and on the Continent.
Their stance on economic issues stressed equal protection of the law for
all and special favors for none. "The Democrats are for elevating and
improving the character and condition of *the whole people*," said the
Post. It was not the job of government to pass laws for the benefit of "a
privileged few." All laws should have a general applicability, aiding the
entire populace. The party, said its state committee, holds "that justice
and sound policy forbid the federal government to foster one branch of
industry to the detriment of any other, or to cherish the interests of one
portion to the injury of another portion of our common country." The
same principle applied within Massachusetts. Government was to be
deaf to the inveigling of special interests and classes, consulting one
criterion only — the good of the whole.[14]

A like egalitarianism informed their views of society and the economy,
although with significant reservations. Antebellum Democrats were not
a species of primitive socialists, a fact often forgotten by their more
enthusiastic modern admirers. They fully conceded that a certain degree of inequality was inevitable in even the best of societies. Even a
"radical" Democrat like Marcus Morton could say, in a gubernatorial
address: "Perfect equality, moral, social or pecuniary, is not attainable.
God created men with unequal physical and intellectual powers." This
feature made them "better adapted . . . to the ever varying duties and
employments of life" and was "doubtless the best calculated to promote
the general happiness." The *Post* vigorously denied the Whigs' charge
that Democrats wanted to divide property equally. The people (for
whom it claimed to be speaking) were willing to grant, it said, "that
equality OF CONDITION is not, in the nature of things, possible. For

different citizens do not possess equal capability of mental and physical exertion. All have not equal integrity of character. All have not equal wants and necessities and tastes to gratify." Indeed, it concluded, "They are the uncompromising enemies of EQUALITY OF CONDITION. . . . They know that where *equal* rights of property are protected by standing laws, every man will attain precisely that *condition* to which his exertions entitle him."[15]

Men, therefore, would naturally array themselves in different ranks, according to their native talents and ambition. What the Democrats objected to was superimposing upon this beneficent natural ordering a system of "artificial" inequality. When some attained high position through special favors awarded by the state — or when others were reduced to poverty and subservience by those possessed of such favors — an injustice had been committed. The institution of that kind of system invariably created wide disparities of wealth, which Democrats regarded as definitely abnormal, even dangerous. "Left to natural causes, wealth," one of their conventions observed,

> would not accumulate in masses sufficient to disturb, materially, our relative independence. The useless gathered hoard, provoking extravagance and pride, is seen in one or two generations to be decomposed. . . . Nature is a most potent leveller — far greater than the radicals. Her universal law is diffusion, equalization, and reorganization.

To violate that "universal law" was to invite trouble. "Great inequalities of condition," wrote Morton, "— the extremes of poverty and wealth, are alike unfavorable to free institutions, and to the virtue, intelligence, and happiness of the people."[16]

How far inequality had actually progressed in Massachusetts was a question Democrats differed on. They assumed that there already existed an expanding cadre of powerful capitalists, whose bloated and undeserved wealth had skewed the "normal" curve of property holdings, but how, they asked, did this phenomenon affect the rest of society? Some held it must inevitably prove deleterious, simply because the money that filled the pockets of the rich would normally go to the masses. "In proportion to the number of idle persons in a population, who must necessarily be supported by the active, will the proceeds of the laborer's industry be diverted from its legitimate object, his own support." Thus ran the *Post*'s analysis, and it was a common one. Others emphasized that the economic institutions and programs established by the rich would impoverish the general populace. Some worried, as will be shown later, that the large business enterprises the laws made possible might oppress the employees who worked there. Finally, the very fact that the wealthy received preferential treatment from the government in itself created an invidious distinction. Said the central committee: "It divides society into two circles: an outer circle, embracing the unprivileged many: and an inner, smaller and upper circle, embracing the privileged few. For the outer, there is labor, wages, subsistence; for the inner, leisure, dividends, sumptuousness — too often, prodigality."[17]

While inequality was undoubtedly the unmistakable tendency of the system of special privilege, most Democrats believed that so far this tendency had not advanced very much. True, some were alarmist. According to Frederick Robinson, "a state of inequality now exists in the Commonwealth, in consequence of our numerous acts of incorporation, which could not have been brought about in many ages by all other means, which individual labour and enterprise could contrive." And he spoke compassionately of "the poverty, degradation, and wretchedness of multitudes, whose lives are devoted to labor." However, such radical criticism was uncommon. Conspicuously absent from Democratic writings and speeches was any sustained reference to an actual impoverishment of the great mass of the population. On the contrary, they often remarked on the superior position of the American laborer and the relative lack of poverty here. Rantoul, as firmly radical as Robinson, argued that "never was wealth before distributed among so many millions." In his view, the reputed wealth of landlords, merchants, and manufacturers was exaggerated and probably temporary, and in any case, under the American system, had little power to overawe the people. "With free schools, and a free press, . . . we need have no fear of the aristocratical tendencies of accumulated masses of capital." To Democrats who thought along these lines, serious, widespread social repercussions of the system of privileged wealth were a prospective rather than an actual danger. In seeking a concrete example of that system's inevitable effects, they usually got no nearer to home than England.[18]

Thus, the essential work of the Democratic party was one of preservation: to prevent the excrescences of the system of privilege from disfiguring a basically sound social order. That done, little else was necessary. Men would at last be free to become all they could, without fear of being hindered by a privileged elite. The circulatory network of economic enterprise would come unclogged, and its life-giving fluid flow smoothly again to all parts of the body politic.

These were matters they cared deeply about. The Democrats were worldly strivers, engrossed in business concerns, thoroughly bourgeois. The right of every man to amass wealth was not, for them, an abstraction but the key to human happiness. To Whig charges that their program threatened property rights they indignantly retorted that nothing could be further from the truth. Such rights *should be deemed sacred,*" wrote Morton. The *Post* labeled them "among those fundamental rights which lie at the foundation of society, and upon the sacredness of which depend not only its order and harmony, but also its civilization and progress." Were they to be impaired "there would exist no motive for individual enterprise or public improvement — neither incentive to private interest nor devotion to the state." The Democrats only wanted to make sure that everyone's right to property (and implied in that was the ability to acquire as well as hold property) was *equal.* As Morton put it, "Civil institutions should aim to encourage each one faithfully to employ his talents in that sphere of action to which they are best adapted, and in which they will contribute the most to the welfare of himself and his fellow-creatures. And this end can best be attained by securing to everyone the fruits of his own industry." The Democratic national administration, declared an 1838 convention, aims at "opening an unrestricted competition to all classes of our citizens in the pursuit of wealth." That was best done, according to the *Post,* through "equal and just laws — laws which shall secure a free field for the action and energies of any class, and protect the lives and property and liberties of every one."[19]

In other words, the Democrats stood for the classic liberal ideal of unrestricted competition for the world's goods under a system of equality of opportunity for all. Only that equality was defined narrowly and in the negative sense: The government should abstain from granting special favors or treatment. In their view there was very little in a positive way that the government could, or should, do (outside of providing free public education) to correct other inequalities. The *Post* derided communitarians and others who wanted to remake society by redistributing wealth. That kind of scheme

> is Utopian because it is unnatural; and above all, unnatural in this land which owes its triumphs to *individualism*, such as never was developed in the history of man. Here is a social state which leaves the individual all rights, power, capacities and triumphs, and yet links together all in a community of interests and destiny. However plausible and however philanthropic Fourierism may be, at the bottom it belongs to the old, Asiatic, aristocratic, *paternal* system of government; the system that assumes to do *for* the people — to take care *of* the people — and does not respect and act on the principle that God has given man reason and capacity enough to *do for and take care of himself.*

Or, as it submitted in another editorial: "All the agency of government can do is *to protect . . . each individual, when assailed in his rights, with the whole force of society.* It is not the proper function of government to supply every good nor to remedy every evil."[20]

The thrust of this entire appeal is to align the Democrats clearly with the aspirations of what Richard Hofstadter called the "expectant capitalist," the "hard-working, ambitious person for whom enterprise was a kind of religion." Their sympathies lay with the man on the rise. Everyone, said Rantoul, possesses an "instinct of perfectibility" which leads him to want to perfect his condition. The Democrats themselves were conscious of their natural constituency and made no apologies for it. The state committee boasted that the party represented "the broad table-land of the middle classes and middling interests. The democratic party therefore naturally embraces the great classes of men that constitute the physical, the intellectual, the moral force of the state; the producers of wealth; the yeomanry who till the soil; mechanics, manufacturers, operatives, traders, whose labor sustains the state." Or, in the *Post*'s words, the party was composed of "the pure, *clarified*, wholesome, *middle* portion of the people":

> They are mostly persons of some little property, and expecting to earn and lay up more. They are industrious, economical, prudent, inde-

> pendent in their feelings and opinions, and generally heads of families.
> . . . This class, it will be seen, includes the great body of the farmers
> and country mechanics, with many of the city mechanics and laboring
> persons.

These humble, upright, mobile types comprised "the people" whose interests they claimed to have so much at heart.[21]

At this point one can begin to fathom the Democrats' reaction to the working class. This group's entire outlook rests on the proposition that the "natural" state of society is essentially benign. They were not Pollyannas: They saw great injustice in the world. But these, they held, were artificial, stemming from the overweening power of the great capitalists and their political allies. Strip them of their power, curtail the influence of the great corporations, restrict government to its proper sphere, they said, and the major social ills will be solved and the social order that existed before the capitalists took over restored. And what type of society was that? One with some gradations of wealth, to be sure, but fundamentally a *society without classes* — a mass of atomistic economic units, individuals competing with each other in an open field to gain a decent living for themselves and their families. In a society such as that, property would never become locked in certain hands, never accrete in huge sums to deprive the many of the wealth they have created. In short, the very idea of "class" was for the Democrats an unnatural one.

Couple with this fundamental assumption the party's other principles and biases. It saw no inherent evil in manufacturing enterprise, which was merely another kind of economic activity. It found, for the most part, that the inequities against which it was struggling had not yet succeeded in exploiting and impoverishing a significant portion of the citizenry. Its entire philosophy of government resisted recognizing the possibility that there might be special groups in the population with distinct needs and interests. To even entertain such a notion was "favoritism": One should think and act only in terms of "the whole people." In any case, government had no business interfering with the natural apportionment of wealth in society. Finally, this was a party whose whole outlook was entrepreneurial. It courted the middle class by promising equal opportunity and equal treatment for all. Its attention was directed primarily to this class — dwindling, but still important —

and away from the growing number whose prospects of joining the ranks of the comfortable were rapidly fading.

Is it any wonder that the Democratic party failed to challenge the image of the respectable worker? Could it have even conceived of a working class, much less made an honest appraisal of its true situation — or still less sympathized with its plight? Hardly. To do so would have meant admitting that a vast transformation of the benign natural order had taken place — that an economic and social system was developing in which most would inevitably have to assume nonentrepreneurial, dependent positions. Such an admission would have implied that government might have to intervene in ordinary social processes to come to the aid of less-favored classes. Most crucial, it would have undercut the entire Democratic effort to maintain equality of opportunity. Posit a world dominated by big business and factories, and that effort becomes quixotic.

For the Democrats to recognize that a working class existed and constituted a major social problem would be tantamount to conceding that the world they were trying so feverishly to restore was never going to return. Take that fateful step, and the raison d'être of their party would vanish. So their collective vision turned resolutely away from the modern industrial economy and its social ramifications. It was much easier to blame the problems of the day on a few evil, grasping capitalists and their political toadies. Hoping against hope, they continued their struggle, ignoring the fundamental changes taking place around them. As time went on, their efforts became more and more ineffectual. To the voters they became irrelevant. By the late fifties Democratic leaders, their fortunes at a low point, decided on a change of strategy. Dropping the old rhetoric, the old platforms, instead they concentrated almost exclusively on national issues in a vain effort to chip away at the impregnable fortress of Republicanism. Yet even then, habits of thought deeply ingrained over three decades of political combat kept them from dealing forthrightly with the now huge working class.

Can it be, then, that the Democrats merely ignored the working class? Certainly historians like Schlesinger do not think so. The party of "the people," he says, often presented itself as the party of "labor." And so it did. "To defend the rights of labor, is the glory of the age," a group of Democratic legislators asserted. "The democracy demands, as the test of its measures, their tendency to elevate the laboring classes." And George Bancroft, in a funeral oration for Jackson, claimed that the Old Hero displayed a

> deep devotedness . . . to the cause and to the rights of the laboring classes. It was for their welfare that he defied all the storms of political hostility. He desired to ensure to them the fruits of their own industry; and he unceasingly opposed every system which tended to lessen their reward, or which exposed them to be defrauded of their dues.

"Why, what is the democratic party in the United States?" asked Robert Rantoul. "It is the mass of the laboring people of the United States."[22]

But these and countless similar statements have no relation to the working class, properly understood. For the Democrats — as imprecise on this point as their opponents — "labor" included nearly everyone who did not belong to the privileged, wealthy elite. It meant, simply, those who did honest, real work, who actually produced the world's goods. All others were "non-producers," the drones of society. Rantoul's analysis was succinct: "Society, as you very well know, is divided into two classes — those who do something for their living, and those who do not." The latter included paupers, "idlers," swindlers, beggars, spendthrifts, "the vagabond demagogue," and "the disorganizer." "But all who do something for a living, who furnish to society some equivalent for the protection which society affords them, in whatever field of industry they exert their strength or their talents, or employ their time or their capital, by whatever title the world may designate their labors, have common interests with one another, and belong without question to the party of genuine workingmen." This vast group was the only one to which Democrats consistently applied the words "labor" or "workingmen," which they refused to narrow down any further. One Democratic propagandist went so far as to attack a Whig speech for its "anti-republican tendency to establish classes and orders of men, and to single out laborers as a sort of lower order in society dependent upon the more favored classes for subsistence and support." Such doctrine "is only adopted to governments in which permanent and distinct classes are to be established, and in which the laboring man is to be rendered patient under his toils, from the settled conviction that he can never go beyond his circle, and can never change the laws that govern him." It was obviously inappropriate in America.[23]

This unwillingness to focus on the special concerns of employed laborers was reflected in much of the party's response to labor-related issues — a response that in fact was quite different from what Schlesinger leads one to believe. For instance, the trade union movement, which was fairly strong in Massachusetts, embraced almost exclusively skilled handicraft workers — one of those hard-working groups of "producers" the Democrats claimed so earnestly to represent. Yet aside from Frederick Robinson and a few others who joined the party directly from labor activities, Democrats were strangely silent about trade unionism, declining it open or clear support. A few even criticized it: Rantoul wrote that all combinations to raise wages were an inexcusable infringement on the worker's right to set his own wages. David Henshaw, for many years the party's leading organizer, called a union "a monopoly placed in a few hands" which would "compel a workman against his own will to adopt their prices and hours of labor." To him this was "as reprehensible as the trades union of the Bar, or of the Physicians." When the state Supreme Court decided the landmark case of *Commonwealth* v. *Hunt*, in which trade unions were declared lawful (Rantoul, evidently repressing his earlier reservations, represented the defendants), all that appeared in the *Post* was a brief, noncommital notice of the arguments before the bench. And the great shoemakers' strike of February 1860 — the most impressive demonstration of labor strength in the antebellum period — elicited from the *Post* the analysis that bad conditions in the industry were due to southern reluctance to purchase Massachusetts-made shoes, a reluctance stemming from resentment over the heavy vote shoemakers gave to the Republicans. "The remedy for them and their employers is not a strike against low wages but a strike against anti-slavery agitation." Union organizing was foreign to the Democrats' individualistic, entrepreneurial creed, unworthy of serious consideration.[24]

As for working-class political agitation, Democrats revealed themselves time and again as lukewarm or even hostile toward separate "labor" parties. They split over cooperating with the Working Men's party of the early thirties, and many fought against attempts to persuade the Democratic organization to back its cause. (The *Post*'s comment: "In a country like ours, where all our institutions are framed to foster the industry and to promote the acquisition of property to the whole people, the idea of founding any party, and particularly the democratic party, which is composed, proverbially, of the industrious, upon pauperism, is . . . a perfect absurdity.") It is true that the party eventually supported several planks of the Working Men's platform, such as public education, a mechanics' lien law, and abolition of imprisonment for debt. But then, so did many Whigs; these measures were part of the age's general enthusiasm for reform.[25]

One of the party's most revealing stands concerned the chief worker political demand of the forties and fifties, a law regulating the hours of labor. Again one can find individual Democrats who were enthusiastic about the proposal. Ben Butler, closely associated with Lowell, became a leader in the fight, and Democrats cooperated with Free Soilers in introducing hours bills into a hostile, Whig-dominated legislature. But there was no clear consensus within the party in favor of such a law. Only once, in 1850, did its state convention explicitly support one, and even then carefully specified that it merely advocated an advisory law declaring the number of hours that *should* constitute a fair day's work — not a law enforcing such a maximum. In a letter responding to a query from a group of Charlestown laborers, asking whether he supported the "ten hour system," Marcus Morton probably spoke for most Democrats: "Each laborer is a freeman, and has a right to labor as many or as few days, and as many or as few hours in each day, as he may judge right. And no human power has a right to decide for him, how much or how little he shall labor." He sympathized, he explained, with the workers' demand for a ten-hour day — indeed he thought ten hours was about as much toil as a human being could bear — but the solution to overwork "must depend mainly upon the laborers themselves. Much, very much, may be expected from their independence, their moral firmness, and their self-respect." The only concession he would make was to grant that in certain fields — those dominated by large corporations — an overall standard work day should be set. But, he insisted, it should be arrived at "by mutual consultation between laborers and employers." He did not endorse (or even mention) a ten-hour *law*.[26]

To give the Schlesinger interpretation its due, Democrats often did exhibit a solicitous interest in the predicament of one group of workers, the factory operatives. Ever anxious to ferret out the abuses of great corporations, they pounced on any indication these workers were being exploited by their bosses. Regularly the owners were charged with "gouging" their employees by holding down wages. "Capital," Representative Henry Williams asserted, "is powerful, coercive, and grasping. It naturally seeks the largest profits, and does not, therefore, generally allow an increase of wages . . . , until forced to do so."[27] Another favorite target of theirs was the textile mills' practice of blacklisting "unsatisfactory" workers.[28] Above all the Democrats were the prime movers in the campaign for a secret ballot law, a proposal inspired by reports that factory workers were being coerced to vote Whig. As early as 1834 they denounced this intimidation, and by the early forties the *Post*'s editorial page was making frequent mention of the need for a secret ballot, at one point calling it "the most important measure the democracy can achieve." That claim was a bit exaggerated: The party seems to have regarded it as a desirable but minor reform. In any case, its enthusiasm for the issue abruptly died away after 1845. But when the Democratic–Free Soil coalition took power briefly in the early fifties the secret ballot was revived and a law finally passed. The actual progress of this campaign — and the arguments employed during it — will be treated in more detail later on. Suffice it to say that on this issue the Democrats did align themselves with a leading grievance of the factory operatives.[29]

Yet party leaders seemed hesitant to take these attacks to their logical conclusion: a general examination of the condition of the entire working class. In fact, sometimes they purposely stepped back from further criticism. One *Post* editorial, observing that the blacklist "tends" to make employees "servile and submissive," then commented: "*We do not say that this evil has been experienced to any great extent yet*, but it is a natural consequence of the present system." An address by the central committee denounced Whigs for coercing the votes of laborers, "who are dependent, *it may be*, upon others for subsistence or employment."[30] Given the Democrats' usual penchant for extravagant rhetoric and blanket charges, these qualifications are curious . . . and revealing. Their sympathy with the factory workers' plight was leading them into realms for which their ideology had not prepared them and which they were reluctant to explore. It was obviously far easier to confine their condemnation to the great capitalists and to end it there.

Massachusetts Democracy, then, despite its self-anointed title of "the party of labor," never in more than a limited, half-hearted way identified itself with the aspirations of the working class. Its leaders were concerned for "the whole people" — and particularly, the upwardly mobile, self-employed portion. Their vision was directed toward what was, for them, the larger problem of the danger of concentrated wealth. These preconceptions and biases steered them away from even a recognition of an entity like the working class. Such a party could hardly be expected to generate searching criticism of the image of the respectable worker. Indeed, it is surprising that Democrats mentioned the respectable worker as frequently as they did — which was rarely. It was principally a Whig-Republican concoction to which they merely nodded occasionally in assent. Most crucial, the majority of Democrats made little attempt (aside from their defense of factory workers) to join the labor-oriented critics of the image. When, in 1840, Orestes Brownson published his essay "The Laboring Classes" — probably the most trenchant analysis of the worker's situation to appear in antebellum America — he was shunned by his party. George Bancroft, then the state's leading Democrat, and others across the nation publicly repudiated him.[31] Such "wild" doctrines had no place in the world view of a party toiling so earnestly for bourgeois respectability and political power.

Challenging the Whig-Republican hegemony from a different tack, but no less vigorously, were the reformers. Antebellum Massachusetts spawned an impressive variety of reform movements, all fervently devoted to correcting what they conceived to be great flaws in society. The most prominent, of course, were the abolitionists, but working alongside them were men and women promoting such causes as temperance, public education, the abolition of capital punishment, peace, utopian communes, women's rights, better treatment of the insane, as well as many others. No matter what their particular interest, though, all were united in a deep dissatisfaction with some aspect of the world about them. To their minds the oft-repeated claim that Americans lived in a perfect, or even progressing, society was delusive, if not downright outrageous. They were, in short, concerned, socially aware, skeptical, aroused by insensitivity to suffering and injustice and sympathetic with the underdog. What group might better be expected to expose the image of the respectable worker?

These reformers all had very different ideas about how best to achieve their goals. Some were content to work within the major parties as full-time politicians. Men like Charles Sumner, Horace Mann, or Robert Rantoul in effect fought two battles at once: one, as good Whigs or Democrats, and the other as advocates for their favorite reforms. Usually, however, they were so thoroughly enmeshed in the political infighting of the day that I have chosen to treat them with their non-reformist colleagues. Other reformers were not closely identified with any party organization — indeed, their primary careers were outside of politics — but they did occasionally enter the lists for some specific purpose, withdrawing when done. Such, for example, was Samuel Gridley Howe, famed teacher of the blind, who ran successfully for the lower house of the state legislature in 1842 to help Dorothea Dix's crusade for better care of the insane. But most unique of all — and in many ways, the purest examples of the reform mentality — were those who steadfastly resisted getting involved in the normal course of politics. They were the true outsiders, purposely spurning the lure of office and power in order to wage, without compromise, their campaign for reform. "Agitators," they often called themselves, working directly on public opinion to mobilize it for great ends. It is this group that I wish to discuss next.

Most revealing are three prominent figures in this camp, all men who have left behind a voluminous record of their thought on many topics. They were engaged primarily in the struggle against slavery, but their interests encompassed numerous other reforms as well. The first, and best known, is William Lloyd Garrison, the contentious editor of the *Liberator* and, for many, the voice of New England abolitionism. Closely allied with him was the movement's foremost orator, Wendell Phillips, a bold, forthright man with a knack for burrowing to the core of a question. Finally, there is Theodore Parker, a scholarly minister who, after settling in Boston in 1845, shifted his attention from transcendentalism to a wide range of antislavery activities. Working through the press, pulpit, and the speaker's rostrum, this triumvirate became a powerful phalanx for reform — so powerful that, by the fifties, each one of them had a national as well as a local reputation.[32]

An essential belief of all three of these men was that the duty of the reformer was to pierce through the smokescreen of received ideas wherever they masked injustice and oppression. In this respect, they held, reformers were a breed apart from the politicians, who merely rode along with the prevailing tides of opinion for fear of losing votes. For such trimmers they had nothing but contempt. "The politician," Phillips said,

> must conceal half his principles, to carry forward the other half — must regard, not rigid principle and strict right, but only such a degree of right as will allow him at the same time to secure *numbers*. His object is immediate success. When he alters his war cry, he ever looks back over his shoulder to see how many follow.

The man who yearned for political power could never be expected to truly lead the people: to discover the path of righteousness and guide them to it. "His office is, not to instruct public opinion, but to represent it."[33]

How different the approach of the reformer, who above all else was a teacher. "The reformer is careless of numbers," announced Phillips, "disregards popularity, and deals only with ideas, conscience, and common sense." He aimed "to tear a question open and riddle it with light." This did not mean he was always right.

> He may be often wrong . . . but he says something that sets every-body thinking — he says something that stirs the whole atmosphere. We are crystallizing constantly down into unwise rest intellectually, and he comes and disturbs the process and sets all the elements and atoms into general movement and they crystallize around a new centre.

The reformer was thus by definition an iconoclast. Casting a suspicious eye on even the most universally accepted ideas and conventions, he stood ever ready to challenge them and, if need be, to offer alternatives. In this he performed a valuable social function: "to refine the taste, mould the character, lift the purpose, and educate the moral sense of the masses on whose intelligence and self-respect rests the State." Always he was guided by certain immutable principles of morality and divine justice — searchlights with which he disclosed the fraudulence and hypocrisy of so much that passes for truth.[34]

Challenging accepted ideas, in fact, was for these men a task of great importance during the antebellum years. Their prime target was the collection of tendentious propositions used to justify slavery, but from this they (Garrison especially) often moved on to question other widely cherished beliefs: those concerning religion, for instance, or the place of women, the role of the church, the obligation to obey the law, and the proper function of government. Here were men, in short, undaunted by the weight of public opinion and prepared, even eager, to do battle against it when it conspired to oppress (or just ignore) such groups as slaves, women, prisoners, the insane. Would it not have been natural for them to take up the cause of the poor laborer and, in so doing, "riddle with light" the image of the respectable worker?

Indeed, this was just what they did — to a limited degree. Other struggles remained closest to their hearts. Yet despite the assertions by some historians that abolitionists were indifferent or even hostile to the plight of labor, this was not the case for these three men. Significantly, all of them made trips to England early in their careers (Garrison in 1833 and 1840, Phillips in 1840, Parker in 1843–44), where they encountered the blatant poverty of the workers and talked with labor-oriented reformers like the Chartists and Owenites. Out of these contacts would grow a concern for the lot of the worker in America.[35] And while this never became a matter of great import for them, neither was it an issue they ignored.

Garrison's flirtation with the cause of the working man was the most curious. On the face of it, he should have been the most sympathetic of the three. Unlike the others, he came decidedly from the wrong side of the tracks: Raised in a poor Newburyport family which his father abandoned when William was only three, he peddled candy and begged for food as a boy, never had any formal schooling, and was apprenticed to a printer at age thirteen. He surely must have known most concretely the condition of the average laborer. Yet he never evinced more than a moderate, intermittent interest in labor-related questions. Perhaps his early association with the Federalist party taught him to distrust the volatile masses. Certainly his first public pronouncement on the matter — in the very first issue of the *Liberator* — reeked of old-line Federalism. Alluding to unnamed labor organizations, he characterized them as attempts "to enflame [sic] the minds of our working classes against the more opulent, and to persuade men that they are contemned and oppressed by a wealthy aristocracy." His ire rising, he warned that it was "in the highest degree criminal . . . to exasperate our mechanics

to deeds of violence, or to array them under a party banner." They were
not "the objects of reproach," nor was their toil "dishonorable." "We are
the friends of reform; but this is not reform." Shortly after, he remarked
complacently that under a republican form of government society was
always "full of inequalities"; this could occur, he said, "without even a
semblance of oppression." Those who taught the "pernicious doctrine"
that the wealthy were the enemies of the poor were blind to the realities
of life.[36]

This is not, however, the sum total of Garrison's thoughts on labor —
and those historians who emphasize these early passages do him an
injustice. Indeed, even in these editorials he granted that the wealthy
often abused their exalted position ("perverted opulence," he called it);
and soon he was acknowledging the "lamentable truth, that wealth has
more power than knowledge or merit in society. Every moral effort,
therefore, which is made to reverse this unnatural superiority, deserves
praise." By 1836 Garrison, no doubt embittered by the hostility with
which the rich greeted abolitionism, was moved to declare there was a
"real danger" that the masses "will not long be regarded as men and as
brethren, but as a servile and distinct race; . . . they will be defrauded
by grinding monopolies, and reduced by systematic processes." Everyone knows, he wrote, "that there is a growing aristocracy in our land;
that privileges are granted to the wealthy few, to the injury and impoverishment of the laborious many." For it is "in the nature of wealth
to be extortionate." The result was inevitable:

> Our laboring population, whether white or colored, are not held in due
> estimation; they are generally overtasked; they are seldom adequately
> remunerated . . . ; they are valued according to the strength of their
> bodies, rather than to the intelligence of their minds and the im-
> provement of their hearts. The lower they are found in degradation,
> the nearer they approach to starvation, . . . the less sympathy is ex-
> tended to them — the less aid do they find.[37]

Throughout the forties Garrison returned sporadically to these same
themes. On a visit to Glasgow, Scotland, in 1840 he was shocked to learn
from a meeting of abolitonists that they were not concerned with the
plight of the poor British laborer. "The people of England are in a state
of subjugation," he wrote when he returned; for English abolitionists to

ignore this was "hollow-hearted philanthropy." American abolitionists "sympathize with the oppressed, as well as the enslaved, throughout the world." In general, he stated several years later, humanity suffers because of "existing social arrangements." For the poor, labor is a task of "unreasonable severity, and with inadequate compensation." They are "debased by ignorance and crime, by the conflict of passions and interests, by moral pollution, and by positive want and starvation." Throughout the decade he recommended the various Fourierite communities then being established to the attention of his readers. Although he felt they had serious shortcomings, still, they were a step in the right direction. "In view of the present unequal state of society, who can honestly doubt that this is a subject worthy of the earnest consideration of all classes of men." By 1849 he was writing of the " 'perishing classes' which abound in such numbers among us": "Shall not their supplicating voice be heard, and more systematic and energetic measures adopted to rescue those already sinking in the mire and filth of poverty and crime, and to prevent others [from] being swept into the same vortex . . . ?" In sum, Garrison did not devote much attention to the worker, but what he said indicates he had strong reservations about the respectable worker image. [38]

Of the three reformers, Wendell Phillips was probably the least concerned with the question of labor. This statement may seem puzzling to some, for history books often portray him as an ardent champion of the worker. So he became, *after* the Civil War. Before 1865 he rarely spoke of the subject. When he did, though, he displayed a definite solicitude for the working class. He directed public attention to the low wages paid female laborers and to the problem of crime in large cities. He was forcibly impressed with the plight of English workers. He subscribed to, and evidently found appealing, *Young America*, the journal of the labor reformer George Henry Evans. At the first meeting of the New England Workingmen's Association (1845) he served as an active delegate. Perhaps his patrician background dissuaded him from pursuing this matter further, but at least he was clearly aware that the lot of the worker was no cause for complacency. [39]

It may seem ironic that, of the three, it should be the minister who paid the most attention to the condition of the working class. But unlike the stereotype, Theodore Parker was neither naïve nor other-worldly.

Ministers, he firmly believed, must concern themselves with the "morals of society." They should "look at the dealings of men in their relations of industry and of charity, and set forth the mutual duty of the strong and the weak, the employer and the employed, the educated and the ignorant, the many and the few." And always they should strive to eliminate suffering and injustice from the world. "It is for the minister to make ready the materials with which better forms of society shall one day be made. If possible he is to prepare the idea thereof; nay, to organize if he can."[40] This was the activist mold into which Parker sought to fit his own ministerial career. Eventually he would lend his formidable intellect — far more subtle, inquisitive, and incisive than either Garrison's or Phillips' — to a wide variety of reform efforts.

Since the thirties, apparently, Parker had been privately disturbed about the status of labor. In 1841 he wrote an essay on the subject for the transcendentalist journal, the *Dial*, but it was not until he took a trip to Europe and moved from the village of West Roxbury to Boston that his interest was really aroused. Thrust among reformers, he became one himself. With typical enthusiasm he attended meetings, joined organizations, circulated petitions. Most important, he devoted his sermons to reform topics, and it is through these and other talks — half religious, half political — that his views on the working class may be discerned.[41]

Parker was convinced that poverty was "the dark side of modern society." It was worst, of course, in Britain, but even in advanced New England the gap between rich and poor "remains in a painful form and extended to a pitiful degree." He felt it his duty to break through the crust of complacency and bring the horrendous conditions of the poor to light. "This class of men are perishing; yes, perishing in the nineteenth century; perishing in Boston, wealthy charitable Boston; perishing soul and body, contrary to God's will; and perishing all the worse because they die slow, and corrupt by inches."[42]

The poor, he insisted, did not include simply widows and orphans, the "transiently poor" (those just starting their life's careers), or the lazy. Subtract these and the majority of the poor still remained: "the class who are permanently poor." It was a large class, and included many who had jobs (though apparently, in his view, mostly unskilled or day-labor types of jobs).[43] He bluntly informed his parishioners of the sordid facts of their existence:

The poor are miserable. Their food is the least that will sustain nature,
— not agreeable, not healthy; their clothing scanty and mean, their
dwellings inconvenient and uncomfortable, with roof and walls that let
in the cold and the rain — dwellings that are painful and unhealthy; in
their personal habits they are commonly unclean.

At their jobs the poor often received just enough wages to survive, a
situation "only one remove" from slavery. Almost always they were
overworked. Parker had nothing against work — "Manual labor is a
blessing and a dignity" — but only if undertaken in reasonable amounts.
"Too much of it wears out the body before its time, cripples the mind,
debases the soul, and chills the affections." Sadly, this was precisely
what happened among the poor.[44]

The ramifications of their poverty were extensive, especially in two
vital areas, education and morality. The Commonwealth's vaunted
common school system by and large "grossly neglected" the poor, he
contended. "They are ignorant; they have no time to attend school in
childhood, no time to read or to think in manhood. . . . If they have the
time, few men can think to any profit while the body is uncomfortable."
It was not surprising they often became "unthrifty, reckless and desperate." He also spoke with passion of how poverty "tends to barbarize
men," to stifle their best moral impulses and leave them open to illicit
temptations. Destitution was the main cause of crime, he asserted, and
he backed up his claim with statistics.[45]

Admittedly, in most of these passages Parker focused on "the poor" as
a group, not the working class per se. The two were evidently not
coequal for him. In an outline of the major divisions of society he included a large middle class, comprising "the mass of people in all the
callings of life." By that definition the middle class would subsume many
workers.[46] However, from the manner in which he talked about the
poor it is obvious that the vast majority of them were workers; hence,
the trends he was pointing out touched an indeterminate but clearly
large portion of that class. Thus Parker joined Garrison and Phillips in
carving large slices out of the image of the respectable worker, replacing
them with pieces of a far more somber hue.

In short, the evidence discussed suggests that in this area the reformers of Massachusetts carried on with the courage and perspicacity they
demonstrated in so many others. Although the question of the working

class was not uppermost in their minds, they understood almost instinctively the inadequacies of popular opinion and proceeded to challenge it forcefully. But unfortunately, this account does not tell the whole story, for there are other statements by these three men, statements not yet examined which show them sharply qualifying their indictment of the workers' condition, or even contradicting it. And there appears to be no way of reconciling these two sides of their thought.

For example, what is one to make of the debate that erupted in 1847 between abolitionists and labor agitators over the issue of "white slavery"? Many of the latter had long maintained that the situation of the "wage slaves" (that is, workers) of the North was fully comparable to that of black slaves in the South, and that abolitionists and other reformers would do well to drop their campaign to eradicate southern slavery and concentrate instead on the evil closer to home. As early as 1840 Garrison had countered this argument in England. He virtually had to: it attacked, from a moral perspective, all that he and his friends were so fervently trying to accomplish. Early in 1847 he decided to set the dispute to rest. There is no such thing, properly understood, he wrote, as "wage slavery." "The evil in society is not that labor receives wages, but that the wages given are not generally in proportion to the value of the labor performed." Yet the issue went deeper, he contended. To call a worker a "wage slave" was to ignore the freedoms and opportunities he possessed, ones that the black slave so woefully lacked. He was free to "work for whom he pleases, when he pleases, and where he pleases," could make his own contracts, had a wide range of personal freedoms, was equal with everyone else in the eyes of the law, was paid for his toil. Slavery therefore was the far greater evil; anyone who doubted this had lost his sense of perspective.[47]

Phillips, in an editorial several months later, took the argument further.

> Except in a few crowded cities and a few manufacturing towns, I believe the terms "wage slavery" and "white slavery" would be utterly unintelligible to an audience of laboring people, as applied to themselves. There are two prominent points which distinguish the laborers in this country from the slaves. First, the laborers, as a class, are neither wronged nor oppressed: secondly, if they were, they possess ample power to defend themselves, by the exercise of their own

acknowledged rights. Does legislation bear hard upon them? — their votes can alter it. Does capital wrong them? — economy will make them capitalists. Does the crowded competition of cities reduce their wages? — they have only to stay at home, devoted to other pursuits, and soon diminished supply will bring the remedy.

He granted that "imperfections" in "social and political arrangements" still bore hard on the worker and that much could be done (better allocation of public lands, a fairer system of taxation, and so forth) to change this. "But to economy, self-denial, temperance, education, and moral and religious character, the laboring class . . . must owe its elevation and improvement. Without these, political and social changes are vain and futile." He closed, significantly, by warning that men must stop "looking at American questions through European spectacles."[48]

During this debate Garrison and Phillips accepted blithely one of the chief postulates of the respectable worker image: that the worker possessed great economic freedom and opportunity. He was not "bound" to the wage system in any real sense, could choose and change jobs with ease, could amass capital, was even able to indulge in the luxury of staying home to drive up wages. Parker too seems to have subscribed to such notions. In a speech before a group of New York teachers he extolled the North because there "the career is open to talent, to industry; open to every man; the career of letters, business, and politics. Our rich men were poor men; our farmers men come from sires else not heard of." Or, in a sermon on Daniel Webster: "In this country the swift decay of powerful families is a remarkable fact. Nature produces only individuals, not classes."[49] Like the Democrats, these reformers held so firmly to the idea of opportunity that they could not consider the possibility it might be fast eroding for many. Its bright promise warped their entire view of the working class.

A more serious defect in their approach to the worker surfaces when one tries to locate some account of the *causes* of the worker's situation. Incredibly, for a group so absorbed in the roots of such evils as slavery, they rarely talked of this. Outside of vague indictments of "imperfections" in the social and political system, they offered no criticisms of industrialism in their writings, nor was there any comprehension of the economic basis of the worker's condition. Parker, the only one to deal with this question, proposed that "natural and organic" factors were chiefly responsible for poverty: the upbringing of the poor in environ-ments of poverty and crime; "lack of ability, power of body and of mind"; the propensity of the poor to bear too many children; their slender opportunity for self-development; their intemperance. He identified few "political" causes, and as for "social" causes, he listed only the prevailing lack of respect for hard work and the demise of charity. That other, institutional factors might be responsible was never considered.[50]

A possible explanation for these omissions, in Garrison's case mainly, though to a lesser extent in Parker's too, may be that both men, deeply concerned with matters of religion, saw social injustice not as a problem of institutional arrangements but as a product of the unregenerate human heart. Sin, Garrison declared, was "the origin of oppression, the fountain of wretchedness," and so long as men remained its slaves "they cannot escape from grinding taxation, from abject poverty, from hope-less misery." Those untouched by the benevolent influence of true Christianity would continue to oppress, exploit, enslave their fellow man — *that* was the central truth of human affairs. To suppose that the source of injustice lay in the economic or political institutions men have contrived, they felt, was to mistake the secondary for the essential cause. For this reason both Garrison and Parker, while acknowledging the good intentions of the communitarians, held out little hope that their efforts might eventually lead to the elimination of poverty or other evils. They were working on "external" matters only. In Garrison's view, "an internal reorganization must precede the external salvation of mankind from sin and misery." What was needed was "a regeneration of mind and a oneness of spirit in righteousness, which shall 'overturn, and overturn,' all that is oppressive and unjust, until the form of society shall be simple, beautiful, the outward symbol of an inward redemption." Parker similarly, while conceding that new laws and charitable efforts might mitigate poverty, insisted that its ultimate eradication would de-pend on "the general advance of mankind." In a sermon on the mal-treatment and neglect of the poor, the "intemperate," orphans, and other social outcasts, he concluded by observing: "What we want to remove the cause of all this is the application of Christianity to social life. Nothing less will do the work." Men thinking along such lines could hardly be expected to discern the true nature of the worker's situation.[51]

One can find other, isolated statements by these men illustrating their

unconcern for the plight of the·worker or their antipathy to working
class grievances. Parker and Phillips, despite their "radicalism," were
not above eulogizing Massachusetts (or the North generally) as almost
perfect societies, with an industrious, moral population and wealth divided more equally than anywhere else in the world.[52] Parker decried
any attempt to regulate employer-employee relations by law (and privately Phillips took the same position, scoffing at strikes as well.)[53]
Again, these sorts of statements are hard to reconcile with others they
made on worker-related questions. Models of consistency in their discussions of slavery, they evidently did not deem it necessary to take the
same care with this subject.

These reformers, then, were willing to go only so far in their criticisms of the worker's condition. It was a question with which they were
obviously uncomfortable. Certainly part of the reason for their hesitancy
must have been the indifference, and even hostility, with which a
substantial portion of the working class and its leaders regarded
abolitionism. Abolitionists had hoped to rally workers to their cause and
must have been extremely disappointed when they did not respond.[54] It
must be recalled too that, with the forties and fifties, more and more of
the working class consisted of Irish immigrants, notorious for their
abhorrence of antislavery. For this they earned the enmity of the
abolitionists and of reformers generally; Parker, in particular, became
virulent on the subject. Perhaps the most accurate gauge of the reformers' feelings about the worker was the position they took after the Civil
War ended and slavery was abolished. Parker had died by then, but
Garrison emphatically refused to take up the worker's cause. And in this
he was joined by many of the state's other old reformers, like Samuel
Gridley Howe and Samuel May, Jr. (the latter branding labor agitators
as "a set of idle and noisy men and women").[55] Only Wendell Phillips —
who had paid the least attention to the worker before the war — carried
the fight for reform into this new area.

Whatever their motivation, the fact remains that the accomplishment
of these reformers on the question of labor was strangely limited. On the
one hand, they attacked powerfully some of the most crucial tenets of
the respectable worker image. Workers, they held, were often under-
paid, overworked, and subjected to other forms of oppression, and this
constituted a social problem of major dimensions. However, their chal-

lenge to the image was incomplete, even superficial. They seem to have accepted a good part of it, especially those aspects dealing with the worker's freedom and opportunity to rise, and never undertook the type of searching probe that often made their discussions of slavery and other social ills so illuminating. Nor did the worker's situation elicit from them the compassion inspired by other victims of social injustice. Without that compassion, their eagerness to prick the easy complacency of the age lost a good deal of its edge.

Through all these "variations and dissents," then, the image of the respectable worker held up surprisingly well. Most of the groups examined in this chapter chose to ratify it in their own way, contributing ornamental variety but very little of substance. Of those who had reservations — the mercantile critics of the twenties, the Democratic defenders of the factory worker, the reformers — only the last made more than half-hearted assaults on the image, few of which had a major impact. (And, it should be remembered, relatively few people in antebellum Massachusetts paid them serious heed anyway.) So the image remained alive.

Upon reflection, one can hardly have expected anything different. Many of these various groups, particularly their leaders, had little contact with and hence little feeling for workers. They all considered themselves to be of the respectable portion of society. If the Whigs and Republicans went around claiming the workers were respectable too, who were they to deny it? Besides, they had their own concerns and battles to attend to. The *fervor* necessary for a long, sustained assault on the prevailing views of the worker was absent. Without that, their occasional criticisms never amounted to more than feeble nit-picking.

PART III
The Emergence of
"The Labor Question,"
1840–1880

"We believe that the time has arrived when every friend of human advancement should calmly and deliberately consider the evil tendencies of our present system of manufacturing."

— Report of a joint committee of the Massachusetts legislature, 1855

Chapter 6

The Generation of Doubt

THE FAITH OF Massachusetts politicians in the image of the respectable worker was destined to be challenged, and when it was, their tight coil of serenity slowly came unwound. Starting in the 1840s, and with much greater force after the Civil War, a campaign was mounted against this cherished image. New, skeptical voices questioned it, strenuously, and offered in its place a much darker view of the worker's condition (and by extension, of industrial society generally). This is not to say the image was scuttled. With alacrity its adherents marshaled their counterarguments — and with suprisingly effective results. Ultimately this clash of ideas would form the core of what came to be known as "the labor question."

The emergence of this controversy was inevitable. The respectable worker image had not won dominance by force of its vague, often half-formed arguments. Moreover, as time passed those arguments, since they did not present an accurate picture of the worker, must have seemed increasingly deficient: They supplied the wrong answers, missed the point, or left untouched large realms of social experience. Yet history is replete with all sorts of improbable, inadequate, even silly ideas that have lasted for amazingly long periods of time. (One has only to consult the history of science for numerous examples.) The respectable worker image, defective as it was, did not generate its own counterattack. Other forces were at work.

The last chapter examined some groups in the political arena that furnished modifications of the image (though little more) and others that one might expect to be skeptical but in fact were not. Turning from politics to the larger society, this chapter deals with discontents generally agreed to be present in these years, and seeks to locate in them the impulse that finally found expression in a persistent attack on the respectable worker image.

Recently some historians have identified a pervasive unease festering at the heart of antebellum America, an unease centering on that very "progress" so often extolled as its most precious achievement. There was a growing suspicion, these historians say, that prosperity was exacting too high a price. In the haste to get rich, much that was praiseworthy about America was fast disappearing. Some people talked of how a stable and supportive social order was dissolving into chaos. The extreme fluidity of American life had supposedly undermined the valuable disciplinary restraints normally imposed by family, church, and village. The resulting stresses had already provoked an alarming rise in social deviance and dependence. Others fretted over the way traditional social and personal standards of morality were being dismissed as old-fashioned in this new, fast-paced world. Where wealth could be obtained easily by manipulating paper currency or securing privileges from the government, men conveniently forgot about the dignity of hard, honest labor, mercantile rectitude, the tangible value of real coin. Outside the economic sphere they sensed a disquieting spread of mercenary selfishness and a corresponding disregard for the older virtues. For many the most serious manifestation of these trends was the lack of a deeply felt, all-central religion to guide men along the path of righteousness. The people who voiced these fears were a varied lot: Some were Democrats; some members of the professions which designed institutions for the care of the insane, the criminal, and other social outcasts; others were evangelical Protestants. But no doubt these kinds of fears disturbed a goodly fraction, maybe even a majority, of the populace. Even so staunch a Whig as Robert Winthrop could be found assailing "the influence of Commerce upon the social and political condition of man" as "the most destructive feature of the age in which we live." Could it have been this uneasiness about the value of progress that inspired the challenges to the respectable worker image?[1]

If this is so, I would submit, it is only in the most general sense. By questioning the value of industrial society as a whole — by pointing out the insufficiency of a purely economic reckoning of modern means of production, so common among contemporaries (see chapter 3) — these skeptics performed a valuable service: They subverted the fragile and unthinking optimism of the times. Thereby, in all likelihood, they helped pave the way for a more objective view of the working class.

However, the evidence indicates that they did not, themselves, propound such a view. The Democratic party, as already indicated, did not.
Nor did the asylum builders or the evangelicals: They were too busy
proposing "corrective" measures (institutions, conversions) to coun-
teract the baneful tendencies of the age. None of these groups cared
about or inquired seriously into the situation of the worker. In fact, they
seem to have accepted most of the respectable worker image even as
they lamented the condition of society.[2] These skeptics, in other words,
contributed a *mood*, but little else.

Two other groups would seem to merit attention. The first is writers.
Massachusetts harbored in the antebellum decades the most brilliant
galaxy of writers in America — Emerson, Thoreau, Hawthorne, and
(during the years he wrote *Moby Dick* and the later fictional pieces)
Melville. A recent critic, Leo Marx, has discovered some most relevant
common themes about contemporary life in their writings: a keen
awareness of the jarring, destructive intrusion of the machine into pastoral America and a concomitant revulsion at the whole technological
mentality. Might they, therefore, have contributed to the assault on the
respectable worker image?

I think not. The examples Marx plucks from the compositions of
Emerson and Hawthorne form but a tiny part of their collected work. In
their other (and much more popular) pieces, they were evidently unconcerned with these themes. And, while he does locate these themes
in Thoreau's and Melville's major writings (though I find that his analysis
of *Moby Dick* is strained and unfocused), it must be remembered that
these books and essays — indeed, all of both authors' entire output —
were virtually unread during their lifetimes. And no matter how large
such themes may figure in all these men's works, one must question how
much of their message reached their audience. A perusal of the abysmally superficial book reviews in even the most learned journals of the
day reveals a woeful insensitivity to deeper literary meanings. It is hard
to imagine that many people in antebellum Massachusetts, after reading
these authors, came away deeply disturbed about the dangers of industrialization.[3]

Another group apparently worthy of attention is the communitarians.
The antebellum period witnessed scores of communitarian experiments,
many of which sought to demonstrate the feasibility of new patterns of

social order. "We are a little wild here with numberless projects of social reform," Emerson wrote Thomas Carlyle in 1840. "Not a reading man but has a draft of a new community in his waistcoat pocket."[4] The most important for this study were those based on the theories of the Frenchman Charles Fourier. Fourier considered modern industrial society chaotic, the wage system a grave injustice, and offered in their place a community organized around a rotation of tasks and a more equitable system of remuneration. Taking their inspiration from his indefatigable American disciple, Albert Brisbane, Fourierist "phalanxes" were established all across the United States. Surely communitarians must have had some influence?

Here again, closer examination reveals this is not so. Fourierism was popular, but *not* — pace Emerson — in Massachusetts. Almost all the Fourierist (and Owenite) communities set up in America were located outside New England. In Massachusetts only the short-lived Northampton Association (1842–1845) was conceived along these lines, and even its debt to Fourierism was, according to one student, "limited." It is true that in its final years Brook Farm was turned into a Fourierist phalanx, but it is no accident that at precisely this juncture most people lost interest in it. For the most part, the Commonwealth paid little attention to these communities or the ideas they embodied. William H. Channing was the only important figure to embrace Fourierist doctrines. Outside of him and a small knot at the fringe of the reform movement, they stirred little excitement or debate.[5]

It seems highly unlikely, then, that these various social critics were responsible, in any but the most general way, for the new, darker picture of the worker that began to emerge in the 1840s. To find out who was responsible one must turn to an entirely different stratum of the social order. For, I would argue, the attacks by politicians on the respectable worker image between 1840 and 1880 were directly inspired by workers — or to be more accurate, workers and a small group of middle-class reformers and agitators who allied with their cause.

The laborers of the Bay State were not dumb, passive witnesses to the events of their age, nor did they sit idly by as their economic and social status was being transformed by industrialization. Quite a few had definite ideas about these matters and were determined to make them known. As the decades passed, moreover, they began to forge links among themselves. People began to speak of a labor "movement." The use of this term is slightly misleading, as their endeavors fell into two separate (though related) categories. On the one hand, there was the effort to set up trade unions or at the very least to engage in union-type activities, like collective bargaining and strikes. And, growing out of these activities there were, in the loosest sense of the word, the workers' "political" activities: their continual attempts to present their point of view to the larger public and to influence government policy. An indeterminate but substantial portion of the working class supported both these endeavors.

In point of fact, worker unrest predates the 1840s, first surfacing in the decade between the mid-twenties and mid-thirties.[6] In these years the trade union movement was born. Unions had existed before (Boston's printers established the first one early in the century), but never had they been so numerous or bold. Primarily, they were adopted by skilled workers. For some time fundamental changes in marketing arrangements had gradually undermined the status of the typical journeyman. His chances of eventually becoming an independent master were slipping fast; his wages failed to keep up with the rise in prices; increasingly he resented the traditional long work day. Through the union he was able to fight these trends. In the Commonwealth's larger towns, and especially in Boston, many new unions were begun, principally in the construction and shipbuilding trades. Vigorously they attempted to enforce apprenticeship rules or to impose what today is called a closed shop. Most often, however, they were concerned with bread-and-butter issues: higher wages and, particularly, shorter hours. A series of bitter strikes was fought to attain the ten-hour day, most notably by Boston's house carpenters in 1825, its ship carpenters in 1832, and the building trades in 1835. All failed. Strike fervor even spread to unorganized factory workers, as supposedly contented mill girls across the state conducted brief, abortive turnouts, chiefly for higher wages.[7] When the panic of 1837 finally put an end to these efforts, their record of accomplishment was modest. Compared with other industrializing states like New York or Pennsylvania, the Commonwealth's unions never achieved great strength. (Boston was, by

1836, the only major city in the nation whose skilled workers had not won a ten-hour day.) Nevertheless they had, at least, made their presence — and their grievances — known.

The same unrest that inspired unionization also fueled the first crude attempts by Massachusetts workers to enter the political arena. There they were joined by quite a few independent craftsmen, resentful at their recent loss of status and the competition of factory production. The most overtly political organization associated with these groups' demands was a new Working Men's party, established in the early thirties to nominate candidates for local and state offices. The "workingmen" this party claimed to represent were defined, in the fashion of the day, broadly: They included, in the words of some Boston organizers, all those "who, by their honest industry, render an equivalent to society for the means of subsistence which they draw therefrom."[8] Also, their specific demands — an improved system of public education, a mechanics' lien law, reform of the militia system, abolition of imprisonment for debt, opposition to the Bank of the United States — were ones which many besides workers cared about. Probably as a result of the vagueness of its appeal, the party never managed to garner much support. Samuel Clesson Allen, its nominee for governor, attracted only 6% and 3% of the total vote in the two years he ran, 1833 and 1834. More embarrassing still, indications are that little of its support came from workers, who continued voting primarily for the two major parties. Farmers in the western part of the state contributed a large share of the Working Men's total. Workers evidently saw little prospect of relief through this form of political action.[9]

Another avenue of agitation seemed more promising. In September 1832 there was held in Boston the first convention of a rather unique labor organization, the New England Association of Farmers, Mechanics, and Other Working Men. While backed chiefly by skilled artisans, the association, as its name indicates, sought to attract other groups of "producers." It also tried (although with limited success) to sign up factory workers and for this reason has been called the first "industrial union" in the nation's history. And it was indeed, in part, a union. Its main goal, initially, was to coordinate efforts by urban artisans to win a ten-hour day through strikes. Auxiliaries were set up in major cities and a strike fund collected. With the failure of the Boston ship carpenters' strike, however, the association turned more to obtaining direct relief from the state government. Over the next two years, in addition to allying itself with the demands of the Working Men's party, it agitated for laws regulating the hours of labor (especially for women and children in factories) and establishing a system of schools to educate effectively child operatives. This was the first time these issues — destined to become significant later on — were mentioned in political discourse. For the association they were crucial, and its members worked tirelessly for them. By the time it expired in 1834 it had made a definite impress on the public mind.

Finally, the efforts of certain men closely allied with these organizations and with the cause of labor generally must be mentioned, men such as Charles Douglas, Samuel C. Allen, Seth Luther, Theophilus Fisk, even professed Democrats like Frederick Robinson and Orestes Brownson. These spokesmen conveyed the workers' half-formed discontents to the public in more polished form. In so doing they articulated with precision and force a mounting dissatisfaction with the image of the respectable worker. The "producing classes" (what most of them rose to defend) were, they continually argued, getting shortchanged. Modern economic trends, coupled with unjust government policies, were conspiring to rob them of a just portion of the fruits of their labor. What should be theirs was going instead to bloated capitalists and money-changers. Thus far, this argument resembled the Democrats' line, but these men carried it much further. There had *already* developed, they maintained, a sharp inequality of wealth. Poverty was spreading extensively among the laboring classes, and it was this poverty that was the source of most social ills. They drew special attention as well to the plight of factory workers, talking of the debilitating effects of overwork, their meager pay, the stultifying influence of industrial toil on the intellects of child operatives. "The whole system of labour in New England, more especially in cotton mills," charged Luther, "is a cruel system of exaction on the bodies and minds of the producing classes, destroying the energies of both, and for no other object than to enable the 'rich' to 'take care of themselves' while the poor must work or starve." No trace of the respectable worker here.[10]

The culmination of their efforts came in Orestes Brownson's striking essay on "The Laboring Classes" in his *Boston Quarterly Review* of 1840. As the record of his life shows, Brownson was an iconoclast of the first order: He cut straight to the core of the matter. "The great evil of all modern society, in relation to the material order, is the separation of the capitalist from the laborer." The working class (which he defined, significantly, as all those, and *only* those, who were employees) already constituted a large segment of the populace. It was poor and depressed, even as everyone else was prospering. The workers' poverty, he explained, was directly tied to the wage system, which made them hapless potential victims of their employers. "Wages is [sic] a cunning device of the devil, for the benefit of tender consciences, who would retain all the advantages of the slave system, without the expense, trouble, and odium of being slave-holders." In the current scheme of things, a laborer's ambition to become self-employed was a foolish dream. He did grant that the worker in America was noticeably better off than his counterpart abroad; his condition "has been made as good as it can be." Yet, Brownson insisted, it "is now not improving but growing worse." Indeed, over the past fifty years it had declined considerably, and he took pains to demonstrate that this bleak state of affairs was not due to any failings of the worker, nor could it be ameliorated by exhorting him to "improve" himself. "The evil we speak of is inherent in all our social arrangements, and cannot be cured without a radical change of these arrangements." Brownson thus became the first social theorist to define clearly the plight of the workers (or as he sometimes called them, the "proletaries") and the causes thereof.[11]

Brownson's essay provides a link with the second great wave of worker unrest and agitation, which formed after the depression of the late thirties and grew until deflected by the intense sectional controversy of the fifties and, of course, by the Civil War itself. Again, two distinct strands of unrest can be identified. The trade union movement, after almost disappearing during the depression, slowly and haltingly came back. By the 1850s it was making good progress, as before, largely among the skilled trades. Unfortunately, little has been written about this phase of unionism in Massachusetts. It is known that the new unions generally abstained from political activities, concentrating instead on collective bargaining, and that they still were not overwhelmingly powerful. Whether unionized or not, though, workers often resorted to

THE GENERATION OF DOUBT

strikes. Important ones were waged in this era by Boston seamstresses (1844), various groups of textile workers (Fall River, 1848, 1850–1851; Chicopee, 1857–1858), and, most noteworthy, shoemakers (Natick, 1859; Lynn, 1860). The Lynn effort has been called "the greatest strike in American history before the Civil War."[12] A reduction in wages brought the journeymen shoemakers and female binders out; long processions of strikers demonstrated in the streets; violence ensued, provoking local authorities to call in police all the way from Boston. Within weeks the strike spread to most of the major shoe-producing towns in New England, and at its height possibly as many as 20,000 workers were involved. After several more weeks the strike collapsed, but not before stirring the entire Commonwealth.[13]

A new form of "union" essayed by workers in these years was the cooperative. Several producers' cooperatives were set up, as, for example, by Lynn shoemakers. But a great deal more important were consumers' cooperatives, which started in Boston in 1845 and spread quickly through the state, eventually uniting in a New England Protective Union. When the movement peaked in the early fifties more than 30,000 workers were members; the stores themselves at one point did an annual retail business of $4 million. New England was in fact far ahead of the rest of the nation in adopting this new organization.

It was, however, in the revived political agitation of the forties and fifties that the working class had its most vivid impact. At this point a new force made its appearance: the unskilled industrial workers toiling in the factories and large craft shops. Previously quiescent, these operatives had new grievances, and were determined that something be done about them.

The lot of the factory worker had never been easy, even in the Jacksonian years. The glowing picture that has come down to us of the fairly idyllic life led by Lowell mill girls *is* partially correct (certainly the wages they received were higher than in any other occupation then open to women). Yet even for them, the hours were long, the work tedious and unhealthy; and the circumstances in the company boarding houses left much to be desired. The working and living conditions of many other factory workers — other textile mill operatives (those employed under the "Rhode Island" system, largely in southeastern Massachusetts), as well as the general run of industrial or craft shop employees in such fields as shoes, machinery, or ready-made clothing — were also demonstrably poor.

The situation of all these men and women underwent a marked decline in the two decades preceding the Civil War. Equally significant, that decline continued, unrelieved, until 1880. This is hard to perceive at first, for in some respects their circumstances *improved*, when measured in absolute terms. But if they are compared to those of nonindustrial workers (not to mention the self-employed segment of the labor force), one finds a growing divergence in the status of the two groups — with industrial workers at the bottom of the heap.

There is, for instance, the vital matter of wages. The people of Massachusetts, as mentioned in chapter 2, were on the whole one of the wealthiest in the Union during the period 1840–1880. This included its manufacturing workers as well.[14] Moreover, wages in manufacturing appear to have increased steadily in these years (except in the 1870s, when the depression forced a heavy cut). Yet so did the cost of living and, more important, the wages of nonindustrial workers. The result was that the wage gap between skilled workers and the largely unskilled industrial workers — a significant one even in the Jacksonian years — remained and even widened. One study of the wage records of seven mills in the Waltham-Lowell group of cotton textile plants (the highest paying in the United States) reveals that starting in 1840 workers in these plants had, in most years, lower real earnings than the average for all workers in the United States; during the war and in the 1870s they were substantially lower. And, as the author points out, these wages were earned increasingly by adult males with families to support rather than single farm girls, making the hardship that much greater.[15] A state census for 1875 placed workers in cotton and woolen manufacturing among the lowest paid of all those involved in manufacturing. Male workers in the boot and shoe industry were near the middle ranks (they were able to hold their ground through a one-third increase in real wages between 1860 and 1876). Only in some specialized industries, such as arms and ammunition or clocks and watches, did industrial wages match those given skilled artisans. The census also showed that in all manufacturing women and children were paid abysmally, far less than men.[16] In a prosperous age, the industrial worker was being left behind.[17]

The factory operatives' working conditions were more onerous as well. With regard to the hours of labor, it is true there was some improvement. For cotton textile workers the twelve- to thirteen-hour day common earlier gave way to roughly eleven by the late fifties, and ten by 1874. A similar reduction seems to have occurred in other industries. Skilled artisans, however, had secured ten in the *forties;* after the Civil War many were working only eight. Furthermore, in the textile industry, at least, the operatives were working harder, as machines were speeded up to compensate for time lost.[18] Working conditions in large factories remained just as unhealthy as ever. Poor ventilation and dangerous machinery were ever-present hazards. Occasionally disaster would strike, as when a fire swept through the upper floors of the Granite Mill, a cotton plant in Fall River, in 1874, killing twenty-three and injuring more than thirty; almost all of the victims were women and children.[19] Then too, there was always the precarious nature of the job itself to consider. The blacklist became a common device at this time: "troublemakers" of any sort (not to speak of union organizers) could not only be fired but effectively banished from an entire industry. And thousands of workers lost their jobs in periods of economic failure, as in 1857–1858, or the severe depression commencing in 1873. Cotton textile workers also were dismissed en masse during the war years, when supplies of southern cotton were cut off. The result was that turnover in industrial occupations was high, with many operatives moving from town to town seeking a better job or any job at all.[20] All this pressed especially hard on a group now fairly effectively locked into factory-type jobs, with only a modest chance to advance or escape.[21]

It is not surprising, then, that factory workers began to complain loudly about their situation. And, as their proportion of the total work force rose — from almost one-third in 1837 to almost one-half from 1855 on[22] — it became increasingly harder for the public, or the politicians, to ignore them. Far more than any other group, it was these workers who were responsible for generating the new dissents from the image of the respectable worker. Conversely, in the popular mind the term "worker" became much more closely associated with those who toiled in factories.

The focus of the operatives' agitation in these years was their demand for a law fixing a ten-hour maximum work day in manufacturing establishments. As early as 1842 petitions started trickling into the legislature from such mill towns as Fall River and Lowell, signed by thousands of employees, requesting action in this area. Over the next six years the lawmakers were inundated with similar petitions. Typical was one presented by Mary Healy and 411 other workers at Lowell, charging that the prevailing system of long hours produced a "weariness of body, lassitude of mind, neglect of many of the nobler duties of life, and a consequent disrelish for domestic, mental and moral pursuits."[23] Mill girls in that city founded the Female Labor Reform Association (1845), which, under the effective leadership of Sarah Bagley, sponsored a labor newspaper and rounded up support for the measure. As enthusiasm for a ten-hour law grew across the Commonwealth, other groups arose. In 1845 the New England Workingman's Association was formed to coordinate a statewide drive. However, its conventions were soon taken over by associationists, land reformers, and other middle-class "labor agitators" and transformed into a sounding board for their schemes. Significantly, as this happened the workers themselves lost interest in the association. By 1849, after several changes of name, it was defunct. Yet the issue did not disappear. All through the forties, in newspapers and pamphlets, the question of overwork in the mills was hotly debated. Other industrial states in this period had ten-hour movements, but nowhere were they so energetic or well-organized as in Massachusetts.

The unwillingness of the General Court to act disheartened the movement in the late forties, but early in the ensuing decade it revived. In 1852 a Ten-Hour State Convention, held in Boston, resolved to work exclusively for a ten-hour law. Soon auxiliaries were set up throughout the state, which began to agitate vigorously. Ten-hour rallies were held, petitions circulated, and, most important, the auxiliaries began selectively endorsing political candidates sympathetic to the proposal. The movement got valuable backing from such state legislators as Ben Butler, James M. Stone, and William S. Robinson. Despite all this, the legislature still refused to do anything. The workers did win a victory of sorts when the textile corporations, under pressure, voluntarily reduced the work day to eleven hours. In any event, by the mid-fifties the campaign came to a halt.[24]

The sectional antagonisms of the decade, and then the Civil War itself, inhibited labor agitation of all kinds. When the conflict ended, though, worker unrest burst forth anew, this time with remarkable force. Indeed, the decade or so after Appomattox marks the high point of labor strength and influence in the period covered by this study. This holds true for both spheres of worker activities — unions and politics — although at this stage the division between the two grew muddled.

Even during the war, labor, while throwing itself wholeheartedly behind the Union effort, was not particularly content. The cotton textile workers suffered greatly, and all workers were forced to cope with an unprecedented inflation. Union organizing therefore proceeded apace; by the close of the war the Commonwealth had finally pulled even with the other major industrial states in the number of unions it harbored. Over the next ten years the trend continued. By far the most powerful union of the time was that of the male shoeworkers, the Knights of St. Crispin. These workers, fighting to maintain a decent living wage in their now highly mechanized field, flocked to the Crispins after they organized nationally in 1867. At its peak in 1869–1870 the national union was easily the largest in the land, with 50,000 members, well over half of whom were located in Massachusetts. Its female affiliate, the Daughters of St. Crispin, was almost as powerful in its sphere. Both unions proceeded to set a new example of militance. Between 1868 and 1872 they conducted strikes (mainly over wages) in most of the major shoe-producing towns, strikes that were well-run and sometimes violent. The biggest, in Lynn in 1872, met with crushing defeat. As the others were none too successful either, the union thereafter went into abrupt decline, but not before having sent a shiver of apprehension through the state.[25]

The Crispins were the most noteworthy instance of a mood sweeping many trades. Everywhere, it seemed, workers were readier than ever before to use strikes to combat the growing power of large corporations. Nailmakers, granite cutters, the engineers and firemen of the Boston & Maine Railroad — these and numerous others struck, principally for higher wages. It was the textile workers, though, who proved the most persistent. In this volatile industry wages were cut with every decline in trade. This practice, and the continuing unwillingness of the bosses to reduce the eleven-hour day, sparked many strikes by their still unorganized employees. No mill town was immune, but the most severe strikes occurred in two rapidly expanding textile-producing cities in the southeast: New Bedford (1867, 1877) and Fall River (1868, 1870, 1872, 1875, 1879). Fall River, in fact, became synonymous in this period with bitter labor unrest. Its strikes were well-organized (thanks to the large number of spinners from England with previous union experience), lengthy, and often erupted into violence, directed largely against "scabs." While they were also no more effective than most others, they — like those of the Crispins — attracted much public attention.[26]

The long depression that set in in 1873 wiped out most of the union gains of the preceding decade. Strikes continued, but formal unions disintegrated. For a while worker cooperatives became quite popular again. The organizing spirit only lay dormant, however, and as the hard times lifted workers once more sought out union affiliation — this time with the newly emerging Knights of Labor.[27]

With their growing enthusiasm for (and expertise in) organization, it was only natural that the workers should turn once more to political agitation. In the postwar period they succeeded in gaining far more political influence than they ever had before. Most of their efforts were bent towards the campaign they had abandoned in the fifties: legislation for shorter hours. Only now many of them fought for an *eight*-hour day. Similar movements arose in other northern states, but again the strongest was in Massachusetts. In 1864 the guiding spirit behind much of this agitation, a Boston machinist, Ira Steward, helped create the Labor Reform Association, a union-based affair that became the first eight-hour organization in the state. Later he transferred his prodigious energies to more openly political groups: the Eight-Hour League of Massachusetts (1865) and the Boston Eight-Hour League (1869), both of which labored tirelessly for hours legislation. Steward also contributed a flood of pamphlets on the subject, most based on the quite modern notion that workers who toiled fewer hours would cultivate a taste for the finer things in life and, goaded by these new wants, would strive to earn more and work harder. All this activity peaked in the late sixties and began to produce results. The state legislature ordered investigations into the question, debated several proposals, and in 1874 passed a measure that to a great extent met the workers' demands.[28] During this time workers were also successful in getting action on more modest proposals, such as outlawing contract laborers from abroad, incorporation of the Knights of St. Crispin, and creation of a permanent state agency to look into the condition of labor.

Finally, the postwar period saw a revival of specifically working class political movements. The purest example is the Independent (later, Labor Reform) party, formed in 1869 at a convention of trade union representatives (Crispins, mainly) and various labor sympathizers. Its primary interest was currency reform, but it also endorsed hours legislation, a federal department of labor, incorporation of the Crispins, and other labor measures. The party won its greatest victories in 1869 and 1870. In the former year it elected one senator and twenty-two representatives and garnered 10% of the vote for its gubernatorial candidate, Edwin M. Chamberlin. In 1870 Wendell Phillips ran for governor on its ticket (and on the prohibitionists'), polled 15% of the vote, and in the process shocked many major party politicians. Eleven representatives were elected. From then on the party declined rapidly, in part because of a split within its ranks over whether to stress currency reform or hours legislation.[29]

In the remainder of the seventies two other political movements managed, through overt appeals to workers, to draw their support. The Greenback movement attracted some of the currency reformers among labor's friends, including Phillips, but never won a popular following. Much more significant was the enthusiastic mass that gathered in the seventies around the personality of Ben Butler. Historians still debate whether Butler was a devoted advocate of labor or a self-serving, corrupt demagogue. Yet it is undeniable that he made labor-oriented proposals a large part of his appeal. Moreover, he had a folksy stump-speaking style that apparently won him a good many working-class votes, especially among the Irish. His perennial campaigns for the governorship — first as a Republican, after 1877 as a Democrat — kept labor issues alive.[30]

All of these labor reformers — particularly such prominent figures as Phillips, Butler, and Steward — served to present the grievances of the working class before the larger public. In so doing they made people aware of the increasingly precarious situation of most members of that class. In speeches and pamphlets these men continually emphasized the worker's poverty and the disproportion between what he contributed to social prosperity and what he actually earned. They also talked despairingly about his growing inability to overcome his plight. He had no choice, they contended, but to accept the terms offered by his employer. He was a virtual slave to the wage system, "which demoralizes alike the hirer and the hired," as Phillips put it, "cheats both, and enslaves the working-man." There was not even "one chance in ten, compared with what there was, that the children of these men shall lift themselves." A wide array of measures were suggested to help the worker, most involving legislation and requiring that voters take steps to reduce the "inordinate power of capital," another favorite theme. All were based on the simple proposition that "capital should have less and labor should have more than it now does." An *organized* working class, these spokesmen were confident, could achieve these vital reforms. The labor movement, Phillips proclaimed, is "the grandest and most comprehensive movement of the age." It represented the determination of the masses "peaceably to take possession of their own."[31]

For a period of more than half a century, therefore — from the 1820s to the 1870s — many Massachusetts workers and their sympathizers carried on, with only brief interruptions, a strident, forceful campaign to protect their interests through unions and to impress upon the public and the government the seriousness of their progressively deteriorating situation. In time that campaign became more and more effective. With factory operatives in the lead, the agitators maintained a continual drumbeat of discontent which, by the postwar decades, it was impossible for any public figure with the slightest sensitivity to ignore. It was this effort, based as it was on an utter denial of most everything the respectable worker image affirmed about the working class, which was chiefly responsible for the doubts about this image that began filtering into the political arena after 1840. One by one important politicians, responding to the unrest, started to question some of the image's most crucial tenets. Gradually, confusedly, out of this dissent emerged new perspectives on the worker's situation. With that "the labor question" was at last joined.

The dissent from the respectable worker image was not clearly associated, over these four decades, with any one political party. In the antebellum years certain members of the Democratic and Free Soil parties fired the opening salvos. I intend to examine what they said, but the major emphasis of the ensuing discussion will be on the twenty years *after* 1860. It was then that the full flowering of dissent came to pass. Here the focus will be specifically on the Republican party.

The Republicans enjoyed a virtual monopoly over state politics in the two postwar decades. In almost every election, particularly during the war itself, their victory margins were substantial. Every governor but one was a Republican. The only Democrat to win (William Gaston, in 1875) did so only because of the depression and a split among Republicans over prohibition. In the General Court both houses were always Republican, usually (the senate especially) by a healthy majority. The same trend obtained for national offices. Of the forty-nine representatives elected to Congress between 1860 and 1878, forty were Republicans; seven were Democrats, one a "Conservative Unionist," and one independent. (Most of the Democrats were elected in 1874, again because of the depression.) All the Commonwealth's United States Senators in these years were Republicans. It cast its electoral votes, without fail, for that party's candidates for president. Every prominent figure the state contributed to national affairs — Boutwell, Sumner, Wilson, the Hoars, Banks, Dawes, Butler (to 1877) — all were Republicans. Overwhelmed by this cascade of victories, the Democrats sank into impotent opposition. Well could their regular gubernatorial candidate in the late sixties, John Quincy Adams, Jr., write to Wade Hampton of South Carolina: "I represent nothing in Massachusetts, but a comparatively small and very unpopular minority, and am regarded as hardly less objectionable, though for more insignificant than yourselves by the majority."[32]

But the Republicans, for all their power (or perhaps because of it), were not a monolithic group. They were split into competing factions, most notably on national issues but on state issues as well. With party regularity weak, it was possible for some of them — Radical Republicans, chiefly — to criticize the respectable worker image and to side with labor. These politicians were to manufacture most of the dissent on this issue after the war, so it is their views that I will examine most closely.

After 1840 all politicians, whether they subscribed to the respectable worker image or not, had to deal with the fact that the ethnic composition of the working class was changing, radically, due to immigration. Most of them preferred to ignore this unsettling phenomenon, continuing to talk about an undifferentiated mass of "workers"; others mused openly on the far-reaching implications of this change. Nevertheless, the subject of the immigrant managed to insinuate itself, subtly and implicitly, into many discussions of the working class. The emerging dissent from the respectable worker image in these years cannot be understood without reference to the way immigration helped shape politicians' thinking about workers.

As already mentioned, Massachusetts, starting in the 1840s, was swept by a flood of immigration, first from Ireland, then from Canada, Germany, Great Britain, and other nations. It was an unexpected, even startling inundation. When the state entered the Union in 1788 it had had a more homogeneous population, ethnically, than any other: The vast majority of its inhabitants were of English or Scottish descent. Even as late as 1840 only 5% of its people were foreign-born. By 1880 fully one-quarter fell into that category, and another quarter were the children of recent immigrants. The old Puritan stock had been elbowed aside by hordes of aliens.[33]

Modern studies on the history of immigration disclose that the natives did not adjust easily to these newcomers. They were foreign in more than origin: Usually, their religion, poverty, mores, and manners, and even their speech set them off noticeably. The natives quickly decided they were "inferior," even threatening, and had no qualms about letting them know it. Faced with such an unfriendly welcome, the various immigrant groups banded together for mutual assistance. Their "clannishness" only excited the natives' suspicions further. Those who arrived first — mainly the Irish — bore the brunt of nativist hostility, but at no time was the immigrant fully accepted by the original inhabitants. At best he was merely tolerated.[34]

Nearly all the immigrants of these decades joined the labor force as members of the working class, swelling its numbers immensely. And since most of them were unskilled (or possessed skills unsuitable to an industrializing, commercial state), they took their place at the bottom rungs of that class. The only important exception to this rule were some German and English immigrants, who had a craft or profession or a knowledge of the more complex machinery to be found in factories and therefore could command decent wages. The great majority, however, took jobs as factory workers, domestic servants, field hands, peddlers, dockworkers, or simply as day laborers. After a while (though usually not until the second generation) some progressed to semiskilled jobs, opened small shops, or perhaps worked their way up in the factory. But their mobility was limited, and in any case unnoticed: For every one who secured a better position, many more arrived from abroad to fill the slots left vacant below. The result was that in most of the jobs mentioned above there was a rapid turnover of personnel. Immigrants simply replaced on a wholesale basis the native-born incumbents, who usually moved on to better positions. This trend was particularly common in the textile industry, where as early as the fifties immigrants came to constitute over half the labor force. Given the fact that male immigrant heads of families were much more likely than their native-born counterparts to send their wives out to work, I would estimate that between 1850 and 1880 at least 30% to 35%, and probably even more, of the entire working class was foreign-born. If the second generation is included, it was doubtless a clear majority.[35]

It should be added that, just as immigrants transformed the working class, so they altered the Commonwealth's cities. The proportion of immigrants in most cities was noticeably higher than in the state as a whole. Boston alone accounted for roughly one-quarter of all the state's foreign-born. This swarming into urban areas increased their visibility, impressing them that much more forcibly on the awareness of the native-born.[36]

Changes of this magnitude aroused grave anxieties among the native-born majority and obviously called for some response from political leaders. Would a working class composed of large numbers of foreign-born (and their immediate descendants) be able to maintain the same high standards allegedly set by their native-born predecessors? (For the respectable worker image had presupposed a native-born working class. It was rarely stated explicitly; there had been no need to before.) Or, conversely, if the influx of aliens was causing a deterioration of the working class, what implications might this have for Massachusetts society as a whole, and what could be done about it?

It is tempting to summarize the political response to the immigrant by citing its most blatant manifestation, the Know-Nothing movement of the 1850s. Certainly this was, for a time, a significant feature of Massachusetts politics. Indeed, of all the states swept by nativist fervor during these years, Massachusetts was the scene of the movement's greatest victories. In 1854, the very year that its political wing, the American party, was formed, it carried the state, and Henry Gardner, its gubernatorial candidate, triumphed by a big margin. Its nominees also won every seat in the state senate and all but three in the house. In 1855 and 1856 its strength declined somewhat, but Gardner managed to get reelected and it still held a majority in each house of the legislature. During these years quite a few rising politicians — notably Nathaniel P. Banks and Henry Wilson — abandoned their former parties to ally themselves with nativism. At the same time, however, a new political force — the Republican party — was making even more converts. The nativists could not compete. In 1857 the new party captured the state, in the process attracting a goodly portion of the nativist vote. The American party continued to nominate candidates for a few years more, but its career was over.

On the surface the party's impressive showing would seem to indicate a deep reservoir of hatred among the native-born population toward the immigrant. In their public statements its leaders constantly stressed the "threat" the immigrant posed to the state's well-being: the way he allegedly took jobs away from native workers; his eagerness to join potentially dangerous foreign-born military companies; the burden he and his fellows placed on the state's charities; his attempt to undermine public education by securing state aid for parochial schools; and most important, his role in "subverting" cherished political institutions. The Irish were pictured as nothing less than docile tools of the "spiritual despotism" of the Roman Catholic church, scheming to employ their fast-increasing votes to further its own malevolent ends. "The alien born who has lived among foreign customs and institutions," warned Governor Gardner, "however honest and well disposed, cannot be competent to enter into the spirit and comprehend the genius of our institutions like one born and educated among them." The thrust of much of the party's platform was to eliminate the influence of the immigrant from politics until sufficient time had elapsed for him to become "Americanized." To do otherwise, they prophesied, would be to court disaster. Said Gardner: "Every additional naturalization tends to denationalize, to Europeanize, America. The universal record of History teaches that all republics that have risen and fallen owe their destruction to foreign influence, unseen at first, permitted till too strong for resistance, at last fatal."[37]

To assume, however, that this rabid antagonism toward the immigrant accurately describes the feelings of most politicians of the day would be an error. The nativist victories of the mid-fifties are deceptive indicators of the movement's true strength. Students of the subject have demonstrated that the American party was a unique beneficiary of the chaotic political conditions of this decade. Many of its adherents were, in fact, Free Soilers who, while none too enchanted with the immigrant's stand on slavery, saw the party primarily as a vehicle for their own ends. There is no other explanation for the spate of Free Soil measures passed by the nativist-controlled legislatures or for the state party's adamant antiexpansionist stand at the Americans' national conventions. This also accounts for the party's strange failure to pass any significant nativist legislation during the three years it was in power. Obviously, quite a few of those elected under its banner (and, presumably, of the people who voted for them) did not see immigration as a pressing problem. Furthermore, one should remember that, aside from opportunists like Banks and Wilson, most practicing politicians did *not* back the nativist cause. The American party was chiefly an amateur affair; many of its nominees had had little previous political experience. The majority of the political leaders of the day either abstained from the movement, waiting for the storm to pass, or forthrightly attacked it for its proscriptive policies.[38]

The nativist stance toward the foreign-born should, therefore, be construed as but a part of the political response to immigration, not its underlying theme. It was in fact the extreme end of a spectrum that started with hatred, eased into suspicion, and then moved on to guarded acceptance and finally even open solicitation of the foreign vote. Most politicians tended to fall somewhere in the middle of this range.

Since the great majority of the politicians of these decades were native-born Protestants — even in the Democratic party, which had a sizable contingent of Irish supporters[39] — there was naturally a certain distance between them and the foreign-born. Even among the immigrants' defenders one discovers little overt sympathy for their plight or appreciation of their culture. Yet whatever their private feelings in the matter, most politicians were cautious, evidently determined, especially in the forties and fifties, not to publicly criticize the immigrant and his ways. To do so would only have encouraged nativism — and cost them immigrant votes.

In the antebellum decades it was very uncommon for nonnativist politicians to disparage the foreign-born. There were occasional exceptions. For example, a delegate at the 1853 constitutional convention warned against granting the vote to the alien too soon after his arrival because he was unprepared, due to the "dwarfing and paralyzing influence of the institutions under which he has been reared," to exercise that right properly. Or another delegate, fearful that unless "Irish children" were properly educated, they might "grow up amongst us, ignorant and vicious, first to rob our hen-roosts, and afterwards to commit more serious offences." Barnas Sears, Horace Mann's successor as secretary of the state Board of Education, bemoaned "the introduction of . . . demoralizing foreign influences," which have brought about a decline in "the purity and nationality of our manners." Sears's successor, George Boutwell, observed that "the intellectual and moral character of the operative population has deteriorated within twenty years" as "foreign born persons have been introduced in great numbers into nearly all the mills." And the chairman of the Board of Alien Commissioners branded foreign-born state paupers as "lazy, ignorant, prejudiced, and to the last degree unreasonable."[40]

It is worth noting, however, that most of these critical comments came from government officials holding *appointive* posts. Politicians who had to campaign for votes did not enjoy the luxury of expressing their opinions so freely. Yet they did manage to do so indirectly — and revealingly.

Their misgivings come through clearly in the efflorescence of concern during the fifties about the "dangers" posed by the Commonwealth's cities. Massachusetts politicians had always been ambivalent about urban life. They admired cities for their bustling enterprise and their contributions to "civilization," at the same time they frowned upon the inordinate influence of their wealth and their immorality. With the vast influx of foreign-born, their character had changed markedly. A distressed Robert Winthrop, born and raised in Boston, remarked: "I am not an old man quite yet; but I confess it sometimes seems to me almost as difficult to realize that this is the Boston of my boyhood, as it was for Rip Van Winkle . . . to recognize his home, when he returned from that memorable visit to Sleepy Hollow."[41] He and others saw the cities as entering into a period of decline, and the (usually) unspoken assumption was that the immigrant was largely to blame.

Quite a few politicians, for instance, lamented the apparent upsurge of "immorality" in Massachusetts cities. They adverted often to the prototypical innocent country lad making his way to the city to seek his fortune only to fall victim to its myriad temptations. "In cities," said George Boutwell, "we find vice, not only hereditary in families, but local and social; so that streets and squares are given up, as it were, to the idle and vicious, whose numbers and influences produce and perpetuate a public sentiment in support of their daily practices." Edward Everett noted that "the contagion of vice and crime produces in a crowded population a depravity of character from which the more thinly inhabited country, though far enough from being immaculate, is comparatively free." It was enough, he added, to make him "anxious for the future."[42] None of these men openly stated that the foreign-born were responsible for these trends, but since aliens *were* flooding into the cities and since it was well-known that their crime rates far exceeded those of the native-born, it probably was not very difficult for politicians' audiences to make the implicit connection. Just as today "crime" has become a political code word for "Negro," so in the 1850s "vice" was one for "immigrant."

Other politicians addressed the broader urban dilemma. The hordes of newcomers streaming into the cities — and then moving from one to another in search of jobs — were transforming them into places in which the inhabitants had no real roots, for which they had no affection — in short, arenas of social chaos. "Our cities are peculiar . . . ," remarked Richard Henry Dana. "They are, to a certain extent, mere platforms on which rest the immense transient mass of immigrant population." The social conditions that grew out of this instability were fraught with peril. The poverty of many urban dwellers was too extensive to be contained by traditional remedies and so constituted a threat to the community.

George Hillard described Boston as

> a city of refuge for those social outlaws and outcasts whom the country
> throws off from its green lap . . . for that poverty whose roots are sin
> and whose fruit is death. This is a poverty which is rebellious, destruc-
> tive, hopeless, homeless, and Godless. This is the poverty which
> prowls around our dwellings as wolves around a sheepcote, seeking an
> unguarded point where they might enter. It is a poverty embittered by
> the sight of enormous wealth. . . . It is now a cloud no bigger than a
> man's hand, but swelled as it is daily by foreign and domestic accre-
> tions, who shall say whether, in the future, we are to be as safe from it
> as we are now.

Most of all leaders worried about the political effects of cities. Give the
rootless, alien urban masses too much power, they argued, and you
invite ruin. "Cities," said Ben Butler, "have ever been the fountains, as
they ever must be the fountains, out of which tyranny and oppression
have drawn forth their waters." Their various fears were well summed
up by John Palfrey, reflecting on Boston's masses of foreign-born. Puritan Boston was "magnificent," but that glorious age was over: "on the
whole, the primitive virtue has been left behind in the historical period.
The ancient high tone of public sentiment is gone."[43]

Not all politicians took this stance: Some defended the cities or at least
criticized them on different grounds.[44] But those who did voice these
fears were important figures, and what they were implicitly suggesting
was that the immigrant was a detrimental addition to Massachusetts
society. His numbers posed unprecedented problems; his "character"
— formed out of desperation, anomie, and poverty — could only vitiate
the Commonwealth's traditionally high standards of public virtue.

Yet despite this dissatisfaction the immigrant *was* welcomed, albeit
not very graciously, for one very simple reason: His labor was needed.
Throughout the antebellum decades the influx of foreign-born was vi-
talizing the state's economy. In places like Boston and Fall River especially, this new large pool of cheap labor stimulated rapid progress in
construction and in many areas of manufacturing.[45] Politicians quickly
grasped the implications of this and repeatedly asserted that immigration, no matter what its other drawbacks, was an economic necessity.
Typical was George Boutwell's balanced assessment:

> This population is not altogether desirable, but, as a whole, it is benefi-
> cial. We can lose nothing by Europeans coming among us, if they do
> not bring *Europe* with them. They produce and they consume, — they
> increase our burdens and they bear our burdens. They make roads,
> railways, and canals, which our native population have neither the
> ability nor the disposition to accomplish. They purchase and settle our
> public lands. . . . Production and consumption are wonderfully on the
> increase.

In these terms immigration was a beneficial trend — and *only* in these
terms. The alien was never lauded for his potential cultural or social
contributions, for it was assumed he had none to make. He won acceptance solely on the basis of his strong back.[46]

This pinched, calculating reception gave way, in the years after the
war, to a cautious toleration. By then much had changed. The shock of
the great Irish immigration had abated, and although the foreign-born
would soon stream in anew, there was no repetition of the massive wave
of the antebellum years. Then too, many of the later newcomers hailed
from Britain or Germany, nationalities with which natives felt more
kinship. Meanwhile, the antebellum immigrants had managed to settle
down to a more or less routine existence — an "appearance of stability"
that impressed those of Yankee stock. As they found their appropriate
niches and demonstrated their economic value, they fulfilled the
prophecies of the politicians. Most important, the war had certified their
worthiness. Natives were pleased — and no doubt surprised — when
large numbers of these supposed "aliens" went off to fight bravely for
the Union. In 1863, as a token of gratitude, the constitutional amendment barring voting until two years after naturalization was ostentatiously repealed. The foreign-born had proved themselves good citizens
in the most patriotic way possible.[47]

As Massachusetts learned of these facts, the comments on the immigrant often turned good-natured. And for this one has the testimony not
only of politicians themselves but also of the Boston *Daily Advertiser,* in
these years the leading Republican newspaper in the state and an accurate barometer of opinion within the party.[48] From this point on there
was a notable lack of opposition to immigration per se. The consensus
was that more newcomers meant more willing workers, and that could
only aid the Commonwealth. In fact, some said immigration should be
encouraged. "It has come to pass," observed Franklin Sanborn, secre-

tary of the Board of State Charities, "that they perform a very large proportion of the physical labor throughout the State, whether it be in the mill or in the shop, whether in the family or upon the farm. As far as muscular exercise is concerned, they constitute 'the bone and sinew' of the land, and it would be very difficult, if not impossible, to dispense with their services." By 1871 the *Advertiser* could justly remark: "There is no longer a declared purpose anywhere to discourage immigration. It is one of the sources of national wealth and power which the ignorant alone despise." The only immigrant group that encountered any overt hostility in this period was Chinese contract laborers, imported into Massachusetts mainly as strikebreakers. But, while they caused a brief stir, their numbers were insignificant and they were soon forgotten. Immigration had proved a manifest good.[49]

One trend often noted approvingly was that immigrants seemed to be losing the distinctive (and, the implication was, inferior) traits that so clearly marked them when they arrived. It was a loss devoutly desired by the native-born. The *Advertiser* took care to specify that newcomers were welcome from abroad only "with the understanding that they seek us to become part of us, — anxious to be adopted as our citizens and to adopt [sic] themselves to our ideas and institutions, — not as migratory colonies of foreigners, without sympathy with us or interest in us." For the most part the process of assimilation appeared to be moving ahead nicely. "The character of the great body of immigrants has been wonderfully improved. They are no longer outcasts and victims. They are educated to some extent; they have acquired small estates; they are capable of labor requiring intelligence and skill. . . . They make industrious citizens and give a fair return for all the advantages they find." Another editorial stated: "It is remarkable how readily our foreign population, as a whole, adapts itself to our institutions, and it should be the effort of every well-wisher to his country to use whatever influence he may possess to nationalize the whole mass, obliterate distinctions of race, language and habits, and make these aliens 'part of one harmonious whole.' " Also, the signs for the future were encouraging. The more recent immigrants, it was predicted, would adjust to American life even faster, and in any case the *children* of the foreign-born "*are* Americans, to all intents and purposes, by birth, by language, and by education."[50]

At other times, however, these spokesmen were not so optimistic.

Despite the observations cited above, the assimilation process was far from completed. The foreign-born were unhappy with demands that they "become part of us" and clung to their old ways fervently. They were not really integrated socially or economically either. In their more sober moments postwar politicians recognized this, and grew quite anxious.

There was abundant evidence, for instance, that poverty was still a chronic feature of immigrant life. If the noisome immigrant ghettos of Boston and other cities were not sufficient proof, one could always resort to statistics. Expenditures for charitable relief of extreme poverty reached record levels after the war. Inquiry revealed that much of this was due to persistent destitution among the foreign-born. The Board of State Charities reported in 1876 that two-thirds of the state's paupers were "of recent foreign origin." A similarly high proportion of the inmates at the state's almshouses fell into that category. Perhaps the most glaring sign of their desperation was the common practice, in their frantic search for more income, of having the entire family work, even small children. Also, there was the large "tramp" population of the time which, consisting largely of transient aliens roaming from job to job, prompted a long overdue modification of the laws of settlement in 1870. The older laws, presupposing a stable, limited pauper class, had proved totally inadequate to relieving the wandering immigrant poor. During the depression of the seventies the number of these homeless laborers rose drastically, exciting fear and resentment.[51]

It must have been dispiriting, too, to learn that some of the prime causes of immigrant poverty seemed no nearer to eradication. Illiteracy rates among the foreign-born remained high. The first generation had received no education in Europe; their children were often kept out of the much-vaunted common schools either because they had to work or because their parents distrusted the Protestant orientation of those schools. Immigrant birthrates continued to be far higher than those of the native-born, a trend much remarked on. The Bureau of Statistics of Labor found that while "Massachusetts mothers" averaged only 3.55 births each, their Irish counterparts registered 5.03, Canadians 4.78, "other British" 4.40, and Germans 4.23. Most disturbing was the connection between the immigrant and public intemperance. The popularity of saloons in immigrant districts was notorious; enforcement of regulatory liquor laws there was almost impossible. Arrest records showed that most of those taken in for drunkenness were of foreign origin. It was considered a well-established fact — not only among prohibitionists but even by such agencies as the Board of State Charities — that intemperance was a major cause of poverty. Obviously, there could be little hope for a people hindered by illiteracy and sodden with drink — and with too many children as well.[52]

Finally, there were ominous signs that the foreign-born, given their background and present circumstances, might well constitute a serious threat to the good order of society and government. It was a most difficult admission to make, and many politicians chose not to, if only on the principle that avoiding the issue might deprive it of encouragement. Others put up a pretense of optimism. "The foundations of public order," the *Advertiser* offered bravely, "are as stable today as they have been at any time in the history of the State." Yet in the very same sentence the editor was forced to recognize the presence of "an element in the population to which mischievous demagogues may appeal with some show of success," and the context made it clear he was speaking of the foreign-born.[53] The problem inevitably became part of the political dialogue.

The most common manifestation of this threat was crime and general lawlessness. Crime rates in Massachusetts surged after the war to unprecedented levels. Police arrest records and surveys of offenders lodged in prisons and juvenile reformatories showed that a disproportionately large number came from the immigrant ranks. Yet distressing as this was, it seemed to natives but part of a more general phenomenon: that the foreign-born as a whole were more prone to disregard the law. Their massive disobedience of liquor regulations was one often-cited example. Far graver was their alleged inclination to riot. Massachusetts itself was spared serious incidents of this nature during these years, but the activities of the Molly Maguires in Pennsylvania and then the great railroad strike of 1877 sent shivers through the Commonwealth. After the strike the *Advertiser* made an interesting distinction between the largely native-born strikers and the mob that wreaked most of the destruction. The former, it contended, failed stupidly to realize the potential consequences of their acts, for "there is always and everywhere an ignorant, vicious, reckless substratum of society, ready and willing to take advantage of any disorder to make war with devilish lust upon those who live lawfully and industriously." The clear implication in the rest of the editorial was that that "substratum" was composed primarily of immigrants. "The foreign element in [the laboring] population is now controlling and has introduced the dangerous and unrepublican methods of lawlessness resorted to elsewhere."[54]

With these apprehensions, politicians naturally felt ambivalent about the growing influence of the foreign-born in politics itself. Those who benefited from their vote — the Democrats chiefly, though also a Republican like Butler (who, significantly, found a more congenial home in the Democratic party after 1877) — of course preferred to say nothing derogatory about their impact. Most Republicans were not so reticent. They worried openly about voting frauds and violations of the naturalization laws in immigrant neighborhoods. They fought hard (and successfully) to keep an English literacy test for voting in the state constitution. They were frightened that someone like Butler, whom they regarded as a wild, sinister demagogue, could gain such a strong following among the foreign-born. On occasion they blamed the immigrant for "radicalism" in politics: the ten-hour movement, or worse, socialism. (The *Advertiser:* "In this country there are no native communists, and the foreigners who think they are socialists are, with very rare exceptions, ignorant, idle and vicious.") And they sternly reproached the Irish for their role in the Fenian movement and their agitation for a free Ireland generally. All these aspects of immigrant political power seemed direct threats to stable, "progressive" government.[55]

Over these four decades, then, the political spokesmen of Massachusetts were of two minds regarding the immigrant. On the one hand, there was a clear recognition that immigrants were necessary, indeed that in some respects they were slowly proving themselves worthy citizens of the Commonwealth. Yet for most politicians the foreign-born were a group for which they had little sympathy or respect. Their abiding poverty, their strange religion and customs, their clannishness and "lawlessness," made it difficult to believe they would be anything but an undigested, unsettling lump in the body politic for a long time to come.

How did these perceptions influence their view of the working class? In one important sense, they could have had no other effect than to weaken the image of the respectable worker. When the working class was mostly native-born there was a bond between it and political spokesmen that made admitting any significant "deterioration" difficult. But when a large proportion of that class was no longer "one of us" — moreover, belonged to a group that public opinion stigmatized as inferior — that damaging admission was a lot easier to make. Unpleasant social trends can more readily be credited when one is able to maintain some distance from them. Hence, as the ensuing pages will demonstrate, some politicians were now willing to assert that the working class was quite different from what it (supposedly) used to be — that it was becoming increasingly "degraded." To have said that about native workers bordered on an insult; to say it about immigrants was "realistic," even charitable.

At the same time, though, the immigrant question had another effect. While it was drawing notice to, and making it possible to grant, the declining condition of the working class, it simultaneously diverted public attention from the causes of that decline. It was not necessary to inquire into the workings (and potential defects) of a modern industrial, capitalist economy for explanations, when a simpler, more attractive answer lay readily at hand. The worker's plight could now be attributed to his peculiar background and character, rather than to the system in which he was enmeshed. In fact many of those politicians who eventually challenged the image of the respectable worker usually implied as much in their simplistic "solutions" to the problem of poverty. Educate the worker (and his children), they argued; provide him with usable skills; rescue him from the lure of alcohol — do this, and poverty will be eradicated.

Occasionally public figures openly asserted the immigrant's personal culpability for poverty. The Board of State Charities felt it knew why Massachusetts had more paupers per capita than any other state: "We are providing . . . for much pauperism that had its root in England, Ireland, the British Provinces, or at the South, and has only been transplanted to our soil." Therefore, it concluded, its "chief occasion or proximate cause is immigration." At other times this line of reasoning verged on racism, as when the Board declared the "chief cause" of pauperism and crime to be "inherited organic imperfection" or "poor stock." (This was of two kinds: "lack of vital force" and "inherited tendencies to vice.") The board did not explicitly connect "poor stock" with the aliens, but the implication was plainly there. In another example, the *Advertiser* dismissed allegations of the factory operatives' declining status by pointing out: "The entire character of our factory population has changed; the foreign element largely predominates; and there is undoubtedly among the operatives relatively less interest in their own social improvement and in the education of their children than there was in the last generation." Similarly, in the midst of the depression of the seventies it discounted the large number of new charity cases by noting that "we are constantly receiving large accessions of population from other countries, of a class which is in the first generation more liable to become criminal or pauper, or both, than is the case with older residents." The constant temptation was to trace all these urgent social problems to the immigrant.[56]

More than mere callousness is at issue here. The immigrant's broad back was made to carry not only the actual burdens of the working class but the blame for those burdens. Its degradation, finally acknowledged, was simultaneously seen as something transferred from Europe (where the laborer, as everyone knew, suffered abject poverty and misery). Insofar as politicians thought in these terms, the image of the respectable worker was not so much challenged as eclipsed. And ultimately, the worker's plight was not so much explained as explained away.

Chapter 7

Three Disquieting Issues:

Secret Ballot, Child Labor, Hours Law

THE CHALLENGE to the respectable worker image was conveyed into the political arena chiefly in discussions of labor-related issues. In these decades three issues in particular performed this function: the demands for protection of the franchise through a secret ballot, for the restriction of child labor (especially in factories), and for the regulation of the working hours of female factory operatives by law. The advocates of these measures, responding to worker discontent, brought a fresh perspective to the labor question. Discarding the baggage of old ideas, they delved earnestly into the worker's condition and came up with some startling new truths. Broadcast to the general public, their findings shook the respectable worker image to its roots.

Of these issues, the proposal for a secret ballot was most briefly in the political spotlight, but nevertheless, proved capable of arousing deep emotions. The Commonwealth's republican form of government was predicated on the unfettered exercise of the elective franchise. "The genius of liberty requires of every rational soul, a free and honest expression of his unbiassed [sic] convictions and volitions," said Marcus Morton. "And whoever would infringe this right, and corrupt, at its source, the freedom of elections, . . . cannot be a real friend of the equal rights of man, nor a sincere supporter of the true principles of the government under which he lives."[1] So firm was this belief that when it was found that attempts were regularly being made to control the votes of workers, many politicians turned to the secret ballot for remedy. And in the course of debates over the issue, questions were raised as to why workers were so susceptible to this kind of intimidation in the first place.

With that a large breach was opened in the idea of the respectable worker.

The likelihood that the wealthy and powerful might try to sway the votes of the poorer masses had long worried the state's politicians. Back in the colonial period Great Britain had furnished them with numerous instances of this problem at every parliamentary election. In many constituencies, even allegedly "popular" ones, candidates were notoriously successful in lining up support among the poor with bribes, drink, and other temptations. For many decades one of the principal arguments for a property qualification for the suffrage in Massachusetts was the prevention of precisely that evil. By cutting the poor out of the electorate, there would be far less opportunity for manipulating votes. When the existing (and fairly low) property qualification came under fire at the constitutional convention of 1820, this argument was repeatedly used. As Josiah Quincy put it, "The theory of our constitution is, that extreme poverty — that is, pauperism — is inconsistent with independence." Several delegates even wondered if the votes of the state's nascent class of factory workers might not in the future be controlled by their employers.[2]

These Cassandras, however, were drowned out by the swelling chorus of optimism. The property qualification was struck in favor of a small poll tax. Over the next several decades most politicians congratulated themselves on their foresight. As the respectable worker image took hold they were convinced that laborers, even factory laborers, were as politically independent as any other group. "Show me a capitalist who attempts to influence an election by the power of wealth," commented Representative John Davis, "and I will show you a proud, spirited people, that will brand him as a wretch and hiss [him] from the community."[3]

In 1839 this universal complacency suddenly came to an end. A Whig-controlled legislature passed a law requiring that ballots be inserted into ballot boxes "open and unfolded." (Evidently there was no provision one way or the other before this.) Soon complaints were heard that employers were taking advantage of the law to ascertain how their workers were voting. Some Democrats seized upon these reports, and the secret ballot issue was born.

From this point on the secret ballot would be identified primarily as a

Democratic measure. As mentioned in chapter 4, it was not of vital importance for them, but they did push for it. In his inaugural address to the legislature in 1840 Marcus Morton recommended legislation "rendering more secure the secrecy of ballot." A bill he proposed passed the senate but got stalled in the house. During his second term, two years later, B. F. Hallett led the Democratic forces in the house in another effort, only to see their proposal lose by one vote. For the remainder of the decade the *Post* and successive Democratic conventions labored to keep the issue alive but in vain. In 1850 Amasa Walker presented a bill to the senate which was, he later recalled, "literally laughed down."[4]

Very shortly help came from an unexpected quarter. The state's Free Soilers were growing increasingly angry at the reluctance of the "lords of the loom" to aid the antislavery cause and took up the secret ballot issue as a way of striking back. Said Horace Mann, one of their leaders: "A southern slave stands higher, practically, than a northern laborer, if the latter must vote as his employer dictates." When they joined up with the Democrats in the coalition that captured the General Court in 1851, the measure at last found strong support. Walker reintroduced his bill — which provided that all ballots be sealed in identical envelopes — and it passed. That fall a widely reported incident in Lowell dramatically confirmed the need for such a law. On a flimsy pretext the city's Whig administration threw out the results of the regular legislative election and called for a new poll. When it looked as if the coalition candidates might triumph again — which, it turned out, would assure coalition control of the General Court — the cotton mills' agents passed the word that the corporations wanted the operatives to vote for the Whig candidates. The Hamilton Company allegedly went so far as to place a notice outside the plant gates warning, "Whoever, employed by this Corporation, votes the Ben Butler, Ten-Hour ticket on Monday next will be discharged." The threats did not work. Enough coalitionists were returned from Lowell to give them a slight majority in the legislature. When news of the corporations' strong-arm tactics leaked out, an uproar ensued. Eventually a house committee substantiated most of the charges against them and bluntly chastised them for violating the freedom of elections.[5]

The Lowell episode prompted the new legislature to pass a law making it an offense to coerce or influence a voter through bribery or by threatening to reduce his wages or fire him. But when the Whigs swept back into power in 1853, they repealed this law. At the constitutional convention held that year Democrats and Free Soilers fought to have privacy of suffrage written into the new state constitution. After extensive debate a secret ballot clause was included, only to go down to defeat when voters later rejected the entire document. Thereafter the issue faded away. An effective secret ballot law would not be enacted until 1888.

Throughout this controversy the proponents of the secret ballot insisted that the coercion of factory workers by their employers was a commonplace event. "Whig capitalists," ran a typical *Post* editorial, operate on "the ancient feudal principle" that "along with the labor they buy the vote also of the independent laboring man." By 1853 the Democrat Henry Williams was advising the constitutional convention that "the practice of intimidation, has become with us an evil of great magnitude," and even more frightening, seemed to be *succeeding*. Factory operatives feared antagonizing their boss by voting against him. One delegate at the convention reported he had "had men come to me, time and again, with tears in their eyes, complaining of this restriction upon their rights, and many men would keep away from the polls, entirely, because they could not vote their own views, and would not vote against what they considered to be right." How else was one to explain the Whigs' ability to consistently carry the factory towns, when their well-known affiliation with the state's manufacturers demonstrated how little they cared for the workers' interests? (They opposed the law, said the *Post*, because "they know that if their power to overawe and control the workingman at the polls is taken away from them, they cannot retain a city or large town in the state.") Here was but another proof of the inordinate influence of the great corporations in the social and political life of the Commonwealth.[6]

This picture of masses of workers cowering before their Whiggish employers posed an unanticipated question: How was it possible? The respectable worker image taught that there was a parity of economic power between employer and employee. The latter was "independent"; he could not be intimidated by his boss. Yet if the employers' threats were in fact proving effective, evidently laborers feared deeply having their wages cut, being denied a promotion, or simply being fired. Marcus Morton, obviously troubled by the contradiction, fumbled to describe what was happening. The worker, he said, "should be the truly independent man": "He in reality is no more dependent upon his employer, than his employer is upon him." But the repeated infringements of his right to vote showed that "the dependence of the one upon the other, although imaginary, is scarcely less effective or less the means of coercion and oppression than if it were real." What Morton was actually saying was that the theory of the respectable worker could not account for the very real economic coercion he knew the worker was suffering from.[7]

By the fifties some of those favoring a secret ballot started to refer to workers in terms alien to the respectable worker image. The worker, they suggested, was economically *dependent* and must therefore be guarded by the state. At the constitutional convention, for instance, delegate Samuel French claimed to speak on behalf of "a large class of people who are laborers," remarking that "many of them [are] unable to protect themselves; and they ask us to afford them that protection which they need in the exercise of their rights of voting." Delegate Henry Wilson lashed into the state's "vast commercial interests . . . employing thousands of men, in counting-houses, shops, stores, and factories, . . . who are dependent upon it for employment and support," and the "vast manufacturing interest" which attempts to control the votes of "the laborers and mechanics dependent upon that interest." In a speech before a Free Soil convention Horace Mann painted a gloomy portrait of the class the secret ballot was designed to help:

> Let us look in [sic] the thousands of day-laborers, of workmen on corporation grounds, of dependent clerks, of subordinates at custom-houses and other public offices, and so forth, who have no capital but their industry, no resources but their daily earnings, who have an aged mother or dependent sisters to support, or a family of children to be fed, clothed, and educated; who may be turned out even of the humble tenements where they live, as winter is coming on; who may be refused promotion or advancement in their work and in their wages; and in regard to some of whom the wolf of hunger sits growling at the door; let us look at these, I say, and then answer the question, whether they ought not to be protected in voting according to their judgment and conscience.

The legislative committee investigating the Lowell election irregularities pointed up the urgency of insuring a free ballot in these terms:

. . . as wealth increases, and concentrates itself in fewer hands, the
protection of the mass of working-men, who must be dependent in a
very great degree upon the wealthy for employment, becomes doubly
important. If we are never to have such painful toils and struggles,
such frequent failures, and such slow and wearisome progress upward,
as the masses of England are enduring and making, it will be because
we live in an age when the encroaching power of wealth can be stayed
before the people are ground to the dust.[8]

Explicit statements like these, as well as the thrust of the secret ballot
issue generally, served to place before the public a new concept of the
worker: a figure weak, vulnerable, an economic pawn callously pushed
around by his powerful employer. It was a picture described in a few
quick strokes; its vast implications were never adequately explored. But
at least the point was made. The opponents of the secret ballot scoffed at
it as a maudlin, gross distortion of the worker's true situation. Old-line
Whigs such as George Briggs continued to maintain that "the sun of
heaven does not shine upon any class of laborers in any community on
the earth, that is more intelligent, that is better paid, or more independent, than the laborers of Massachusetts." To William Schouler the
reports of extensive intimidation of workers at the polls were "all mere
romance."[9] Yet these reiterations of the old optimism could not repair
the damage done. Mainstream politicians had asserted that the much-
vaunted economic independence of the worker was a myth. Although
tentative and imperfect, their attack went to the very heart of the respectable worker image.

The first calls for the regulation of child labor were sounded almost at
the outset of the Bay State's industrial career. Even then, the actual
practice had long antedated the issue. Children had always worked in
Massachusetts, to an extent that would today seem harsh. In an era
when adult labor was usually performed in or near the home, children
were not only expected to do household chores but were often used by
their parents to help bring in the harvest, take care of small tasks at the
shop, aid in various types of domestic manufacture in the winter, clean
fish when the catch was brought in, and do numerous other jobs that did
not require adult strength or skill. Also, it was not at all uncommon for
children to be contracted as apprentices by their parents when they

reached their early teens. To most people this was nothing to apologize for. The child was assisting the family economically, while at the same time doing something that was good for him. Parents firmly believed their offspring should be inculcated as soon as possible with the talents and "character" they would need in later years. They had to be steadily weaned from what was childlike about them — their playfulness, spontaneity, aimlessness, selfishness — and taught to "act like adults." Work (even school work was justified in these terms) disciplined the child and instilled habits of regularity, industry, and sobriety.

With industrialization, however, a new kind of child labor appeared. Children started working outside the home, for people other than their parents, as wage earners. It was a logical development: Mechanization and the increasing division of labor in manufacturing created many unskilled jobs that children could fill quite adequately — and at a fraction of the wage an adult could command. As might be expected, child labor became most prevalent in the very highly mechanized fields. Cotton mills, especially of the "Rhode Island," or family variety, hired children in large numbers. An incomplete survey in 1820 discovered that they comprised 45% of the employees in Massachusetts cotton mills; by 1832 that figure was cut in half (to 21%), but was still substantial. Woolen mills also used many children. When immigrants took over these jobs in the fifties, they often brought their offspring into the plants with them. An official inquiry in 1867 estimated that one-fourth the employees of the state's twenty-five largest woolen and cotton mills were children. For manufacturing as a whole only crude statistics exist for the postwar period, which, as they rely on testimony from employers, no doubt underestimate the total number of child laborers. Yet they demonstrate that the practice was still a common one. In both the 1870 and 1880 census tabulations, employed youngsters ten to fifteen years of age represented over 10% of all children those ages in the Commonwealth. Most of them were engaged in manufacturing, where they constituted about 5% of the total number of employees. Even in the latter year, when the stiffest child labor laws were in effect, this meant that over 21,000 children under fifteen were wage earners. Child labor was a small but persistent feature of the state's economy.[10]

Children working outside the home, mainly in factories, posed new and disturbing questions. Removed from the beneficent supervision of their parents, they were thrust into a large shop or mill — filled with adult employees of varying backgrounds and character — where they fell under the watchful eye of the employer, who cared about little other than extracting as much labor as he could. To keep their jobs they were forced to stay at work all year and for the long hours of a typical work day. Their contact with their parents — not to mention school — was, necessarily, sharply curtailed. In short, work, which had formerly been deemed a valuable part, but only a part, of a child's upbringing, now threatened to consume almost his entire waking existence. It is not surprising that child labor quickly became the subject of inquiry and legislation.

It was the conflict between child labor and a sound education that first drew the notice of politicians, and henceforth this theme dominated the debate. As early as 1816 Governor Caleb Strong expressed concern about the possibility that young factory operatives might be deprived of proper schooling and recommended to the legislature "that effectual measures be taken for the instruction of such children." His warnings went unheeded. The General Court remained unperturbed; even by the mid-twenties a senate committee looking into the matter saw no need for remedial legislation. Evidently the number of children affected was still too small to warrant action.[11]

However, in 1836 a hard-hitting report by the house committee on education at last succeeded in awakening concern. Penned by James G. Carter, the noted educational reformer, it prophesied that New England's "peculiar character for general intelligence and virtue" might well decay unless something were done about the deleterious effect of factory labor on children. A powerfully written piece, backed by hard statistics, it can be said to mark the birth of child labor as a political issue. The General Court responded by passing a landmark bill. The first of many laws regulating child labor, it prohibited children under fifteen from working in any "manufacturing establishment" unless they had attended a public or private school for three months of the twelve preceding each year they were employed.[12]

Even this modicum of education proved difficult to secure. Over the next three decades various secretaries of the state Board of Education protested that the laws were being evaded widely. The 1836 act left unmentioned the means of enforcing compliance; six years later the task was handed over to local school committees, hardly an advance. The legislature addressed itself sporadically to the problem, at one point making it illegal to employ children under twelve in a factory for more than ten hours a day. But most of its efforts went for nought; the law remained a dead letter.[13]

After Appomattox the issue was revived, in fact, took on unprecedented importance. It was not a particularly "popular" issue. Politicians rarely mentioned child labor in stump speeches, newspapers did not editorialize on it much. But within the government itself — in legislative halls and the various executive agencies — it was a persistent topic of discussion. Much of the impetus behind this new interest came from a report in 1866 by a commission appointed by the legislature to investigate the hours of labor and the "condition and prospects" of "the industrial classes." Branding child labor "the most marked and inexcusable evil" brought to its attention, the commission substantiated the "frequent and gross violation" of existing laws, assailed public apathy on the subject, and issued ominous forecasts of what would happen if the situation were not corrected. This body and its successor, created one year later, recommended stringent new legislation or, failing that, stricter enforcement of the old. The General Court moved promptly, enacting two laws that prohibited children under ten from working at all in a "manufacturing or mechanical establishment" and allowing children ten to fifteen to do so only if they attended school three months a year (or its equivalent); and in either case they could not be employed more than sixty hours a week. Better enforcement procedures were established, including a clause fining *parents* who allowed their children to work in violation of the law. (Previous laws had fined only the employer.) On paper, these were the most rigorous attempts yet to curtail child labor.[14]

However, they were not sufficient. For over a decade more Massachusetts politicians continued to wrestle with the problem. The acts of 1866 and 1867 proved hardly more effective than their predecessors; official confirmation of their inadequacy came quickly. In 1868 and 1869 two reports were issued by the deputy state constable named in the 1867 act to supervise its enforcement. The constable (Henry K. Oliver, a conscientious civil servant) told of widespread violations of the new law and recommended reforms. Later, Oliver's successor to the post had similarly bad news to report, while Oliver himself continued to lament the situation in his new position as chief of the Bureau of Statistics of Labor. Joseph White, secretary of the state Board of Education, added his voice to the doleful chorus, as did the state Board of Health. Finally, in 1874 Governor William Washburn made prominent mention of the subject in his annual address to the legislature, alluding to recent evidence which showed there were "many thousand children in our crowded cities and manufacturing establishments, who never enter a school-room, and are growing up without even the rudiments of what we call education. The number of this class seems to be increasing yearly." It was an area, he suggested, in which "important changes are imperatively demanded as soon as they can be brought about." Once again the legislature made the attempt: A new law prohibited children under eighteen (rather than fifteen) from working more than ten hours a day — or sixty a week — in manufacturing. But the enforcement procedures were left untouched.[15]

Not surprisingly, this measure hardly helped at all. The very next year the new deputy state constable in charge of enforcing the law, George McNeill, issued the most pessimistic report yet. From 60,000 to 80,000 children between five and fifteen habitually did not attend school, he estimated — about one-fifth of the children of those ages in the state. The figure was far higher than any given before. The reason, he offered, was that most of the truants were out working: The child labor laws were "inoperative." Much more stringent measures were needed. So, in 1876 and 1878 two further acts were passed which stipulated that no factory or workshop (or "mercantile establishment," a new provision) could employ children under fourteen at all, "unless such child can read and write." The education requirement was expanded from three to five months a year (though the age through which it applied was reduced a year). Enforcement was tightened: Employers had to keep on hand a certificate from the local school committee stating that the employed child had completed the required schooling. Failure to produce this certificate upon demand of the local truant officer was prima facie evidence that the employer was guilty of violating the law. By 1881 Governor John Long could at last report that the state's child labor laws were in general being complied with.[16]

Throughout this long controversy the overriding complaint of the critics of child labor was that it made it impossible to educate adequately these young workers. The argument was every effective. The state's common school system was regarded with the utmost pride. Nothing was more crucial than making certain that all children could avail themselves of this great gift. Governor Washburn, alarmed at the extent of child labor, put it this way:

> The assumption of our laws is, that the highest intelligence is the highest good of the entire people. Ignorance is dwarfing to the individual and dangerous to society. . . . The State assumes that the physical, mental and moral treasures embraced in what we call childhood, are so much capital belonging to the community as well as to the parents. And it has been well said that the State undertakes to provide for, invest, develop, and look after this childhood treasure, in such a way that it shall pay the highest dividends to the Commonwealth. No distinction of outward condition, whether it be of wealth or poverty, of birth or race, can be allowed to interfere with the purpose of the State. She claims the right and responsibility of providing a good common-school education for every child within her borders at the public expense. She starts them all upon the highway toward useful and honorable manhood and womanhood. That she advances and maintains this theory is one of the crowning honors of our good Commonwealth.[17]

To some minds the solution to the child labor problem was simply to moderate the demands of the factory on the child's time. After the war the English system of "half-time" schools for young factory operatives drew wide notice (the child would labor for half the normal work day, then go to school the rest of the time). The adoption of such a system was often recommended for Massachusetts. Evidently its proponents saw nothing wrong with children toiling in factories, so long as it was not pushed to excess. A similar assumption underlay the contemporary vogue for teaching "industrial art" (that is, mechanical drawing) and mechanical skills of various sorts in the public schools. Education has a proper role, said Governor Alexander Rice, "in fitting young men and young women to properly enter upon the industrial career which choice or circumstances will naturally open before them." That children *should* enter upon such a career — at the right age — did not trouble them.[18]

But more often than not the rhetoric of child labor law advocates suggested that factory work — and the industrial system generally — did trouble them, deeply. Many of them were convinced that employment in a factory or craft shop harmed children, not only because they worked there too long, but because of *the very nature of that type of work*. It is significant that through most of this period few were disturbed about children working on farms or aboard ships or in stores. All the child labor laws except the last set maximum hour limits only for manufacturing. It was true that most child workers were in manufacturing, but there was another reason. Toiling at a machine was held to be deleterious and stultifying.

Children were vulnerable: their bodies frail, their minds unformed. Factory work, many charged, injured their health. It was dangerous; the air was "impure"; the labor often debilitating. The state Board of Health estimated that death rates were higher among "factory children" than among youngsters not exposed to that type of work. It was also pointed out that child operatives were less likely than adults to protest against overwork and thus stood the risk of being driven beyond their physical capacities by unscrupulous factory owners who cared little about their employees. Joseph White, secretary of the state Board of Education, stressed that they were a

> helpless class. Between the pressure of the heavy hand of capital, sometimes blind and relentless, and the behests of ignorant or vicious or necessitous parents, those children can look alone to the Commonwealth as a protector or guardian. Like the blind, and the deaf-mute, and hardly less helpless than these, they are the wards of the State, and claim, not as charity but as justice, the privileges of knowledge and of healthful training.

Others contended that factory work had a dreary, deadening effect on young minds, at the precise moment in their lives when they needed to be stimulated and developed. As far back as 1836 the Carter report charged that "that minute subdivision of labor, upon which the success of manufacturing industry depends, is not a circumstance favorable to intellectual development." In such work "the operative is reduced, in some degree, to the humble sphere of a part of the machinery." The word "drudgery" began to be used to describe the regimen of the plants.[19]

To allow children to continue under these conditions, they were sure, would end disastrously. Deputy state constable George McNeill drew a bleak portrait of the young laborer turned adult operative:

> Brought up in the mill from childhood; lulled to sleep by buzz of the spindles, or the incessant thud of the loom; short of stature, mostly without beard, narrow-chested, somewhat stooped; a walk not like the sailor's but equally characteristic; not muscular, but tough; flesh with a tinge as though often greased; cheeks thin, eyes sharp, — a man pretty quick to observe, and quick to act, impulsive and generous, with a good deal of inward rebellion and outward submission.

This was a far cry from the manly, proud respectable worker, indeed, more like the much-maligned European laborer. The first special commission on the hours of labor made the connection explicitly: "We are rushing into the same fearful condition in which England found her manufacturing districts years ago. The long hours for children, placed at an early age in factories, and the consequent neglect of education, led . . . directly to the deterioration in health and character, to a letting down of the whole nature and constitution, physical, intellectual, and moral." If child labor were not restricted, who knew what European-type unrest might result? McNeill used plain language. "They can and must be saved from the brutalizing influence of ignorance and want, or else their testimony will be given in worse grammar, and not before a bureau of investigation, but before a terrified and at last an awakened populace."[20]

Child labor law advocates reached still gloomier conclusions when they sought to establish why children were submitted to this noxious toil in the first place. For the most part their attention centered on the children's parents. What caused these mothers and fathers to disregard the normal guardian impulse of every parent? The answers they came up with were unsettling.

Usually they were forced to recognize that in this matter the parents were driven by abject poverty. Over and over they remarked that adult operatives had such a difficult time making ends meet that even the pittance a child laborer could contribute helped. A survey by the Bureau of Statistics of Labor found that fathers relied on what their employed children brought in for one-quarter to one-third of the entire family's earnings. (Even children under fifteen contributed one-eighth to one-sixth of the family's income.) Indeed, noted the bureau, without their wages the majority of workers' families would be in poverty or debt. In Governor Washburn's words, "The anxiety of parents to reap the fruits of the constant labor of their children is so great, that they are quite willing to neglect all provision for their mental or moral culture." Henry Oliver concurred. "Their great thought is acquisition, and they consider that every pair of hands, (that brains help hands they do not realize,) should contribute to the common earnings." And to some extent he even conceded their point. "Men and children in rags need clothing more than spelling books."[21]

In some treatments of this question the blame was laid directly on the immigrant. Unschooled in his native land, he arrived here without what McNeill called "the old New England pride of education" that native-born factory workers used to possess. The French Canadians crowding into the mills, Oliver wrote, are "generally with almost no thought nor opinion upon educational matters. Utterly ignorant as a class, uncleanly in person and habit and habitation, unambitious, and thinking solely of the immediate supply of mere bodily wants, they have no such idea of the value of education as, from childhood upward, it has been presented to the minds of the people of New England." Their coming, some politicians claimed, had worked a "deterioration" of the intellect (and "moral character") of the operative class. The education of their offspring was vitally necessary to prevent any further decay. Oliver again: "The condition of these adults will be, nay is, the condition of their children whom they brought with them, who are working with them, and who will repeat the life and the habits of their parents, unless they receive what their parents were denied at home, the unspeakably great blessings of education, an education which shall educate them completely and inseparably, out of the tastes, the habits and the degradations of these parents." A few went even further, recommending the establishment of evening schools for *adults* — their object, largely, to remedy the deplorable lack of schooling among immigrants. Such schools, according to one secretary of the Board of Education, "cannot fail of doing much to remove from society that lower stratum, of which ignorance is the primitive formation, and from which comes much of the improvidence, unthrift, poverty, and most of the vices and crimes which we deplore."[22]

Yet the responsibility for child labor lay not with the parents alone. The employer who hired the child was responsible too. In the early decades of the century this practice had been easier to excuse: Laborers of any age were hard to come by for factory work, and if children did not fill the jobs nobody would. But by the fifties Massachusetts no longer suffered from a labor shortage. The only reason for hiring children was to hold down labor costs. When report after report revealed how willing (eager, even) employers were to violate the law to keep children on the payroll, many people must have been shocked. The state's great corporations (especially the textile giants), which had long been praised for their benevolent attitude toward their employees, were found to be taking advantage of the most defenseless of all workers. The unscrupulous boss began to be portrayed by critics as a chief villain in the child labor problem. The implications of this new perception of the corporation were far-reaching: If employers were so ready to run their factories on a strictly economic accounting, with hardly a care for the more intangible cost in human lives, how precarious was the position of other, adult workers? What good was the industrial system generally, if it encouraged a cold disregard for such manifestly important considerations as public health, intelligence, and virtue? What was happening to children was only the cutting edge of a much greater social problem.[23]

This determination by child labor law advocates that all was not well with the industrial order in turn reinforced their commitment to educating young workers. Brimming with enthusiasm, they invested the state's common schools with the task of halting what they saw as a decline in the condition and prospects of the working class. The commission on the hours of labor was sure that if the regulatory laws were enforced, "the happy influence would flow out into all places where children are employed, enriching the farms and factories with a higher class of laborers, and giving to the whole State a more healthy, intelligent, and virtuous population." They continually repeated the old maxim that the educated worker was a more productive worker. The more schooling he received, the better for him and for the Commonwealth. "Education, the simple capacity to read and write, adds twenty-five per cent. to the wages of the working classes of a State," claimed Representative George F. Hoar. Horace Mann, convinced that Massachusetts, like Europe, was "verging towards those extremes of opulence and penury, each of which unhumanizes the human mind," was similarly optimistic. "If education be equably diffused, it will draw property after it, by the strongest of all attractions; for such a thing never did happen, and never can happen, as that an intelligent and practical body of men should be permanently poor." Education was, "beyond all other devices of human origin, . . . the great equalizer of the conditions of men."[24]

Others chose to predict welcome improvements in the virtue and attitudes of the working class. "The farmer is always secure in his home, and he is also guarded in health and morals by the circumstances of his life," noted one secretary of the Board of Education. "But the corresponding wants of the operatives in the mills must be met, as far as practicable, by physical, moral, and mental training. The public schools are the only means that can affect the whole population." The strong moral component of contemporary education would keep the workers on the path of rectitude. Educate them, Oliver forecast, and "they shall shrink away, with a sort of moral shudder, from intemperance, licentiousness, debauchery, gin-shops, dancing-saloons and nasty homes. . . . Achieve all this, . . . and you will preserve the New-England character." He even claimed they would be neater. ("Clean shirts follow clean thoughts.") Finally, education was said to make workers content with their lot and thus less disposed to striking and forming unions and less willing to listen to "demagogues" spouting wild, anticapitalist doctrines. The curtailment of child labor, in sum, would lead to an across-the-board amelioration of the fortunes of the worker. Yet the very idea that schools had to, much less could do all these things must have set many to wondering.[25]

Thus, the debate over child labor introduced into political discourse a whole range of unsettling ideas: the harmful and stunting nature of factory work; the grinding poverty and ignorance of much of the adult working class; the inordinate power and rapacity of employers; the general slippage in the tone and well-being of all of society. It was, in other words, one of those issues whose ramifications extended to almost every facet of the status quo. And sympathetic politicians proved very willing to explore those ramifications. The fate of working children excited tender concern. Inherently dependent and powerless, they were uniquely capable of being imposed upon, exploited, beaten down. Moreover, what happened to them in early life would go a long way toward shaping the future of the Commonwealth. As politicians strove to understand and expose the plight of children, they ended up confessing doubts about their society that they otherwise might have dismissed out of hand. The innocence of childhood had illuminated the darker side of the industrial order.

The issue that was more potent than any other in generating new perspectives on the working class was the proposal to shorten, by law, the workday in factories for adult laborers. The contention that factory operatives worked too many hours was the major political grievance of the working class itself during this period. In response to their agitation, Massachusetts politicians undertook a host of inquiries into their job conditions and lives. These efforts ultimately yielded penetrating analyses of the worker's situation. Still more supports under the respectable worker image were knocked away.

From the start the hours issue was intertwined with another: the position of *female* workers in general. The idea of regulating the hours that men worked encountered stiff opposition: men supposedly were strong, assertive, independent types who could take care of themselves. But women were different. The "weaker sex" was placed in almost the same category as children: Susceptible to exploitation and unable to fight back, they qualified as potential wards of the state. Eventually, hours law proponents concentrated more and more on securing protection for female workers only. Most probably would have preferred to include both sexes, but politically that goal was unrealistic.

As in the case of children, women had always had an important economic role within the family and only became workers in large numbers with the advent of industry. The Lowell mill girls are well known, but women filled many other jobs as well. They were active in household manufactures, mainly spinning and the making of straw hats and bonnets. Besides cotton and woolen manufacturing, they were hired in other important industries. They performed the simpler tasks associated with boot and shoe making and worked in the state's growing ready-made clothing industry, as well as in the production of hats, paper, and carpets. And, of course, many were engaged as domestic servants. Yet as with children, it was their toil in factories and craft shops that excited the most interest. The supposedly idyllic life of the mill girls for a long while enchanted the public into believing that female operatives in general were well cared for and protected by solicitous employers. But when these women started striking and joining in the call for shorter hours in the thirties and forties, many took notice. By the postwar years a number of official investigations confirmed women's position at the lower rungs of the industrial ladder: their long hours, poor working conditions, unstable employment, and particularly their low wages. Female operatives clearly were faring much more poorly than their male counterparts, and the notion grew that they should be treated differently by the state.[26]

From the reformers' point of view little was sacrificed, tactically, in narrowing their campaign to women. In most of the state's major industries women were a key part of the labor force. In straw bonnets and clothing they totally dominated. The proportion of women employees (both adult and child) in the all-important cotton textile field was slowly falling (from around 90% in the 1820s to 60% in the 1870s), but they still were crucial there. In woolen textiles (including worsteds) they constituted 40% to 50% of all employees throughout the period; in paper, about half; in carpeting, a growing majority. Even in boots and shoes, a male-dominated field, there were a substantial (though declining) number of women. In all manufacturing fields combined, census figures show that in 1850 women were 39% of the labor force, in 1875, 26%. Since these overall figures included self-employed artisans, the proportion of female *workers* was undoubtedly higher, for very few women were self-employed.[27] The implications of these figures were obvious: Limit the working hours of women, and employers in the major industries would be forced to limit the hours for *all* employees. Women were used so extensively it was impossible to run the factories and shops without them.

It was not until the mid-forties that Massachusetts politicians began confronting the hours issue. Petitions from factory towns and worker agitation generally prompted the state house of representatives to appoint a special committee to look into the matter. Headed by William Schouler, a Whig newspaper editor from Lowell and a known friend of the manufacturing interests, it proceeded to hear testimony from workers and to visit the Lowell mills. Its findings were predictable. The operatives' health was *not* being injured, it maintained, by the prevailing workday, and any attempt to regulate hours by law would place

Massachusetts industry at a competitive disadvantage. It would also constitute an unwarranted abridgment of the workers' right to arrange their own terms of employment. ("Labor is intelligent enough to make its own bargains, and look out for its own interest without any interference from us.") While acknowledging that "abuses" existed, the report concluded that correction would have to come only "in the progressive improvement in art and science, in a higher appreciation of man's destiny, in a less love for money, and a more ardent love for social happiness and intellectual superiority."[28]

The Schouler report set the tone for most of the investigations that followed over the next decade. Time and again legislative committees rejected regulatory legislation as unnecessary, improper, and unfair to both manufacturing corporations and the worker. In the early fifties ten-hour bills were repeatedly introduced in the legislature, and although they won substantial support from Democrats and Free Soilers, they were all voted down. A half-century later George F. Hoar would recall how a speech he gave on the house floor in favor of such a bill was "received with great derision." Some progress was made, though. In 1850 Representative James M. Stone wrote a report for the minority of a house committee which advocated an hours law. An exceptionally strong piece, it anticipated virtually all the arguments used by proponents of the measure over the next three decades. The prevailing workday, Stone charged, "is a great evil, which, not only immediately affects the laborers themselves, but is diffused into society, and will entail serious effects upon posterity." Two years later William S. Robinson, along with Stone the leading champion of hours regulation in the legislature, also penned a cogent minority report. Finally, in 1855 and 1856 majorities of house and senate investigating committees came out for the first time in favor of a ten-hour bill. Still, the legislature balked.[29]

At the close of the Civil War the question surfaced with new vigor. Quickly, it was taken up by working-class political organizations and labor unions and became an important political issue. So confident were its backers that they now began campaigning for an *eight*-hour law. The movement was given strong impetus by a new legislative inquiry. A joint committee filed a report avidly recommending hours restriction and branding the existing workday in manufacturing "a disgrace, in our opinion, to Massachusetts, and an outrage on humanity." The document's alarmist tone inspired the legislature to create a special five-man commission to look into, not only the hours of labor, but the general "condition and prospects of the industrial classes."[30]

As it became obvious the question could no longer be evaded, politicians began to take sides. The line-ups were muddled. The Democratic party's convention of 1866 came out explicitly for an eight-hour law, and its adherents generally seem to have supported it. But the key to the measure's fate rested with the dominant Republicans. Here, a curious division developed. Opposing the measure was the party's conservative wing, closely allied with the state's business interests. Yet it also was attacked by quite a few Radical Republicans, disturbed by the way an hours law would undermine the worker's freedom of contract and the rights of property. This group found a powerful spokesman in the *Daily Advertiser*, which from the beginning criticized hours legislation severely.[31] On the other hand, another group of Radical Republicans were notably sympathetic to the measure. During the war Governor John Andrew had cultivated the support of labor. After his death a small corps of Radicals sought to continue this policy of cooperation. Governor Alexander Bullock was a recognized friend of labor; James Stone was now speaker of the house and William Robinson the house clerk. Ben Butler, not yet out of favor with the party, stood ready to help. With such well-placed allies labor reformers looked forward to an easy victory.[32]

They were quickly disappointed. Early in 1866 the special commission on the hours of labor, although appointed by Bullock, issued an adverse report. While in favor of child labor laws and even conceding the evils of excessive labor in the abstract, it nevertheless rejected hours regulation as an improper exercise of legislative power, unfair to different classes of workers, and an unnecessary restriction of freedom of contract. If work hours needed to be curtailed (and the commissioners granted this would probably be beneficial), it should be done voluntarily. The report effectively squelched the rising enthusiasm for an hours law. Two months later the house defeated an eight-hour bill by a two-to-one margin. A second commission the next year issued another report that was almost as hostile. It agreed that the workday should be reduced to ten hours, but insisted this could be done by restricting *child* labor (a doubtful proposition). It specifically opposed either an eight- or ten-hour law, which, it said, would only reduce wages and productivity and increase commodity prices. So, the "experts" had spoken; the issue seemed dead. In 1868 another bill went down to defeat.[33]

Yet labor would not allow politicians to dispose of the issue that easily. The agitation, instead of expiring, gained momentum. Indeed, by the late sixties it had reached a crescendo. In 1867 and 1868 many other northern states passed hours laws. While most of them were ineffectual, they had major symbolic value. Even Congress passed one for federal employees. Significantly, that bill was introduced by the Commonwealth's Nathaniel P. Banks and received the outspoken support of Senator Henry Wilson (though Sumner voted against it). Shortly other sympathetic voices were raised. Henry Oliver, in his capacity as chief of the newly created Bureau of Statistics of Labor, regularly devoted large sections of that agency's annual reports to approving testimony on shorter hours from employers and employees and made a ten-hour law the leading recommendation of his office. Governor William Claflin suggested that the General Court take up the question anew. At the Republican state convention of 1871 George F. Hoar, now a dominant figure in party councils, asked the convention to endorse an hours law. Over the next several years it did so, although in vague language and with qualifications. Even Sumner backed away from his earlier opposition. Finally, in 1874, Governor William Washburn, universally regarded as "sound" on most issues, came out for the measure in strong terms. His support was especially significant. A few years before he had been skeptical, but now, he said, he had reached the conclusion that "the State cannot afford to be utterly regardless of the health and social well-being of a large class of its citizens for fear of interfering with some established custom or some prevailing system."[34]

By the early seventies hours bills were perennial items on the legislature's agenda. Several times they passed the house, only to fail in the senate. A minority report from a house committee, and then, in 1874, a majority report from a senate committee proposed a ten-hour law for women. Both reports were brief: at this point all the relevant arguments had been thoroughly aired. The latter report, coupled with Washburn's speech, finally pushed the measure over. Nathaniel Banks, now a state senator, shepherded the bill through the legislature, and it was signed by the governor. The act prohibited women from working in any "manufacturing establishment" more than ten hours a day (or, alternatively, a total of sixty hours a week). Enthusiasm carried over into a related area as, over the next few years, the legislature also passed laws establishing state supervision of safety conditions in factories.[35]

Over the long course of this struggle the arguments set forth by hours law advocates were few and simple. What they did, essentially, was to boldly transfer the indictments of factory work used in the child labor debates to adult laborers — and, interestingly, to *all* adult laborers: in their manifestos, at least, they often made no distinction between men and women. The "excessive" hours put in by factory workers were said to cause grave damage to their health, intellect, and morals. The question of health was raised frequently. Toiling in factories and shops eleven, twelve hours a day and longer, six days a week, with only short breaks for eating was, they charged, more than the human body could bear. The operatives' regimented existence was described poignantly in James M. Stone's minority report of 1850. "They get up in the morning and hurry to their work — they go at stated times to their boarding houses and eat their hasty meals, and hasten back to the mills again, and there remain, till they quit work for the day, and return to their boarding houses, tired and exhausted." This enervating pace could not fail to exact its physical toll. Medical testimony was cited to prove that textile mills were unsafe and poorly ventilated, that workers were not allotted sufficient time to digest their food, that the incidence of disease and death were higher among factory operatives than in other trades. Employers were fond of dismissing this kind of evidence by noting the scarcity of complaints on company illness reports. But then they also said unhealthy workers (especially the mill girls) could always return home to convalesce. The Stone report pounced on the contradiction: Sick employees did indeed return home, which is why they did not show up on illness reports; they had had to quit. The company reports were therefore worthless. Besides, as aliens replaced native operatives, the recourse of recuperating under some rural familial roof was obviously no longer available. By the postwar years even the commissioners on the hours of labor were conceding that long hours, where they obtained, could injure health. In 1874 Governor Washburn confidently declared: "That the strength of the operatives in many of our mills is becoming exhausted, that they are growing prematurely old, and that they are losing the vitality requisite to the healthy enjoyment of social opportunity, are facts that no careful and candid observer will deny."[36]

From the physical, hours law advocates moved on to the spiritual effects of the long workday. Here their warnings grew more strident. Allow the laborer only a few hours day leisure, they argued, and you sap the intellectual and moral foundations of society. He will become a simulacrum of a human being, without the energy or ambition to pursue goodness or knowledge, without even the time to do so. How, they asked, would he find the opportunity to read, to undertake that lifelong effort to better himself that marked the upright citizen? Said the special commission of 1867:

> It is not enough that the laborer have education in childhood; he must have the means of constant improvement and progress in manhood. He must not only know something of the past, but be familiar with the events of the present. New ideas, new discoveries, new issues are made from day to day, and the laborer must have the means of knowing what these are. All this requires time, and not only time, but rest from toil in such a condition that the mind can engage with its full strength in intellectual pursuits.

Long hours doomed the worker to a state of intellectual stagnation, cutting him off from the formative ideas of his age. Bad enough for native workers, what would be the effect on the foreign-born, deprived of a common school training?

> What is to be done with them? How are we to protect ourselves from the ignorance that is generally their misfortune rather than their fault? How are we to educate them into unity of aspiration and purpose with native-born citizens? Shall we work them so many hours a day that they will have neither strength, interest, nor time, for becoming acquainted with our institutions and our aims as a people? Or shall we, by shortening their hours of labor, and the establishment of evening schools, if need be, fit them for the duties of citizenship, and make them a part of ourselves?

These were the alternatives posed by Governor Washburn. James Stone predicted the inevitable outcome of continued neglect. Soon, he held, the influx of aliens will bring about "an entire modification, and depression of the state of society in and about manufacturing places." Keep them locked in ignorance and the result will be "a strictly manufacturing population, permanently bound by circumstances, to factory employ-ments, similar in character to the factory population of England."[37]

For the same reasons, they were convinced, long hours would lead to moral degradation. It was common knowledge (to their minds) that the proverbial licentiousness of the British working class before the Factory Acts was due to overwork. Excessive toil dulled the mind: The laborer returned home from the plant seeking stimulation, and usually found it in liquor. The same thing could happen in America. Again they worried particularly about the immigrant, raised without the stern moral up-bringing of a Yankee and hence an easier prey, allegedly, to temptation.[38]

The burden of long hours finally depressed the worth of labor itself. Labor, one must recall, had traditionally been regarded as a fulfilling and sustaining enterprise. But how could it continue to be so under these onerous conditions? It is doubtful that hours law advocates would have had any great esteem for factory toil in any case, but they firmly believed the duration of the workday made it an irksome, unrewarding chore. The authors of the 1865 joint committee report were astonished when operatives came before them and described themselves as "slaves." "It was painful to listen to the unanimous evidence showing a steady demoralization of the men who are the bulwarks of our national life." Yet that evidence revealed workers did indeed resemble slaves:

> Instead of that manly and sturdy independence which once distin-guished the mechanic and the workingman, we have cringing servility and supineness. Instead of self-respect and intelligence, we have want of confidence and growing ignorance. Instead of honest pride in the dignity of labor, we have the consciousness of inferiority. Instead of a desire to enter the mechanic arts, we have loathing and disgust of their drudgery and degradation. Instead of labor being the patent of nobil-ity, it is the badge of servitude.[39]

The word "drudgery" came to be used often to describe factory work. No longer did that work serve as something that gave meaning to the operative's life or exalted him in the eyes of the world. It was a brutish expenditure of energy, nothing more.

After unraveling this long string of oppression, hours law proponents still had one vital question to answer: Why did the worker endure it? He was obviously being made to work longer than he wanted to, yet the respectable worker image taught that that was impossible. The supposedly "independent" worker faced with these conditions should quit — or bargain to get his hours reduced. The record showed, however, that he stayed, and "bargaining" succeeded only when done collectively and usually after costly strikes. Plainly there was something wrong with the theory. This question probably troubled many, but James Stone was the only politician to address the problem explicitly. The rise of great industrial corporations, he held, had destroyed "that natural equality of condition" that ought to exist between employer and employee, that "which would enable each party to exercise its due share of influence in fixing the rate of wages, the hours of labor, and all other relations, by mutual arrangement and agreement." The corporations are "immense artificial persons, with far larger powers than are possessed by individuals." They are directed solely to turning a profit, and "are not chastened and restrained in their dealings with the laborers, by human sympathy and direct personal responsibility to conscience and to the bar of public opinion." Hence it is not surprising that the employee has no control over the length of the workday. The corporations can

> fix inexorably, without consultation with the laboring class, all the terms and conditions of labor. The will of the corporations thus becomes law, and declares how many hours the laborers shall work. . . . From this decision of these powerful employers, large masses of the laboring people have practically no escape. Circumstances, practically compel them to submit to the offered terms. Many of them must do so, or have no work at all; and to some, this is equivalent to having no honest means of support. The power of the corporations, thus exercised in determining the conditions of labor of large numbers of the laboring classes, not only oppresses those whom they employ, but also exerts a powerful influence to depress the condition and prolong the hours of labor in every branch of industrial pursuits.

In a flash of insight, Stone had identified the crux of the worker's problem under industrialism. The worker had nowhere else to go, he was powerless — in short, he was *dependent*.[40]

This, then, was the factory operative as he was drawn by the friends of hours legislation. He was tired, broken, deprived of a happy home life, sunk in vicious habits, ignorant of the world around him, listless, bored, powerless. There could hardly have been a more vivid contrast with the cherished image of the respectable worker. That spirited, independent figure in fact seemed to be fast disappearing from the scene. In the state's rush to erect the new industrial order, they were saying, it had extracted from the worker more than he could reasonably be expected to yield. Like a gold coin passed too often from hand to hand, labor was losing its luster, and ultimately, its value.

Chapter 8

The Postwar Years: Closing Ranks

RESOUNDING DISCORDANTLY through Massachusetts politics for four decades, the issues just discussed disrupted the soothing harmonies of the respectable worker image. The inquiries of those who advocated the secret ballot, child labor laws, and hours laws for adult operatives — and the charges growing out of those inquiries — cast doubt on nearly every facet of that image. Moreover, its whole thrust seemed increasingly irrelevant for a working class now composed so heavily of the foreign-born and their descendants. Inevitably, this persistent questioning had its effect. By the postwar years it was clear that the image had been seriously challenged — and damaged.

Nevertheless, the damage was contained. Studying political discourse in the decade and a half after Appomattox, one is impressed by the *lack* of any general debate over the circumstances, future, or impact of the working class. True, politicians spoke of "the labor question" and matters touching directly the mass of workers received more attention than they ever had before the war. But "the labor question" consisted, principally, of these three issues. The debates they engendered did not blossom into an extended discussion of the working class itself. The criticisms of the respectable worker image were confined to a narrow sphere. Rarely, except among the few labor-oriented politicians like Phillips and Butler, did they take on a life of their own. It is as if the collective political leadership of Massachusetts made a conscious effort to ignore the unsettling questions that they themselves had raised.

As a result, there never was, outside the debates over these issues, a confrontation between two distinct approaches to the working class. Most of the politicians who backed these reforms did not try to draw together their disparate findings into a coherent alternate view — a "counter-image," so to speak. Their attacks on the older image remained haphazard and confused — and consequently, not nearly so effective as they might have been.[1] Their failure may have been one of imagination, but I think it is more accurate to describe it as one of interest and of will.

How receptive the political climate of the day might have been to a frontal assault on the respectable worker image may be judged by the experience of one man who made the attempt: Henry K. Oliver. His story is so instructive that it is worth a digression.

On the face of it, Oliver would seem one of the least likely candidates to lead an attack on established wisdom. His career up to this point bespoke an earnest competence, but not much more. The son of an orthodox Puritan minister, he was connected with old, respected New England families. At various times before the war he had been a teacher, high school principal, headmaster of his own school, adjutant-general of Massachusetts, director of a cotton textile corporation based in Lawrence, and mayor of Lawrence. During the war itself he was treasurer of the state. Thereafter, then in his late sixties, he served as deputy state constable in charge of enforcing the child labor laws. That, coupled with his involvement in cotton manufacturing, made him a natural choice to head the state Bureau of Statistics of Labor when it was formed, in 1869, in response to labor demands.[2]

While Oliver had always been considered sympathetic to the problems of workers — and no doubt his stint as deputy state constable reinforced his concern — no one expected what followed. The bureau was created to collect information on "the laboring classes," and he went about his task with gusto. With only one assistant he sent out circular surveys, conducted extensive research, and even made personal tours to find out as much as he could about the worker's condition. The results were laid out before the Commonwealth in the bureau's first four annual reports (1870–1873).

What Oliver presented was a scene of almost unrelieved misery. The evidence he compiled pointed straight to one overwhelming fact: that *poverty* "always has been, and is," as he put it, "the normal condition of wage-laborers." His surveys of employers and employees disclosed that most workers lived at the edge (and sometimes over the edge) of actual pauperism. The average yearly earnings of all wage earners in the state he estimated at about $600, a very inadequate sum. For some, things were desperate. Agricultural laborers, women laborers, and most important, factory operatives almost all were struggling to survive. The latter, he charged, "are the worst sufferers under the wage-system. Their pay is put at at the lowest point that will keep off positive want, so that the labor of wives and children must be added to that of fathers, in order to yield the family a proper support." The workers' penury, he went on, pervaded every aspect of their existence. His investigations into accounts in savings banks showed that most laborers were unable to put away more than meager amounts; many were in debt. His eyewitness reports on the squalid conditions in working class districts of Boston were brutally honest. All across the nation, he wrote, "will be found, in the labyrinthal slums of cities, in narrow courts, dark lanes, and nasty alleys, wretched tenements, with small rooms, dismal, dark, unventilated, into which the sun, God's free gift, never sends a shimmering ray; packed full of men, women, and children, as thick as smoked herrings in a grocer's box." Such circumstances drove the workers to drastic steps to surmount them. He detailed the enervating toll of the long hours they labored, their wanderings in search of better jobs, their constant resort to the deleterious routine of factory labor. (He was convinced that "factory life any way, . . . is a bad life, physically, morally, socially, and intellectually.") But these efforts, he insisted, would prove futile, for the chances of the average worker's rising above his lowly status were slim.[3]

Beyond this, Oliver had a keen appreciation of the self-perpetuating nature of poverty. Poverty, he wrote, "generates a stagnation in everything, a stagnation of knowledge, of culture, of refinement, of success." It was debilitating and demoralizing; it robbed the worker of self-respect, ambition, aspiration. To expect a man in these straits to "improve" himself was to ask, if not the impossible, certainly the unreasonable. He had little patience with those who harped on the venality and ignorance of the working class, especially of immigrants. They may indeed exhibit such traits, he said, but they were hardly to blame. "Their whole life and surroundings have been always antagonistic to goodness and purity, and failing, therefore, to appreciate the beneficent moral influences of innocent recreation, . . . and their own human nature . . . demanding some relief from the delving [sic] monotony of daily toil, and the jading realities that beset and torment them, they grasp at those that are nearest, most familiar, cheap and exciting." In short, the working class was not only "degraded" at present: It looked as if it would remain that way for a long time to come. Indeed, the signs indicated its situation was deteriorating. Massachusetts laborers, he claimed, were fast approaching their counterparts abroad. In the large cities, in fact, he could see practically no difference.[4]

To remedy this situation Oliver insisted first that the true causes of the workers' poverty be acknowledged. Their background and circumstances must be taken into account, but the public must also be made aware that the whole "wage system," by creating a deep division between capitalist and employee, kept the worker down. Hence, it would do no good to exhort the worker himself to greater efforts. Even labor unions, to which Oliver was sympathetic, probably could not accomplish much. (Strikes, to his mind, were "a crude, costly, and awkward way of accomplishing a purpose.") What was required was for the state to step in and interpose its power on behalf of the worker. Oliver advocated hours laws, child labor laws, factory safety acts, and health inspections of slums — the whole panoply of protective legislation — as well as a general movement by workers themselves toward what he vaguely termed a system of "cooperation." Only in this way could the labor question, "the problem of the age," be solved.[5]

Oliver's reports represent the only coherent, sustained critique of the respectable worker image by a mainstream politician for the entire postwar period. (As he rather ingenuously admitted, his findings were "opposed to the generally received opinions; the general impression being, that labor is well enough paid, and therefore well enough provided for.") Coming from such a respected figure — a solid Republican of high standing — and from an agency of the state government, the reports stirred wide interest, being taken up in the press and debated in the halls of the legislature. His accounts of the notorious Boston tenements prompted the formation of a citizens' committee to end the most glaring evils. Soon requests were coming in from other states for copies, and even Congress took notice. If, as he said, "labor, in this country, has not, until recently, come prominently into public sight and discussion," he singlehandedly had much to do with correcting that oversight.[6]

Doubtless, though, he was not pleased with the tenor of the response his efforts elicited in Massachusetts. Initially the bureau had widespread support, but as soon as its first report came out the tide quickly turned against it. Almost universally, its findings were excoriated and dismissed. The state's powerful real estate, financial, and manufacturing interests all attacked the reports vigorously. Soon prominent political spokesmen and even labor leaders, for some reason, joined the chorus. The *Advertiser* lambasted the reports as "a libel upon the State and upon the people." They were based, it charged, on inadequate data, which were poorly interpreted as well. One report it labeled "a mass of false assumptions, bungling calculations and absurd conclusions." The bureau had "a case to make out," and "ignored or falsified all the facts that would lead to results different from those it had set itself to find." It should "collect facts" only, and not try to "establish theories." On the floor of Congress Henry Dawes, a leading Republican, denounced the bureau's methodology: "The instances they have dragged to light no more prove the general condition of the operative than the marching into open court of a criminal for trial proves the general prevalence of crime in any community." By 1873 Governor Washburn was reiterating these allegations in his message to the General Court. The bureau's investigations must be lifted, he said, "to a higher and broader level." That same year Oliver was replaced as bureau chief by Carroll Wright.[7]

There were in fact grounds for criticizing Oliver's work. He had had no training as a labor economist or statistician, and his reports, as he himself admitted, *were* built on skimpy data. It is also true that he was openly sympathetic with the goals of the labor movement. Nevertheless, his findings were, in a broad sense, an accurate summation of the condition of most members of the working class. Yet Massachusetts politicians were not ready to accept that, and probably would not have even if he had been a neutral expert in the field and had access to a mass of statistics. So, instead of serving as a catalyst for a full-scale discussion of the working class, his investigations were rejected out of hand and fell into oblivion. The common objection that he was trying to "establish theories" rested on the easy assumption that an unbiased observer, unswayed by the oddball theories of the labor movement, could not possibly come up with such depressing conclusions. It is not surprising, then, that politicians refrained from developing further the charges that arose during the debates over labor-related issues. And without that, there could never be a true dialogue on "the labor question."

For added evidence of their reluctance to pursue the matter, one has only to consult the broader currents of state politics during these years. While politicians did display an unprecedented interest in labor issues, none became an important question except for the hours law proposal and even that got shunted aside. The main arena of contention between Republicans and Democrats centered primarily on national issues: Above all, Reconstruction, but also currency, the tariff, civil service reform, and similar items. On the state level the principal issue was, for a long time, prohibition, while others included state finances, state involvement in railroad construction, and political corruption. After all these points had been argued, little time remained to inquire into the worker's problems. Indeed, if one examines the situation closely it is clear that politicians engaged in continual maneuvers to insure that this would be so. They did respond to labor agitation, but only as much as was necessary to survive. They were obviously not genuinely interested in labor issues. As soon as they could safely do so, they dropped the matter entirely.

The predicament of the Democrats was a vexing one. Once again reduced to an impotent minority, their organization was in a shambles. The war had tainted them with the stain of disloyalty. Never having been fully accepted as respectable by the Commonwealth's voters to begin with, they now had to work feverishly to reestablish their legitimacy. It is no accident that in these years they gave the gubernatorial nomination on six occasions to a pair of *bona fide* Adamses — John Quincy, Jr. and Charles Francis. They also took care to embrace a "correct" position on monetary policy, a sensitive issue in the state. In any event, they had to be very careful about whom they allied themselves with. They needed workers' votes, yet to go too far in support of the labor movement and "labor principles" would scare away solid, middle-class types. They also needed the immigrants' votes, but since generally they already *had* that, there was no need to ostentatiously solicit them. All through these years Irish politicians were conspicuously absent from the Democratic leadership (with the exception, in the late seventies, of Patrick Collins). To complicate matters further, their strong contingent of immigrant supporters made them reluctant to back labor too openly. Relationships between most immigrants and organized labor were not good. (Union membership was overwhelmingly Protestant, and the conservative Catholic clergy frowned on union activities and strikes.) The foreign-born might be displeased if the party was perceived as leaning too far towards the labor movement.

For most of this period, therefore, the Democrats remained . . . the best way to put it is, quietly sympathetic to labor. Their opposition to civil rights for southern blacks and to a protective tariff were seized by Republicans as signs of hostility to the working man. They had to defend themselves. So, at the same time they tried to play the issue down, they came out early in favor of an eight-hour law. In the legislature, the small Democratic contingent tended to back ten-hour bills, and fought strongly to abolish contract labor and condemn the use of Chinese workers as strikebreakers. Their state conventions were always careful to include a plank boasting of the party's solicitude for labor. A typical resolution, in 1874, promised "to foster with care the interest of labor, the basis of material prosperity, and of the industrial classes on whose moral and intellectual condition must ever depend the character and success of popular political institutions." Yet they were usually hesitant to go beyond such smiling generalities, and if they did take a prolabor position fairly consistently, they also did so without making a great stir. For them, national issues and the other state issues were far more important. As if to reaffirm their "soundness" on the question, the party included in its resolutions for 1875 a plank reading: "The interests of capital and labor are identical, and any attempts to produce antagonism between the two must be injurious to both. We favor such legislation as will secure to both an open field and fair play, and to both equal rights and just rewards under the law."[8]

Only at the very end of the period did the party abandon this cautious line. Ben Butler's belated conversion to Democracy set the stage for a riotous state convention in 1878, as Butler supporters overwhelmed party regulars and captured the gubernatorial nomination for their hero. Although the angry regulars, at a rump convention, named a candidate of their own, Butler's immense popularity carried the great majority of Democratic votes. From that point on the party took on the character of its new leader, beginning to appeal more openly for workers' (and immigrants') votes, attack the power of "monopolies," and in general justify its program in terms of its benefits for labor. Ultimately that strategy succeeded. In 1882 a Democratic alliance with the Greenback-Labor party propelled Butler into the governor's chair. Despite all this, though, the fact remains that for most of the years being considered in this chapter the Democrats did little to spread dissent from the image of the respectable worker.

The dominant Republican party came at the labor question from an entirely different angle. Securely entrenched in power at the war's end, they had no pressing need to recruit workers' votes. In all likelihood, a substantial proportion of those votes already went to the Republicans out of respect for the party's association with the war effort. (Almost two-thirds of the ballots in Boston were cast for Lincoln in 1864, the second-highest proportion of any city in the nation.) But as time wore on the swollen Republican majorities of the war years dwindled. This was especially true in the seventies, when wartime loyalties had started to fade and the party seemed to lapse from the high moral purpose it had displayed at its inception. The depression of that decade hurt too. Now it became crucial not to antagonize any more voters than necessary while still holding true to traditional Republican policies — which meant primarily, at this stage, fiscal and tariff policies.

The Republicans, like the Democrats, also had a problem of establishing their legitimacy — or rather, sustaining their legitimacy. The party at the close of the war was barely a decade old. The goals for which it had originally been formed were largely realized. Soon its vaunted unity would start crumbling, as issues like women's suffrage, state aid to railroads, and the particularly volatile one of prohibition caused dissension. Some serious questions thus were posed: Would the emotional bonds forged during the war be enough to maintain its support? Would voters be attracted in great numbers now that the issues the party concerned itself with were more complex, divisive, and dull? Republican leaders worried about the fragility of their new position and were inordinately sensitive about possible inroads into their power base.

The challenge of the Democrats could be met easily enough by "waving the bloody shirt" and pointing with alarm to their connection with immigrants and urban political corruption. But the challenge of labor-oriented political movements presented a new and potentially more threatening dilemma. Republicans were upset at the size of Wendell Phillips' vote in the 1870 gubernatorial race and, even more alarming, the rising influence of Butler. In fact, all through the seventies party leaders were obsessed with Butler, whose open appeals for worker support and emphasis on labor issues (and unorthodox monetary policies) seemed to be succeeding. Such "demagoguery," they feared, might mobilize enough public enthusiasm to overturn the Republican hegemony. Throughout the decade the regular organization, led by George F. Hoar and Henry Dawes, labored mightily to repulse Butler's attacks, first from within the party and then, after 1877, via the Democrats. This entailed making a special effort to cut into his formidable popularity among workers and the foreign-born.

But — and this is the crucial point — their strategy was based on political calculation, little more. There was, to be sure, a residue of idealism within the party which found an outlet in concern for the working class. It has been shown that in the debates over the hours law, a group of Radical Republicans fought tirelessly for the measure and finally managed to push it through (many in this group were also active in the struggle for child labor laws). Nevertheless, the influence of these men waned, rather than grew, during the seventies. Most Republicans came to adopt the businessman's view of labor matters. What acknowledgment they made of worker demands was inspired mainly by a careful estimate of how much they had to give up in order to stay in power.

The easiest way to appear friendly toward labor was to make purely verbal concessions — to proclaim solicitude for the worker without offering anything substantive. Often Republicans would point to the party's long fight to restrict (and then abolish) slavery as an earnest of their devotion to "free labor" everywhere. The ending of human bondage for blacks, they argued, elevated all workers. "We have made labor honorable," boasted Henry Wilson, "even in the rice swamps of the Carolinas and Georgia; we have taken the brand of dishonor from the brow of labor throughout the country; and in doing that grand work we have done more for labor, for the honor and dignity of laboring men, than was ever achieved by all the parties that arose in this country from the time the Pilgrims put their feet upon Plymouth Rock up to the year 1860." Wilson's hosannas were echoed by the Republican state committee. "So far from being the slave of capital," it said of the party, "it is the child of the people, liberal and progressive from the first moment of its history, and in this respect, as in all others, broadly distinguished from that party of stubborn conservatism which sustained the institution of slavery to the very latest moment, and is now held together by the cohesive power of prejudice and caste." Republican spokesmen extolled the solid benefits workers derived from their programs. The abolition of slavery was said to have given the working man new opportunities to move south. The homestead law offered him even greater rewards out west. Traditional Republican interest in education, charity, and other efforts "to sustain a high standard of social condition" testified to their concern for the fate of the common man. And their goal of promoting prosperity would inevitably redound to the good of the worker. When the tariff and currency issues became prominent, they took care to specify how the party's stand there would help workers. Claimed the *Advertiser:* "Its whole career has illustrated its devotion to the rights and interests of the poor."[9]

Fine language and vague promises, however, satisfied few workers; by the late sixties they were demanding more specific commitments. Republicans were slow to respond. To some extent they probably underestimated the growing impact of worker agitation. Perhaps they hoped the reports of the special commissions of 1866 and 1867 would stifle public interest in these matters. In any case, until 1869 no Republican state convention even mentioned a labor-related issue in its address to the voters. Yet sympathetic Radicals did keep concern for labor issues alive, and soon others joined in. In Congress, Nathaniel Banks came out, in 1866, for a federal eight-hour law after initially opposing it. The next year Henry Wilson endorsed Banks's bill in the Senate (though confessing uncertainty about its wisdom). Both began making political capital of their support when the measure proved popular. Interestingly, Banks and Wilson each had poor, working-class backgrounds.

In 1869 the party suddenly awoke to the gravity of its situation. Working class agitation and union organization had become strong currents. The rather stupid refusal of the Republican legislature to grant a charter of incorporation to the Crispins was a prime factor in the formation of the Labor Reform party. Soon politicians were scrambling to make amends. The state convention of 1869 endorsed charters for organized labor; the following year for the first time it adopted a vaguely prolabor plank. The *Advertiser*, long hostile to labor, admitted the party now had to take a firm stand "in favor of laws which, without violence, will tend to equalize the burdens and adjust the rewards of labor, and contribute to the prosperity and contentment of all" (although it continued to oppose "penal statutes on the hours of labor"). The Crispins got their charter, and the Republican legislature also set up the Bureau of Statistics of Labor.[10]

Wendell Phillips' strong showing in 1870 prompted new efforts to win workers' support. At the Republican convention a year later George Hoar, president of the gathering, warned that the party would have to address itself to the problems of labor, and he told the delegates that he favored official investigations, child labor laws, workers' cooperatives, and even hours laws for women and children. After beating back a strong challenge by Butler for the gubernatorial nomination, the convention chose William Washburn as its candidate. Later given the honor twice more, Washburn, while not an overly enthusiastic friend of labor, at least had an open mind in the matter, and would prove to be the most sympathetic Republican governor of the period. Under his three administrations support for effective child labor and hours laws gained and finally triumphed in the General Court. By 1874 the state convention was advertising its "sympathy with that legislation which will promote the best interests of labor and tend to the moral and intellectual elevation of all persons engaged in industrial pursuits." In Congress, Hoar sponsored a bill creating a national commission to investigate the condition of labor. Even Charles Sumner, before almost completely uninterested in labor questions, was forced when seeking reelection in 1873 to recant his earlier opposition to hours laws and to seek endorsements from the state's labor leaders. Republicans knew that to ignore labor demands was to invite trouble.[11]

Yet their support was grudging; as soon as it proved politically feasible, it was withdrawn. With the passage of the major child labor, hours restriction, and factory inspection laws in the mid-seventies (almost all the opposition to these measures coming from die-hard Republican legislators), public demand for action in this area abated. The depression curtailed sharply labor agitation and organizing efforts. While Republican senators and congressmen continued to take a prolabor stand in Washington, back home the party's enthusiasm for the worker sensibly diminished. Resolutions sympathetic to labor began to be dropped from party platforms. When Republicans confronted a new challenge from Butler in 1878, the change in tone was noticeable. The party, the *Advertiser* recommended, should "decline to commit itself to the enforcement of crude and doubtful measures for the relief of labor." The convention that year declared that Massachusetts had prospered "because her citizens have believed that the interests of each is [sic] the interest of all, and have labored together for the Commonwealth." Those who "foment discord by falsely teaching that our community is composed of hostile classes whose interests are antagonistic, are public enemies whose defeat is essential to the public welfare." Not surprisingly, there were no kind words for the worker in this platform. The Republican state committee issued an address warning that a "covert and persistent attempt" was under way to deliver the state over to "repudiationists and communists": "In aid of this attempt an effort is made to establish a war of classes, a thing unknown and foreign to a free Commonwealth, the honorable and natural alliance between labor and capital is denounced, the manly independence of honest toil is represented as servitude." In the thick of the campaign the *Advertiser* charged Butler with trying to stir up class hatred. "Between capital and labor there is no cause of enmity. Their interests are one. . . . As a rule the employers of labor in Massachusetts take an honest and lively interest in the welfare of their workmen." Through these and similar statements, the party signaled its retreat from its half-hearted, brief coalition with the working class.[12]

It is plain, then, from the maneuverings of Massachusetts Democrats and Republicans in these years that the labor question was an issue most of them simply were uncomfortable with. Given the rising interest of the working class in politics, public figures knew they had to take some stand, but by the gingerly way they handled the matter it is obvious they would have preferred not to deal with it at all. Maybe it was too explosive, or just unpleasant. Possibly they were so unprepared for it they did not know *how* to cope with it, preferring instead to fall back on more traditional kinds of issues. Whatever the reason, this hesitancy dominated their approach to all matters relating to the working class. The seminal criticisms made by the advocates of labor-oriented legislation were, by and large, *not* taken up and explored further. They remained festering, embarrassing reminders of a social disfigurement politicians all hoped would fade away.

With the impact of its critics thus contained, the respectable worker image survived, battered but still strong, into the postwar years. Predictably, some of its old confidence was gone. Its authority now challenged, it became more defensive, belligerent. But despite the attacks, it continued to provide the terms with which many, if not most, politicians understood the working class. A mode of thought formed over half a century was difficult to give up.

Sustaining the image, as it had before, was the politicians' abiding preoccupation with the course of the state's economy. More than ever the Commonwealth's prosperity was tied to the progress of manufacturing and commerce. However, the prospect that that progress would continue unhampered suddenly seemed in doubt. Other states were catching up to, even surpassing Massachusetts in industrial production and volume of trade; it would have to fight harder to retain its former share of the nation's wealth. Then too, Massachusetts, like all industrial states, was hit hard by the depression of the seventies, which made one thing clear: No matter how well the state fared competitively, the path to prosperity would not be smooth. These forebodings about the Commonwealth's ongoing economic health made politicians more attentive than ever to the protection and advancement of industry. They celebrated its past triumphs and labored hard to assure future success. High tariffs, better railroads and harbors, trade schools, a sound monetary system — all these and more were touted as vital to industrial progress. Concomitantly they became more sensitive about attacks on business. Labor groups that chided corporations for making fat profits were told they should instead be praising those corporations and helping them to do better. Even a "prolabor" politician like Butler defended big businesses as "the conduit through which . . . the wealth produced by labor as the fountain-head must be at last distributed and accumulated." Let the corporations amass wealth, it was said: Inevitably they will pass the benefits along to the workers. "The great object to be sought," said the *Advertiser*, "is to broaden and enlarge the field in which industry may be made tributary to human happiness." From these premises, the politicians of this period would continue to find appealing an optimistic view of the worker's condition. That would be yet another sign of the fundamental soundness of the whole industrial order.[13]

Most often the old respectable worker image surfaced in repeated assertions that the average worker was well off economically. The American laborer's "facilities for acquiring domestic comfort, social consideration, and competency if not independence of fortune, are," said the

Advertiser, "the envy of workingmen the world over." Numerous statistics were brought forward to confirm this wonderful fact. Especially popular were comparative analyses of the wages and cost of living of American and European workers. All allegations of extensive poverty among workers were vigorously refuted. "The masses in New England," wrote an indignant Charles Francis Adams, "are no more afflicted with poverty than they are with disease." (In this connection politicians also denied that factory operatives were overworked or in poor health.) Actual pauperism among workers was supposedly a minor — and diminishing — problem (although after the depression optimism about that disappears). What little poverty remained was traceable to the deficiencies of the foreign-born and general laziness or lack of "character" among the poor. Unemployment was held to be minimal too, even during the depression. Apparently nothing could shake their conviction that the "plight" of the worker was an invention of addled labor reformers, with no basis in fact. And they were confident that, as economic conditions improved, the worker would grow still richer.[14]

Whether the worker continued to enjoy abundant opportunities to advance was evidently less clear, but on balance the answer here was affirmative too. Certainly, according to most politicians, he was not lacking in aid: free reading rooms and libraries, low-cost housing, night schools, savings banks, and above all the common school system furnished him throughout his life with the means he needed for self-improvement. At their most hopeful they claimed it was still eminently possible for the worker to enter the ranks of the self-employed. "Few men of energy, capacity, and common sense, expect to be dependent upon wages for a lifetime," an *Advertiser* editorial asserted.

> The history of labor shows no other country in the world where laboring men who start without fortunes of any kind so often become employers of labor themselves as in the United States. There is no such thing among us as an hereditary working class; the least fortunate is ambitious to become superior to fortune, and if he has ordinary strength of will and of hand he seldom fails. Failure, when it does come, is almost always owing, not to want of opportunities, but to want of health, of prudence, and of effort.

In more sober moments, however, even this adamantly optimistic journal conceded that the average laborer's chances of becoming self-employed were limited and growing more so. Trying to set up a small shop or firm was usually futile in an economic arena dominated by large corporations. At the same time, the paper insisted that he could progress *as a worker*. "With individuals the condition is constantly changing, and must inevitably change for the better in a state of society where everybody reads, where the facilities for moving from place to place are so abundant, where men can change their employers as often as it is for their interest to do so, and where every intelligent workman is under constant stimulation to do his best." George F. Hoar agreed, claiming that, while "the lowest class may have poor wages . . . the man who was in the lowest class five or ten years ago is not found in that class today." The laborers' invariable upward progress was clearly manifested in their "large deposits in savings banks" and "the homes which are growing up like mushrooms year by year" in and around manufacturing towns, "homes of comfort, of thrift, of wealth, indicating increasing means of their occupants." The mobile, independent worker was virtually assured of a better life.[15]

Political spokesmen thus made a strong effort to uphold the major economic components of the image of the respectable worker. To them the laborer was still well off and had good prospects of raising his estate. Yet the situation was different with respect to the more spiritual side of the old image. By these years it was very rare, except in passing remarks, to find politicians praising the working class as virtuous and intelligent or as making a worthy contribution to democracy. Interestingly, they did not claim the opposite was true; they simply kept silent about the whole subject. Here, I think, the weight of the evidence — or of what was perceived as evidence — was too much to deny. The facts brought to light by proponents of protective legislation, coupled with the continual charges of immorality and ignorance among the foreign-born, made it obvious to all that there had indeed occurred a "degradation" of the working class. This was the area, then, where the critics of the image inflicted the greatest damage. Still, by not admitting the change openly — or by emphasizing that it was due to immigration alone — the average politician could remain hopeful about the industrial order. It may have been a truncated version of the respectable worker image that he retained, but it served its purpose.[16]

His tenacity was eventually to win official approval. Henry Oliver's replacement as chief of the Bureau of Statistics of Labor, Carroll Wright, was determined to set the agency on a new course. Wright was a young man with little political experience. Starting out as a poor farm boy in New Hampshire, he educated himself, rose to colonel during the war, and later, settling in Reading as a lawyer, served two terms as state senator. Having exhibited no overt sympathy for the cause of labor, he was as good a choice as any to head the "reformed" bureau. In his first report he quoted approvingly from a letter sent him by Francis Walker, director of the national census, which observed that "your office has only to prove itself superior alike to partisan dictation and to the seductions of theory, in order to command the cordial support of the press and of the body of citizens."[17]

Wright sought assiduously to follow Walker's advice. His reports (he headed the bureau until 1888) could not have been more unlike his predecessor's. Eschewing as much as possible all "theorizing," he dedicated the bureau to amassing a huge body of statistics relating to all aspects of the condition of labor. (Indeed, in this respect it became a model of its kind.) The reports were simply compilations of the results, with little interpretation of the data and few recommendations. Under the guise of impartial fact-gatherer, Wright could present himself as a neutral in the struggles between capital and labor.

But neutral he decidedly was not. Whereas Oliver's reports were suffused with anger at the circumstances of the typical worker, Wright's breathed satisfaction and hope. This is not to say he ignored *all* unpleasant facts. In his first two reports he directed attention to the workers' sometimes inadequate housing, poor safety conditions in factories, the dangers of excessive hours for the health of women, and similar evils. He became positively indignant about child labor, calling for "the extremest legislation in this direction." Yet these problems were not uppermost in his mind. As became clear with the passage of time, Wright was sanguine about the status of the worker. For him, as for other adherents of the respectable worker image, the most significant feature of that status was the worker's material well-being. In 1875 and 1876 he presented the results of extensive surveys into the matter, designed to find out whether the "wage system" was "natural and just." His answer was that, in balance, it was. While dismayed that it forced women and children to labor, and that it kept about 10% of all workers in poverty (his estimate), he pointed happily to the obverse: that the vast majority of working class families had an adequate income (even managed to save some of it), were well-fed and clothed, and enjoyed decent housing; and that quite a few (usually skilled) workers possessed such luxuries as sewing machines and pianos. Later, when the workday for adults was reduced to ten hours, he was satisfied that employees were no longer overworked and even came out against a further reduction. Continually he would stress that the Massachusetts worker was noticeably better off than the European laborer, compiling extensive data on conditions in England, France, and Germany to prove his point. As for the future, he had great faith that the worker's situation would improve, indeed *had* to improve. Skeptical about all "panaceas" for the problems of labor, he felt it was far better to trust in the general progress of the age to gradually and inevitably eliminate them. The most the state should do was to provide for helpless women and children, and above all, to assure everyone easy access to schooling. At one point he wrote that "when the state earnestly and actively undertakes the education or elementary training of the child-workers of the state, she will find no vexed labor questions which will at all disturb her peace."[18]

This was what most politicians wanted to hear. While not totally optimistic, in the main Wright's reports validated their own cursory impression that the worker's economic health was essentially sound. From all quarters — even the business community — there came enthusiastic praise for Wright's efforts. The *Advertiser*, a virulent foe of the bureau under Oliver, now found its work valuable. "The bureau, under its new organization, professes a disposition to ascertain and publish the exact truth, and to let the facts speak for themselves." It added, significantly, "It would be difficult for any person to learn . . . whether Colonel Wright belongs to or sympathizes with the labor reformers or not."[19] The bureau's reports furnished the foundation of hard facts so necessary to bolster the sagging image of the respectable worker.

Yet as one reads through the ruminations of these politicians, the feeling is inescapable that much of the life had indeed gone out of the image. It is a theme repeated almost as if by rote, an incantation to ward off disturbing visions. The realization had begun to set in that, for all its superficial resemblance to the prewar "laboring classes," the working class had changed and was now to some extent strange and even threatening. By reassuring themselves of its solid economic base, politicians could at least hope that it would eventually "elevate" itself, join the comfortable middle classes, and become absorbed into the mainstream of society. However, there was always the possibility it might not. Any sign that the working class was coalescing into a separate, antagonistic group, conceiving its interests as separate from the rest of society's, was pounced on with alarm.

These fears come through most vividly in the reaction to labor unions. When so devoted a friend of the workers as Wendell Phillips opposed strikes, one can imagine how the ordinary politician felt about the subject. Nearly everyone granted that workers had a right to form unions. Nor was any objection raised when they sought to bargain collectively. But when workers started using unions to attain economic leverage, they were invariably attacked. If a union tried to force nonmembers to join or to obey union rules, it was accused of violating individual freedom. More grievous still was the strike. While it was assumed unions had an abstract right to strike, few politicians were happy when they actually did. Strikes, many claimed, were useless. The iron law of wages, based on supply and demand, guaranteed that workers would always receive the highest pay that current economic conditions would allow. To try to extract more from the capitalist would eventually drive him out of business, forcing him to fire his employees. Even if the company survived, the worker almost always lost more pay for the time he was out than he made up for with his new wages. Therefore, it was held, workers should accept the wages offered, even in hard times, and hope for a general improvement in their trade. This was the position of nearly everyone who addressed the subject. Throughout these years the *Advertiser* kept up a drumbeat of criticism of the many strikes conducted by workers. Hardly any, in its view, were justifiable: All were harmful to the economy and ultimately futile. Carroll Wright concluded from a survey of strikes in Massachusetts between 1830 and 1880 that *"strikes generally prove powerless to benefit the condition of the wage classes."* The task was to convince the worker of this. "Strikes are born of ignorance, distrust, and the lack of that spirit of brotherhood between employer and employed upon which the best interests of both depend. These interests are mutual, and when this truth is recognized and acted upon in their mutual relations, strikes will cease."[20]

When strikes resulted in violence, the hostility to unions reached a fever pitch. The use of force to intimidate nonmembers or to keep out scabs was common in the turnouts of these years and always came in for heated condemnation. To the *Advertiser* such outrages "are the natural fruit of combinations which seek to dictate the manner in which men shall sell the labor of their hands and to compel the acquiescence of such as prefer to make terms for themselves." On this score nothing excited more indignation than the great railway strikes of 1877. None of these strikes actually spread to Massachusetts itself, but that was little solace. The shaken *Advertiser* called the episode "the most formidable revolt against capital ever witnessed in this country." That the strikers tried to prevent scabs from taking their place was bad enough, but when they interfered with railroad operations, and then when rioting and violence broke out in Chicago, Pittsburgh, Baltimore, Philadelphia, and a host of other cities, the reaction among "respectable" people was furious. Interestingly, as mentioned before, the *Advertiser* claimed that the mobs were not composed of "sturdy, honest laboring men," but rather were drawn from "an ignorant, vicious, reckless substratum of society," composed mainly of the foreign-born. The "extraordinary number" of such types in large eastern cities posed a threat to social order and deserved no leniency. (A mob such as the one in Chicago, said the paper, is like a "wild beast": "It is to be shot at sight when it begins to show its teeth.") Yet the strikers themselves were not absolved from blame: They should have foreseen the consequences of their acts, and in the long run it was they who would pay for the immense damage caused. As for their principal apologists, they were nothing but "immigrants who have not got rid of the notion that a man who is not a laborer for wages belongs to another class, which has prescriptive rights and privileges, between the members of which and his own class there is nothing in common, and can be no good understanding or free sympathy." It added: "The better class of American workmen know better"; capitalists did not "oppress" them. Still, the railroad strikes served as startling new evidence of the malice most workers bore towards their employers. Two years later the paper recommended arbitration of labor disputes with an interesting admission: "Much as there may be to be said about the common interest of labor and capital, they have relations that are in a degree antagonistic and which provoke serious differences."[21]

Working-class political activities bred similar anxieties. Besides the eight-hour movements, "labor reform" parties, and Ben Butler, politicians also had to contend with the rise of socialism in the United States and Europe. All were attacked vigorously, either by dismissing them as mere demagogues, office-seekers, muddle-headed fanatics, or Democrats in sheep's clothing or by ridiculing their beliefs. In a typical comment, the *Advertiser* asserted: "In a free country like ours both capital and labor can live and thrive without antagonism, if each will submit to reason and refuse to be led astray by jealousy and false theories." During the sixties these movements seemed little more than irritations, but over the following decade labor violence, the Paris Commune, and the rise of Butler showed that working-class agitation was going to be a persistent — and increasingly dangerous — phenomenon. More and more an effort was made to tie it to immigrants and their "foreign" ideas, or to "so-called 'social philosophers,' who go about preaching to men more ignorant, but not more malevolent, than themselves, that it is a crime for some men to be more industrious, more saving and more prosperous than others, and that all accumulated wealth is the result of stealing and oppression which it would be heroic to punish." By 1878 the paper was calling "the growth of the communistic spirit in our central and western cities" one of the most "disturbing forces" of the times. The Republican victory over Butler that year was viewed as a major triumph for the defenders of order and peace:

> The intelligent, industrious and sober citizens of Massachusetts have won an honorable and decisive victory over the factions of ignorance, discontent and disorder, marshalled by desperate demagogues, to capture the State. There was never before so favorable an occasion for the onslaught of the communistic elements, and there is not likely to be another in our generation. . . . If the cause which is overwhelmingly defeated had triumphed, a revolution would have been begun which would not only have degraded Massachusetts, but in its progress would have threatened the existence of the republic.

Plainly, worker agitation posed a threat to the very foundations of society, which it was the duty of every right-minded citizen to resist.[22]

Interwoven in the political dialogue of these years, then, was a growing tendency to see unions and workers' political activities as evidence of an alienated, unified, and even at times a dangerous working class. The fragile mask of optimism built upon the respectable worker image was beginning to show large cracks. How deep or common these fears were is difficult to determine. As the preceding paragraphs illustrate, they were voiced primarily by the leading Republican newspaper (one that, moreover, was the spokesman of nervous State Street financial interests) as well as by such elevated souls as Charles Francis Adams, who, in typical Adams fashion, worried that "the collision between the forces of associated capital and those of associated labor is likely to make itself felt throughout all the wide extent of human civilization."[23] More ordinary politicians, however, even if they agreed with the *Advertiser*'s forebodings, could hardly make such statements publicly. Criticism of unions or of worker agitation might be interpreted by their opponents as hostility to the aspirations of labor, costing them a sizable body of votes. So usually they said nothing.

Yet certainly one can detect a noticeable shift in their attitude toward the working class. They might continue to praise it, but in many respects they were a good deal less enthusiastic. At times it still could evoke their sympathy. An example is Governor William Washburn, exhorting the legislature to "fairly and honestly examine the condition of the laboring classes, upon whom the whole superstructure of the social organism rests":

> Because they are a part of ourselves, it devolves upon us to relieve them, as far as possible, from the grievances to which they are subjected. Their existence is not separate from the existence of the State; what tends to their welfare is calculated to promote the general welfare; in the last analysis their interest is identical with the interest of the upper classes; the least additon to their comfort is a gain to the whole community; and if their case is considered in the right spirit there is no good cause for antagonistic feeling.[24]

But even this eloquent plea comes in the same address in which Washburn rejects any proposal to restrict the workday! The simple fact was that workers were perceived less and less as "part of ourselves." Except among a decreasing minority of politicians, they excited no genuine concern. It is significant that postwar opponents of hours legislation used as one of their principal arguments the idea that helping workers in this way was an "improper" function of the government. (Before the war, opponents explicitly conceded the government had a right to pass such laws; they had been against them on other grounds.) Men who had bemoaned the plight of the insane, the uneducated, and particularly the enslaved — and who had countenanced unprecedented extensions of the state's power to aid these afflicted groups — could summon up little compassion for the problems of the worker.

At its most extreme their indifference could take the form of stern warnings against setting up public soup kitchens in the winter in the very depths of the depression. Such indiscriminate charity, it was said, was "virtually offering a bounty to pauperism. It promotes lying, deceit, unthriftiness, instability." More common was the constant practice of lecturing workers on their duty to help themselves, instead of looking to the government for protection. If they would only work harder without whining about excessive hours, if they would shun liquor, attend night school, turn away from sordid entertainments, and save money, whatever difficulties they might be having were sure to disappear. As the special commission of 1866 put it:

> Never was there a more glorious opportunity opened to the working men of any country, than of ours; but opportunity alone is not all that is needed; it is only as the opportunity is seized and used, wisely and manfully, by the working men themselves, that they can rise to the position of useful and honorable citizenship, . . . or reach that goal of true and noble manhood, that constitutes the only order of nobility recognized by the genius and spirit of our National Government.

Having dispensed this brave advice, the politician could then dismiss from his mind the possibility that these were people who might require his attention and, eventually, his aid.[25]

So, one by one, Massachusetts politicians closed ranks to repair the image of the respectable worker — and the *state*'s image as a progressive, prosperous, happy place. Through some desperate scrambling they managed to rescue it, ignored what was damaged beyond repair, slapped a new coat of statistical paint on the rest, and brandished it defiantly before the critics. Yet as with any myth persistently and tellingly challenged, their old trust in it was shaken. Their loud invocations masked its hollow core, and one senses that they knew it. Despite

their best efforts, a new note of uncertainty crept into political discourse, apprehension too. The working class was not behaving according
to the image: It was angry, threatening, no longer comprehensible.
Sooner or later it would have to be confronted as it really was. Meanwhile the reiteration of the respectable worker image could postpone
the inevitable — a fragile defense against despair, a prop under the
fading glory of the Commonwealth.

PART IV
Conclusion

"Our history seems a great political ro-mance."

— Edward Everett, 1830

Chapter 9

The Image As Invention

IN THE END, it is the disproportion that strikes us most of all.

The machine transformed Massachusetts. It offered a powerful new means for creating wealth. For nearly three-quarters of a century the state's citizens busily set about constructing the factories, cities, and the transportation, supply, and distribution mechanisms needed to exploit its advantages most effectively. True to its promise, it provided much — but demanded more. It fundamentally reordered society, arranging people in different groupings of class and status, altering the very pattern and tempo of their lives, fashioning a new environment and endowing them with a new destiny. It changed them. They become "a mechanical people."

Yet in searching for their response to this great transformation, we find so very little. Their leaders react with barely a shrug. They are not fascinated, exhilarated, perturbed, or deeply moved at all. They look at what is happening, and then turn away satisfied, leaving us open-mouthed at their equanimity.

The mystery deepens when we focus on what little they did say. Early in their industrial career they encountered the most significant and enduring of the machine's social consequences, the modern working class. This, one would think, was a phenomenon so novel, so unlike anything they had ever experienced before, that surely it must have excited curiosity. Fitfully, it did, but what came out of their half-hearted investigation was a complex of ideas — the image of the respectable worker — that had precious little to do with what it purported to describe. The working class was satisfyingly "elevated," the image reported; no need to worry. Nothing important had really changed. This fantastic concoction stifled further examination. Lulled by its assuring features, the state was able to proceed undaunted on its industrial course. True, after a while the image was questioned, its defects revealed, alternatives proposed. Yet, though damaged, it maintained tenaciously its hold over men's minds. It was too alluring to let go.

Why this disproportion? Why such a startling lack of concern, and such gross misapprehensions when politicians did address the subject? What could they have been thinking? There is no neat, simple answer to these questions. The more one probes, the clearer it becomes that what is called for is a series of explanations, layered one on top of another. Each must be examined, then peeled away, as one might an onion, to reveal the next layer underneath.

The first hypothesis that must be considered concerns these leaders themselves — as well as the entire premise upon which this study has been based. In chapter 1 it was posited that the best way of discovering how the people of Massachusetts thought and felt about industrialization was to see what their public figures said about it; that the imperatives of a competitive, democratic political system would virtually force them to make contact with and articulate the popular reaction to this vital social change. But is it possible this assumption has been misleading? Could these politicians have had a strong motive for ignoring, or distorting, the public's impression of the industrial order, and somehow succeeded in short-circuiting the political mechanism that would have made them come to terms with it?

This is in fact the kind of argument that would be made by someone who held to a class-based interpretation of history, such as a Marxist. In a developing capitalist economy like Massachusetts', the argument would run, the major political parties, though they might appear sharply divided, would in reality be closely allied with the dominant social class, the bourgeoisie. Politicians themselves would most likely hail from that class, certainly very few would arise from the working class, and almost all would probably share the goals and outlook of the leading businessmen of the day. Even if they were not virtual tools of these men, they would be so well-attuned to the capitalist point of view as to be in effect their spokesmen. If this is true, the respectable worker image or a similar complex of ideas was almost inevitable. It was what every capitalist dreamed his employees should be like, and if he could convince the public that that was indeed what they were like, he would have, with one stroke, removed the major objection to industrial progress under capitalism. With this in mind, the politicians gladly donned the rose-colored glasses. The image of the respectable worker was propounded, and received nearly unanimous assent in the political arena. Since no other choices were offered, the public was forced to buy these tawdry goods — at the very moment (this would be the other side of the Marxist argument) they themselves were deeply troubled over the impact of industrialization on their lives. The image was thus the product of a narrow class bias, devised by men who had a clear stake in the success of the factory system, and a gross distortion not only of the actual situation of the worker, but of the way in which the great mass of the population conceived the profound changes going on around them.

There is certainly something to be said for this argument. The politicians of Massachusetts do seem to have been "bourgeois," in the widest sense of the word. Thus far there have been no comprehensive studies of the social status of political leaders in this period. But impressionistic evidence testifies overwhelmingly to their comfortable situation. Nearly all, even on the Democratic side, came from the ranks of merchants, lawyers, clergymen, editors, shopkeepers, industrialists, investors and entrepreneurs, managers, or well-to-do farmers. This was true even for local posts in cities and towns. Only rarely did a self-employed artisan, much less a grimy-handed worker, run for office. There was apparently some easing of this rule as time went on. By the fifties men of relatively humble origins started to make a name for themselves in politics. The two most famous examples are Henry Wilson, who began life as a cobbler, and Nathaniel Banks, who worked as a bobbin-boy in a cotton factory. After the war urban political machines began to serve as avenues of upward mobility for the lowly. But even then success in politics was relatively rare for men of this type: Government remained the preserve of the bourgeois. It would hardly be surprising if these politicians were profoundly influenced by their social class. If they were Whigs they probably knew personally, might even have been related to, the leading businessmen of their locality. Even if they were not, they must have accepted easily business values and the capitalist way of looking at things. Moreover, it is equally probable that they had little contact with the laboring classes, little sense of their real situation, and, as the years passed, little sympathy for whatever they knew of their plight. For the gulf between the poor and the well-off, always deep in Massachusetts, was widening all the time. Fitted with this sort of class blinders, these men naturally embraced the image of the respectable worker. Their background, values, desires, told them this was the way things must be, and their limited social experience did not tell them anything different.

Yet does it follow from this set of facts that the respectable worker image was *simply* the product of narrow class bias and unreflective of the larger social concerns of the day? I think not. The course of Massachusetts political history, and what is known of popular attitudes of the time, suggest strongly that politicians' views could not have been, and in fact were not, very dissimilar from those of most of their constituents.

First, it must be recalled that the political system of Massachusetts did exhibit, in the most forceful way possible, the corrective mechanisms described in chapter 1. Leaders who tried to ignore or distort popular perceptions and attitudes paid the political price; those who catered to them were rewarded. In the 1840s and 1850s the dominant Whig party made a concerted effort to avoid taking anything more than a timid, equivocal stand on slavery and its expansion. Dissenters tried initially to work within the organization to change its stand. When that failed, they left to form the Free Soil and then the Republican parties. Those who remained never wavered from their original course, only to find the party's ranks seriously depleted by the tide of antislavery sentiment surging through the state. The final blow, however, came with the nativist episode of the mid-fifties. Once again the Whig leadership tried to ignore the problem, refusing (to their credit) to give in to the growing nativist hysteria that was especially acute among Whig voters. But once again they suffered by it, only this time the cost was the extinction of their organization. In short, the strongest, best-financed, best-connected political party of its day lost, in the space of one decade, almost all its support when it failed to respond in a satisfactory way to a growing, sharply emotional, widespread concern over slavery and the "threat" of immigration. The voters simply would not be placated by honeyed words or half-hearted, muddled pronouncements and in the end proved perfectly willing to abandon the party when a better alternative came along. This presents an important question: If the Whigs could not fool the voters in these instances, why should one assume they (or any other party) would have been able to disregard a festering unease among the public about industrialization, to soothe its anxieties with the respectable worker image? Is it not far more likely that there was little such unease, and thus they were able to propound that image and not incur losses thereby?

The historical record poses still another question. If the public was far more distressed about industrialization than the statements of mainstream politicians would indicate, would not the time have been ripe for a new political organization to come to the fore, to seize upon this distress and make it the basis of a successful campaign? Such an organization could have charged the Whigs/Republicans with failing to respond to the plight of the huge working class, with a nearly total reluctance to recognize, much less deal with, the serious social consequences of industrialization. But what in fact happened? It has already been shown how the Democrats, who supposedly would have had everything to gain, did not adopt this strategy in any but a very limited way. Even more telling is the fate of the two "labor" parties of this period, the Working Men's and Labor Reform parties. They did take this line, and played a major role in injecting new ideas about the worker into the political arena. Yet both were incredibly short-lived. The heyday of the Working Men's party was 1833–1834; at its peak it garnered 6% of the vote. The Labor Reform party, a stronger effort, managed (with the help of the prohibitionists) to capture as much as 15% of the vote and several legislative seats, but it too passed quickly (1869–1871). If there was widespread concern about industrialization, surely these were the two parties that most emphatically addressed that concern, but they expired almost as soon as they appeared. (One could argue they failed because they were poorly financed, amateur efforts; so was the nativist American party, and it swept to power within two years.) Either they were extraordinarily inept, or their appeals fell on unreceptive ears.

Finally, one comes to an intriguing puzzle: The politicians who set forth the respectable worker image were continually returned to office by an electorate that contained large numbers of workers — who supposedly should have known that the image did not describe their situation.[1] What is even stranger is that far more often than not, the leading factory towns and the major cities, including many of the hotbeds of labor agitation, voted *Whig* (or Republican).[2] How can this be? In the

absence of a secret ballot, intimidation by employers may account partially for it, but the full answer has to lie elsewhere.

It is useful to try to reconstruct how the typical worker must have
conceived his situation. He lived, first, in a state (and nation) where
capitalist enterprise on a small scale had a very long popular tradition;
chances are that at one time or another he (or certainly most of his
immediate ancestors, if he was born in America) had been involved in it.
The ways of business, the acquisitive spirit, and the ethos of individual
economic competition and advancement were almost inbred in him. It is
for this reason that he so reluctantly abandoned the idea he could improve his condition in the same manner as the self-employed. Although
labor agitation was very strong in this period, it must be remembered
that quite a few workers did not join in. They wanted to better themselves through their own efforts: hard work, extra jobs, finding employment for the rest of their family, saving their small wages, grabbing at
every opportunity to elevate themselves. Even in a town of extreme
labor solidarity like Lynn a great many workers thought in these terms.
Among skilled artisan workers, the dream of eventually opening their
own shop died very slowly, even when it was clear such efforts had little
chance of surviving in a modern industrial economy. In other words,
many workers were "bourgeois," not in status, but in outlook. Enterprise and improvement were constantly on their minds and colored
their image of themselves.[3]

It is important to remember also the all-pervading rootlessness and
confusion of the average worker's existence. Before mid-century he
most likely drifted into this way of life. He was a farmer whose land had
given out, an immigrant just off the boat, an independent artisan who
could not compete with factory-made goods; or *she* was someone who
had never held a job before. He thus came to his new situation unprepared, not knowing what to expect or how to make sense of it. Doubtless
he did not foresee what followed: the instability of employment, the
continual search for new jobs, the movement from place to place, never
putting down deep roots or forming lasting ties. It was a hard life,
dispiriting, demeaning, but above all very difficult to fathom.

Imagine now this man confronted by some politician reciting the
many-splendored virtues of the laborers of Massachusetts. How would
he react? Some historians have contended that workers in these years
generally subscribed to a full-fledged "labor ideology," a mirror which

held before them a clear picture of their true situation. Some of them evidently did, especially in places like Lynn, with its close-knit, stable, knowledgeable artisan community. Among most other workers, though, particularly before the Civil War, this was probably not so. They may have joined a union, attended a ten-hour rally, even gone out on strike to express their discontent, but discontent does not necessarily translate into ideology. Most were probably not at all certain what to make of the respectable worker image. Although it did not seem to describe their own experience, still, it did have flattering bourgeois overtones. Many must have felt they *should* believe it. Most important, workers usually had (as yet) no well-formed model of their own, no separate tradition to deploy against it. For the moment, they were simply confused. Thus, no doubt vaguely aware that all was not right, they voted for these mainstream politicians, even for Whigs and Republicans, so closely identified with their bosses and the most articulate and aggressive proponents of the respectable worker. (They were not the only workers to react this way: Western European socialists have long lamented the large numbers of workers who vote conservative, even when there exist well-established socialist parties.) In ratifying the respectable worker image, they expressed their hope of what they might still become, declaring their trust in the promise of a new order that had not yet disillusioned them.

What was happening in Massachusetts, then, does not quite follow a Marxist script. While the respectable worker image did grow, in part, out of the class consciousness of the politicians who devised it, this does not mean it was, for that reason, grounded solely in class. For in their society the "bourgeois" outlook was common, even among the workers themselves. These politicians' backgrounds were not special sources of illumination, foreign to the masses. They acted rather as refracting lenses, bringing into sharper focus — indeed, creating a definite image out of — a vague penumbra of popular attitudes, ideas, values, and desires. Conversely, there is little evidence — in fact, strong reason to doubt — that there existed some deeply felt, pervasive popular discontent about industrialization which politicians were able to ignore. True, not everyone welcomed the respectable worker image with enthusiasm: A substantial (and growing) number of laborers and their middle-class sympathizers had their doubts. But the bulk of the population does not appear to have been disturbed by it. They did not know what to make of

the new economic and social changes. Looking to their leaders for guidance, they were provided with answers that did not seem improbable.

Hence the search for the origins of the image of the respectable
worker cannot end with the argument from class bias. That argument,
however, does suggest a further line of inquiry. If politicians and public
did share the same bourgeois outlook, might there not have been other
ideas, values, aspirations held in common that might help explain this
peculiar construction? What is it about their circumstances and experi-
ences that would account for their strange readiness to believe the
respectable worker image?

The broadest answer to these questions lies in the trait that these
people shared with all humanity, a simple reluctance to accept change.
What seems like unconcern really masks a fear of the unknown and the
unfamiliar. The respectable worker image, according to this interpretation, was a way of denying unpleasant new realities. It was a disguise for
the working class, a trick outfit to convince people that the worker was
nothing more than a newfangled version of the old "mechanic," with
more or less the same steady virtues and qualities. This type of explanation has long been popular among historians. Ever since Marx, it has
been recognized that in the past most people have demonstrated a
marked unwillingness to come to grips with large social changes. There
is usually a lag between social perception and evolving circumstances.
The mechanics of this lag were perceptively explained by William
James. "Our minds," he wrote,

> . . . grow in spots; and like grease-spots, the spots spread. But we let
> them spread as little as possible: we keep unaltered as much of our old
> knowledge, as many of our old prejudices and beliefs, as we can. We
> patch and tinker more than we renew. The novelty soaks in; it stains
> the ancient mass; but it is also tinged by what absorbs it. Our past
> apperceives and cooperates; and in the equilibrium in which each step
> forward in the process of learning terminates, it happens relatively
> seldom that the new fact is added *raw*. More usually it is embedded
> cooked, as one might say, or stewed down in the sauce of the old. New
> truths thus are the resultants of new experiences and of old truths
> combined and mutually modifying one another.[4]

Man, in this analysis, is a conservative creature. Throughout his life he
is engaged in constructing a world view, a body of ideas that furnishes

explanations and guidance as to how things work (and should work). Through these ideas he is linked with others in his society in a community of shared beliefs. Understandably, such a dearly obtained instrument is not lightly tampered with, much less discarded. New information, new thoughts must undergo close scrutiny, not simply to find out whether they are true or good, but often for the more elemental reason that they are *inherently unsettling*, no matter what their real value. It is therefore the inevitable fate of new ideas to be questioned, attacked, resisted, to make their way slowly and hesitantly into men's minds. For every one to be adopted many more are discarded. Those that gain favor are so frequently "stewed down in the sauce of the old" that they emerge, as in some of the more fanciful creations of French cuisine, an almost unrecognizable shell of their former selves. New ideas and old influence and fertilize one another, and the whole process is imbued with no little passion.

Obviously, a comparable process was occurring in nineteenth-century Massachusetts. Yet this interpretation can explain only so much, for it comes up against one overwhelming objection: The people of Britain (and, I submit, practically every industrializing nation in history) did not exhibit anywhere near as much reluctance to admit the significance and gravity of the social changes wrought by the machine. Why such a short "lag" in Britain and such a long and extensive one in the United States? Other explanations are patently called for.

The next logical step is to examine the social and economic context of industrialization in Massachusetts, and its actual progress there. In these areas, as already noted, there were several factors that predisposed the state to the machine. The Massachusetts economy was already diversified and market-oriented. Its businessmen were willing to take risks. There was a fair degree of occupational and geographic mobility among its people. Important groups closely associated with the preindustrial order were able to make their separate peace with the factory. All these traits produced a certain adaptability, so that the introduction of the machine was not nearly so jarring as it might otherwise have been. Likewise, the impact of industrialization on the working class could have been much worse. The lot of the Massachusetts worker was hardly easy, but it still was markedly better than his British counterpart's, a fact often remarked by contemporaries. The well-publicized horrors of England's mills and mines (and its cities generally) were rare in the Bay State. Conversely, one must remember that a good deal of public attention was centered on the factory girls of Lowell and Waltham. The benign paternalism of the mill owners in these cities, while not typical of Massachusetts employers, earned widespread praise, eventually achieving national, even worldwide renown. The happy factory girl became the symbol of the state's industrial system, reassuring many of its benevolent tendencies.

These points carry us further toward a full explanation, but they too have their limitations. The favorable preconditions to industrialization plainly helped to pave the way for the factory, but we should recall once again that many of these preconditions existed in Britain too. And the milder course of industrialization on American shores was hardly so strikingly different from what occurred in Britain as to account for the sharp divergence in response. Still one must search further.

I propose that better progress can be made by approaching the problem from a different perspective. All of the preceding explanations are predicated on the assumption that the Commonwealth's "response" to industrialization is to be taken literally as that: a pure response, a mechanical reaction to concrete social and economic changes. This paradigm — a common one with those who study the evolution of social thought — sees man's ideas about society as essentially a narrow attempt to make sense of the world about him and to justify (or criticize) the way that world functions. That social thought serves such purposes is undeniably true, but to view it as that alone is to miss a good part of what goes into the making of these ideas. Social thought is more than an abstract effort of perception and judgment: It is an *invention*, and, as such, reflects the ideals, expectations, anxieties, assumptions, and hopes of the people who created it. Inevitably, then, it becomes "distorted," mirroring not only the realities it seeks to describe but also the minds of the people themselves. To some extent they *impose* a vision of the reality they want to see, or at least one they can accept. It is only when social thought is viewed from this angle that one can finally account for the singular way in which Massachusetts came to terms with the machine.

I believe that two sets of concerns are at work here.[5] The first is the state's intense preoccupation with economic endeavor. The people of

Massachusetts in these years were — and had always been — an enterprising lot. All over the state they were busy setting up shops and businesses, coaxing harvests from the niggardly soil, combating the elements to haul fish from the sea, braving countless hazards to trade in every ocean on the globe. On their own terms, these were remarkable achievements. And the Bay Staters' persistence was rewarded with wealth beyond that of almost every other state.

A people devoted so fervently to making a living, to establishing a working economy and amassing worldly goods, to seeking out new opportunities, were likely to approach industrialization from a very particular focus. They were not going to be overly concerned with its possible social consequences. Their first question would be: Will it help us materially? As they became acquainted with the factory's advantages, they answered in a strong affirmative; from then on they wanted to hear nothing derogatory about it. It was bringing them all the wealth they had hoped for, and more. So they became fervently attached to it and, like some moon-struck lover, blind to its faults.

Out of this preoccupation with money-getting came much of the impetus for the respectable worker image. In antebellum Massachusetts it was taken for granted that he who worked was an eminently worthwhile citizen, helping himself achieve a position of comfort and respect within the community and aiding society in its continuing advance toward prosperity. The very history of Massachusetts proved that axiom. Is it thus surprising that they found so appealing the idea that the worker *had to be* a well-rewarded, elevated, favored individual? The employee, previously a peripheral figure, had become central to the operations of the economy. It was inconceivable that he should not be its beneficiary. From his own unique position, and in his own way, he did what everyone else was doing. How could he be all that different? The people of Massachusetts, with their entrepreneurial bent, wanted very much to believe in a respectable worker as the perfect complement to a "progressive" economy. Since they did not care to examine too closely the actual situation of the working class, they were no doubt gratified when their leaders presented him in this favorable light.

The other force shaping Massachusetts' reaction to industrialization is not as easy to define. It can be termed, loosely, the "spirit of the age," one which Bay Staters shared with their fellow Americans throughout the half-century before the Civil War. However difficult to pin down, this spirit is not at all hard to sense. One has only to peruse a random selection of the political speeches of the era to be struck by it immediately: a remarkably naïve optimism about the capacities of human nature and of America as a nation.

These people were convinced they lived in a special place, a special time. To be sure, they admitted imperfection. The United States was faced with some disturbing temptations and dilemmas, suffering from, among other things, a certain crudeness and restlessness of spirit, excessive partisanship, an undue regard for the dollar, and, most frightening, sharp sectional hostility. Still, they preferred to dwell on the nation's uniqueness. America was conceived in freedom and justice. With the Revolution it had thrown off the decaying ideas, traditions, institutions of a benighted Europe. It had created the freest, most enlightened government on earth, with a system of laws that treated all men alike. It possessed a social order with no oppressed masses or privileged elite. In short, it had established an environment that would unleash the full potential of man's powers. All that had held people down in Europe was miraculously gone. They would carry the race to its highest possibilities.

A people with such a Promethean self-image were going to have an exaggerated sense of their own power. They refused to be bound by the experience of the past or of others. Everything about their nation scorned the idea of limitations. They seemed capable of realizing whatever they might imagine, and, starting from scratch, they might imagine anything. Their society was fluid, forming, amenable to conscious shaping. It could and would be whatever they wanted it to be.

Among these people was introduced the machine. Quickly they assumed that what had happened to the British would not happen to them. The United States, they were convinced, could bypass the failures of European industrialism and fashion a factory system on a new model, bringing unprecedented wealth to all and oppression to none. All that was needed was native intelligence and resourcefulness, good will, common sense, and a healthy awareness of the moral verities. They went even further: The very act of setting the factory down in pastoral America would strip it of any potential for harm. The machine would be tamed by the garden, and rendered benign.

Given these expectations, the respectable worker followed naturally.

He was the fulfillment of the prophecy, the confirmation of their uniqueness — the living proof for the Old World that society could be founded on principles of freedom, equality, and opportunity. He substantiated their faith in all they were doing and hoped to do. With him they announced to the world that a working class could come forth without any faltering in the march of human progress.

Ultimately, it was from this paradoxical combination of materialism and innocence that Massachusetts would develop its response to the machine. Each of these qualities can drive men powerfully; in tandem they become formidable indeed. A people thus inspired can obscure sordid reality with cheap visions, dispel forebodings with facile hopes. And they can go onward, barely conscious of what they are making of themselves and of their land.

Appendices, Notes,
Bibliographical Note,
and Index

Appendices

APPENDIX A: THE CALCULATION OF TABLES 5 AND 6

Tables 5 and 6 in chapter 2 present estimates of the size of various divisons of the Massachusetts labor force, estimates which have been derived from census data and other contemporary records. Since the material in the tables is particularly important for the thesis of this work, an explanation of how I arrived at these figures is in order.

To start with, I must emphasize again that these *are* only estimates. The censuses upon which they are based not only do not use the classifications employed here, they do not even provide data from which these estimates may be computed directly. None of the tabulations consulted, for instance, breaks down comprehensively independent and nonindependent (employed) persons. None but those of 1870 and 1880 breaks down agricultural and nonagricultural labor the way it is done in Tables 5 and 6 — and even those two do so only roughly. Furthermore, none of these censuses is terribly reliable. The estimates for 1837, 1845, and 1855 are drawn from state censuses of manufactures, which were compiled mainly for the purpose of providing information on factory production and only incidentally to discover facts about the labor force. People were counted only if they were involved in "manufacturing establishments," as defined by the census takers — definitions that usually omitted very small businesses and those working at home (not to mention many enterprises that are now considered to be manufacturing). Farm owners and laborers were not counted at all (their numbers are inferred here from the United States censuses of the intervening years). The estimates for 1870 and 1880, based on national censuses, are much more reliable. Still, they contain discrepancies and tend to undercount women and children engaged in manufacturing.

In drawing up these tables I confronted two problems: translating the figures given in the censuses into the categories I wanted to investigate, and making an estimate of the total labor force. The first was the most difficult, especially in determining the number of independent and nonindependent persons. Occasionally, the censuses supplied hints about the number of employees in a given industry or trade. Sometimes the figure could be guessed by comparing the total work force in an industry or trade with the number of "establishments" given. Most often, however, my estimate was based on my own knowledge of the stage of development of the field at that particular time.

With certain types of occupations, a fair amount of guesswork was necessary. For example, agricultural laborers were counted only in 1870 and 1880; before that they were included with all farmers or not counted at all. Even in 1870 and 1880 a number of agricultural laborers were returned under "laborers (not specified)," so the estimates in the tables are larger than those of the corresponding censuses. The labor force in transportation and commerce was hardly counted at all in 1837, 1845, and 1855. The estimates in the tables are therefore speculative. The labor force under "fishing and extractive" consists principally of fishermen. Many of these men worked at fishing only seasonally and may have described themselves as something else for the census taker. Often they declared themselves "mariners" (as did those in ocean-going commerce). These factors were taken into account for the "fishing and extractive" classification. The estimates for domestic service for 1837, 1845, and 1855 are extrapolations from the 1850 and 1860 national censuses, which list the number of male servants only. Female servants were guessed. The white-collar figures for those three years are likewise based on scanty information and guesswork.

The second problem was the vital one of determining the total labor force, in order to fix the proportion of the total for each classification and to find out how many workers were left unaccounted for by the various censuses. The 1870 and 1880 censuses conveniently tabulate the total. For 1855 the figure was found by, first, averaging the total state populations for 1850 and 1860 to get an estimate for 1855, then, multiplying the labor force figures for 1860 by the same proportion that the 1855 estimate bore to the 1860 population. The most problematic years were 1837 and 1845. Here the number of female workers seems to have been counted carefully (outside of domestic servants), the number of male workers very incompletely. I noticed that in the more accurate later censuses, as the figures below indicate,[1] approximately 90% of all males over fifteen in Massachusetts worked. So, to the female worker figures for these years I added a sum equivalent of 90% of the male population over fifteen to arrive at an estimate of the total labor force.

	1855 (estimate)	1870	1880
Males over 15	358,900	480,600	600,700
Male workers over 15	333,500	439,400	534,300
Male workers as percentage of total males over 15	93%	91%	89%

These tables, then, should be read with all the foregoing qualifications in mind. They are not the kind of statistics that would satisfy a demographer or social historian. Rather, they aim to provide approximations of certain broad trends over a long period of time. Some of the estimates, though, are more reliable then others. The figures for 1870 and 1880 are probably very close to the actual occupational breakdowns. Those for 1845 and 1855 are a rougher approximation. Those for 1837 are largely guesswork. And among the various occupational classifications, the figures for nonindependent workers in manufacturing are by far the most accurate — for every year, including 1837. If anything, the

numbers under this heading are probably too low, since the relevant censuses
failed to count those engaged in domestic manufacturing. These tables, therefore, are above all a useful record of the growth of the factory working class —
and by extension, of the entire working class, of which the operatives formed so
large a part.

APPENDIX B: POLITICIANS SYSTEMATICALLY STUDIED FOR THIS WORK

Listed below are the names of the forty-two political figures whose extant public
writings were examined for this study. Some of the writings of other politicians
were also eventually included in my survey, but these were the only ones whose
entire output was systematically researched.

Adams, Charles Francis, Sr.	Henshaw, David
Adams, John Quincy	Hoar, George F.
Allen, Samuel C.	Lincoln, Levi, Jr.
Appleton, Nathan	Lloyd, James
Bancroft, George	Lyman, Theodore
Banks, Nathaniel P.	Mann, Horace
Boutwell, George	Mills, Elijah
Brooks, John	Morton, Marcus
Bullock, Alexander H.	Otis, Harrison Gray
Butler, Benjamin F.	Palfrey, John Gorham
Choate, Rufus	Pickering, Timothy
Curtis, Benjamin R.	Quincy, Josiah
Cushing, Caleb	Rantoul, Robert, Jr.
Dana, Richard Henry, Jr.	Schouler, William
Davis, John	Sedgwick, Theodore, Jr.
Dawes, Henry	Strong, Caleb
Eustis, William	Sumner, Charles
Everett, Alexander H.	Walker, Amasa
Everett, Edward	Webster, Daniel
Gore, Christopher	Wilson, Henry
Hallett, Benjamin F.	Winthrop, Robert C.

APPENDIX C: VOTING BEHAVIOR OF SOME PRINCIPAL CITIES, 1830–1880

Tables C-1 and C-2, below, offer evidence concerning the voting behavior of
some of the leading commercial and industrial towns and cities of Massachusetts
between 1830 and 1880.[1] Two questions are addressed here: How popular were
the Whig and Republican parties in these localities? And how well did various
minor parties fare?

TABLE C-1. Percentage of Total Vote for Whig (to 1854) or Republican (from 1855) Gubernatorial Candidates, 1830–1880[a]

00*	less than majority (or plurality) of total
00	more than 5 percentage points below party's statewide tally
00	more than 10 percentage points below party's statewide tally

	Statewide	Boston	Worcester	Springfield	Chicopee	Haverhill	Lynn	Lowell	Lawrence	Waltham	Fall River	New Bedford	Taunton
1830	72	82	74	62		55	67	60		90	98	76	na
1831	54	71	47	51		61	34*	53		50	61	50	61
1832	53	61	56	61		51	24*	59		46	33*	38*	33*
1833	40	48	64	55		74	18*	42		29*	21*	24*	16*
1834	58	66	77	63		52	30*	57		41	44*	51	33*
1835	58	62	60	55		47*	53	52		61	71	45*	33*
1836	54	62	65	54		42*	37*	49*		41*	45*	45*	38*
1837	61	72	65	60		53	49*	63		57	53	56	59
1838	55	64	66	60		56	42*	63		47*	51	55	49*
1839	50*	57	60	49		57	44*	56		47*	54	53	46*
1840	56	62	69	57		59	49*	60		53	51	54	50
1841	52	58	66	49*		57	44*	53		47*	46*	49*	45*
1842	47*	51	59	48*		45*	37*	47*		44*	42*	50	42*
1843	48	59	57	48		43	41*	52		43*	46*	56	39*
1844	52	63	60	51		51	45*	50		45*	46*	59	47*
1845	49	50	46	49		51	45	58		39*	53	56	49
1846	54	66	58	57		49	45*	64		45*	64	64	60
1847	51	56	59	55		53	42*	53		41*	57	61	58
1848	50	69	30*	57		45	30*	54		41	63	59	57
1849	49	68	30*	51		44	39	54		44*	52	58	59
1850	47	67	26*	46	52	48	34*	52	55	46	61	57	56
1851	47	60	32*	49	57	44	39*	49	53	47	45	53	55
1852	45	63	30*	44	55	41	44	42	44	48	42	51	54
1853	48	66	30*	42*	65	43	42	50	48	47	na	52	56
1854	21*	31*	14*	16*	19*	16*	15*	22*	8*	27*	16*	21*	14*
1855	27*	14*	37	23*	34	41	33*	24*	14*	18*	34*	33*	17*
1856	No Republican candidate												
1857	47	31*	57	49	48	65	49	43	47	51	51	55	43
1858	58	43*	65	50	52	67	63	54	57	59	64	59	62
1859	54	44	63	49	57	59	60	52	55	54	57	53	28*
1860	64	48	65	62	67	71	57	66	59	52	79	78	73
1861	68	55	66	74	92	78	69	68	60	57	84	86	78
1862	60	45*	68	60	61	69	63	58	54	47*	79	82	69
1863	71	62	76	72	74	77	81	72	63	67	90	85	79
1864	72	61	76	74	71	73	79	68	68	70	81	87	77
1865	77	64	79	75	73	80	86	76	68	76	77	86	85
1866	78	69	81	79	68	76	86	77	69	80	86	88	88
1867	58	45*	58	61	57	60	56	60	51	55	68	77	75
1868	68	53	73	66	58	73	70	66	57	64	70	78	76
1869	54	41*	60	50	51	48	44	58	39*	49*	60	71	58

	Statewide	Boston	Worcester	Springfield	Chicopee	Haverhill	Lynn	Lowell	Lawrence	Waltham	Fall River	New Bedford	Taunton
1870	53	46	55	49	48	50	31*	55	43*	47	49	55	59
1871	55	49	56	54	27*	55	41	54	37*	53	49	52	61
1872	69	60	67	64	57	69	66	67	51	58	72	81	79
1873	55	46*	36*	42*	50*	55	49*	42*	43*	44*	54	75	80
1874	48*	36*	47*	33*	32*	55	50	53	45*	43*	41*	49*	45*
1875	49	49	44*	54	46*	54	40*	50	46*	47*	49*	45	52
1876	54	44*	52	54	47*	56	51	55	53	53	60	49	54
1877	50	48*	51	55	47	47	44	42*	46*	54	40*	41*	62
1878	53	44*	52	52	42*	51	39*	46*	41*	58	43*	60	57
1879	51	42*	51	50	41*	48	40*	42*	39*	50	36*	57	54
1880	59	48*	59	62	48*	58	52	54	50	60	58	70	65

a All figures rounded to nearest whole percent.

Table C-1 presents the percentage of the vote gained by Whig or Republican gubernatorial candidates in these towns and cities and in the state as a whole.[2] In the fifty elections covered by the table the Whig or Republican candidates carried the state forty-five times. In every city but two (Lynn and Waltham) they won either a majority or plurality in at least two out of every three elections. In five of the thirteen cities (Worcester, Springfield, Haverhill, Lawrence, New Bedford) they won at least four out of every five (and just missed with Lawrence). Even in the two cities where they were the least popular, Lynn and Waltham, they won, respectively, twenty-five and thirty-one times.

The table also indicates those instances when the vote in each city was more than five percentage points below the party's statewide vote, and more than ten percentage points below. Here, Whigs and Republicans show up less well, but still strong. In a clear majority of cases the Whig/Republican vote was *not* more than 5% lower than the statewide vote. In quite a few cases, in fact, it was higher. Only Lynn, Lawrence, and (after the mid-fifties) Boston proved regularly unable to match these parties' statewide percentages.

Since workers formed the great mass of the electorate in these towns and cities, the evidence suggests strongly that they were only slightly less enthusiastic about the Whig/Republican hegemony than voters elsewhere in the state.

Table C-2 deals with the willingness of these towns and cities to abandon the major parties to support minor party candidates for governor. Six minor parties are covered. In the case of the Working Men's party of 1833–1834, the results were mixed. In some places it did quite well, in others (including, oddly, Lynn) very poorly. With the Liberty and Free Soil parties, an equally confusing picture emerges. The former attracted significant support only in Haverhill; elsewhere, it did as well as in the rest of the state (the two major seaports,

TABLE C-2. Percentage of Total Vote for Gubernatorial Candidates of Selected Minor Parties, for Selected Years, 1833–1880[a]

1833–1834	Working Men's party
1842–1847	Liberty party
1848–1853	Free Soil party
1854–1858	American party (nativist)
1869–1871	Labor Reform party (combined in 1870 with Prohibition party)
1880	Greenback party

	Statewide	Sample avg.	Boston	Worcester	Springfield	Chicopee	Haverhill	Lynn	Lowell	Lawrence	Waltham	Fall River	New Bedford	Taunton
1830														
1831														
1832														
1833	6	6	9	0	7		0	0	12		6	11	9	7
1834	3	2	5	0	2		0	0	0		0	1	0	13
1835														
1836														
1837														
1838														
1839														
1840														
1841														
1842	5	4	3	3	2		9	9	5		0	5	2	4
1843	7	6	4	7	6		17	7	7		0	6	2	7
1844	7	6	4	7	6		9	5	8		2	8	2	6
1845	8	5	3	7	5		12	6	6		3	2	1	6
1846	10	8	9	10	8		20	6	9		2	6	1	5
1847	9	6	4	12	5		9	9	6		2	6	1	5
1848	29	30	21	57	16		31	46	34		19	24	24	29
1849	23	21	12	50	9		21	25	22		11	24	18	21
1850	23	19	12	51	11	7	21	23	22	14	9	19	22	17
1851	21	17	10	42	12	3	19	21	17	8	8	29	24	14
1852	27	25	17	44	17	11	22	32	28	15	13	39	34	23
1853	24	20	12	40	10	7	23	31	25	14	12	na	27	18
1854	63	68	57	62	68	70	75	73	68	78	55	67	63	77
1855	38	41	38	27	33	31	31	38	43	59	39	52	46	53
1856	62	63	44	56	54	53	74	70	67	66	48	80	71	70
1857	29	27	38	18	8	20	17	34	29	29	25	36	31	36
1858	10	9	13	5	4	11	5	14	12	11	4	9	11	7
1859														
1860														
1861														
1862														
1863														
1864														
1865														
1866														
1867														

	Statewide	Sample avg.	Boston	Worcester	Springfield	Chicopee	Haverhill	Lynn	Lowell	Lawrence	Waltham	Fall River	New Bedford	Taunton
1868														
1869	10	11	3	14	20	5	33	37	6	5	0	5	7	0
1870	15	17	9	9	18	9	25	47	18	12	8	24	15	12
1871	5	8	1	3	2	15	8	24	8	10	1	18	1	8
1872														
1873														
1874														
1875														
1876														
1877														
1878														
1879														
1880	2	2	1	2	2	1	5	7	0	2	1	3	0	1

[a] All figures rounded to nearest whole percent

Boston and New Bedford, being notably unenthusiastic). The Free Soil party, however, picked up impressive support in some of the cities, particularly Worcester. Boston as well as the small cotton textile towns of Chicopee, Lawrence, and Waltham were still cool. The nativist American party of the mid-fifties captured cities with relatively few recent immigrants and was less successful in those with many (like Boston), for the largely Catholic immigrants voted overwhelmingly against it. The Labor Reform and Greenback parties did exceptionally well in Lynn, Haverhill, and Fall River; in the other cities, the gains were fair to poor.

Two key trends emerge from this table. The first is the great disparity among the various cities in their support of each of these very dissimilar minor parties. There is no consistent pattern. But second, and more important, the overall average support for minor parties in the sample cities varied by just a few percentage points from that of the state as a whole. Voters in these cities evidently did not feel any more disenchanted with mainstream politicians than those living elsewhere.

The two tables together disclose some important facts about the political behavior of these key cities. Boston, until the party's demise, was clearly a Whig stronghold, every year doing better (usually substantially better) than the statewide average. (This is corroborated in its choice of mayors, all of whom were Whig, except in 1834–1835, 1845, and 1854). From 1855 on, however, the situation changed. For five years lingering support for nativists and old-line Whigs prevented the Republicans from gaining a foothold. During the 1860s it was usually Republican, but noticeably less so than the state as a whole, and by the 1870s Democrats were carrying the city fairly regularly (and electing most of its mayors too). The efficient Democratic machine and its Irish backers had taken the citadel at last. Fall River is also worth looking at. After the war it became synonymous with bitter labor unrest, yet it was not until the mid-seventies that its Republican orientation began to shift. Its enthusiastic support of the Labor Reform party, though, furnished a clear sign that its devotion to Republicanism was fragile.

Finally, there is Lynn. The recent work of Paul Faler and Alan Dawley has focused renewed attention on this city as a vortex of labor agitation. This is fully borne out by the voting statistics. Lynn was far and away the least enthusiastically Whig/Republican of the sample cities (except during and immediately after the war). It was also unusually prone to embrace third parties, particularly the labor-oriented parties of the 1870s. But these same figures should caution us about making generalizations from Lynn to the entire state. Its shoeworkers were *not* representative of the working class of Massachusetts; their class consciousness and political awareness were exceptional. They may not even have been typical of other shoeworkers. Compare Lynn's Whig/Republican percentages with those of neighboring Haverhill, also heavily dependent on the shoe industry. The latter is an almost perfect mirror of the statewide Whig/Republican totals. Lynn's workers became an important source of criticism of the industrial order, but one must remember that in these years they were far more iconoclastic than their fellows across the state.

Notes

CHAPTER 1. CONFRONTING INDUSTRIALIZATION

1. It is important to keep in mind, though, that, despite the presence of "factory towns," manufacturing has never engaged a majority of the population. At no time in American history has the proportion of the labor force engaged in manufacturing gone beyond 20% to 25%; in fact, it has hovered steadily at those limits since the 1880s. The most accurate statistics on this subject are in Stanley Lebergott, *Manpower in Economic Growth: The American Record since 1800* (New York, 1964), p. 510.

2. On the piecework system in various industries in nineteenth-century Massachusetts, see Blanche Evans Hazard, *The Organization of the Boot and Shoe Industry in Massachusetts before 1875* (Cambridge, Mass., 1921), pp. 42–64; Felicia Johnson Deyrup, *Arms Makers of the Connecticut Valley: A Regional Study of the Economic Development of the Small Arms Industry, 1798–1870* (Northampton, Mass., 1948), p. 109. As late as 1875, 37% of all employees engaged in manufacturing in the state were paid on a piecework basis. See figures in Carroll D. Wright, *The Census of Massachusetts: 1875*, 4 vols. (Boston, 1877), 2: 753–754.

3. Of course, this was not the sole factor in determining wages: Such criteria as skill, experience, strength required, or the danger of the job were also taken into account. But it was still a wage based on time put in.

4. As is evident from the foregoing discussion, the term "working class" in this study will fairly well ignore what is today an important component of that group, white-collar workers. As the next chapter will show, during most of the nineteenth century the proportion of such workers to the total was very small, usually less than 10%. So, throughout the text, for "working class" read blue-collar working class.

5. Marvin Meyers, *The Jacksonian Persuasion: Politics and Belief*, rev. ed. (New York, 1960), pp. 7–8.

6. On the "Commonwealth ideal" and its practical applications, see Oscar and Mary Flug Handlin, *Commonwealth: A Study of the Role of Government in the American Economy: Massachusetts, 1774–1861*, rev. ed. (Cambridge, Mass., 1969).

CHAPTER 2. MASSACHUSETTS: BUILDING AN INDUSTRIAL STATE

1. [United States] *Census for 1820* [Fourth Census] (Washington, D.C., 1821). (Hereafter, all United States censuses will be cited as *U.S. Census*, preceded by a cardinal number corresponding to the number of the census and followed, in parentheses, by the census year.) On farm conditions for the entire

southern New England region in this period, see Percy W. Bidwell, "The Agricultural Revolution in New England," *American Historical Review*, 26 (1921): 684. A more optimistic picture is presented in Paul W. Gates, *The Farmer's Age: Agriculture 1815–1860* (New York, 1960), pp. 22–29.

2. Daniel J. Boorstin, *The Americans: The National Experience* (New York, 1965), p. 10. Boorstin's discussion of this New England trait of "versatility," as he calls it, is on pp. 3–48.

3. And perhaps, toward the middle of the century, turn positively envious, as big Boston capitalists discovered the handsome profits to be made in western land!

4. Caroline Ware has a good discussion of these factors for the entire New England region in her *The Early New England Cotton Manufacture* (Boston, 1931), pp. 4–18.

5. Figures from Handlin, *Commonwealth*, p. 162.

6. The standard works on the leading industries are Arthur H. Cole, *The American Wool Manufacture*, 2 vols. (Cambridge, Mass., 1926); Ware, *Early New England Cotton Manufacture;* Hazard, *Organization of the Boot and Shoe Industry.* Information on other industries can be found in Victor S. Clark, *History of Manufactures in the United States*, 2 vols. (Washington, D.C., 1916–1928), vols. 1 and 2, *passim.*

7. Census totals can be recomputed using the more modern definition of manufacturing, but nothing can compensate for incomplete counts. The following figures were drawn from various state and national censuses between 1837 and 1860 and represent the value of manufactures produced in Massachusets for the years given. The figures were arrived at mainly by excluding agricultural products and products of agricultural processing, such as milling, from the totals given in the censuses. (All figures rounded off to the nearest hundred.)

1837	$ 77,415,200
1840	53,415,200
1845	86,417,600
1855	233,420,500
1860	234,067,000

Even taking into account the effects of the depression of 1837–1839, this progression is highly improbable. Source: John P. Bigelow, *Statistical Tables: Exhibiting the Condition and Products of Certain Branches of Industry in Massachusetts, for the Year Ending April 1, 1837* (Boston, 1838), pp. 201–204 (for 1837); U.S. Department of State, *Compendium of the . . . Sixth Census* (Washington, D.C., 1841), pp. 110–117 (for 1840); John G. Palfrey, *Statistics of the Condition and Products of Certain Branches of Industry in Massachusetts, for the Year Ending April 1, 1845* (Boston, 1846), pp. 373–377 (for 1845); Francis DeWitt, *Statistical Information Relating to Certain Branches of Industry in Massachusetts, for the Year Ending June 1, 1855* (Boston, 1856), pp. 634–643 (for 1855); 8 *U.S. Census (1860), Manufactures*, pp. 251–257 (for 1860).

8. Source for Table 1: *12 U.S. Census (1900)*, vol. 8, *Manufactures*, pt. 2, p. 347.

9. *Population Redistribution and Economic Growth, United States, 1870–1950*, 3 vols., ed. Simon Kuznets and Dorothy S. Thomas (Philadelphia, 1957–1964), 1: 692, 697. For further comparative data, see Albert W. Niemi, Jr., *State and Regional Patterns in American Manufacturing 1860–1900* (Westport, Conn., 1974), chap. 2 and *passim*.

10. Source for Table 2: Kuznets and Thomas, *Population Redistribution and Economic Growth*, 2: 85. The absolute numbers represented by these percentages are given in 1: 626.

11. *Ibid.*, 2: 85–92, 194.

12. Richard A. Easterlin, "Interregional Differences in Per Capita Income, Population, and Total Income, 1840–1950," in *Trends in the American Economy in the Nineteenth Century*, National Bureau of Economic Research: Studies in Income and Wealth, vol. 24 (Princeton, N.J., 1960), pp. 97–98. States west of the Mississippi have such high wage rates because of transportation difficulties (as does, say, Alaska today) that comparisons with them would be misleading.

13. *Ibid.*, p. 99–101. Again, these rankings compare only those states east of the Mississippi. In this and in the preceding set of figures for 1840, income per worker refers to total income averaged out over *all* those in the labor force — self-employed and employees.

14. Kuznets and Thomas, *Population Redistribution and Economic Growth*, 1: 753.

15. The standard source on agricultural developments in the antebellum period is Bidwell, "Agricultural Revolution," pp. 683–702. A convenient summary of agricultural product statistics for ten-year intervals between 1845 and 1875 can be found in Wright, *Census of Massachusetts: 1875*, 3: xiii–xviii. On the farmer's situation after the Civil War, see Massachusetts Bureau of Statistics of Labor, *Second Annual Report (1871)*, pp. 157–171 (hereafter, these reports cited as *MBSL*, followed by a number indicating the volume of the report and, in parentheses, date of publication); *MBSL 3 (1872)*, pp. 25–44; Thomas Talbot, *Address . . . to the Two Branches of the Legislature of Massachusetts, January 2, 1879. Mass. Senate Doc. No. 1 (1879)*, p. 31. Quotes are from *MBSL 3 (1872)*, pp. 30, 40.

16. The most thorough source of information on this subject is Samuel Eliot Morison, *The Maritime History of Massachusetts 1783–1860*, rev. ed. (Boston, 1961), *passim*. See also Percy W. Bidwell, "Population Growth in Southern New England, 1810–1860," *Quarterly Publications of the American Statistical Association*, n.s., no. 120 (December 1917): 817–828, and, for post–Civil War developments, Edward C. Kirkland, *Men Cities and Transportation: A Study in New England History 1820–1900*, 2 vols. (Cambridge, Mass., 1948), 2: 111–229.

17. *12 U.S. Census (1900)*, vol. 8, *Manufactures*, pt. 2, p. 347. An estimate of out-of-state products consumed in Massachusetts can be found in Representa-

tive Charles Hudson's speech, U.S., Congress, House, *Congressional Globe*, 27th Cong., 2nd sess., 8 July 1842, 11, Appendix: 931. Albert W. Niemi, Jr., has demonstrated Massachusetts' large share in the interstate export of manufactured goods for 1860, in his *State and Regional Patterns*, pp. 59–60.

18. Kirkland, *Men Cities and Transportation*, vols. 1 and 2, *passim*. Figures on the growth of railroad mileage are in 1: 284 and 2: 350.

19. Jesse Chickering, *Statistical View of the Population of Massachusetts, from 1765 to 1840* (Boston, 1846), p. 3.

20. Source for Table 3: *12 U.S. Census (1900), Population*, pt. 1, pp. xxiv–xxv.

21. A stagnant agriculture as the explanation for the low rates of increase from 1800 to 1830 is cited by Chickering, *Statistical View*, p. 42; and Bidwell, "Population Growth," 814.

22. Comparative figures on population density may be found in *12 U.S. Census (1900), Population*, pt. 1, p. xxxiii. See Table 3 for an explanation of the "North Atlantic region."

23. Sources for Table 4: *5 U.S. Census (1830)*, p. 22 (for 1830); Massachusetts Board of State Charities, *Annual Report No. 3* (1867), p. 23 (for 1840) (hereafter, these reports cited as *MBSC*, followed by number of report and, in parentheses, date of publication) — there is no indication here where this 1840 figure comes from; presumably it was the 1840 United States Census, but I was unable to locate it there; *7 U.S. Census (1850)*, pp. xxxvi–xxxvii (for 1850); Francis De-Witt, *Abstract of the Census of the Commonwealth of Massachusetts . . . 1855* (Boston, 1857), p. 230 (for 1855); *8 U.S. Census (1860), Population*, pp. xxix, xxxiii (for 1860); Oliver Warner, *Abstract of the Census of Massachusetts, 1865 . . .* (Boston, 1867), p. 56 (for 1865); *9 U.S. Census (1870)*, 1: 328–342 (for 1870); Wright, *Census of Massachusetts: 1875*, 1: 284 (for 1875); U.S. Census Office, *Compendium of the Tenth Census . . .* (Washington, D.C., 1883), pt. 1, pp. 426, 464–469 (for 1880).

24. In 1880, 439,341 of the state's 1,783,085 population had parents one or both of whom were born in a foreign country. *10 U.S. Census (1880)*, 1: 685.

25. For a discussion of this subject with reference to the city of Boston, see Peter R. Knights, *The Plain People of Boston, 1830–1860* (New York, 1971), chap. 3.

26. Chickering, *Statistical View*, pp. 42–43, 107, and *passim;* quote on p. 43.

27. George W. Chase, *Abstract of the Census of Massachusetts, 1860, from the Eighth U.S. Census . . .* (Boston, 1863), pp. 296–298.

28. Bidwell, "Population Growth," pp. 834–839.

29. A study by Jeffrey G. Williamson is dubious of explanations that claim manufacturing as the chief cause of urbanization in antebellum America. Yet one must allow that he is talking of the country as a whole. His own data show that New England cities were heavily dependent on manufacturing, and conversely, that Massachusetts, the most industrialized state, had very high "incremental

urbanization ratios" for the years covered by the present work. See Jeffrey G. Williamson, "Antebellum Urbanization in the American Northeast," *Journal of Economic History*, 25 (1965): 592–608, and especially pp. 600, 604.

30. A comparative study of the conditions and history of these three cities can be found in *MBSL 13 (1882)*. More recent examinations are Donald B. Cole, *Immigrant City: Lawrence, Massachusetts, 1845–1921* (Chapel Hill, N.C., 1963), pp. 17–67; Margaret T. Parker, *Lowell: A Study of Industrial Development* (1940; reprint ed., New York, 1970), pp. 59–117 *passim*. While it was not exactly a factory town, Springfield mushroomed as an urban center under the impetus of a manufacturing boom wrought by the Civil War. See Michael H. Frisch, *Town into City: Springfield, Massachusetts, and the Meaning of Community, 1840–1880* (Cambridge, Mass., 1972), chaps. 3–5.

31. The population of the entire nation at the latter date was only 28.2% urban. Urbanization trends for Massachusetts and other states in the nineteenth century have been conveniently collected in *17 U.S. Census (1950)*, vol. 2, *Characteristics of the Population*, pt. 1, pp. 18–23 (but see the corrections made in Kuznets and Thomas, *Population Redistribution and Economic Growth*, vol. 3). For town life in Massachusetts before 1820, see Richard D. Brown, "The Emergence of Urban Society in Rural Massachusetts, 1760–1820," *Journal of American History*, 61 (1974): 29–51.

32. Data emphasizing the central position of Boston can be found in Chickering, *Statistical View*, p. 79; Warner, *Abstract of the Census, 1865*, p. 277; Wright, *Census of Massachusetts: 1875*, 1: xxviii. See also Knights, *Plain People of Boston*, chap. 2.

33. *Ibid.*, pp. 37, 59; see, in general, chaps. 3 and 4. For comparative statistics for a much smaller town, Waltham, see Howard M. Gitelman, *Workingmen of Waltham: Mobility in American Urban Industrial Development, 1850–1890* (Baltimore, 1974), chap. 2.

34. The classification system used in these tables was suggested by the one devised by David Montgomery in his *Beyond Equality: Labor and the Radical Republicans, 1862–1872* (New York, 1967), pp. 448–452. Appendix A of this work explains how these tables were derived. Sources for Tables 5 and 6: Bigelow, *Statistical Tables, 1837*, 169–204; *6 U.S. Census (1840)*, pp. 48–49 (for 1837). Palfrey, *Statistics, 1845*, pp. 329–377; *7 U.S. Census (1850)*, pp. 48–49, 57–58 (for 1845). DeWitt, *Statistical Information, 1855*, pp. 570–643; *8 U.S. Census (1860)*, pp. 218–219, 227–229 (for 1855). *9 U.S. Census (1870)*, 1: 674–695 and 3: 528–532 (for 1870). *10 U.S. Census (1880)*, 1: 760–775, 792–807 and 2: 130–134 (for 1880).

35. The recent work on Boston is in James Henretta, "Economic Development and Social Structure in Colonial Boston," *William and Mary Quarterly*, 22 (1965): 75–92; and Allan Kulikoff, "The Progress of Inequality in Revolutionary Boston," *William and Mary Quarterly*, 28 (1971): 375–411. For corroborating evidence from another Massachusetts town, Newburyport, see Stephan

Thernstrom, *Poverty and Progress: Social Mobility in a Nineteenth Century City* (Cambridge, Mass., 1964), pp. 34–42.

36. Data for 1820 from *4 U.S. Census (1820)*, under Massachusetts (no page numbers). G. B. Warden has pointed up some important shortcomings in the Henretta and Kulikoff studies in his articles, "The Distribution of Property in Boston, 1692–1775," *Perspectives in American History*, 10 (1976): 81–128 and "Inequality and Instability in Eighteenth-Century Boston: A Reappraisal," *Journal of Interdisciplinary History*, 6 (1976): 585–620. If his criticisms are valid, this would further tend to weaken the hypothesis that a large working class existed in the preindustrial period.

37. Source for Table 7: Montgomery, *Beyond Equality*, p. 449.

38. Source for Table 8: same as for Tables 5 and 6 (see note 34, *supra*). All the figures in this table are by necessity (from the limitations of the censuses from which they are drawn) *minimal* figures and may not represent the total number of workers in any given group.

CHAPTER 3. THE BOUNTEOUS FACTORY

1. T. S. Ashton, *An Economic History of England: The 18th Century* (London, 1955), p. 125. Phyllis Deane, a leading student of British industrialization, has disputed the choosing of this period, arguing that many of the trends apparent then actually had their genesis earlier. Yet it seems to me that her own evidence fails to support her. See *The First Industrial Revolution* (Cambridge, 1965), pp. 87, 101, 108, 116–118 and (with W. A. Cole) *British Economic Growth 1688–1959* (Cambridge, 1962), p. 40, note 2, and pp. 75–82, especially p. 78, note 1.

2. In the case of Massachusetts this included trade with other states.

3. Of the voluminous literature on this subject, I have found most helpful Harold Perkin's *The Origins of Modern English Society 1780–1880* (London, 1969).

4. Sources are as follows: For Figure 1, data for England and Wales and London, 1688–1801, are estimates given by Deane and Cole, *British Economic Growth*, pp. 3, 7. Data for England and Wales and London, 1841–1881, are from Geoffrey Best, *Mid-Victorian Britain, 1851–1875* (New York, 1971), pp. 6, 7. Data for Massachusetts, 1790–1880, are from *17 U.S. Census (1950)*, vol. 2, *Characteristics of the Population*, pt. 1, p. 18. For Figure 2, Deane and Cole, *British Economic Growth*, p. 137 estimates the nonagricultural population of England and Wales at 20% to 40% in 1688. Data for 1801–1881 are from *ibid.*, p. 142. Data for Massachusetts, 1820–1880, are from *4 U.S. Census (1820)*, under Massachusetts (no page numbers) and Tables 5 and 6, pp. 33, 34. For Great Britain, "nonagricultural population" for 1801–1881 includes all not engaged in agriculture, forestry, and fisheries. For Massachusetts, "nonagricultural population" for 1820 includes all not engaged in agriculture only; for 1837–1880 it includes all not engaged in agriculture, foresty, fishing, and mining. For Figure

3, data for Great Britain (Definition I) are from Deane and Cole, *British Economic Growth*, p. 142. Data for England and Wales (Definition II) are derived from W. A. Armstrong, "The Use of Information About Occupation," in *Nineteenth Century Society*, ed. E. A. Wrigley (Cambridge, 1972), pp. 230, 268, 280. Data for Massachusetts are from *4 U.S. Census (1820)*, under Massachusetts (no page numbers); Francis A. Walker, *A Compendium of the Ninth Census* (Washington, D.C., 1872), pp. 797–799; and *10 U.S. Census (1880)*, vol. 2, *Manufactures*, p. xii. Total labor force for Massachusetts, 1850–1880, used in computing percentages in Figure 3, is that given in Table 5 (or averages derived therefrom), and *not* that given in the above census reports.

5. For figures on this trend in manufacturing and other areas, see Perkin, *Origins*, pp. 107–124.

6. For much of what follows I am indebted (in addition to the sources cited in subsequent notes) to Asa Briggs' masterful survey *The Making of Modern England, 1783–1867* [originally published as *The Age of Improvement*] (1959; reprint ed., New York, 1965); and to Robert K. Webb, *Modern England* (New York, 1968), intro. and chaps. 1–7.

7. This was important, but it can be overestimated. See Perkin, *Origins*, pp. 63–73, 183–195; and E. J. Hobsbawm, *Industry and Empire* (New York, 1968), pp. 33–34.

8. For this episode and its international ramifications, see Reginald Horsman, *The Causes of the War of 1812* (New York, 1962), especially pp. 128–138, 245–258.

9. On the continuing political domination of the landed aristocracy through the first half of the nineteenth century, see G. S. R. Kitson Clark, *An Expanding Society: Britain 1830–1900* (Cambridge, 1967), chap. 2. For a still later period (1852–1867) see W. L. Burn, *The Age of Equipoise* (New York, 1964), pp. 313–326.

10. E. P. Thompson, *The Making of the English Working Class* (New York, 1963), chaps. 13–16; Perkin, *Origins*, pp. 208–217.

11. For a treatment of the rioting see George Rudé, *The Crowd in History* (New York, 1964), chaps. 4, 5, 9, 10, 12.

12. For illuminating discussions of this controversy, see Perkin, *Origins*, chaps. 7–10; Burn, *Age of Equipoise*, chap. 3; and Raymond Williams, *Culture and Society 1780–1950* (New York, 1958), pt. 1. The way the worker was conceptualized by his contemporaries is treated in Asa Briggs, "The Language of 'Class' in Early Nineteenth-Century England," in *Essays in Labour History*, ed. Asa Briggs and John Saville (London, 1960), pp. 43–73.

13. In this area I have benefited from reading John T. Ward, *The Factory Movement, 1830–1855* (London, 1962).

14. The forty-two politicians are listed in Appendix B. The disproportionately large sample from the pre-Jacksonian years was included to compensate for the scarcity of their surviving writings. I examined all the pamphlets, published

speeches, and other public political statements appearing even remotely relevant that I could find in the Boston Public Library, the Boston Atheneum, and the Harvard College Library. Considering the wealth of these libraries' holdings in this period of Massachusetts history, I assume that I thereby looked at most of the extant writings. I should add here that I also examined the writings of three "reformers" who are discussed in chapter 5. See note 32 of that chapter for sources consulted.

15. Alexander H. Rice, *Address . . . to the Two Branches of the Legislature of Massachusetts, January 3, 1878. Mass. Senate Doc. No. 1 (1878)*, pp. 17–18. It is only fair to add that this topic had for quite a while been considered in the main body of various messages.

16. Daniel Webster, "The Tariff" (Speech in Congress, April 1 and 2, 1824) in *Writings and Speeches . . .* 18 vols. (Boston, 1903), 5: 136; Edward Everett, "The Circumstances Favorable to the Progress of Literature in America" (Speech before the Society of Phi Beta Kappa, Cambridge, August 26, 1824) in *Orations and Speeches on Various Occasions*, 4 vols. (Boston, 1850–1868), 1: 17. For similar statements, see the "Answer of the Senate to the Governor's Message" (June 1818) in *Acts and Resolves Passed by the General Court of Massachusetts, 1818*, p. 588 (from 1795 to 1880 this series is published under various titles; hereafter cited as *Mass. Acts and Resolves*); Representative John Davis' speech in U.S., Congress, House, *Register of Debates*, 19th Cong., 2nd sess., 31 January, 1827, p. 886; Edward Everett, "The Cattle Show at Dedham" (September 26, 1849), in *Speeches*, 2: 646–647.

17. Daniel Webster, "Speech on the Tariff" (Boston, October 2, 1820), in *Speeches*, 13: 17; Levi Lincoln, *Speech . . . to Both Branches of the Legislature, Delivered June 2, 1825* (n.p., n.d.), p. 11; Edward Everett, "The Cattle Show at Danvers" (September 28, 1836), in *Speeches*, 2: 185. For other examples of this argument, see Josiah Quincy, *An Address Delivered Before the Massachusetts Agricultural Society, October 12th, 1819* (n.p., n.d.), p. 2; Benjamin F. Hallett, *Oration Before the Democratic Citizens of Worcester County, . . . at Millbury, July 4, 1839* (Worcester, 1839), p. 35; Caleb Cushing, *Address. Delivered September 26, 1850, at Salem, Before the Essex Agricultural Society . . .* (Salem, Mass., 1850), pp. 10–11; Daniel Webster, "Speeches at the State Agricultural Fair, Rochester, N.Y." (September 20 and 21, 1843), in *Speeches*, 13: 177.

18. Senator Isaac Bates's speech, U.S., Congress, Senate, *Congressional Globe*, 28th Cong., 1st sess., 21 February 1844, vol. 13, Appendix, p. 295; George S. Boutwell, "A System of Agricultural Education" (Speech, October 8, 1857), in *Thoughts on Educational Topics and Institutions* (Boston, 1859), p. 345; Robert C. Winthrop, "Agriculture" (Speech before Middlesex Agricultural Society, Lowell, September 24, 1851), in *Addresses and Speeches on Various Occasions . . .*, 4 vols. (Boston, 1852–1886), 1: 745; Winthrop, "American Agriculture" (Speech before Bristol County Agricultural Society, Taunton, October 15, 1852), in *ibid.*, 2: 78. For similar comments see [Alexander H. Everett], *America: Or A General Survey of the Political Situation of the Several Powers of*

the Western Continent . . . (Philadelphia, 1827), p. 156; Charles P. Huntington's speech at the Massachusetts Constitutional Convention of 1853, *Official Report of the Debates and Proceedings in the State Convention, Assembled May 4th, 1853, To Revise and Amend the Constitution of the Commonwealth of Massachusetts*, 2 vols. (Boston, 1853), 1: 493 (hereafter cited as *Constitutional Convention Report, 1853*); George Boutwell, *Address Delivered at Concord, September 18, 1850* . . . (Boston, 1850), p. 13.

19. "Answer of the Senate to the Governor's Message" (June 9, 1808), in *Mass. Acts and Resolves, 1808*, p. 171; Elbridge Gerry, "Message to the Legislature" (June 7, 1810), in *Mass. Acts and Resolves, 1810*, p. 21; "Answer of the House of Representatives to the Governor's Message" (June 1809), in *Mass. Acts and Resolves, 1809*, p. 322. See also "Answer of the House of Representatives to the Governor's Message" (June 9, 1808), in *Mass. Acts and Resolves, 1808*, p. 168; Levi Lincoln, "Message of the Lieutenant Governor to the Legislature" (January 26, 1809), in *Mass. Acts and Resolves, 1809*, p. 229; Christopher Gore, "Message to the Legislature" (June 7, 1809), in *ibid.*, pp. 308–309.

20. John Brooks, "Message to the Legislature" (January 20, 1819), in *Mass. Acts and Resolves, 1819*, p. 654. For other examples, see "Answer of the House of Representatives to the Governor's Message" (May–June 1817), in *Mass. Acts and Resolves, 1817*, p. 406; "Answer of the Senate to the Governor's Message" (June, 1818), in *Mass. Acts and Resolves, 1818*, p. 591; Levi Lincoln, *Address Delivered Before the Worcester Agricultural Society, October 7, 1819* . . . (Worcester, 1819), pp. 4, 13, 14; Edward Everett, "American Manufactures" (Speech before the American Institute, New York, N.Y., October 14, 1831), in *Speeches*, 2: 72–76.

21. "Answer of the Senate to the Governor's Message" (May–June, 1817), in *Mass. Acts and Resolves, 1817*, p. 402; John Brooks, "Message to the Legislature" (May 31, 1817), in *ibid.*, p. 395; Representative John Reed's speech, U.S., Congress, House, *Register of Debates*, 20th Cong., 1st sess., 3 April 1828, p. 2156. Cf. Representative Francis Baylies' speech, U.S., Congress, House, *Annals of Congress*, 18th Cong., 1st sess., 27 February 1824, p. 1690; Edward Everett, "The Principle of the American Constitutions" (Speech at Cambridge, July 4, 1826), in *Speeches*, 1: 121; Caleb Cushing, *An Oration, Delivered Before the Citizens of Newburyport, on the Fifty-Sixth Anniversary of American Independence*, July 4, 1832 (Newburyport, Mass., 1832), pp. 24–27; John Davis, *Duties on Woollens.* [sic] *Speech . . . in the House of Representatives* . . . (n.p., [1827]), pp. 5–6; A. H. Everett, *America*, pp. 156–158; Representative John Davis' speech, U.S., Congress, House, *Register of Debates*, 20th Cong., 1st sess., 13 March 1828, p. 1898; Levi Lincoln, *Message . . . Communicated to the Two Branches of the Legislature, January 6, 1830. Mass. House Doc. No. 1 (1830)*, pp. 26–27; Representative John Reed's speech, U.S., Congress, House, *Register of Debates*, 20th Cong., 1st sess., 3 April 1828, p. 2156.

22. Webster, "Speech on the Tariff," in *Speeches*, 13: 16–17; Representative Benjamin Crowninshield's speech, U.S., Congress, House, *Annals of Congress*,

18th Cong., 1st sess., 24 March 1824, p. 1896. For other examples of this line of argument, see "Answer of the House of Representatives to the Governor's Message" (June 1820), *Mass. Acts and Resolves, 1820,* pp. 239–240; Senator Harrison Gray Otis' speech, U.S., Congress, Senate, *Annals of Congress,* 16th Cong., 1st sess., 4 May 1820, p. 667; remonstrance of Boston merchants, February 9, 1824, reprinted in *ibid.,* 18th Cong., 1st sess., Appendix, pp. 3079–3091; [James T. Austin], "The Proposed New Tariff," *North American Review,* 13 (1821): 60–88; [Edward Everett], "Commerce and Manufactures," *ibid.,* 17 (1823): 186–228; [Edward Everett], "The Tariff Question," *ibid.,* 19 (1824): 223–253.

23. Edward Everett, "The Fourth of July at Lowell" (Speech, July 5, 1830), in *Speeches,* 2: 59; Everett, "American Manufactures," *ibid.,* p. 75; John Davis, *Inaugural Address . . . to the Two Branches of the Legislature of Massachusetts. January 9, 1841. Mass. House Doc. No. 1 (1841),* p. 10; Winthrop, "Agriculture," in *Speeches,* 1: 746; Marcus Morton, *Address . . . to the Two Branches of the Legislature, . . . for the Political Year Commencing January 1, 1840. Mass. House Doc. No. 9* (1840), p. 14. For other statements of these themes, see Robert Winthrop, "Protection to Domestic Industry" (Speech, Massachusetts House of Representatives, February 15, 1837), in *Speeches,* 1: 211; Representative Charles Hudson's speech, U.S. Congress, House, *Congressional Globe,* 27th Cong., 2nd sess., 8 July 1842, 11, Appendix, p. 931; Senator Isaac Bates' speech, U.S., Congress, Senate, *Congressional Globe,* 28th Cong., 1st sess., 21 February 1844, 13, Appendix, p. 295; Winthrop, "American Agriculture," in *Speeches,* 2: 74–78; Edward Everett, "The Progress of Agriculture" (Speech before the Hampshire, Franklin, and Hampden Agricultural Society, Northampton, October 7, 1852), in *Speeches,* 3: 147–154; Massachusetts Board of Education, *Twentieth Annual Report (1857),* p. 37 (hereafter, these reports cited as *MBE* followed by number of report and, in parentheses, date of publication. All quotes are from the report of the secretary of the board); and, of course, the statement of Horace Mann that gives this book its title (from *MBE 8* [*1845*], p. 106).

24. For examples of such measures in the period 1780–1810, see Handlin, *Commonwealth,* pp. 37–38, 48, 52–53, 68–80.

25. Massachusetts Constitution of 1780, chap. 5, sec. 2; Levi Lincoln, "Message of Lieutenant Governor to the Legislature" (January 26, 1809), *Mass. Acts and Resolves, 1809,* pp. 229–230; "Answer of the House of Representatives to the Governor's Message" (January 1809), *ibid.,* p. 243. Similar statements can be found in Samuel Adams, "Message to the Legislature" (May 31, 1796), *Mass. Acts and Resolves, 1796,* p. 622; Christopher Gore, "Message to the Legislature" (June 7, 1809), *Mass. Acts and Resolves, 1809,* p. 309; Christopher Gore, "Message to the Legislature" (January 25, 1810), *Mass. Acts and Resolves, 1810,* p. 374; "Answer of the House of Representatives to the Governor's Message" (June 1810), *ibid.,* p. 32.

26. See, for example, Samuel Adams, "Message to the Legislature" (January

19, 1795), *Mass. Acts and Resolves, 1795* p. 616; "Answer of the House of Representatives to the Governor's Speech at the Opening of the Session" (January 22, 1796), *ibid.*, p. 515.

27. Gerry, "Message to the Legislature" (June 7, 1810), *Mass. Acts and Resolves, 1810*, p. 21; Everett, "Fourth of July at Lowell," in *Speeches*, 2: 54–55. Other examples of this argument can be found in "Answer of the House of Representatives to the Governor's Message" (June 1810), *Mass. Acts and Resolves, 1810*, p. 32; "Answer of the House of Representatives to the Governor's Message" (June 13, 1811), *Mass. Acts and Resolves, 1811*, p. 199; Lincoln, *Address, Oct. 7, 1819*, p. 13; A. H. Everett, *America*, pp. 142–148; Everett, "American Manufactures," in *Speeches*, 2: 75–76; [Alexander H. Everett], "Life of Henry Clay," *North American Review*, 33 (1831): p. 375. Even long after this period, politicians occasionally rehearsed this aspect of its achievements. See Levi Lincoln, *Speech . . . Delivered to the Two Branches of the Legislature. May 25, 1831. Mass. Senate Doc. No. 1 (1831)*, p. 20; John H. Clifford, *Address . . . to the Two Branches of the Legislature of Massachusetts, January 14, 1853. Mass. Senate Doc. No. 5 (1853)*, p. 16.

28. Daniel Webster, "Second Speech on the Sub-Treasury" (Speech in Senate, March 12, 1838), in *Speeches*, 8: 177. See also his "Lecture before the Society for the Diffusion of Useful Knowledge" (Speech at Boston, November 11, 1836), in *ibid.*, 13: 68–69.

29. *MBE 9 (1846)*, p. 73; Everett, "Fourth of July at Lowell," in *Speeches*, 2: 56.

30. [Caleb Cushing], *Summary of the Practical Principles of Political Economy . . .* (Cambridge, Mass., 1826), pp. 26–27.

31. Edward Everett, "The First Settlement of New England" (Speech, Plymouth, December 22, 1824), in *Speeches*, 1: 54; Lincoln, *Speech, June 2, 1825*, p. 12; Levi Lincoln, *Speech . . . Delivered Before the Legislature, June 6, 1826* (Boston, 1826), p. 10; George Bancroft, *Oration, Delivered on the Fourth of July, 1826, at Northampton, Mass.* (Northampton, Mass., 1826), p. 14.

32. Lincoln, *Speech, June 6, 1826*, p. 10; A. H. Everett, *America*, p. 140; Cushing, *Oration, Delivered Before the Citizens of Newburyport*, pp. 49–50; Everett, "Fourth of July at Lowell," in *Speeches*, 2: 55; Edward Everett, "Accumulation, Property, Capital, Credit" (Speech before the Mercantile Library Association, Boston, September 13, 1838), in *ibid.*, pp. 297–298. Lowell became a showplace of industry for visitors from other states and abroad. See Marvin Fisher, *Workshops in the Wilderness: The European Response to American Industrialization, 1830–1860* (New York, 1967), pp. 90–112.

33. It should be noted, however, that Democrats tended to mention this (and, in fact, all the other ideas discussed in this chapter) notably less frequently than politicians of the other major parties. The architects and principal owners of the factory system were usually Whigs (or later, Republicans), and there was no political sense in praising the works of such prominent opponents. Signifi-

cantly, though, Democrats never attacked the system either. For more on Democratic attitudes, see below, chapter 5.

34. Morton, *Address, Jan. 1, 1840*, p. 16; Horace Mann, "Speech, Delivered at Dedham" (November 6, 1850), in *Slavery: Letters and Speeches* (Boston, 1851), p. 361; George N. Briggs, *Address . . . to the Two Branches of the Legislature of Massachusetts, January 10, 1849. Mass. Senate Doc. No. 2 (1849)*, p. 4. Cf. *MBE 8 (1845)*, p. 106; [Edward Everett], *Address . . . to the Two Branches of the Legislature . . ., for the Political Year Commencing January 6, 1836. Mass. House Doc. No. 6 (1836)*, p. 8; George Bancroft, *Address at Hartford, Before the Delegates to the Democratic Convention of the Young Men of Connecticut, on . . . February 18, 1840* (n.p., n.d.), pp. 12–14.

35. First Annual Message, December 6, 1825, in *A Compilation of the Messages and Papers of the Presidents 1789–1897* 10 vols., ed. James D. Richardson (Washington, D.C., 1896–1899), 2: 316 (cf. p. 311). For some similar statements, see Cushing, *Oration, Delivered Before the Citizens of Newburyport*, pp. 5–11; Alexander H. Everett, *A Discourse on the Progress and Limits of Social Improvement . . .* (Boston, 1834), p. iii; Bancroft, *Address at Hartford*, pp. 9–10. A handy compendium of the uses of this notion is in Arthur A. Ekirch, Jr., *The Idea of Progress in America, 1815–1860* (New York, 1944). See also Rush Welter, "The Idea of Progress in America," *Journal of the History of Ideas*, 16 (1955): 401–415.

36. A. H. Everett, *Discourse on Social Improvement*, p. 40; Amasa Walker, "Political Economy, As a Study for Common Schools," in *The Lectures Delivered Before the American Institute of Instruction, at Northampton, Mass., Aug. 1850 . . .* (Boston, 1851), p. 29 (italics mine).

37. Rufus Choate, *Speech . . . on the Bill to Alter and Amend the Several Acts Imposing Duties on Imposts* [sic] *. . . House of Representatives, U.S., June 13, 1832* (n.p., n.d.), p. 11; Everett, "American Manufactures," in *Speeches*, 2: 71. For other examples, see John Quincy Adams, *The Great Design: Two Lectures on the Smithson Bequest by John Quincy Adams. Delivered at Quincy and Boston in November 1839 . . .* [November 14 and 21, 1839], ed. Wilcomb E. Washburn (Washington, D.C., 1965), pp. 89–91. Cf. John Quincy Adams, "Society and Civilization," *American Whig Review*, 2 (1845): 80–87; Rufus Choate, "Speech Upon the Subject of Protecting American Labor by Duties on Imports" (Senate, April 12 and 15, 1844), in *Works*, 2 vols. (Boston, 1862), 2: 212.

CHAPTER 4. THE RESPECTABLE WORKER

1. Representative Henry Williams's speech, U.S., Congress, House, *Congressional Globe*, 26th Cong., 1st sess., 4 June 1840, 7, Appendix, p. 532; Edward Everett, "Fourth of July at Lowell," in *Speeches*, 2: 63. For some other examples, among many, see quotation from Everett's speech in Congress, March 9, 1826, in Paul R. Frothingham, *Edward Everett: Orator and Statesman* (Boston, 1925), p. 105; Cushing, *Oration, Delivered Before the Citizens of Newburyport*,

p. 44; Caleb Cushing, *Introductory Discourse, Delivered Before the American Institute of Instruction, . . . in Boston, August, 1834* (Boston, 1834), p. 19; Senator John Davis's speech, U.S., Congress, Senate, *Register of Debates*, 24th Cong., 1st sess., 2 May 1836, 13, pp. 1378–1379; Robert Winthrop, "The Wants of the Government and the Wages of Labor" (Speech, House of Representatives, June 26, 1846), in *Speeches*, 1: 545–546, 558–560.

2. Mann, "Speech at Dedham," in *Slavery*, 385; Webster, "Lecture Before the Society for the Diffusion of Useful Knowledge," in *Speeches*, 13: 76. These kinds of arguments can be found in Webster, "Speech on the Tariff," *ibid.*, 13: 17–18; Edward Everett, "On the Importance of Scientific Knowledge to Practical Men . . ." (Speech before several "institutions for scientific improvement," ca. 1830), in *Speeches*, 1: 267; Daniel Webster, "Mass Meeting at Saratoga" (August 19, 1840), in *Speeches*, 3: 24–25; *Report* [of the Special Committee]. *Mass. House Doc. No. 50 (1845)*, p. 10; *Minority Report* [of Joint Special Committee on alteration of hours of labor]. *Mass. Senate Doc. No. 112 (1856)*, p. 5.

3. Webster, "Speech on the Tariff," in *Speeches*, 13: 18; *MBE 7 (1844)*, p. 189 (cf. p. 39). A similar analysis is in George Boutwell, "The Intrinsic Nature and Value of Learning, and Its Influence upon Labor," in *The Lectures Delivered Before the American Institute of Instruction, at Springfield, Mass., August 19, 1856* (Boston, 1857), p. 51.

4. See, for example, Boston *Post*, December 20, 1841; *MBE 7 (1844)*, p. 188; Representative Charles Hudson's speech, U.S., Congress, House, *Congressional Globe*, 27th Cong., 2nd sess., 8 July 1842, 11, Appendix, p. 930; *Minority Report* [of Joint Special Committee on alteration of hours of labor]. *Mass. Senate Doc. No. 112 (1856)*, p. 5.

5. Kinley J. Brauer, *Cotton versus Conscience: Massachusetts Whig Politics and Southwestern Expansion, 1843–1848* (Lexington, Ky., 1967), p. 19.

6. The Whigs' position as spokesmen of the state's economic and social elite is a truism of the standard histories of the period. See Arthur B. Darling, *Political Changes in Massachusetts 1824–1848: A Study of Liberal Movements in Politics* (1925; reprint ed., Cos Cob, Conn., 1968), pp. 6–22; William G. Bean, "Party Transformation in Massachusetts With Special Reference to the Antecedents of Republicanism 1848–1860" (Ph.D. dissertation, Harvard University, 1922), pp. 4–8; Arthur M. Schlesinger, Jr., *The Age of Jackson* (Boston, 1945), chaps. 12–13 (especially pp. 144–146) and *passim*.

7. It was not always possible to discover the party affiliation of members of the constitutional convention of 1853. Remarks from the record of the convention will be included here for any speaker who I know was not a Democrat (see slate of Democratic candidates in *Post*, March 2, 1853). The same applies to legislative committee reports cited here.

8. Samuel Adams, "Message to the Legislature" (January 19, 1795), *Mass. Acts and Resolves, 1795*, p. 616; John Brooks, "Message to the Legislature" (June 6, 1820), *Mass. Acts and Resolves, 1820*, p. 226; Horace Mann, "Speech,

Delivered at Lancaster" (May 19, 1851), in *Slavery*, p. 519.

9. *Ibid.;* Rufus Choate, "The Power of a State Developed by Mental Culture" (Lecture before the Mercantile Library Association, Boston, November 18, 1844), in *Works*, 1: 402.

10. Daniel Webster, "The Removal of the Deposits" (Speech, Senate, January 20–February 22, 1834), in *Speeches*, 6: 268; Choate, "Power of a State Developed by Mental Culture," in *Works*, 1: 402–403; Webster, "Second Speech on the Sub-Treasury," in *Speeches*, 8: 176–177; Nathan Appleton, *Labor, Its Relations in Europe and the United States Compared* (Boston, 1844), p. 3; Edward Everett, "Lecture on the Workingmen's Party" (Speech, Charlestown, October 1830), in *Speeches*, 1: 283; John Brooks, "Message to the Legislature" (June 5, 1821), *Mass. Acts and Resolves, 1821*, p. 337; George N. Briggs, *Address . . . to the Two Branches of the Legislature of Massachusetts, January 12, 1847. Mass. Senate Doc. No. 2 (1847)*, p. 18. For other examples of these themes, see James Sullivan, "Message to the Legislature" (June 3, 1807), *Mass. Acts and Resolves, 1807*, p. 14; Caleb Strong, "Message to the Legislature" (January 15, 1801), *Mass. Acts and Resolves, 1801*, p. 583; Caleb Strong, "Message to the Legislature" (June 5, 1804), *Mass. Acts and Resolves, 1804*, p. 711; John Davis, *Speech . . . on the Bill for the More Effectual Collection of Impost Duties. . . . House of Representatives, May 4, 1830* (Washington, D.C., 1830), p. 20; Senator Isaac Bates' speech, U.S., Congress, Senate, *Congressional Globe*, 28th Cong., 1st sess., 21 February 1844, 13, pt. 2, Appendix, p. 295; Daniel Webster, "The Tariff" (Speech, Senate, July 27, 1846), in *Speeches*, 9: 227. Politicians were occasionally capable of more prosaic definitions of labor. See John Davis's description of it as simply "a commodity bought and sold like merchandise in the market" in his *Sub-Treasury Bill. Reply . . . to Mr. Buchanan, of Pennsylvania, . . . Delivered in the Senate of the United States, January 23, 1840* (Washington, D.C., 1840), p. 9.

11. For more on this, see Peter Laslett, *The World We Have Lost* (New York, 1965), chap. 2.

12. Everett, "On the Importance of Scientific Knowledge," in *Speeches*, 1: 267; Adams quoted in Samuel F. Bemis, *John Quincy Adams and the Union* (New York, 1956), p. 330; Rufus Choate, "Speech on the Power and Duty of Congress to Continue the Policy of Protecting American Labor" (Speech, Senate, March 14, 1842), in *Works*, 2: 73; Rufus Choate, *Speech . . . on the Question of the Removal of the Deposites* [sic]. *Delivered in the House of Representatives, March 28, 1834* (Washington, D.C., 1834), p. 4; Daniel Webster, "Reception at Pittsburg" [sic] (July 8, 1833), in *Speeches*, 2: 148–149; Webster, "Mass Meeting at Saratoga," *ibid.*, 3: 24; Representative Levi Lincoln's speech, U.S., Congress, House, *Register of Debates*, 23rd Cong., 1st sess., 17 March 1834, 10, p. 3019. For Democratic views, see Robert Rantoul, "An Address to the Workingmen of the United States of America," (1833) in *Memoirs, Speeches and Writings of Robert Rantoul, Jr.*, ed. Luther Hamilton (Boston, 1854), pp.

219–223; Hallett, *Oration, July 4, 1839*, p. 35; George Boutwell, *Address, Sept. 18, 1850*, pp. 4, 10–11.

13. The first use of these terms that I found occurs in a speech by Governor John Brooks, "Message to the Legislature" (June 6, 1820), *Mass. Acts and Resolves, 1820*, p. 226. For examples of the various ways they were used, see Representative John Davis' speech, U.S., Congress, House, *Register of Debates*, 22nd Cong., 1st sess., 6 June 1832, p. 3309; Webster, "Removal of the Deposits," in *Speeches*, 6: 267; Webster, "Lecture before the Society for the Diffusion of Useful Knowledge," *ibid.*, 13: 76; Everett, "Accumulation, Property, Capital, Credit," in *Speeches*, 2: 289; Appleton, *Labor*, pp. 4, 11–12; Daniel Webster, "Public Dinner at Philadelphia" (Speech, December 2, 1846), in *Speeches*, 4: 47; Edward Everett, "Dinner to Thomas Baring, Esq." (Speech, September 16, 22, 1852), in *Speeches*, 31: 135. For Democratic variants, see Rantoul, "Address to the Workingmen of the United States," in *Speeches*, 219–223; Theodore Sedgwick, *Public and Private Economy*, 3 vols. (New York, 1836–1839), 1: 225; Hallett, *Oration, July 4, 1839*, p. 35; George Bancroft, "Oration, Delivered at the Commemoration, in Washington, of the Death of Andrew Jackson" (June 27, 1845), in *Literary and Historical Miscellanies* (New York, 1855), p. 465; Robert Rantoul, "Speech in Answer to Davis" (House of Representatives, January 24, 1852), in *Speeches*, p. 781.

14. Appleton, *Labor*, p. 4; Webster, "Second Speech on the Sub-Treasury," in *Speeches*, 8: 167; Webster, "Lecture Before the Society for the Diffusion of Useful Knowledge," *ibid.*, 13: 76–77 (cf. 72–75); Everett, "Fourth of July at Lowell," in *Speeches*, 2: 64. See also Webster, "The Tariff," in *Speeches*, 5: 141; Caleb Cushing, *Speeches Delivered in the House of Representatives of Massachusetts, on the Subject of the Currency and Public Deposites* [sic] (Salem, Mass., 1834), pp. 26–27; Winthrop, "Protection to Domestic Industry," in *Speeches*, 1: 209; Representative Charles W. Upham's speech, U.S., Congress, House, *Congressional Globe*, 33rd Cong., 2nd sess., 27 February 1855, 31, Appendix, p. 255.

15. Representative William B. Calhoun's speech, U.S., Congress, House, *Register of Debates*, 25th Cong., 1st sess., 12 October 1837, 14, p. 1469; Everett, "Lecture on the Workingmen's Party," in *Speeches*, 1: 290; Representative Isaac Bates's speech, U.S., Congress, House, *Register of Debates*, 20th Cong., 1st sess., 26 March 1828, p. 2014.

16. See [Caleb Cushing], "M'Culloch's Political Economy," *North American Review*, 25 (1827): 119; Cushing, *Speeches on the Currency*, pp. 12–13; Rufus Choate, "Speech Upon the Subject of Protecting American Labor by Duties on Imports" (Senate, April 12 and 15, 1844), in *Works*, 2: 212; Daniel Webster, "Speech at Pepperell, Mass." (November 5, 1844), in *Speeches*, 13: 290; Winthrop, "The Wants of the Government and the Wages of Labor," in *Speeches*, 1: 542, 544; John G. Palfrey, *Speech . . . on the Bill Creating a Territorial Government for Upper California, Delivered in the House of Representatives of the*

United States, February 26, 1849 (n.p., n.d.), p. 5. For Democratic examples, see Robert Rantoul, "The Education of a Free People" (Speech before the American Institute of Instruction, 1839), in *Speeches*, 138; Hallett, *Oration, July 4, 1839*, p. 19; Morton, *Address, Jan. 1, 1840*, p. 38; Bancroft, *Address at Hartford*, p. 14. The first mention I found of "the laboring *class*," in the singular, refers to factory workers. *Report* [of the Special Committee on limiting the hours of labor]. *Mass House Doc. No. 153 (1850)*, p. 24.

17. Webster, "The Tariff," *Speeches*, 5: 141. For typical statements on high wages, see Cushing, *Summary*, p. 44; Webster, "Reception at Pittsburg," in *Speeches*, 2: 148–149; John Davis, *Address . . . Delivered Before the Two Branches of the Legislature, January 21, 1834. Mass. House Doc. No. 14 (1834)*, p. 6; Winthrop, "Protection to Domestic Industry," in *Speeches*, 1: 206; George N. Briggs, *Address . . . to the Two Branches of the Legislature of Massachusetts, January 8, 1850. Mass. Senate Doc. No. 2 (1850)*, p. 18; Winthrop, "The Wants of the Government and the Wages of Labor," in *Speeches*, 1: 544; Appleton, *Labor*, pp. 8, 12.

18. For attempts at explanation, see Everett, "Fourth of July at Lowell," in *Speeches*, 2: 55–62; Everett, "On the Importance of Scientific Knowledge," *ibid.*, 1: 260–265 (quote in text from p. 260); Webster, "Lecture before the Society for the Diffusion of Useful Knowledge," in *Speeches*, 13: 72–75; Representative Charles Hudson's speech, U.S., Congress, House, *Congressional Globe*, 27th Cong., 2nd sess., 8 July 1842, 11, Appendix, p. 930; Appleton, *Labor*, pp. 12–13. Cf., for a Democratic view, Bancroft, *Address at Hartford*, p. 14.

19. Representative John Davis' speech, U.S., Congress, House, *Register of Debates*, 22nd Cong., 1st sess., 6 June 1832, p. 3309. Davis was to return to this theme. See his *Address, Jan. 21, 1834*, p. 6; *Sub-Treasury Bill*, p. 14.

20. Appleton, *Labor*, pp. 13–14; Representative John Davis' speech, U.S., Congress, House, *Register of Debates*, 22nd Cong., 1st sess., 6 June 1832, p. 3310. See the sources cited in note 14 of chapter 4, and also Webster, "Mass Meeting at Saratoga," in *Speeches*, 3: 24; Clifford, *Address, Jan. 14, 1853*, p. 17; Henry Wilson, *Are Working-Men "Slaves?" Speech . . . in Reply to the Hon. J. H. Hammond, of South Carolina, in the Senate, March 20, 1858 . . .* (Washington, D.C., 1858), p. 14. For a Democrat, see Sedgwick, *Public and Private Economy*, 1: 14–26, 241–242.

21. Rufus Choate's speech, *Constitutional Convention Report, 1853*, 1: 458. See Webster, "Lecture Before the Society for the Diffusion of Useful Knowledge," in *Speeches*, 13: 77; Webster, "Second Speech on the Sub-Treasury," *ibid.*, 8: 166–167, 175; Appleton, *Labor*, pp. 8–10; Webster, "The Tariff," *Speeches*, 9: 226–227.

22. Brooks, "Message to the Legislature" (June 6, 1820), *Mass. Acts and Resolves, 1820*, p. 226; Joseph Story's speech in Massachusetts Constitutional Convention of 1820, *Journal of Debates and Proceedings in the Convention of*

*Delegates, Chosen to Revise the Constitution of Massachusetts, Begun and hol-
den in Boston, November 15, 1820, and continued by Adjournment to January 9,
1821*, rev. ed. (Boston, 1853), p. 285 (italics added) (hereafter cited as *Constitutional Convention Report, 1820*). See also Appleton, *Labor*, p. 8; *MBE 7 (1844)*,
p. 193. Mann's concern about the polarization of wealth in Massachusetts is in
MBE 12 (1849), pp. 57–59. For a similar emphasis on *in*equality, see, oddly
enough, Edward Everett, *The Prospect of Reform in Europe*, 3rd ed. (London,
1831), pp. 41–42. It may be significant that this was intended for foreign consumption.

   23. Story's speech, *Constitutional Convention Report, 1820*, p. 286; Josiah
Quincy, *An Address to the Citizens of Boston* . . . [September 17, 1830] (Boston, 1830), p. 49; Webster, "Second Speech on the Sub-Treasury," in *Speeches*,
8: 167; Representative Edward Everett's speech, U.S., Congress, House, *Register of Debates*, 21st Cong., 1st sess., 8 May 1830, p. 910; Everett, "Accumulation, Property, Capital, Credit," in *Speeches*, 2: 294. See also [Nathaniel
Greene], *An Exposition of the Principles and Views of the Middling Interest. In
the City of Boston* (Boston, 1822), p. 8; Representative William B. Calhoun's
speech, U.S., Congress, House, *Register of Debates*, 25th Cong., 1st sess., 12
October 1837, 14, p. 1470; [John G. Palfrey], "Massachusetts Common
Schools," *North American Review*, 44 (1837): 516–517; Appleton, *Labor*, pp.
4–5, 7–9. Here is one component of the respectable worker image that not all
Democrats could support. To them, one of the chief dangers of the "monopolies"
and legislative charters against which they fought was that such instruments
locked the wealthy into positions of power and insulated them from healthy
competitive processes. Yet at the same time Democrats could also advance the
notion that, *in general*, social mobility in Massachusetts was high. See Theodore
Sedgwick, *An Address* . . . *Delivered Before the Berkshire Association For the
Promotion of Agriculture and Manufactures, at Pittsfield, October 2, 1823* (Pittsfield, Mass., 1823), pp. 4, 14; Rantoul, "The Education of a Free People," in
Speeches, p. 136. See also chap. 5 of the present work.

   24. Everett, "On the Importance of Scientific Knowledge," in *Speeches*, 1:
266; John G. Palfrey, *Papers on the Slave Power, First Published in the "Boston
Whig,"* in . . . *1846*, 3rd ed. (Boston, 1849), p. 53; Representative Charles W.
Upham's speech, U.S., Congress, House, *Congressional Globe*, 33rd Cong.,
2nd sess., 27 February 1855, 31, Appendix, p. 255; Edward L. Keyes' speech,
Constitutional Convention Report, 1853, p. 469; Winthrop, "The Wants of the
Government and the Wages of Labor," in *Speeches*, 1: 543; Story's speech,
Constitutional Convention Report, 1820, p. 286–287. For other examples, see
Representative Edward Everett's speech, U.S., Congress, House, *Register of
Debates*, 21st Cong., 1st sess., 8 May 1830, p. 910; Davis, *Address, Jan. 21,
1834*, p. 7; Webster, "Lecture before the Society for the Diffusion of Useful
Knowledge," in *Speeches*, 13: 76–77; Palfrey, *Speech on the Bill Creating a
Territorial Government for Upper California*, p. 5; *Minority Report* [of Joint

Special Committee on alteration of hours of labor]. *Mass. Senate Doc. No. 112 (1856)*, p. 5; Robert Winthrop, "The Inauguration of the Statue of Franklin" (Speech, Boston, September 17, 1856), in *Speeches*, 2: 287. For Democratic examples, see Sedgwick, *Address, Oct. 2, 1823*, pp. 4, 14; Rantoul, "The Education of a Free People," in *Speeches*, pp. 136–137; Rantoul, "Address to the Workingmen of the United States," *ibid.*, pp. 248–250; Sedgwick, *Public and Private Economy*, 1: 225.

25. Choate, "Speech Upon the Subject of Protecting American Labor," in *Works*, 2: 213 (cf. p. 214). See also Lincoln, *Speech, June 6, 1826*, pp. 10–11; Everett, "The Fourth of July at Lowell," in *Speeches*, 2: 60; *Report* [of the Special Committee]. *Mass. House Doc. No. 50 (1845)*, p. 10; *Minority Report* [of Joint Special Committee on alteration of hours of labor]. *Mass. Senate Doc. No. 112 (1856)*, p. 5.

26. Winthrop, "The Wants of the Government and the Wages of Labor," in *Speeches*, 1: 543. On the Democratic side, see Sedgwick, *Address, Oct. 2, 1843*, pp. 14–15.

27. Brooks, "Message to the Legislature" (June 1, 1819), *Mass. Acts and Resolves, 1819*, p. 28. For other statements of such themes, see Story's speech, *Constitutional Convention Report, 1820*, p. 288; *MBE 12 (1849)*, p. 90.

28. Everett, *Address, Jan. 6, 1836*, p. 6.

29. See the testimony of Nathan Appleton in his *Introduction of the Power Loom, and Origin of Lowell* (Lowell, Mass., 1858), p. 15; Lincoln, *Speech, June 2, 1825*, pp. 12–13; Everett, "On the Importance of Scientific Knowledge," in *Speeches*, 1: 267. See also chap. 5, note 1.

30. Lincoln, *Speech, June 2, 1825*, p. 13; Edward Everett, *Speech . . . on the Proposal of Mr. McDuffie to Repeal the Laws of 1828 and 1824, Imposing Duties on Imports. Delivered in the House of Representatives, on the 7th and 8th of May, 1828* (Washington, D.C., 1830), p. 30; Everett, "On the Importance of Scientific Knowledge," in *Speeches*, 1: 267; Everett, "Fourth of July at Lowell," *ibid.*, 2: 63–64 (cf. Everett's 1850 note to the last speech, p. 67); A. H. Everett, *America*, p. 161; [Alexander H. Everett], "British Opinion on the Protecting System," *North American Review*, 30 (1830): 208–209. See also A. H. Everett, "American System," *North American Review*, 32 (1831): 172.

31. For some later comments, see Webster, "Convention at Andover" (November 9, 1843), in *Speeches*, 3: 176–177; Senator Isaac Bates' speech, U.S., Congress, Senate, *Congressional Globe*, 28th Cong., 1st sess., 21 February 1844, 13, pt. 2, Appendix, p. 296; *Report* [of the Special Committee]. *Mass. House Doc. No. 50 (1845)*, p. 10.

32. See Michael B. Katz, *The Irony of Early School Reform: Educational Innovation in Mid-Nineteenth Century Massachusetts* (Cambridge, Mass., 1968); and Stanley K. Schultz, *The Culture Factory: Boston Public Schools, 1789–1860* (New York, 1973).

33. *MBE 12 (1849)*, pp. 42–43. Bullock's recommendation is in his *Address*

. . . *to the Two Branches of the Legislature of Massachusetts, January 6, 1866.* Mass. Senate Doc. No. 3 (1866), p. 56.

34. Horace Mann, "The Necessity of Education in a Republican Government" (1839), in *Lectures on Education* (Boston, 1855), pp. 123, 127, 151, 124 (cf. pp. 123–137, 151–161); Everett, "On the Importance of Scientific Knowledge," in *Speeches*, 1: 267. See also *MBE 7 (1844)*, p. 194; *MBE 9 (1846)*, pp. 64, 67–68. Interest in the moral benefits of mass education was of long standing and was earlier inspired, in part, by the growing number of poor and other potentially unruly types in the larger towns. Schultz, *Culture Factory*, pp. 8–30. Cf. pp. 55–68 for discussions of public education as a remedy for the faltering influence of family and church.

35. *MBE 11 (1848)*, p. 41; George Boutwell, "Intrinsic Nature and Value of Learning," in *Lectures, Aug. 19, 1856*, pp. 45, 38; *MBE 12 (1849)*, p. 67. For more on this topic, see *MBE 5 (1842)*, pp. 81–120; Choate, "Power of a State Developed by Mental Culture," in *Works*, 1: 401–403; *MBE 12 (1849)*, pp. 67–68; the rest of Boutwell's speech cited above; *MBE 20 (1857)*, p. 37; *MBE 23 (1860)*, pp. 41–54. For Democratic corroboration, see George Boutwell (before 1854 Boutwell was a Democrat), *Address Before the Hillsborough [N.H.] Agricultural and Mechanical Society, September 30, 1852* (Boston, 1853), 12–18, 22; George Boutwell, *Address . . . to the Two Branches of the Legislature of Massachusetts, January 16, 1851. Mass. House Doc. No. 11 (1851)*, p. 3; Rantoul, "The Education of a Free People," in *Speeches*, pp. 135, 138, 140; Sedgwick, *Public and Private Economy*, 1: 238.

36. Webster, "Lecture before the Society for the Diffusion of Useful Knowledge," in *Speeches*, 13: 64, 63 (cf. pp. 65–67); Davis, *Inaugural Address, Jan. 9, 1841*, pp. 4–5. See also A. H. Everett, *America*, pp. 163–164; *MBE 7 (1844)*, pp. 193–194.

37. Levi Lincoln, *Message . . . Transmitted to Both Branches of the Legislature, January 7, 1829* (Boston, 1829), pp. 3–4.

38. Richard McCormick writes that in Massachusetts after 1821 "only a very small minority of adult males were actually disenfranchised." The proportion before that date was probably not very large either. *The Second American Party System: Party Formation in the Jacksonian Era* (Chapel Hill, N.C., 1966), p. 37.

39. Representative Isaac Bates's speech, U.S., Congress, House, *Register of Debates*, 20th Cong., 1st sess., 26 March 1828, p. 2014. Cf. Everett, "On the Importance of Scientific Knowledge," in *Speeches*, 1: 268–270; George Ticknor Curtis, "Letters of Phocion . . .," in *Discussions on the Constitution Proposed to the People of Massachusetts by the Convention of 1853* (Boston, 1854), pp. 58–59. On the Democratic side, see B. F. Hallett, *Oration Before the Democratic Citizens of Oxford, . . . July 5, 1841* (Boston, 1841), p. 9; Bancroft, *Address at Hartford*, p. 14.

40. Edward Everett, *The Progress of Reform in England* (London, 1832), pp. 18–19; Daniel Webster's speech, *Constitutional Convention Report, 1820*, p.

312. See also Joseph Story's speech, *ibid.*, p. 288, and, in general, the entire discussion on pp. 261–322; Representative Isaac Bates' speech, U.S., Congress, House, *Register of Debates*, 20th Cong., 1st sess., 26 March 1828, p. 2014. Cf. George Bancroft's speech before he became a Democrat, *Oration, July, 1826*, pp. 20–21.

41. Webster, "Reception at Pittsburg," in *Speeches*, 2: 150; *MBE 12 (1849)*, p. 76; Daniel Webster, "Reception at Buffalo" (June, 1833), in *Speeches*, 2: 134; Levi Lincoln, *Speech . . . Before the Two Branches of the Legislature, in Convention. June 6, 1827* (Boston, 1827), p. 13; Nathaniel Cogswell's speech, *Constitutional Convention Report, 1853*, p. 168; Daniel Webster's speech, *Constitutional Convention Report, 1820*, p. 315. Cf. *MBE 12 (1849)*, pp. 76–90 for Mann's exposition of this idea.

42. *MBE 9 (1846)*, p. 64; Robert Winthrop, "Free Schools and Free Governments" (Lecture before the Boston Lyceum, December 20, 1838), in *Speeches*, 1: 150 (cf. pp. 150–154). See also Joseph Story's speech, *Constitutional Convention Report, 1820*, p. 288. For the dangers of rampant individualism, see Cushing, *Address, Sept. 26, 1850*, pp. 7–8.

43. Davis, *Inaugural Address, Jan. 9, 1841*, pp. 8–9.

44. Appleton, *Labor*, p. 7 (cf. pp. 4–10); George Boutwell, *An Address Delivered Before the Franklin County Agricultural Society, Greenfield, October 4, 1855* (Greenfield, Mass., 1855), p. 7; Boutwell, "Intrinsic Nature and Value of Learning," *Lectures, Aug. 19, 1856*, pp. 51, 52; Palfrey, *Speech on the Bill Creating a Territorial Government for Upper California*, p. 5.

45. *Ibid.*; Quincy, *Address to the Citizens of Boston* (September 17, 1830), p. 49; Henry Wilson, *How Ought Workingmen to Vote in the Coming Election? Speech . . . at East Boston, Oct. 15, 1860* (Boston, n.d.), p. 2. For other statements of this theme, see Webster, "Convention at Andover," in *Speeches*, 3: 175; Palfrey, *Papers on the Slave Power*, p. 53; Horace Mann, "Thoughts for a Young Man" (Speech before the Boston Mercantile Library Association, 1849), in *Lectures on Various Subjects* (New York, 1859), pt. 1, p. 46; Briggs, *Address, Jan. 8, 1850*, p. 18; Wilson, *Are Working-Men Slaves?*, pp. 13–14. For a Democrat, see Sedgwick, *Address, Oct. 2, 1823*, p. 3.

46. The composite portrait of the worker in antebellum Massachusetts in the following paragraphs is drawn from these sources: Donald B. Cole, *Immigrant City*, chap. 3; Constance M. Green, *Holyoke, Massachusetts: A Case History of the Industrial Revolution in America* (New Haven, 1939), chap. 2; George S. Gibb, *The Saco-Lowell Shops: Textile Machinery Building in New England 1813–1949* (Cambridge, Mass., 1950), pp. 51–55, 88–90, 177–178, 216–220; George S. Gibb, *The Whitesmiths of Taunton: A History of Reed & Barton 1824–1943* (Cambridge, Mass., 1943), pp. 65–72, 135–150; Knights, *Plain People of Boston*, especially chap. 5; Thernstrom, *Poverty and Progress;* Oscar Handlin, *Boston's Immigrants*, rev. ed. (New York, 1959), especially chaps. 3–4; Gitelman, *Workingmen of Waltham;* Alan Dawley, *Class and Community: The Indus-*

trial Revolution in Lynn (Cambridge, Mass., 1976), especially chaps. 2–3, 6; Vera Shlakman, *Economic History of a Factory Town: A Study of Chicopee, Massachusetts* (Northampton, Mass., 1935), pp. 49–56, 139–149; Schultz, *Culture Factory,* chaps. 9–11; Robert G. Layer, *Earnings of Cotton Mill Operatives, 1825–1914* (Cambridge, Mass., 1955); Thomas R. Navin, *The Whitin Machine Works Since 1831* (Cambridge, Mass., 1950), 66–69; Ray Ginger, "Labor in a Massachusetts Cotton Mill, 1853–1860," *Business History Review,* 28 (March 1954): 67–91. (In using the Thernstrom, Gitelman, Layer, and Dawley studies, care must be taken to separate the data and findings on the antebellum period from those of the later decades treated therein. It should also be noted that these authors' general conclusions may not apply to the antebellum period taken by itself.) The account in these paragraphs is also based on sources whose scope is wider than Massachusetts, but which nevertheless contain substantial reference to labor trends within the state: Edith Abbott, *Women in Industry* (New York, 1913); Edward Pessen, *Riches, Class and Power Before the Civil War* (Lexington, Mass., 1973), pp. 38–40; Cole, *American Wool Manufacture,* 1: 233–244, 368–375; Norman Ware, *The Industrial Worker, 1840–1860* (Boston, 1924), chaps. 1–7; Ware, *Early New England Cotton Manufacture,* chaps. 8–9; Deyrup, *Arms Makers of the Connecticut Valley,* pp. 4, 8, 91–109, 217; Lebergott, *Manpower in Economic Growth,* Appendix (contains wage rates for various occupations in Massachusetts).

CHAPTER 5. VARIATIONS AND DISSENTS

1. Daniel Webster, "On the Repeal of the Embargo" (Speech, House of Representatives, April 6, 1814), in *Speeches,* 14: 43–45; Daniel Webster, "Speech on the Tariff," in *Speeches,* 13: 16–19 (quotes in text scattered through pages cited). The first speech above was made when Webster was a representative from New Hampshire and thus not, technically, a Massachusetts politician. However, two years later he moved to Boston, quickly becoming a lawyer for leading shippers there. So his opinions obviously found favor with them.

2. Austin, "The Proposed New Tariff," *North American Review,* 13 (1821): 85–86; Josiah Quincy's speech, *Constitutional Convention Report, 1820,* pp. 251, 252; Everett, "The Tariff Question," *North American Review,* 19 (1824): 246–249.

3. The study referred to here is Lance E. Davis, "Stock Ownership in the Early New England Textile Industry," *Business History Review,* 32 (1958): 204–222. For an interesting insight into the merchants' motives for getting involved in this industry, see Robert F. Dalzell, Jr., "The Rise of the Waltham-Lowell System and Some Thoughts on the Political Economy of Modernization in Ante-Bellum Massachusetts," *Perspectives in American History,* 9 (1975): 229–268.

4. Davis (note 3) finds, strikingly, *no* out-of-state owners in his sample group of stockholders until 1839. Even as late as 1859 they owned only slightly more

than 2% of the total equity surveyed. It is almost certain that the same holds true for the boot and shoe industry.

5. Bancroft, writing in 1843, quoted in Schlesinger, *Age of Jackson*, p. 162.

6. *Ibid.*, pp. 144–176, 254–257, and *passim* (quotes on pp. 144, 154). This interpretation actually originates in an older work, Darling, *Political Changes in Mass.* This is principally an unadorned narrative history, but its largely undeveloped theme is that the Democrats represented the "progressive" forces in the Commonwealth — "the forces outside of or in opposition to the established order" — engaged in battle with a Boston-based aristocracy (quote from p. 39). This treatment was picked up by Schlesinger and refined into the analysis outlined here.

7. *Proceedings and Address of the Massachusetts Democratic State Convention, Held at Worcester, September 26, 1838* . . . (n.p., n.d.), p. 7. For a similar warning, see Amasa Walker, *An Address Delivered Before the Young Men of Boston, Associated for Moral and Intellectual Improvement* . . . [July 4, 1833] (Boston, 1833), p. 27.

8. *Post*, July 16, 1838.

9. Massachusetts Democratic State Central Committee, *Address* . . . *to the Electors of the Commonwealth* . . . *October 26, 1847* (Boston, n.d.), p. 1; Resolutions of the Democratic State Convention, Worcester, September 18, 1850, reprinted in *Post*, September 19, 1850. This theme is an extremely common one and can be found in almost any of the party's pronouncements, especially in the 1830s and 1840s.

10. Paraphrase report of Frederick Robinson's speech in *Post*, March 10, 1835; *ibid.*, October 30, 1833, April 12, 1845, February 24, 1849; Address of the Democratic State Central Committee, reprinted in *ibid.*, November 5, 1852; *ibid.*, June 16, 1858.

11. Representative Henry Williams' speech, U.S., Congress, House, *Congressional Globe*, 26th Cong., 1st sess., 4 June 1840, 8, Appendix, p. 526; *Post*, March 17, 1834; *Proceedings, Mass. Democratic State Convention, Sept. 26, 1838*, p. 7.

12. *Post*, March 26, 1842, July 1, 1843. For the *Post's* treatment of the tariff question, see the issues of September 28, 1839, January 1, 1841, February 6, May 31, 1843. The attack on manufacturing mentioned in the text occurs in an anonymous periodical review (*not* an editorial) in *ibid.*, January 7, 1841.

13. Resolutions of Democratic State Convention, Worcester, September 18, 1850, reprinted in *ibid.*, September 19, 1850. Cf. *ibid.*, November 20, 1838.

14. George Bancroft, *An Oration Delivered Before the Democracy of Springfield and Neighboring Towns, July 4, 1836* (Springfield, 1836), p. 9; *Post*, October 10, 1833 (italics mine); Address and Resolutions of the Democratic State Central Committee, reprinted in *ibid.*, August 6, 1852.

15. Marcus Morton, *Address to the Two Branches of the Legislature of Mas-*

sachusetts. January 20, 1843. Mass. Senate Doc. No. 8 (1843), p. 4; *Post*, October 26, 1836.

16. Address of Democratic State Convention, Worcester, September 1, 1841, reprinted in *ibid.*, September 10, 1841; Letter from Marcus Morton (June 29, 1840) to the Democratic Committee of Arrangements for celebrating the Fourth of July at Worcester, reprinted in *ibid.*, October 20, 1840. Cf. Morton, *Address, Jan. 20, 1843*, p. 5.

17. *Post,* September 14, 1840; Address of the Democratic State Central Committee for 1849, reprinted in *ibid.*, October 19, 1849. For some other considerations of this problem, see *ibid.*, September 12, 1839, November 18, 1840, February 24, 1849; Representative Henry Williams' speech, U.S., Congress, House, *Congressional Globe*, 26th Cong., 1st sess., 4 June 1840, 8, Appendix, p. 533.

18. Frederick Robinson's speech in *Post*, March 10, 1835; Rantoul, "The Education of a Free People," in *Speeches*, pp. 136, 137.

19. Letter from Marcus Morton (June 29, 1840) to the Democratic Committee of Arrangements, *Post,* October 20, 1840; *ibid.*, May 18, 1858; Morton, *Address, Jan. 20, 1843*, p. 4; *Proceedings, Mass. Democratic State Convention, Sept. 26, 1838*, p. 8; *Post,* March 23, 1840 (cf. October 26, 1836, November 20, 1838).

20. *Ibid.*, July 31, 1855, January 28, 1859.

21. Richard Hofstadter, *The American Political Tradition* (New York, 1948), p. 57; Rantoul, "The Education of a Free People," in *Speeches*, p. 118; Address of the Democratic State Central Committee for 1849, reprinted in *Post*, October 19, 1849; *ibid.*, August 30, 1839. Cf. the "Address to the Democratic Electors of Massachusetts" from the convention of Democratic Young Men, Worcester, September 23, 1835, reprinted in *ibid.*, October 16, 1835; *ibid.*, November 10, 1837.

22. "Address of the Democratic Legislative Convention to the People of Massachusetts," reprinted in *ibid.*, April 15, 1840; George Bancroft, "Oration, June 27, 1845," in *Literary and Historical Miscellanies*, p. 465; Robert Rantoul, "Speech at Salem" (October 6, 1848), in *Speeches*, p. 686.

23. Rantoul, "Address to the Workingmen of the United States," in *Speeches*, pp. 219–220, 221, 222; "Examination of the Misrepresentation of Hon. John Davis, as to the Wages of Labor . . . in the U.S. Senate, Jan. 23, 1840," in *Post*, March 19, 1840. (There is no indication of the author, but the *Post* thought enough of this piece to publish copies as an extra sheet for distribution in the forthcoming campaign.)

24. Rantoul, "Address to the Workingmen of the United States," in *Speeches*, pp. 234–235; David Henshaw, *Address . . . at Faneuil Hall . . . Boston, July 4, 1836* (Boston, 1836), p. 27; *Post,* June 18, 1841, February 21, 1860. For more on the shoeworkers' strike, see *ibid.*, February 22, 24, March 5 and 9, 1860.

25. *Ibid.*, July 26, 1836 (cf. November 9 and 10, 1835).

26. Resolutions of Democratic State Convention, Worcester, September 18, 1850, reprinted in *ibid.*, September 19, 1850; Letter from Marcus Morton, August 20, 1840, reprinted in *ibid.*, September 17, 1840. At one point the state central committee did (briefly) criticize the legislature for not passing hours legislation. Mass. Democratic State Central Committee, *Address, Oct. 26, 1847*, p. 1.

27. Representative Henry Williams' speech, U.S., Congress, House, *Congressional Globe*, 26th Cong., 1st sess., 4 June 1840, 8, Appendix: 531. For other examples, see the *Post*, March 10, 1835 (Frederick Robinson's speech), December 26, 1834, April 10, 29, and 30, 1840, October 10, 1840 (Resolutions of the Democratic State Convention, Springfield, September 16, 1840), March 24, 1842, October 17, 1845 (Address of the Democratic State Central Committee, October 15, 1845).

28. See, for instance, *ibid.*, February 8, 1843, February 24, 1849.

29. Quote from *ibid.*, March 18, 1843. Some idea of the trend of Democratic thinking on the secret ballot can be gathered from the following: *ibid.*, December 26, 1834, March 4 and 17, 1840, May 3, 1841 (Address of Democratic members of the Massachusetts legislature), December 14, 1842, February 6, 23, September 14, 1843 (Resolves of the Democratic State Convention, Worcester, September 13, 1843), November 10, 1843 (Address of the Democratic State Central Committee), October 17, 1845 (Address of the Democratic State Central Committee), October 26, 1846 (Address of the Democratic State Central Committee), October 30, 1850, November 1, 1850, August 18 and 22, 1851 (Resolutions of Democratic State Convention, Worcester, August 20, 1851), September 9, 1852 (Resolutions of Democratic State Convention, Fitchburg, September 8, 1852), November 5, 1852 (Address of the Democratic State Central Committee). Most of these contain just brief mention of the measure.

30. *Ibid.*, February 24, October 19, 1849 (Address of the Democratic State Central Committee). (Italics mine in both quotes.)

31. Arthur M. Schlesinger, Jr., *Orestes A. Brownson: A Pilgrim's Progress* (1939; reprint ed., New York: 1963), pp. 100–107.

32. To determine the views of these three reformers on worker-related matters, I used the standard biographies and a large (though not complete) selection of their public speeches and writings. For Garrison, I relied on Wendell Phillips Garrison and Frances Jackson Garrison, *William Lloyd Garrison 1805–1879*, 4 vols. (New York, 1885–1894); Russel B. Nye, *William Lloyd Garrison and the Humanitarian Reformers* (Boston, 1955); Walter M. Merrill, *Against Wind and Tide: A Biography of Wm. Lloyd Garrison* (Cambridge, Mass., 1963); and John L. Thomas, *The Liberator: William Lloyd Garrison* (Boston, 1963). I also found helpful the discussion of Garrison in Aileen S. Kraditor, *Means and Ends in American Abolitionism* (New York, 1967). In these studies I located references to specific worker-related editorials in *The Liberator* from 1831 to 1850, and

proceeded to examine them. For Phillips, I used Oscar Sherwin, *Prophet of Liberty: The Life and Times of Wendell Phillips* (New York, 1958); Irving H. Bartlett, *Wendell Phillips: Brahmin Radical* (Boston, 1961); and the public speeches contained in Wendell Phillips, *Speeches, Lectures, and Letters,* 2 vols. (Boston, 1894, 1900). For Parker, my guide was Henry Steele Commager, *Theodore Parker,* 2nd ed. (Boston, 1947). I used the sermons and writings in his *Collected Works,* Centenary Ed., 15 vols. (Boston, 1910–1913).

33. Quoted in Bartlett, *Phillips,* p. 130; quoted in Sherwin, *Prophet,* p. 282.

34. Quoted in *ibid.,* pp. 282, 291; Wendell Phillips, "The Scholar in a Republic" (Speech, Cambridge, Mass., June 30, 1881), in *Speeches,* 2nd ser., pp. 350, 351. The two latter quotes in the text date from the 1870s but accurately describe Phillips's attitude toward what he was trying to do in the antebellum period. I quoted Phillips extensively because he was much more self-conscious about the role of the agitator than either Parker or Garrison. But there are some interesting parallels in Parker's idea of the role of the minister in his "The Function of a Teacher of Religion" (Sermon, Barre, Mass., June 13, 1855), in *Works,* 4: 288–341 (see especially pp. 322–326).

35. For the influence of their voyages to England, see Commager, *Parker,* pp. 92, 160–161; Bartlett, *Phillips,* p. 338; Thomas, *Liberator,* pp. 297–299. Thomas, it should be noted, sees different implications in Garrison's trip than I do.

36. *Liberator,* January 1 and 29, 1831. Cf. February 5, 1831.

37. *Ibid.,* February 5, 1831, September 24, 1831, August 6, 1836.

38. *Ibid.,* October 23, 1840, December 18, 1840, November 24, 1843, January 5, 1844, July 6, 1849.

39. Wendell Phillips, "Woman's Rights" (Speech, Worcester, October 15 and ·16, 1851), in *Speeches,* 1st ser., pp. 31–33; Wendell Phillips, "A Metropolitan Police" (Speech, Boston, April 5, 1863), in *ibid.,* pp. 495–496; Bartlett, *Phillips,* p. 338. See also Phillips's letter to R. D. Webb, January 13, 1848, quoted in Sherwin, *Prophet,* p. 160.

40. Parker, "The Function of a Teacher of Religion," in *Works,* 4: 325, 326.

41. For the evolution of Parker's thought on labor matters, see Commager, *Parker,* pp. 45–46, 160–164, 171–185.

42. Theodore Parker, "Poverty" (Sermon, January 14, 1849), in *Works,* 9: 263, 265; Theodore Parker, "The Perishing Classes" (Sermon, August 30, 1846), in *ibid.,* 10: 117.

43. For his attempts to analyze the composition of the poor, see Parker, "Poverty," *ibid.,* 9: 273 (quote from this source); Parker, "The Perishing Classes," *ibid.,* 10: 110.

44. Parker, "Poverty," *ibid.,* 9: 264; Theodore Parker, "The Mercantile Classes" (Sermon, November 22, 1846) in *ibid.,* 10: 15; Theodore Parker, "The Laboring Classes (Essay in the *Dial,* April 1841) in *ibid.,* 10: 46, 47 (cf. pp. 49–51).

45. Theodore Parker, "The Education of the Laboring Classes" (Lecture before the American Institute of Instruction, August 1841), in *ibid.*, 10: 78; Parker, "Poverty," *ibid.*, 9: 264; Theodore Parker, "Moral Conditions" (Sermon, February 11, 1849), in *ibid.*, 10: 264 (cf. pp. 264–276). See also Theodore Parker, "The Dangerous Classes" (Sermon, January 31, 1847), in *ibid.*, 10: 166–167; and "The Perishing Classes," *ibid.*, 10: 114, 118–119.

46. Parker, "Poverty," *ibid.*, 9: 263.

47. *Liberator*, March 26 and 19, 1847.

48. *Ibid.*, July 9, 1847.

49. Theodore Parker, "The Public Education of the People" (Address before the Onandaga Teacher's Institute, Syracuse, N.Y., October 4, 1849), in *Works*, 9: 109; Theodore Parker, "Daniel Webster" (Sermon, October 31, 1852), in *ibid.*, 7: 277.

50. Parker, "Poverty," *ibid.*, 9: 273–277 (cf. the general discussion of the causes of poverty on pp. 269–272). Parker did make note of the economic power of the employer over his workers in factories and other large-scale enterprises. But aside from criticizing the employer for trying to control the votes of workers, he failed to draw any conclusions from this. See Parker, "The Mercantile Classes," *ibid.*, 10: 14; Theodore Parker, "The Rights of Man in America" (1854), *ibid.*, 12: 350.

51. *Liberator*, November 19, 1841, January 5, 1844, August 19, 1844; Parker, "Poverty," in *Works*, 9: 286; Parker, "The Perishing Classes," *ibid.*, 10: 134. For more on Garrison's views, see Thomas, *Liberator,* pp. 312–316, 370–371 and Kraditor, *Means and Ends*, pp. 252–255, 268–269 (note 47).

52. See Wendell Phillips, "Capital Punishment" (Speech, Boston, March 16, 1855), in *Speeches*, 2nd ser., p. 106; Parker, "Poverty," in *Works*, 9: 263; Theodore Parker, "The State of the Nation" (1850), *ibid.*, 12: 92–96; Theodore Parker, "The Present Crisis in American Affairs" (1856), *ibid.*, 12: 441.

53. Parker, "The Mercantile Classes," *ibid.*, 10: 14; Bartlett, *Phillips*, p. 428 (note 17).

54. How widespread that indifference or hostility was has been a matter of some debate. For different views, see Joseph G. Rayback, "The American Workingmen and the Antislavery Crusade," *Journal of Economic History*, 3 (1943): 152–163; Williston H. Lofton, "Abolition and Labor," *Journal of Negro History*, 33 (1948): 249–283; Philip S. Foner, *History of the Labor Movement in the United States*, 4 vols. (New York, 1947–1965), 1: 266–296; Bernard Mandel, *Labor: Free and Slave* (New York, 1955), pp. 61–169. Most of these authors find that workers grew notably more sympathetic to antislavery in the late forties and in the fifties — but *only* to the Republican and Free Soil versions, not to abolitionism.

55. See Thomas, *Liberator*, pp. 448–449; Garrison's letter to W. G. H. Smart, August 18, 1875, in Garrison and Garrison, *Garrison*, 4: 248–249; Harold Schwartz, *Samuel Gridley Howe: Social Reformer 1801–1876* (Cambridge,

Mass., 1956), pp. 268–269; Bartlett, *Phillips*, pp. 349–350 (May quote from p. 350).

CHAPTER 6. THE GENERATION OF DOUBT

1. For treatments of this theme, see David J. Rothman, *The Discovery of the Asylum: Social Order and Disorder in the New Republic* (Boston, 1971), especially chaps. 3, 5, 7, 9; Meyers, *Jacksonian Persuasion*; Fred Somkin, *Unquiet Eagle: Memory and Desire in the Idea of American Freedom, 1815–1860* (Ithaca, N.Y., 1967), especially chap. 1; Clifford S. Griffin, *Their Brothers' Keepers: Moral Stewardship in the United States, 1800–1865* (New Brunswick, N.J., 1960), especially chap. 3; Rowland Berthoff, *An Unsettled People: Social Order and Disorder in American History* (New York, 1971), especially chaps. 16–18. Winthrop quote from his "The Influence of Commerce" (Address to the Boston Mercantile Library Association, October 15, 1845), in *Speeches*, 1: 56.

2. See, for instance, the very interesting discussion in Rothman, *Discovery of the Asylum*, chap. 7, of the prevailing view of the asylum builders on the causes of poverty. Although eager to blame social disorganization for the plight of other unfortunates (the insane, criminals), in the case of the poor they pulled back. The poor themselves are primarily responsible for their own plight, they said, because of their intemperance, vice, laziness, and other traits; social factors are of secondary importance. So, although these men drew attention to the growing problem of poverty, they provided no more convincing explanation of it than the average politician. For the origins of this view, see Redmond J. Barnett, "From Philanthropy to Reform: Poverty, Drunkenness, and the Social Order in Massachusetts, 1780–1825" (Ph.D. dissertation, Harvard University, 1973).

3. Leo Marx, *The Machine in the Garden: Technology and the Pastoral Ideal* (New York, 1964), especially chaps. 4–6. I do not mean to deny the importance of this book, which I found, for the most part, very stimulating. My purpose is only to caution against using its thesis in a way the author does not intend: to account for the growing criticism of the respectable worker image in Massachusetts after 1840. Marx, by the way, has some interesting things to say (chap. 4) on how *popular* machines and technology were among antebellum politicians.

4. Quoted in Alice Felt Tyler, *Freedom's Ferment* (1944; reprint ed., Freeport, N.Y., 1970), p. 166.

5. *Ibid.*, pp. 183–184; T. D. Seymour Bassett, "The Secular Utopian Socialists," *Socialism in American Life*, 2 vols., ed. Donald D. Egbert and Stow Persons (Princeton, N.J., 1952), 1: 183–184, 205 ("limited" quote on p. 183). Adin Ballou's Hopedale Community, near Milford, Mass., was supposedly based on "Christian socialism." Yet the main ingredient in its "fraternal communism" was, ironically enough, the very capitalistic device of joint stock ownership. See Tyler, *Freedom's Ferment*, pp. 166–171.

6. Much of what follows, on the antebellum period, is drawn from two classic studies, John R. Commons et al, *History of Labour in the United States*, 4 vols.

APPENDICES, NOTES, BIBLIOGRAPHICAL NOTE, INDEX

(New York, 1918–1935), vol. 1; and Ware, *Industrial Worker*. Despite these two works' many virtues, a more modern inquiry is badly needed. One that serves this purpose well, for a segment of the Massachusetts working class, is Dawley, *Class and Community*.

7. Information on the factory operatives' strikes is sparse. See Ware, *Early New England Cotton Manufacture*, pp. 272–279.

8. Quoted in Commons, *History of Labour*, 1: 292.

9. For analyses of the party's vote, see Arthur B. Darling, "The Workingmen's Party in Massachusetts," *American Historical Review*, 29 (1923): 81–186; and Edward Pessen, "Did Labor Support Jackson? The Boston Story," *Political Science Quarterly*, 64 (1949): 262–274. Darling contends that the party was in effect the "radical wing of the Democratic party"; Arthur Schlesinger maintains that, by 1834–1836, the Workingmen's party was cooperating openly with (if it had not already been absorbed by) the Democrats. Schlesinger, *Age of Jackson*, pp. 155–176. It appears to me, however, that this line of argument has been effectively challenged by Edward Pessen in his *Most Uncommon Jacksonians: The Radical Leaders of the Early Labor Movement* (Albany, N.Y., 1967), pp. 24–25.

10. Luther quoted in *ibid.*, p. 161. See chaps. 7–12 of this work for an excellent analysis of the ideas of American labor reformers in this period.

11. Orestes Brownson, "The Laboring Classes," *Boston Quarterly Review*, 3 (1840): 358–395, 420–512 (quotes on pp. 370, 372, 375, 472). I do not mean to suggest that all of this essay is unalloyed genius. Much of it is silly, as in his insistence that "the priesthood" (i.e., all organized religion) is also a fundamental cause of the worker's plight or his belief that the abolition of hereditary property is the best way to alleviate that plight. Brownson's idiosyncrasies had a way of working against as well as aiding his better judgment. Incidentally, for several years after he wrote this he continued to attack the industrial system and the impoverishment and exploitation of labor. See Schlesinger, *Brownson*, pp. 164–170.

12. George R. Taylor, *The Transportation Revolution 1815–1860* (New York, 1951), p. 284.

13. The outcome of even this strike is uncertain, an indication of how little is known of unionization in this period. Taylor, *ibid.*, p. 285, reports that the workers won substantially all their demands. Ware, *Industrial Worker*, p. 47, says the strike was "utterly lost." The truth is apparently somewhere in between. See the balanced appraisals in John P. Hall, "The Gentle Craft: A Narrative of Yankee Shoemakers" (Ph.D. dissertation, Columbia University, 1953), pp. 279–294; and Dawley, *Class and Community*, pp. 78–89. For a catalog of this and other strikes in the forties and fifties, see *MBSL 11 (1880)*, pp. 3–19.

14. For comparative figures on wages in manufacturing for 1870, see Kuznets and Thomas, *Population Redistribution and Economic Growth*, 2: 129. Easterlin, "Interregional Differences in Per Capita Income," in *Trends in the American*

Economy, has, for 1840, comparative data on nonagricultural income per worker in fields other than commerce (a close approximation of industrial workers) on pp. 97–98. For 1880 he has comparative data on nonagricultural income per worker only for all fields in that category, pp. 99–101.

15. Layer, *Earnings of Cotton Mill Operatives, passim,* but especially pp. 45–51. Even these unfavorable figures overstate the workers' relative prosperity, for they presume the worker was actually employed the maximum number of hours that the mill was in operation, which did not often happen.

16. Wright, *Census of Massachusetts: 1875,* 2: xlvi, 751–752.

17. For more data on wages in this period, see Ware, *Early New England Cotton Manufacture,* pp. 112–113, 240–244; Ware, *Industrial Worker,* pp. xii, chaps. 1, 4; Taylor, *Transportation Revolution,* pp. 294–300. The estimate for male shoeworkers' real wages is by Dawley, *Class and Community,* p. 158 (cf. pp. 149–159).

18. For hours of labor in cotton textiles, see Layer, *Earnings of Cotton Mill Operatives,* pp. 23, 43; Ware, *Early New England Cotton Manufacture,* pp. 249–250, 255–256.

19. On health conditions in the textile mills, see *ibid.,* pp. 251–254. Contemporary medical testimony is presented in Ware, *Industrial Worker,* chap. 5.

20. For information on turnover rates, see Ginger, "Labor in a Massachusetts Cotton Mill," pp. 85–91; Shlakman, *Economic History of a Factory Town,* p. 149; Ware, *Early New England Cotton Manufacture,* pp. 224–226; Dawley, *Class and Community,* pp. 139–142.

21. The dead-end nature of factory work became suddenly real in this period for a large group within the working class, the shoemakers, as the mechanization of their trade between 1840 and 1865 effectively closed off almost any chance for them to make a living as independent craftsmen. See Hall, "Gentle Craft," pp. 243–278. However, their chances of rising into the ranks of shoe *manufacturers* were apparently unaffected, especially if they were skilled cutters to begin with. For data on this type of mobility between 1832 and 1880, see Dawley, *Class and Community,* pp. 55–56, 159–166. A similarly mixed picture emerges in Waltham, where textile mill workers had very limited job mobility, whereas more highly skilled, better paid watch factory workers exhibited relatively high rates of job mobility (especially if they were not Irish). See Gitelman, *Workingmen of Waltham,* pp. 68–74. The present state of knowledge about mobility rates in this period is so incomplete and shows such variations that broad generalizations, in my view, still cannot be made.

22. See Table 6, p. 34.

23. Quoted in *Report* [of the Special Committee upon the petition of Mary W. Healy and 411 others, Lowell operatives]. *Mass. House Doc. No. 48 (1844),* p. 2.

24. In addition to the Commons and Norman Ware studies, I have relied, for information on the ten-hour agitation, on Charles E. Persons, "The Early His-

tory of Factory Legislation in Massachusetts: From 1825 to the Passage of the Ten Hour Law in 1874," in *Labor Laws and their Enforcement With Special Reference to Massachusetts*, ed. Susan M. Kingsbury (New York, 1911), pp. 24–89. Ware argues in *Industrial Worker*, pp. 125–126, that the movement in the fifties was carried out principally by middle-class philanthropists, while the workers lost interest. But even his own evidence (as well as that of Commons and Persons) points to just the opposite conclusion.

25. For the Massachusetts Crispins, see Hall, "Gentle Craft," pp. 295–356; Dawley, *Class and Community*, pp. 143–148, 175–188; and John P. Hall, "The Knights of St. Crispin in Massachusetts, 1869–1878," *Journal of Economic History*, 18 (1958): 161–175.

26. For union activities and strikes in this period, see Commons, *History of Labour*, 2: 16–24, 43–48, 76–79; Montgomery, *Beyond Equality*, pp. 277–295; *MBSL 11 (1880)*, pp. 19–65.

27. For workers' cooperatives in Mass., see Hall, "Gentle Craft," pp. 334–346; Commons, *History of Labour*, 2: 171–175; *MBSL 6 (1875)*, pp. 453–490; *MBSL 8 (1877)*, pp. 51–137. Information on the early organizing of the Knights of Labor in the state can be found in Commons, *History of Labour*, 2: 200; Hall, "Gentle Craft," pp. 359–360; Norman Ware, *The Labor Movement in the United States 1860–1895* (1929; reprint ed., Gloucester, Mass., 1959), p. 200.

28. The progress of this agitation can be traced in Persons, "Early History of Factory Legislation," p. 98; Commons, *History of Labour*, 2: 86–142; Montgomery, *Beyond Equality*, pp. 123–125, 230–277, 296–323.

29. On this party, see Commons, *History of Labour*, 2: 138–144; Edith E. Ware, *Political Opinion in Massachusetts During Civil War and Reconstruction* (New York, 1917), pp. 185–187; Bartlett, *Phillips*, pp. 344–359.

30. The best account of Butler's activities in this decade is Hans L. Trefousse, *Ben Butler: The South Called Him BEAST!* (New York, 1957), pp. 217–243. See also William D. Mallam, "Butlerism in Massachusetts," *New England Quarterly*, 33 (1960): 186–206 (and especially 201–202). On the Greenback movement in Massachusetts, see Bartlett, *Phillips*, pp. 360–364; Commons, *History of Labour*, 2: 243, 246; Robert P. Sharkey, *Money, Class, and Party: An Economic Study of Civil War and Reconstruction* (Baltimore, 1959), pp. 199–206.

31. All quotes in this paragraph from Wendell Phillips, as follows: quoted in Bartlett, *Phillips*, p. 346; "The Foundation of the Labor Movement" (Speech, Labor Reform convention, Worcester, September 4, 1871), in *Speeches*, 2nd ser., pp. 152, 153, 156; *The People Coming to Power! Speech . . . at the Salisbury Beach Gathering, September 13, 1871* (Boston, 1871), p. 10.

32. John Quincy Adams, Jr., *Massachusetts and South Carolina* (Boston, [1868]), p. 3.

33. See *supra*, pp. 28–30; Albert Bushnell Hart, ed., *Commonwealth History of Massachusetts*, 5 vols. (New York, 1927–1930), 4: 143.

34. The classic study of this whole process in Massachusetts — indeed, a path-breaking work in the history of immigration — is Handlin, *Boston's Immi-*

grants. I have relied heavily on it for this section. For evidence on how the Irish were treated — or mistreated — in a small town, see Gitelman, *Workingmen of Waltham, passim.*

35. See especially Handlin, *Boston's Immigrants,* chap. 3 and pp. 216–219. Statistical corroboration of these trends is abundant. Consult *9 U.S. Census (1870),* vol. 1, *Population,* p. 739; *Compendium of the Tenth Census,* pp. 1366–1367; Layer, *Earnings of Cotton Mill Operatives,* pp. 70–71; *MBSL 3 (1872),* pp. 33–34; Cole, *American Wool Manufacture,* 1: 369–370; Persons, "Early History of Factory Legislation," p. 92; Shlakman, *Economic History of a Factory Town,* pp. 138–139; Ware, *Early New England Cotton Manufacture,* pp. 228–232. Only in the boot and shoe industry did foreigners fail to make appreciable headway.

36. For immigrants in cities, see Knights, *Plain People of Boston,* chap. 3; DeWitt, *Abstract of the Census, 1855,* pp. 102–132; Warner, *Abstract of the Census, 1865,* pp. 56–81; Wright, *Census of Massachusetts: 1875,* 1: 3–8, 287–339; Cole, *Immigrant City,* pp. 27–67; and, of course, Handlin, *Boston's Immigrants.* Here again, cities and towns where shoemaking was an important industry were exceptions to this rule.

37. Henry J. Gardner, *Address . . . to the Two Branches of the Legislature of Massachusetts, January 9, 1855. Mass. Senate Doc. No. 3 (1855),* pp. 10, 8. This and Gardner's other two inaugural addresses are a good index of the range and intensity of the nativists' concerns. Cf. his *Address . . . to the Two Branches of the Legislature of Massachusetts, January 3, 1856. Mass. Senate Doc. No. 3 (1856)* and *Address . . . to the Two Branches of the Legislature of Massachusetts, January 9, 1857. Mass. Senate Doc. No. 3 (1857).*

38. See Handlin, *Boston's Immigrants,* chap. 7; Bean, "Party Transformation in Massachusetts," pp. 195–374; George H. Haynes, "The Causes of Know-Nothing Success in Massachusetts," *American Historical Review,* 3 (1897): 67–82; George H. Haynes, "A Know-Nothing Legislature" in American Historical Association, *Annual Report, 1896,* 2 vols., 1 (1897): 175–187; David Donald, *Charles Sumner and the Coming of the Civil War* (New York, 1960), pp. 268–269.

39. As late as the 1870s Irish Democrats had made little headway in the party hierarchy. Its nominees for important posts were invariably native-born. Only Patrick Collins had substantial influence in party councils. The Irish takeover of the Democratic organization did not occur until the 1880s and 1890s.

40. George Hillard's speech, *Constitutional Convention Report, 1853,* 1: 322; Nathaniel Ward's speech, *ibid.,* 2: 630; *MBE 19 (1856),* p. 42; *MBE 23 (1860),* p. 39; report of chairman of the Board of Alien Commissioners, 1858, quoted in *MBSC 1 (1865),* p. 250.

41. Robert Winthrop, "Boston Mechanics and Boston Patriots" (Speech before the Mass. Charitable Mechanic Association, October 11, 1854), in *Speeches,* 2: 190–191.

42. Boutwell quoted in *Account of the Proceedings at the Inauguration of the*

State Industrial School for Girls, at Lancaster, Aug. 27, 1856 (Boston, 1856), p. 45; Edward Everett, "The Importance of Agriculture" (Address, N.Y. State Agricultural Society, Buffalo, N.Y., October 9, 1857), in *Speeches*, 3: 556, 557. For other examples of this theme, see Winthrop, "The Influence of Commerce," in *Speeches*, 1: 42; Mann, "Thoughts for a Young Man," in *Lectures on Various Subjects*, pp. 7–25; Cushing, *Address, Sept. 26, 1850*, pp. 11–12; *MBE 19 (1856)*, p. 43.

43. Richard H. Dana's speech, *Constitutional Convention Report, 1853*, 1: 492; George Hillard's speech, *ibid.*, 1: 584; Ben Butler's speech, *ibid.*, 1: 594; [John G. Palfrey], *A Chapter in American History. Five Years' Progress of the Slave Power . . .* (Boston, 1852), p. 68. This darker view of the cities — especially of their potential political effects — was expressed often at the 1853 constitutional convention, which debated proposals for apportioning representation to give cities more power. See, for example, the rest of Dana's speech cited above, pp. 492–493 and his other comments on pp. 586–587 and vol. 2: 107; Whiting Griswold's speech, *Constitutional Convention Report, 1853*, 1: 431; B. F. Hallett's speech, *ibid.*, 1: 480. For further adverse reactions to the immigrants of antebellum Boston, from politicians and others, see Schultz, *Culture Factory*, pp. 210–251.

44. Apologies for cities can be found in Henry Dawes's speech, *Constitutional Convention Report, 1853*, 1: 540; William Schouler's speech, *ibid.*, 1: 587; Joseph Morss's speech, *ibid.*, 1: 603; Henry Kinsman's speech, *ibid.*, 1: 605; John Gray's speech, *ibid.*, 1: 613; Francis Crowninshield's speech, *ibid.*, 2: 84–85; George White's speech, *ibid.*, 2: 96. Others criticized cities for their excessive wealth and economic power. See John B. Alley's speech, *ibid.*, 1: 592; Ben Butler's speech, *ibid.*, 1: 594–595; B. F. Hallett, *Speech . . . in Faneuil Hall, Oct. 21, 1853, in Favor of the Adoption of the New Constitution* (n.p., n.d.), p. 6; Josiah Quincy, *Considerations Respectfully Submitted to the Citizens of Boston and Charlestown, on the Proposed Annexation of these Two Cities* (Boston, 1854), pp. 6–9.

45. See Handlin, *Boston's Immigrants*, pp. 73–82.

46. Boutwell, *Address, Sept. 18, 1850*, p. 14. For other examples, see Edward Everett, "Effects of Immigration" (Remarks before Association for the support of the Warren St. chapel, Boston, April 18, 1852), in *Speeches*, 3: 106–107; Winthrop, "American Agriculture," in *Speeches*, 2: 72–73; *Post*, May 4, 1844, January 13 and 15, 1855, September 8, 1856; Charles Sumner, "Political Parties and our Foreign-Born Population" (Speech, Boston, November 2, 1855), in *The Works of Charles Sumner*, 15 vols. (Boston, 1870–1883), 4: 78; Caleb Cushing, *Speeches on the Amendment of the Constitution of Massachusetts, Imposing Disabilities on Naturalized Citizens of the United States* (Boston, 1859), p. 16.

47. For more on these developments, see Handlin, *Boston's Immigrants*, chap. 8 (the phrase "appearance of stability" is his); Frisch, *Town into City*, pp. 125–126.

48. The Springfield *Republican* was a close second, but editor Samuel Bowles's independent stance quickly led to apostasy (in the form of Liberal Republicanism) and outright refusal to support certain regular Republican candidates. The *Advertiser*, on the other hand, nearly always spoke for the state party's dominant wing (or wings) throughout this period. In the sixties the paper firmly supported the Radical wing. In the seventies it took a more moderate line, backed Grant and Hays, attacked the Liberal Republican movement, and stood foursquare for a higher tariff and sound currency.

49. *MBSC 3 (1867)*, p. 26; Boston *Daily Advertiser*, May 3, 1871. For other favorable comments on continued immigration, see Nathaniel Banks, *Speech . . . upon the Representation of the United States at the Exhibition of the World's Industry, Paris, 1867 . . .* (Washington, D.C., 1866), p. 22; George F. Hoar, *Claims of the Free Institute of Industrial Science upon the Commonwealth . . . February 11, 1869* (n.p., n.d.), p. 9; and, among many editorials in the *Advertiser*, those of March 20, May 23, July 31 (all 1867), June 25, 1870, August 16, 1878, December 27, 1878, September 29, 1879, April 19, 1880, June 4, 1880. For attacks on "coolie" labor, see Ben Butler, *Address . . . Suggestions of the Effect of an Imported Laboring Class upon American Institutions, Delivered at Woodstock, Conn., July 4, 1870* (Washington, D.C., 1870), pp. 6–8; Wendell Phillips, "The Chinese" (Editorial, *National Standard*, July 30, 1870), in *Speeches*, 2nd ser., pp. 145–147. Cf. *Advertiser*, July 31, 1867, June 25, 1870.

50. *Ibid.*, July 31, 1867, May 31, 1871, March 25, 1868, January 17, 1867. See also September 28, 1868, August 16, 1878, September 29, 1879, April 19, 1880.

51. For indications of concern about all these problems, see Franklin B. Sanborn, "Poverty and Public Charity," *North American Review*, 110 (1870): 341–342; *MBSC 12 (1876)*, pp. lxxii, lxxxi; *Advertiser*, June 27, 1870, January 9, 1874; Rothman, *Discovery of the Asylum*, pp. 290–291; Alexander H. Bullock, *Address . . . to the Two Branches of the Legislature of Massachusetts, January 3, 1868. Mass. Senate Doc. No. 1 (1868)*, pp. 35–36. See also the discussion on the child labor problem in chap. 7.

52. For illiteracy among immigrants, see *MBE 37 (1874)*, pp. 112–116 and chap. 7 of the present work. On immigrant birth rates, consult *MBSC 3 (1867)*, pp. 26–32; *MBSL 9 (1878)*, p. 102 (figures cited in text are from the latter). On intemperance as a cause of poverty, see, among many examples, Wendell Phillips, "The Maine Liquor Law" (Speech, Boston, February 28, 1865), in *Speeches*, 2nd ser., p. 190; *MBSC 4 (1868)*, pp. 133–137 and *MBSC 5 (1869)*, pp. 174–175; D. Leigh Colvin, *Prohibition in the United States* (New York, 1926), pp. 85–86; William Gaston, *Address . . . to the Two Branches of the Legislature of Massachusetts, January 7, 1875. Mass. Senate Doc. No. 1 (1875)*, p. 32; Alexander H. Rice, *Address . . . to the Two Branches of the Legislature of Massachusetts, January 6, 1876. Mass. Senate Doc. No. 1 (1876)*, p. 51.

53. *Advertiser*, August 16, 1878. This editorial also found in Massachusetts cities a large population "not so intelligent as might be wished," and again the

context shows this refers to immigrants. Cf. the similar qualifications in the issue of September 29, 1879.

54. *Ibid.*, July 25, 1877. For similar reactions to immigrant-inspired mob violence (or the threat thereof), see *ibid.*, July 14, 1875, June 21, 1877, July 28, 1877, August 19, 1878; [Charles Francis Adams, Jr.], "The Railroad System," *North American Review*, 104 (1867): 491–492. On crime and lawlessness, see *MBSL 11 (1880)*, pp. 123–195; Talbot, *Address, Jan. 2, 1879*, p. 29; Rothman, *Discovery of the Asylum*, pp. 252–257, 261–262.

55. *Advertiser*, April 17, 1879. For examples of some of these apprehensions, see the issues of March 22, 1867, February 25, 1869, August 13, 1874, January 3, 1880.

56. *MBSC 12 (1876)*, pp. lxxii, lxxxi; *MBSC 2 (1866)*, pp. xxii–xxiii; *MBSC 14 (1878)*, pp. xiv–xvi (cf. *MBSC 8* [1872], p. lxv); *Advertiser*, January 9 and 23, 1874.

CHAPTER 7. THREE DISQUIETING ISSUES: SECRET BALLOT, CHILD LABOR, HOURS LAW

1. Morton, *Address, Jan. 1, 1840*, p. 39.

2. Josiah Quincy's speech, *Constitutional Convention Report, 1820*, p. 251. Cf. Warren Dutton's speech, *ibid.*, pp. 247–248; Samuel Hoar's speech, *ibid.*, p. 248; Israel Thorndike's speech, *ibid.*, p. 253. The votes of factory workers were discussed by Quincy and by James T. Austin, *ibid.*, p. 253.

3. Davis, *Speech on Impost Duties, May 4, 1830*, p. 27. Cf. Edward Everett's speech, U.S., Congress, House, *Register of Debates*, 21st Cong., 1st sess., 8 May 1830, p. 911.

4. Morton, *Address, Jan. 1, 1840*, p. 39. Cf. his *Address, Jan. 20, 1843*, p. 8. The best accounts of the secret ballot agitation prior to 1850 are in the speeches of Foster Hooper, *Constitutional Convention Report, 1853*, 1: 307–308, and of Amasa Walker, *ibid.*, pp. 308–310 (quote on p. 309). See also the Democratic sources cited in note 29 of chap. 5, and Michel Brunet, "The Secret Ballot Issue in Massachusetts Politics From 1851 to 1853," *New England Quarterly*, 25 (1952): 354–362.

5. Horace Mann, "Speech, Delivered at Worcester" (at the Free Soil state convention, September 16, 1851), in *Slavery*, p. 562. On the Lowell incident, see Ware, *Industrial Worker*, pp. 102–103. For the House investigation, see *Report* [of the Special Committee on alleged election irregularities in Lowell]. *Mass. House Doc. No. 230 (1852)*.

6. *Post*, November 1, 1850, March 18, 1843; Henry Williams's speech, *Constitutional Convention Report, 1853*, 1: 285; Foster Hooper's speech, *ibid.*, 1: 308.

7. Morton, *Address, Jan. 1, 1840*, p. 39.

8. Samuel French's speech, *Constitutional Convention Report, 1853*, 1: 313; Henry Wilson's speech, *ibid.*, 1: 303; Mann, "Speech, Delivered at Worcester,"

in *Slavery*, p. 563; *Report* [of the Special Committee on alleged election ir-regularities in Lowell]. *Mass House Doc. No. 230 (1852)*, p. 148.

9. George Briggs's speech, *Constitutional Convention Report, 1853*, 1: 335; William Schouler's speech, *ibid.*, 1: 332. For similar statements on this and the related poll tax issue, see George Hillard's speech, *ibid.*, 1: 321–322; Joseph Morss's speech, *ibid.*, 1: 313–314; Otis Lord's speech, *ibid.*, 1: 298–299; Samuel Lathrop's speech, *ibid.*, 1: 388–390; Curtis, "Letters of Phocion," in *Discussions on the Constitution*, pp. 56–59; George Hillard, "The Letters of Silas Standfast to his Friend Jotham . . . ," in *ibid.*, pp. 111–115.

10. For statistics on child labor in cotton and woolen mills, see Ware, *Early New England Cotton Manufacture*, pp. 198–200, 210–212; Cole, *American Wool Manufacture*, 1: 370–372; Mass. Commissioners on the Hours of Labor, *Reports of Commissioners on the Hours of Labor. Mass. House Doc. No. 44 (1867)*, p. 7. The overall statistics for 1870 and 1880 can be found in *9 U.S. Census (1870)*, 1: 739; *10 U.S. Census (1880)*, vol. 2, *Manufactures*, p. 1358; Carroll Wright, *The Census of Massachusetts: 1880* (Boston, 1883), p. 458.

11. Caleb Strong, "Message to the Legislature" (January 10, 1816), in *Mass. Acts and Resolves, 1816*, p. 84; Persons, "Early History of Factory Legislation," pp. 4–8. Cf. the optimism expressed by Governor Levi Lincoln in his *Speech, June 2, 1825*, p. 13.

12. *Report* [by Committee on Education, Relative to the Education of Chil-dren Employed in Manufacturing Establishments]. *Mass. House Doc. No. 49 (1836)* (quote on p. 6); Persons, "Early History of Factory Legislation," pp. 17–20; *Mass. Acts and Resolves, 1836*, chap. 245, vol. 13.

13. Criticisms of enforcement of the law can be found in *MBE 3 (1840)*, pp. 43–45; *MBE 20 (1857)*, pp. 49–50; *MBE 23 (1860)*, pp. 39, 58–59; *MBE 26 (1863)*, p. 51; *MBE 28 (1865)*, pp. 50–52. The child labor laws of the antebellum period are *Mass. Acts and Resolves, 1837*, chap. 107, vol. 14; *ibid., 1842*, chap. 60; *ibid., 1849*, chap. 220; *ibid., 1855*, chap. 379. The provisions granting en-forcement power to school committees and regulating child labor in factories are in the 1842 act.

14. Mass. Special Commission on the Hours of Labor, *Report of the Special Commission on the Hours of Labor, and the Condition and Prospects of the Industrial Classes. February, 1866. Mass. House Doc. No. 98 (1866)* (quotes on pp. 4, 5); *Reports of Commissioners (1867)*. The two new laws were *Mass. Acts and Resolves, 1866*, chap. 273; *ibid., 1867*, chap. 285. The provisions cited in the text are from the 1867 law; the earlier one, which it amended, was even more stringent. See also *MBE 29 (1866)*, pp. 65–66; Persons, "Early History of Factory Legislation," pp. 93–97; *Advertiser*, March 26, 1867.

15. See Henry K. Oliver, *Report of the Hon. Henry K. Oliver, Deputy State Constable, Specially Appointed to Enforce the Laws Regulating the Employment of Children in Manufacturing and Mechanical Establishments. Mass. Senate Doc. No. 21 (1868)*; Henry K. Oliver, *Report of the Hon. Henry K. Oliver,*

Deputy State Constable, Specially Appointed to Enforce the Laws Regulating the Employment of Children in Manufacturing and Mechanical Establishments . . . for the Year 1868. Mass. Senate Doc. No. 44 (1869); J. Waldo Denny, *Report. Mass. Senate Doc. No. 13 (1870); MBSL 1 (1870),* pp. 134–158; *MBSL 4 (1873),* pp. 381–396; *MBSL 5 (1874),* pp. 1–20; *MBE 31 (1868),* p. 49; *MBE 37 (1874),* pp. 140–142; Massachusetts State Board of Health, *Second Annual Report . . . January, 1871. Mass. Senate Doc. No. 50 (1871),* pp. 410–422; William B. Washburn, *Address . . . to the Two Branches of the Legislature of Massachusetts, January 8, 1874. Mass. Senate Doc. No. 1 (1874)* (quotes on pp. 30, 31–32). The new law was *Mass. Acts and Resolves, 1874,* chap. 221. As it also regulated the working hours of adult females, it will be discussed more fully later in the chapter. Cf. *Advertiser,* March 8, 1869.

16. George E. McNeill, *Report Upon the Schooling and Hours of Labor of Children Employed in the Manufacturing and Mechanical Establishments of Massachusetts. Mass. Senate Doc. No. 50 (1875),* pp. 4, 7, and *passim.* The new laws were *Mass. Acts and Resolves, 1876,* chap. 52 and *Mass. Acts and Resolves, 1878* chap. 257. Long's report is in John D. Long, *Address . . . to the Two Branches of the Legislature of Massachusetts, January 6, 1881. Mass. Senate Doc. No. 1 (1881),* pp. 40–41.

17. Washburn, *Address, Jan. 8, 1874,* pp. 30–31.

18. Alexander H. Rice, *Address . . . to the Two Branches of the Legislature of Massachusetts, January 4, 1877. Mass. Senate Doc. No. 1 (1877),* p. 37. Favorable comment on the half-time system was widespread. For some examples, see *Report of the Special Commission (1866),* p. 49; Oliver, *Report (1869),* pp. 27–35; Washburn, *Address, Jan. 8, 1874,* p. 33; *MBSL 6 (1875),* pp. 5–37; *MBSL 9 (1878),* pp. 22–25 (though, for an attack on such schools as undemocratic, see *MBSL 6 [1875],* pp. 58–59). On industrial art and technical instruction, see *MBE 15 (1852),* pp. 29–30; *MBE 32 (1869),* pp. 9–10; William Claflin, *Address . . . to the Two Branches of the Legislature of Massachusetts, January 7, 1871. Mass. Senate Doc. No. 1 (1871),* pp. 56–57; William B. Washburn, *Address . . . to the Two Branches of the Legislature of Massachusetts, January 5, 1872. Mass. Senate Doc. No. 1 (1872),* pp. 55–56; *MBE 35 (1872),* pp. 109–112; *MBE 36 (1873),* pp. 6–7, 21–37; *MBE 37 (1874),* pp. 33–39, 55–65; *MBE 38 (1875),* pp. 33–50; Rice, *Address, Jan. 3, 1878,* pp. 26–29.

19. State Board of Health, *Second Annual Report (1871),* pp. 410–422 (conclusions on p. 422); *MBE 31 (1868),* p. 49; *Report* [by Committee on Education]. *Mass. House Doc. No. 49 (1836),* p. 8. For other expressions of concern along these lines, see *MBE 23 (1860),* p. 55; *Reports of Commissioners (1867),* p. 20; *Advertiser,* March 26, 1867; Washburn, *Address, Jan. 8, 1874,* pp. 32–33; *MBSL 5 (1874),* p. 3.

20. McNeill, *Report (1875),* pp. 39, 31; *Report of the Special Commission (1866),* p. 9.

21. *MBSL 6 (1875),* pp. 383–385; Washburn, *Address, Jan. 8, 1874,* p. 32;

Oliver, *Report (1868)*, p. 67. Cf. *Report* [by Committee on Education]. *Mass. House Doc. No. 49 (1836)*, pp. 10–12; *MBE 3 (1840)*, pp. 43–45; *MBE 29 (1866)*, p. 66; Oliver, *Report (1869)*, pp. 19, 20; McNeill, *Report (1875)*, pp. 26–27.

22. *Ibid.*, p. 38; Oliver, *Report (1868)*, pp. 66, 81 (cf. pp. 66–82 *passim*); *MBE 25 (1862)*, p. 94 (cf. pp. 75–92). See also *MBE 20 (1857)*, pp. 49–50; *MBE 23 (1860)*, pp. 39–40; *MBE 36 (1873)*, pp. 189–193; *MBE 37 (1874)*, pp. 112–116; Governor Emory Washburn's address at the dedication of the Worcester Normal School Building, reprinted in *MBE 38 (1875)*, pp. 215–216.

23. For some reactions to the employer's role, see the *Report* [by Committee on Education]. *Mass. House Doc. No. 49 (1836)*, p. 10; *MBE 29 (1866)*, p. 66; Oliver, *Report (1868)*, pp. 22–23, 74–75, 93–94; Oliver, *Report (1869)*, pp. 15–20; *MBSL 6 (1875)*, pp. 37–42.

24. *Report of the Special Commission (1866)*, p. 15 (cf. pp. 11–12); George F. Hoar, *Universal Education the only Safeguard of State Rights. Speech . . . in the House of Representatives, January 25, 1872* (Washington, D.C., n.d.), p. 3; *MBE 12 (1849)*, pp. 57, 59. Cf. *MBE 23 (1860)*, pp. 41–53, 57–58; Oliver, *Report (1868)*, pp. 93–94; *MBE 36 (1873)*, pp. 190–193.

25. *MBE 23 (1860)*, p. 55 (cf. pp. 54–59); Oliver, *Report (1868)*, pp. 82, 78. Cf. *MBE 12 (1849)*, p. 60; *MBSL 6 (1875)*, pp. 4, 37–58.

26. For information on female workers in Massachusetts in this period, see the pioneering study by Edith Abbott, *Women in Industry*, pp. 10–245 *passim*; Shlakman, *Economic History of a Factory Town*, pp. 135–139; Ware, *Early New England Cotton Manufacture*, pp. 200–221, 256–268; Lebergott, *Manpower in Economic Growth*, pp. 125–130. Reports of contemporary investigators are in *MBSL 3 (1872)*, pp. 59–118; *MBSL 6 (1875)*, pp. 67–112; *MBSL 9 (1878)*, pp. 99–158.

27. For statistics on the proportion of women workers in various fields, see Abbott, *Women in Industry*, p. 103; Bigelow, *Statistical Tables, 1837*, pp. 169–173; Palfrey, *Statistics, 1845*, pp. 330–355; Joseph G. Kennedy, *Abstract of the Statistics of Manufactures, According to the Returns of the Seventh Census . . .* [1850]. U.S., Congress, Senate, Executive Doc. No. 38, 35th Cong., 2nd sess., pp. 13, 15, 28, 35, 43; DeWitt, *Abstract of the Census, 1855*, pp. 570–590; 8 *U.S. Census (1860), Manufactures*, pp. 251–257; Oliver Warner, *Statistical Information Relating to Certain Branches of Industry in Massachusetts, For the Year Ending May 1, 1865* (Boston, 1866), pp. 660–738; Wright, *Census of Massachusetts: 1875*, 1: 612–613. The cumulative figures for women in manufacturing are from Kennedy, *Abstract of Statistics*, p. 143 (for 1850) and Wright, *Census of Massachusetts: 1875*, 1: 612 (for 1875). It should be pointed out that all these figures include *child* workers of both sexes. Since it appears that slightly more girls worked than boys, the proportion of adult female workers is probably a few percentage points less than those given in the text.

28. *Report* [of the Special Committee]. *Mass. House Doc. No. 50 (1845)*, p. 16.

29. George F. Hoar, *Autobiography of Seventy Years*, 2 vols. (New York, 1903), 1: 163–164. The reports antagonistic to the measure are *Report* [of the Joint Standing Committee on Manufactures]. *Mass. Senate Doc. No. 81 (1846); Report* [of the Special Committee on limiting the hours of labor]. *Mass. House Doc. No. 153 (1850)* (majority report on p. 2); *Report* [of the Special Committee]. *Mass. House Doc. No. 185 (1852)*, (majority report on p. 1); *Report* [of the Joint Special Committee]. *Mass. House Doc. No. 122 (1853)* (majority report on p. 1); *Minority Report* [of Joint Special Committee on alteration of hours of labor]. *Mass. Senate Doc. No. 112 (1856)*. The Stone minority report is contained in pp. 3–31 of the 1850 House report cited above (quote on p. 6). The Robinson minority report is on pp. 2–21 of the 1852 House report cited above. The majority reports favorable to hours regulation are *Report* [of the Joint Committee on regulating hours in incorporated establishments]. *Mass. House Doc. No. 80 (1855)* and *Report* [of the Joint Special Committee on alteration of hours of labor]. *Mass. Senate Doc. No. 107 (1856)*. Cf. the minority report (pp. 2–10) of the 1853 House report cited in this note.

30. *Report* [of the Joint Special Committee on the apprentice system]. *Mass. House Doc. No. 259 (1865)* (quote on p. 3). This report evidently had great national impact. See Montgomery, *Beyond Equality*, p. 125.

31. For the *Advertiser*'s stand on the question in the sixties, see the issues of November 6, 18, and 22 (all 1865), April 21, 1866, February 16, March 8, May 4, June 7 and 17 (all 1867), April 23, 1868.

32. The best guide to the shifting attitudes of Massachusetts Republicans on this issue is Montgomery, *Beyond Equality, passim.*

33. *Report of the Special Commission (1866)* and *Reports of the Commissioners (1867)*. In the latter report, commissioner Edward Rogers wrote a minority opinion advocating hours restrictions for women and children (pp. 41–141).

34. For Oliver's efforts, see *MBSL 1 (1870)*, pp. 111–127, 196–197; *MBSL 2 (1871)*, pp. 557–568. Claflin's opinions are in his *Address . . . to the Two Branches of the Legislature of Massachusetts, January 8, 1870. Mass. Senate Doc. No. 1 (1870)*, pp. 52–53; and *Address, Jan. 7, 1871*, pp. 66–67. Hoar's speech is reprinted in the report of the proceedings of the Republican state convention, Worcester, September 27, 1871, in *Advertiser*, September 28, 1871. The Republican platforms advocating hours legislation are reprinted in *Advertiser*, August 29, 1872, October 8, 1874. Sumner's position is discussed in David Donald, *Charles Sumner and the Rights of Man* (New York, 1970), pp. 346, 576–577. Washburn's advocacy is in his *Address, Jan. 8, 1874*, pp. 33–36 (quote from p. 33). The *Advertiser*, incidentally, continued to oppose the measure. See the issues of April 20 and 27, 1870, March 13, 1871, April 2, 1872, February 11, March 4, April 9 (all 1874).

35. The favorable reports are the minority report contained in the *Report* [of the Committee on the Labor Question]. *Mass. House Doc. No. 318 (1873)*, pp. 3–5 and the *Report* [of the Committee on the Labor Question]. *Mass. Senate*

Doc. No. 33 (1874). The ten-hour law is *Mass. Acts and Resolves, 1874,* chap. 221. The laws regulating safety conditions are *Mass. Acts and Resolves, 1876,* chap. 216 and *ibid.,* 1877, chap. 214. Cf. *MBSL 8 (1877),* pp. 229–291.

36. *Report* [of the Special Committee on limiting the hours of labor]. *Mass. House Doc. No. 153 (1850),* p. 9 (cf. pp. 10–18) for medical testimony); Washburn, *Address, Jan. 8, 1874,* pp. 33–34. For the concessions by the Special Commissions on the Hours of Labor, see *Report of the Special Commission (1866),* pp. 35–43 and *Reports of Commissioners (1867),* pp. 7–8, 22. Practically every proponent of an hours law made mention of the health factor, though few discussed it extensively, as it was considered obvious. For discussions by other state officials, see Boutwell, *Address, September 18, 1850,* p. 6; *MBE 23 (1860),* p. 55; *MBSL 6 (1875),* pp. 67–109.

37. *Reports of Commissioners (1867),* p. 23; Washburn, *Address, Jan. 8, 1874,* pp. 34–35; *Report* [of the Special Committee on limiting the hours of labor]. *Mass. House Doc. No. 153 (1850),* pp. 19, 21.

38. The best exposition of these fears is in *ibid.,* pp. 19–20.

39. *Report* [of the Joint Special Committee on the apprentice system]. *Mass. House Doc. No. 259 (1865),* pp. 4, 5.

40. Report [of the Special Committee on limiting the hours of labor]. *Mass. House Doc. No. 153 (1850),* pp. 23, 24. Cf. *Report* [of the Joint Special Committee]. *Mass. House Doc. No. 122 (1853),* pp. 2–10.

CHAPTER 8. THE POSTWAR YEARS: CLOSING RANKS

1. In an earlier version of this study, written several years ago as a doctoral dissertation, I did indeed label these criticisms collectively as a "counter-image" (Ph.D. dissertation, Brandeis University, 1973). Upon further reflection, I see that I was mistaken. It might be objected that the respectable worker image itself was presented in a piecemeal and confused fashion. To some extent this is true, yet one must remember that its various components had been filtering into the political imagination for three or four decades before the Civil War. Gradually they were sorted and organized into an easily identifiable bank of ideas, from which politicians could draw at will. To challenge that solid structure effectively required an equally coherent alternate view, one which did not take shape after the war. I think it eventually *did* form, but not until the Progressive agitation of the early twentieth century.

2. The best source on Oliver's life is the obituary by Jesse H. Jones in *MBSL 17 (1886),* pp. 3–47.

3. *MBSL 1 (1870),* pp. 88, 131; *MBSL 3 (1872),* pp. 340, 539. This paragraph, and the following ones, summarize Oliver's findings in the reports *MBSL 1 (1870)* through *MBSL 4 (1873).*

4. *MBSL 2 (1871),* p. 534; *MBSL 1 (1870),* p. 194.

5. *MBSL 2 (1871),* p. 46; *MBSL 4 (1873),* p. 5.

6. *MBSL 4 (1873),* p. 397; *MBSL 1 (1870),* p. 39.

7. *Advertiser*, April 29, 1872 (cf. May 5, 1870, April 30, 1872, May 1 and 3, 1872); Henry L. Dawes, *Americans Must Control their own Markets and their own Wares. Speech . . . Delivered in the House of Representatives, May 3, 1872* (Washington, D.C., 1872), p. 12; William B. Washburn, *Address . . . to the Two Branches of the Legislature of Massachusetts, January 2, 1873. Mass. Senate Doc. No. 1 (1873)*, p. 16. For the controversy over the bureau in these years, see James Leiby, *Carroll Wright and Labor Reform: The Origin of Labor Statistics* (Cambridge, Mass., 1960), pp. 54–63. Oliver later returned to politics, serving for four more years as mayor of Lawrence. He died in 1885.

8. Quotes from Resolutions of Democratic State Convention, Worcester, September 9, 1874, in *Advertiser*, September 10, 1874 and Democratic state convention, Worcester, September 22, 1875, in *ibid.*, September 23, 1875.

9. Henry Wilson, *Stand by the Republican Colors! Speech . . . at Great Falls, New Hampshire, February 24, 1872* (Washington, D.C., n.d.), p. 3 (cf. p. 2); [Mass. Republican State Committee], *Address . . .* (n.p., [1869]), p. 3, 4; *Advertiser*, August 9, 1878. Cf. Henry Wilson's speech, U.S., Congress, Senate, *Congressional Globe*, 39th Cong., 1st sess., 22 January 1866, p. 343; *Advertiser*, September 28, 1876; [Mass. Republican State Committee], *The Democratic Record* (n.p., 1880), pp. 29–30.

10. *Advertiser*, October 4, 1870.

11. Quote from Resolutions of Republican state convention, Worcester, October 7, 1874, reprinted in *ibid.*, October 8, 1874. For the interesting maneuvers of Hoar on the labor question, see James W. Hess, "George F. Hoar, 1826–1884" (Ph.D. dissertation, Harvard University, 1964), pp. 140–141, 144–145, 152–153, 160–164, 188–189, 197–198.

12. *Advertiser*, August 9, 1878; Resolutions of Republican State Convention, Worcester, September 18, 1878, reprinted in *ibid.*, September 19, 1878; [Mass. Republican State Committee], *Address . . . 1878* (n.p., 1878), p. 2; *Advertiser*, October 23, 1878. By this time even George F. Hoar had changed his tune. See Hess, "Hoar," pp. 310–311.

13. Ben Butler, *Relief to Labor . . . Speech . . . in the House of Representatives, May 21, 1878* (Washington, D.C., 1878), p. 5; *Advertiser*, October 28, 1871. For other examples of these themes, see *Report of the Special Commission (1866)*, pp. 33–34; Alexander H. Bullock, *Address . . . to the Two Branches of the Legislature of Massachusetts, January 4, 1867. Mass. Senate Doc. No. 1 (1867)*, pp. 30–31; *Report* [of the Committee on the Labor Question]. *Mass. House Doc. No. 318 (1873)*, p. 2; Nathaniel P. Banks, *Speech . . . in the House of Representatives, May 7, 1878* (Washington, D.C., 1878), pp. 15–16, 22–25; *Advertiser*, July 26, 1878.

14. *Ibid.*, August 23, 1869; [Charles F. Adams, Jr.], "The Butler Canvass," *North American Review*, 114 (1872): 155. Similar statements emphasizing the well-being of workers can be found in: *Reports of Commissioners (1867)*, p. 30; Dawes, *Americans Must Control their own Markets*, p. 12; Representative

George F. Hoar's speech, U.S., Congress, House, *Congressional Globe*, 42nd
Cong., 1st sess., 23 March 1872, p. 1911; *Advertiser*, January 29, 1869,
November 22, 1869, March 18, 1870, January 6, 1879, and, in offhand references, many other issues. On the health of workers, see *ibid.*, April 20 and 27,
1870, January 9, 1874. On the lack of pauperism, *ibid.*, January 6, 1865;
Franklin B. Sanborn, "The Poor Laws of New England," *North American Review*, 106 (1868): 484, 507; Sanborn, "Poverty and Public Charity," *ibid.*, 110
(1870): 328–329, 336–342; Franklin B. Sanborn, "Poor-Law Administration in
New England," *ibid.*, 114 (1872): 2–3, 13–16 (see also, in general, the reports of
the Massachusetts Board of State Charities, 1864–1878). On unemployment, see
Advertiser, January 23, 1874, August 19, 1878.

15. *Ibid.*, January 9, 1869, March 22, 1871, April 23, 1868; Representative
George F. Hoar's speech, U.S., Congress, House, *Congressional Globe*, 42nd
Cong., 1st sess., 23 March 1872, p. 1911. Cf. the *Advertiser* issues of May 16,
1867, November 22, 1869, March 13, 1871, October 19, 1872; Adams, "The
Butler Canvass," *North American Review*, 114 (1872): 163–165.

16. For a typical *pro forma* assertion of the worker's high moral and educational attainments, see Dawes, *Americans Must Control their own Markets*, p.
12. The Special Commission on the Hours of Labor of 1867 did worry about this.
See *Reports of Commissioners (1867)*, pp. 26–27.

17. *MBSL 5 (1874)*, p. vii. For Wright and his activities at the Bureau, see
Leiby, *Carroll Wright*, pp. 7–75.

18. This paragraph summarizes Wright's reports for the bureau in the 1870s
(MBSL 5 [1874] to *MBSL 11 [1880])*. Quotes from *MBSL 5 (1874)*, p. 3; *MBSL 6
(1875)*, p. 4. For a critique of his work, see Leiby, *Carroll Wright*, pp. 95–141.
An interesting attempt at placing Wright's thoughts on industrialization (for both
this and the post-1880 periods) in a wider context is Daniel Horowitz, "Insights
into Industrialization: American Conceptions of Economic Development and
Mechanization, 1865–1910" (Ph.D. dissertation, Harvard University, 1966),
passim.

19. *Advertiser*, March 7, 1874. Cf. the issues of March 16, 1875, May 5, 1876,
March 22, 1878, February 21 and 22, 1879.

20. *MBSL 11 (1880)*, pp. 65, 71 (cf. *MBSL 8 [1877]*, p. 3). The *Advertiser* was
in the forefront in proclaiming the uselessness of strikes. For a sample of its
views, see the issues of May 22, 1865, August 14, 1869, September 6, 1869, July
9, 1870, March 22, 1871, October 28, 1871, May 21, 1872, August 12 and 13,
1872, January 18, February 2, March 15, August 4, September 17 and 30 (all
1875), January 19, 1876, September 21, 1876, January 14, 1878, December 28,
1878, June 14, 1879. The paper, it should be noted, did insist employers had an
obligation to pay "fair living wages." It also criticized a yellow-dog contract
imposed by Fall River mill owners as "humiliating" and ascribed part of the
blame for the railroad strike of 1877 to mismanagement by the railroad corporations. See the issues of September 25, 1875, September 21, 1876, and August 2,

1877. Also worth mentioning is the fact that the Springfield *Republican*, often at odds with the *Advertiser* by the 1870s, took much the same attitude towards unions. See Frisch, *Town into City*, pp. 127, 220. For other views on the subject, see Amasa Walker, *The Science of Wealth: A Manual of Political Economy* . . . (Boston, 1866), pp. 269–273; *Reports of Commissioners (1867)*, p. 33; George Boutwell's speech, "Present Questions Affecting Public Prosperity," reprinted in *Advertiser*, October 27, 1871. Phillips' opposition to strikes is related in Bartlett, *Phillips*, p. 340.

21. *Advertiser*, July 13, 1867, July 30, 25, 27, and 28, 1877, July 3, 1879. See also the issues of June 28, 1870, July 20, 23, 24, and 26, 1877, August 2 and 19, 1877.

22. *Ibid.*, September 30, 1869, June 21, 1877, April 29, 1878, November 6, 1878. See also the issues of November 22, 1865, November 9, 1866, June 17, 1867, January 29, 1869, September 9, 1870, May 3, 1871, October 5, 1871, July 13, 1872, August 13, 1874, May 23, 1878, July 26, 1878. Interestingly, the *Advertiser*, despite all its fears, never joined in the lament among "liberal" intellectuals like Godkin that universal suffrage was a mistake. Late in this period, in fact, it specifically repudiated such doctrine. See the issue of February 6, 1879.

23. Charles Francis Adams, *An Address Delivered at Cambridge Before the Society of the Phi Beta Kappa, 26 June, 1873* (Cambridge, Mass., 1873), p. 26.

24. Washburn, *Address, Jan. 5, 1872*, p. 30 (cf. his *Address, Jan. 2, 1873*, p. 19, and *Address, Jan. 8, 1874*, p. 30).

25. *MBSC 11 (1875)*, p. 112 (cf. *Advertiser*, January 6, 1865, November 24, 1873); *Report of the Special Commission (1866)*, p. 48 (cf. pp. 43–50).

CHAPTER 9. THE IMAGE AS INVENTION

1. The exact proportion of workers in the total electorate is quite hard to determine with any accuracy. It is certain that they never had nearly as much political influence as their share of the work force would indicate, since two large groups could not vote: all women workers and male workers under 21. In addition, eligible workers too poor (or unwilling) to pay the small poll tax and immigrant workers not yet naturalized were excluded. There are no comprehensive data for any of these categories. Using the fragmentary evidence available and the figures in Table 6 (p. 34), I would estimate workers were roughly one-third of the electorate in the 1830s, one-half by the 1850s, and three-fifths by the 1870s.

2. See Appendix C.

3. There are helpful discussions of this phenomenon, and of its moral implications, in Paul Faler, "Cultural Aspects of the Industrial Revolution: Lynn, Massachusetts, Shoemakers and Industrial Morality, 1826–1860," *Labor History*, 15 (1974): 367–394; and Alan Dawley and Paul Faler, "Working-Class Culture and Politics in the Industrial Revolution: Sources of Loyalism and Rebellion," *Jour-*

nal of Social History, 9 (1976): 466–480. Faler and Dawley choose to call this cluster of values an "industrial morality," which is odd, since by their own admission it predated industrialization. It was in fact a capitalist morality. They are right, however, to stress that it was not tied to a single class but was widespread throughout the population (see especially "Working-Class Culture and Politics," p. 468). And they make the telling point that even in Lynn, probably a "bare majority" of the workers were, in their term, "loyalists," model workers who shunned collective action (see especially Faler's "Cultural Aspects of the Industrial Revolution," pp. 390–392). Curiously, this crucial group disappears in Dawley's *Class and Community*, where Lynn workers are portrayed as virtually united in their assault on industrial exploitation.

4. William James, *Pragmatism: A New Name for Some Old Ways of Thinking* (New York, 1907), pp. 168–169.

5. Here, I must acknowledge the inspiration of a master historian — and it is fitting that he should be from Massachusetts (and born in this period, as well). The ideas in these concluding paragraphs were developed from certain themes of Henry Adams in chap. 6 of vol. 1 of his classic *History of the United States of America . . .*, 9 vols. (New York, 1889–1898). Explorations of America's preoccupation with economic enterprise are legion. Especially useful have been Meyers, *Jacksonian Persuasion* and David M. Potter, *People of Plenty: Economic Abundance and the American Character* (Chicago, 1954). The themes of American innocence, power, and uniqueness have been explored primarily in their literary manifestations (see, for example, R. W. B. Lewis, *The American Adam: Innocence, Tragedy, and Tradition in the Nineteenth Century* (New York, 1971). The most ambitious attempt to deal with these themes outside of literature has been Boorstin, *The Americans: The National Experience*. Other relevant inquiries are Perry Miller, *The Life of the Mind in America From the Revolution to the Civil War* (New York, 1965); George Fredrickson, *The Inner Civil War: Northern Intellectuals and the Crisis of the Union* (New York, 1965); and Charles Sanford, *The Quest for Paradise: Europe and the American Moral Imagination* (Urbana, Ill., 1961).

APPENDIX A

1. Source: *8 U.S. Census (1860), Population*, pp. 218–219; *9 U.S. Census (1870)*, vol. 1, *Population*, pp. 618–619, and vol. 2, *Vital Statistics*, pp. 564–565; *10 U.S. Census (1880), Population*, pp. 590–593, 714. All numbers to nearest hundred; percentages to nearest percent.

APPENDIX C

1. The voting statistics in these tables were obtained from the state's official annual election tabulations, "Return of Votes: Governor and Lt. Governor," on microfilm at the Massachusetts State Archives, Boston. (The only exception is the totals for the state as a whole in 1874, which are missing from the tabula-

tions. I have used instead the figures given in the *Advertiser*, Nov. 5, 1874.) In those elections where the two major parties had no important competition, the percentages given for each represent its share of the total for both, scattered votes being omitted. In those elections where there were one, or two, significant minor parties, their votes were included in the totals. The minor party candidates thus included are: for 1831 and 1832, Lothrop (Anti-Masonic party); 1833, Adams (A-M) and Allen (Working Men's party); 1834, Bailey (A-M) and Allen (Wkgmn.); 1835, Armstrong (independent); 1842–1847, Sewall (Liberty party); 1845, Shaw (nativist); 1846–1847, Baylies (nativist); 1848–1850, Phillips (Free Soil party); 1851, Palfrey (FS); 1852, Mann (FS); 1853–1854, Wilson (FS); 1854–1857, Gardner (nativist); 1856, Gordon (Fillmore-nativist); 1858, Lawrence (nativist); 1859, Briggs ("Opposition party"); 1860, Lawrence (Constitutional Union party); 1869, Chamberlain (Labor Reform party); 1870, Phillips (LR and Prohibition parties); 1871, Chamberlain (LR) and Pitman (Pro.); 1875–1876, Baker (Pro.); 1877, Pitman (Pro.). In 1855 there were Whig *and* Republican candidates for governor (Walley and Rockwell). In 1878 and 1879 there were "official" Democratic candidates (Abbott and Adams) running in opposition to Butler. Votes from Chicopee and Lawrence were not counted separately until 1850. Votes from Fall River were reported under "Troy," its previous name, until 1834.

2. In Table C-1, the votes for Whig gubernatorial candidates are given until 1854. There was a Whig candidate in 1855, but since a Republican (Rockwell) was also running at this time, I thought it best to shift to Republican gubernatorial candidates at this election (the Whig got 10% of the vote statewide, the Republican 27%). In 1856 the Republicans did not nominate a gubernatorial candidate, though Henry Gardner, a nativist and the eventual winner, was understood to be a "Fremont-American." The Whig candidate that year got 5% of the vote.

Bibliographical Note

THE PURPOSE of this note is to indicate the secondary works most heavily relied on in preparing this study and to provide the interested reader with an introduction to some of the primary sources. (For a more complete listing of primary sources relevant to particular topics, one should consult the notes.) There are two broad areas into which these materials may be divided. The first concerns the progress of industrialization in Massachusetts, and the condition, prospects, and activities of its working class. The second deals more specifically with the reaction of leading public figures to these trends.

INDUSTRY AND THE WORKER

Essential data on the growth of manufacturing and the rise of the working class in Massachusetts can be found in two sets of primary sources: the national census reports (particularly those for the later decades covered in this study), and the various published investigations and compilations of state and local officials. Among the latter, most useful were John P. Bigelow, *Statistical Tables: Exhibiting the Condition and Products of Certain Branches of Industry in Massachusetts, for the Year Ending April 1, 1837* (Boston, 1838); George W. Chase, *Abstract of the Census of Massachusetts, 1860, from the Eighth U.S. Census, With Remarks on the Same* (Boston, 1863); Jesse Chickering, *Statistical View of the Population of Massachusetts, From 1765 to 1840* (Boston, 1846); Francis DeWitt, *Abstract of the Census of the Commonwealth of Massachusetts . . . 1855* (Boston, 1857); Francis DeWitt, *Statistical Information Relating to Certain Branches of Industry in Massachusetts, for the Year Ending June 1, 1855* (Boston, 1856); John G. Palfrey, *Statistics of the Condition and Products of Certain Branches of Industry in Massachusetts, for the Year Ending April 1, 1845* (Boston, 1846); Oliver Warner, *Abstract of the Census of Massachusetts, 1865, With Remarks on the Same, and Supplementary Tables* (Boston, 1867); Oliver Warner, *Statistical Information Relating to Certain Branches of Industry in Massachusetts, for the Year Ending May 1, 1865* (Boston, 1866); Carroll D. Wright, *The Census of Massachusetts: 1875*, 4 vols. (Boston, 1877); Carroll D. Wright, *The Census of Massachusetts: 1880* (Boston, 1883); Carroll D. Wright, *The Census of Massachusetts: 1885*, 3 vols. (Boston, 1887).

The secondary literature on industrialization in Massachusetts is fairly extensive. A number of standard works are devoted wholly or in part to developments in the state: Victor S. Clark, *History of Manufactures in the United States*, 2 vols. (Washington, D.C., 1916–1928); Arthur H. Cole, *The American Wool Manufacture*, 2 vols. (Cambridge, Mass., 1926); Felicia Johnson Deyrup, *Arms*

Makers of the Connecticut Valley: A Regional Study of the Economic Development of the Small Arms Industry, 1798–1870 (Northampton, Mass., 1948); George S. Gibb, *The Saco-Lowell Shops: Textile Machinery Building in New England 1813–1949* (Cambridge, Mass., 1950); George S. Gibb, *The Whitesmiths of Taunton: A History of Reed & Barton 1824–1943* (Cambridge, Mass., 1943); Blanche Evans Hazard, *The Organization of the Boot and Shoe Industry in Massachusetts Before 1875* (Cambridge, Mass., 1921); Edward C. Kirkland, *Men Cities and Transportation: A Study in New England History 1820–1900*, 2 vols. (Cambridge, Mass., 1948); Samuel Eliot Morison, *The Maritime History of Massachusetts 1783–1860*, rev. ed. (Boston, 1961); Thomas R. Navin, *The Whitin Machine Works since 1831: A Textile Machinery Company in an Industrial Village* (Cambridge, Mass., 1950); Thomas R. Smith, *The Cotton Textile Industry of Fall River, Massachusetts: A Study of Industrial Localization* (New York, 1944); Caroline F. Ware, *The Early New England Cotton Manufacture* (Boston, 1931). Oscar and Mary Flug Handlin, *Commonwealth: A Study of the Role of Government in the American Economy: Massachusetts, 1774–1861*, rev. ed (Cambridge, Mass., 1969) is vital to understanding the relationship between state action and industrialization in the antebellum period. Several accounts of individual cities also proved interesting: Donald B. Cole, *Immigrant City: Lawrence, Massachusetts, 1845–1921* (Chapel Hill, N.C., 1963); Michael H. Frisch, *Town into City: Springfield, Massachusetts, and the Meaning of Community, 1840–1880* (Cambridge, Mass., 1972); Constance M. Green, *Holyoke, Massachusetts: A Case History of the Industrial Revolution in America* (New Haven, 1939); Margaret Terrell Parker, *Lowell: A Study of Industrial Development* (1940; reprint ed., Port Washington, N.Y., 1970); Vera Shlakman, *Economic History of a Factory Town: A Study of Chicopee, Massachusetts* (Northampton, Mass., 1935).

For the workers of Massachusetts, there are several older studies which are still quite valuable: Edith Abbott, *Women in Industry* (New York, 1913); John R. Commons et al., *History of Labour in the United States*, 4 vols. (New York, 1918–1935); Philip S. Foner, *History of the Labor Movement in the United States*, 4 vols. (New York, 1947–1965); Ray Ginger, "Labor in a Massachusetts Cotton Mill, 1853–1860," *Business History Review*, 28 (March 1954): 67–91; John P. Hall, "The Gentle Craft: A Narrative of Yankee Shoemakers" (Ph.D. dissertation, Columbia University, 1953); Oscar Handlin, *Boston's Immigrants*, rev. ed. (New York, 1959); Robert G. Layer, *Earnings of Cotton Mill Operatives, 1825–1914* (Cambridge, Mass., 1955); Norman Ware, *The Industrial Worker, 1840–1860* (Boston, 1924). Among the newer investigations, I found especially helpful Alan Dawley, *Class and Community: The Industrial Revolution in Lynn* (Cambridge, Mass., 1976); Alan Dawley and Paul Faler, "Working-Class Culture and Politics in the Industrial Revolution: Sources of Loyalism and Rebellion," *Journal of Social History*, 9 (1976): 466–480; Paul Faler, "Cultural Aspects of the Industrial Revolution: Lynn, Massachusetts,

Shoemakers and Industrial Morality, 1826–1860," *Labor History*, 15 (1974): 367–394; Howard M. Gitelman, *Workingmen of Waltham: Mobility in American Urban Industrial Development, 1850–1890* (Baltimore, 1974); Howard M. Gitelman, "The Waltham System and the Coming of the Irish," *Labor History*, 8 (1967): 227–253; Peter R. Knights, *The Plain People of Boston, 1830–1860* (New York, 1971); Stanley Lebergott, *Manpower in Economic Growth: The American Record since 1800* (New York, 1964); Stephan Thernstrom, *Poverty and Progress: Social Mobility in a Nineteenth Century City* (Cambridge, Mass., 1964).

THE POLITICAL RESPONSE

The course of Massachusetts politics in these years is discussed in Richard H. Abbott, "Massachusetts: Maintaining Hegemony," in *Radical Republicans in the North: State Politics During Reconstruction*, ed. James C. Mohr (Baltimore, 1976), pp. 1–25; William G. Bean, "Party Transformation in Massachusetts With Special Reference to the Antecedents of Republicanism" (Ph.D. dissertation, Harvard University, 1922); Kinley J. Brauer, *Cotton versus Conscience: Massachusetts Whig Politics and Southwestern Expansion, 1843–1848* (Lexington, Ky., 1967); Michel Brunet, "The Secret Ballot Issue in Massachusetts Politics from 1851 to 1853," *New England Quarterly*, 25 (1952): 354–362; Arthur B. Darling, *Political Changes in Massachusetts 1824–1848: A Study of Liberal Movements in Politics* (1925; reprint ed., Cos Cob, Conn., 1968); Arthur B. Darling, "The Workingmen's Party in Massachusetts," *American Historical Review*, 29 (1923): 81–86; George H. Haynes, "The Causes of Know-Nothing Success in Massachusetts," *American Historical Review*, 3 (1897): 67–82; George H. Haynes, "A Know-Nothing Legislature," in American Historical Association, *Annual Report, 1896*, 2 vols., 1 (1897): 175–187; William D. Mallam, "Butlerism in Massachusetts," *New England Quarterly*, 33 (1960): 186–206; David Montgomery, *Beyond Equality: Labor and the Radical Republicans, 1862–1872* (New York, 1967); Thomas H. O'Connor, *Lords of the Loom: The Cotton Whigs and the Coming of the Civil War* (New York, 1968); Charles E. Persons, "The Early History of Factory Legislation in Massachusetts: From 1825 to the Passage of the Ten Hour Law in 1874," in *Labor Laws and their Enforcement With Special Reference to Massachusetts*, ed. Susan M. Kingsbury (New York, 1911); Edward Pessen, *Most Uncommon Jacksonians: The Radical Leaders of the Early Labor Movement* (Albany, N.Y., 1967); Edward Pessen, "Did Labor Support Jackson? The Boston Story," *Political Science Quarterly*, 64 (1949): 262–274; Arthur M. Schlesinger, Jr., *The Age of Jackson* (Boston, 1945); Edith Ellen Ware, *Political Opinion in Massachusetts During Civil War and Reconstruction* (New York, 1917); Sarah S. Whittelsey, *Massachusetts Labor Legislation. Supplement to the Annals of the American Academy of Political and Social Science* (January 1901). There are also literally dozens of biographies of leading political figures, almost all of which furnished enlightening and in some cases essential detail to supplement the more general historical treatments. For a sense of how several public agencies and institutions responded to industrialization, see Michael B. Katz, *The Irony of Early School Reform: Educational Innovation in Mid-Nineteenth Century Massachusetts* (Cambridge, Mass., 1968); James Leiby, *Carroll Wright and Labor Reform: The Origin of Labor Statistics* (Cambridge, Mass., 1960); David J. Rothman, *The Discovery of the Asylum: Social Order and Disorder in the New Republic* (Boston, 1971); Stanley K. Schultz, *The Culture Factory: Boston Public Schools, 1789–1860* (New York, 1973). In a related area, Leo Marx, *The Machine in the Garden: Technology and the Pastoral Ideal* (New York, 1964) is a classic study of the literary response.

The secondary literature is, however, of very limited use in apprehending politicians' attitudes toward industrialization and the worker. For that, one must go directly to the primary sources. I have described elsewhere the nature and extent of the political speeches and writings that were consulted for this study (see pp. 55–56 in text, note 16 of chapter 3, and note 32 of chapter 5). The reader who wishes to sample this very extensive, diverse literature should proceed to where the discussion of industrialization and the working class is richest. Perhaps the best way of doing this is to examine several easily available collections of speeches by politicians who were especially interested in these matters: Rufus Choate, *Works,* 2 vols. (Boston, 1862); Edward Everett, *Orations and Speeches on Various Occasions,* 4 vols. (Boston, 1850–1868); Luther Hamilton, ed., *Memoirs, Speeches and Writings of Robert Rantoul Jr.* (Boston, 1854); Daniel Webster, *The Writings and Speeches of Daniel Webster* (Boston, 1903); Robert C. Winthrop, *Addresses and Speeches on Various Occasions . . . ,* 4 vols. (Boston, 1852–1886). For a reformer's slant, see Theodore Parker, *Collected Works,* 15 vols. (Boston, 1910–1913). Those with access to Massachusetts public documents have several good avenues to explore: the annual addresses by the governor to the General Court, the annual reports of the state Board of Education (particularly when its secretary was Horace Mann) and of the state Bureau of Statistics of Labor, and the reports of the legislative committees and special commissions charged with investigating various aspects of the worker's condition.

Index

Adams, Charles Francis, 213, 251; on poverty, 221; on clash between capital and labor, 228

Adams, John Quincy, 80, 251; on progress, 73; on class, 87

Adams, John Quincy, Jr., 213; on Democratic party, 167

Adams, Samuel: on value of work, 84

Agriculture, Massachusetts: characteristics of, 16; effects of industrialization on, 23–24; employment in, 22, 27, 35–36; politicians' discussions of, 61–65; failure of farmers to combat industrialization, 113

Allen, Samuel C., 120, 156, 157, 251

American party, Massachusetts: progress of, 81, 169–71, 236, 237; vote for, 254–56

Andrew, John, 201

Appleton, Nathan, 116–17, 251; definition of capital, 89; on workers' relationship to capitalists, 91; on esteem accorded labor, 107

Arkwright, Richard, 3

Ashley, Lord, 52, 54

Ashton, T. S., 43

Austin, James T.: on factory workers, 115

Bagley, Sarah, 162

Bancroft, George, 120, 136, 251; on manufacturing, 71; on Democratic party, 119; on democracy, 124–25; on Jackson, 132

Banks, Nathaniel P., 80, 81, 167, 170, 171, 202, 217, 235, 251

Bates, Isaac: on agriculture, 63; on workers, 88–89; on role of workers in goverment, 103

Beverly, 19

Blake, William, 3

Boorstin, Daniel, 18

Boston, 24, 26, 58, 61, 81, 115, 116, 137, 142, 162, 164, 210, 211; shoe industry in, 19–20; as a port, 25; population of, 31–32; working class in preindustrial period, 35–36; trade union activity, 155–56, 159; cooperative movement in, 159; immigrants in, 169, 173, 174, 177; voting record of, 215, 252–56

Boston *Daily Advertiser*: as source, 56, 175; on immigrants, 176, 178, 181; on railroad strike of 1877, 178–79; on socialism, 179; on condition of factory